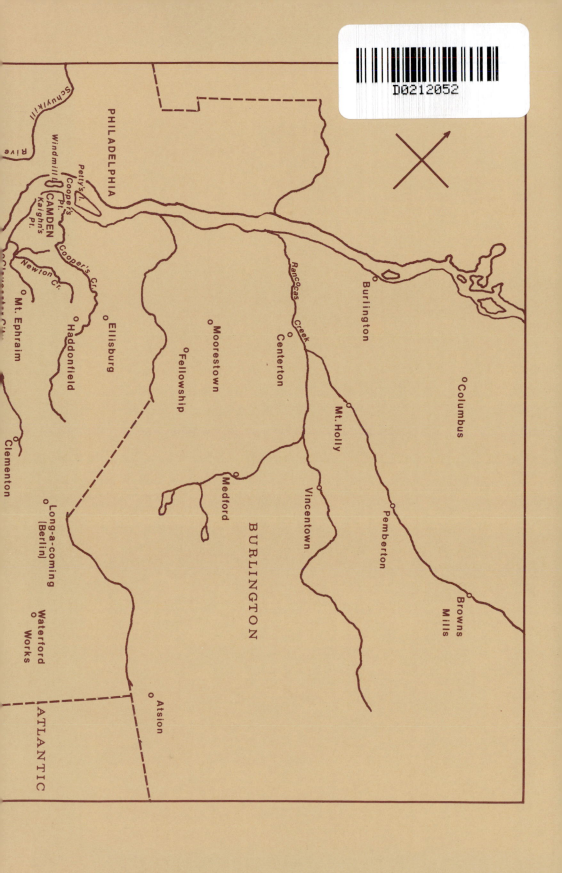

A Gentleman
of Much Promise

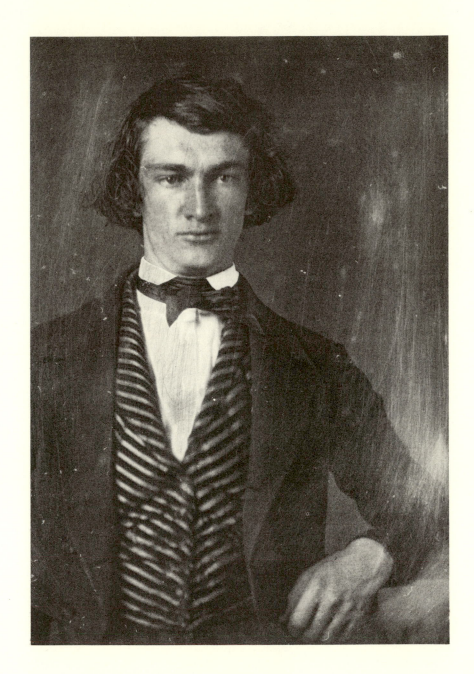

Isaac Mickle, 1846

A Gentleman
of Much Promise

The Diary of
Isaac Mickle
1837-1845

VOLUME TWO

Edited, with an Introduction, by

PHILIP ENGLISH MACKEY

University of Pennsylvania Press

1977

Endpaper maps prepared by Muriel Ketcham

Printed in the United States of America

Library of Congress Cataloging in Publication Data

Mickle, Isaac.
   A gentleman of much promise.

   Includes bibliographical references and index.
   1. Mickle, Isaac. 2. Camden, N. J.--Biography.
I. Mackey, Philip English. II. Title.
F144.C2M52   974.9'8'030924 [B]   76-53190
ISBN 0-8122-7722-8

The Diary

1842-1845

VIEW OF CAMDEN, FROM PHILADELPHIA.

The engraving shows the appearance of Camden, as seen from Walnut Street ferry, Philadelphia. Windmill or Smith's Island appears in front of the city. The canal, for steam ferry boats, through the island, is seen on the right.

Central View of Vincent-town

1842

1 January, Saturday.

The return of this epoch in the annals of the year, affords a fit opportunity to review the past with a view to our improvement in the future. Like the mariner who, in a fog, refers to the wake of his bark to learn if he is going in the right direction, during our voyage upon the hazy sea of life we ought often to look back upon yesterday in order to regulate the morrow. Thus we may be enabled to steer straight for our desired port, and to arrive in safety; thus we may be prevented from becoming bewildered in the whirling eddies of folly, and from drifting out upon the ocean of dissipation, where, without compass anchor or rudder, the boat of youth has but little chance of withstanding the strong gales that always blow towards the Malström of destruction.

In my case, especially, is this a proper occasion for such a review of the past. Beginning, as I now do, a new volume of my diary simultaneous with a new year, what time could be more proper for turning over a new leaf in my life?

During the past twelve months I have begun the study of law; have in a measure come out into company; have undertaken to practice

251

music; and have acquired a knowledge of some games of skill, among which that of billiards is the most interesting and therefore the most dangerous. By the first of these circumstances I have been brought in contact with lawyers, politicians and other public men, from Governors and Senators down to pot-house brawlers about the rights of man; by the second I have been brought into the society of polished, intelligent and virtuous ladies; by the third I have been led to an intimacy with several of the musical professors and amateurs of the day, such as Frank Johnson, Osbourne, Ned King and others; and by the last I have become acquainted with a junto of young men more respectable for their birth than their lives—a bevy who move at once in the highest and lowest circles of society.

The three first of those particulars ought to be subject to certain rules and the last I have determined to deal with by a resolution to forsake it altogether. It was owing to my having but little acquaintance among the ladies, that I began to spend an occasional hour in public places. Reading five or six hours a-day I felt indisposed to study in the evenings; indeed, I was unable to do it. Thus set afloat, as it were, I fell upon the same rock that all young men similarly situated, are apt to fall upon, and soon found myself looking at others playing tenpins and billiards. From looking on to participating in, is but a step. I learned these games, and in the summer played a good deal at the former, and during the fall and winter at the latter, as I have recorded in the last two volumes; and a slight diminution in my *collectis curiosorum numismatum* attests how far my fondness for the billiard-tables was carried. But I have since become a welcome guest at Sheppard's and several other agreeable houses, and as lawyers say, *Cessante causa cessat quoque effectus.* I am no more at a loss for becoming places in which to pass my evenings, and I heartily thank my God that I have sufficient strength of mind to say to temptation, Thus far Shalt thou lead me, and no farther. So long as Mary's smiles and Phoebe's bright eyes, and Hannah's sweet voice and Josephine's bonny face continue to say to me "We are glad to see you," I am resolved to humiliate myself no more by mingling with the dissipated junto at Heyl's or inhaling the thick atmosphere of Elwell's.

With reference to the other three items which I have mentioned, the experience of the past year induces me to make the following regulations.

And first of the law: Of which I will read just so much daily as can be properly digested and reflected upon, and no more. I will go to the office during the winter between nine and ten o'clock in the morning and stay there until a little after two. I will keep some small volume of history or philosophy upon my table to be read as a recreation from the dryness of Coke or Chitty.[1] I will pay most attention to the most uninteresting divisions of the legal science, because to excel in these deserves more praise than to excel in any other. Every ass can understand the easy, and every dolt appreciate the agreeable part of the law; but if the doctrine of estates requires much more study, the mastery of it entitles the student to much greater applause, than a proficiency in criminal law. And finally I will never for a moment forget that a pettifogger is the most contemptible of all animals.

Next of mingling in society: I will avoid flattery and bows, neither of which I conceive to be necessary to true politeness. The latter is a vestige of an age of slavery, and the former a remain of an age of cowardice. I will talk less than it is my nature to do, and always bear in mind the silver rule, "When there is nothing to be said, say nothing." I will try to be in my study by ten o'clock, for bad hours lead to bad morals. And lastly I will fall in love as soon as I can find a sweetheart.

In conclusion, of my music: I will practise much less upon the violin than I have been accustomed to do for the past six months, and hereafter will only play at one tune at a time until I learn it. A little well done is preferable to a good deal done indifferently, and the merit of music, especially, depends not upon its quantity.

Heaven give me power to carry these resolutions into effect!

The New Year comes in with very fine weather. The present winter, so far, has been an extraordinarily mild one. There is no ice at all in the river, and the urchins have as yet had but little skating. The public have had a fine opportunity to enjoy the holydays in a lively manner, and they have availed themselves of it.

For my part I have spent the last three or four days in fiddling, at home, or in walking up and down Chesnut Street to see the happy faces of young and old, as they busily hasten by upon errands of joy. To see others contented always makes me feel so. . . .

2 January, Sunday.

Last Sunday evening Mrs. Sheppard invited me to go to Ide's church on this morning. I did so, and heard a good sermon. I crossed the river with Miss Hannah and had a long talk with her.

In the evening I went to the Camden Baptist Church and heard the new minister. After it was over and before Miss Josephine had fairly taken my arm she began to thank me for my New Year's present. She is a mischievous, a merry lass, as pretty as merry, and as intelligent as pretty.

---

1. Joseph Chitty (1776–1841), like Coke, was an English legal writer whose works were mandatory reading for mid-nineteenth century students of the law.

3 January, Monday.

To-day I began the second volume of Coke upon Littleton. Martin says a student ought to be six months in reading this work, but I shall be more. . . .

5 January, Wednesday.

James T. Sherman, Esq. Editor of the *State Gazette* at Trenton lectured this evening upon the Goths, Vandals and Huns. He is a little man with a big head, a lame leg and a glib tongue; and quite an agreeable fellow. His lecture consisted principally of historical details which no one can remember, but it may do to stir up a curiosity among the youth, and lead them to study the annals of the decline and fall of the Roman Empire; and this he said was his main object. . . .

There was an Eastern gentleman at the office to-day just from the Capitol. He spent several evenings with the President, and describes him as being one of the vainest men that ever lived. He considers the late elections to have resulted as they did, on account of the popularity of his two vetoes; and his visitor thinks he would like to throw himself into the arms of the majority. Unfortunately for the President's vanity, the great change in favour of democracy began before his famous vetoes, and unfortunately for his ambition, the triumphant host have another "Captain" selected on whom they intend to lavish their gifts.

6 January, Thursday.

This evening I attended the meeting of the Episcopal Sewing Society, at Sheppard's. The house was full of company, and of course I did not enjoy myself a great deal. I abhor long letters, dogs, snakes, the devil, and mobs, especially mobs of women. Miss Browning pressed Weight, Ogden and myself so hard to become members that we could not refuse; but neither of us had a quarter of a dollar with which to pay our initiatory fee! Miss Turner also renewed her entreaties for a copy of my march, and I was obliged to tell her I had lost it. Thus it is the ladies compel us to leave the paths of truth and virtue!

8 January, Saturday.

This is the anniversary of Jackson's victory over Packenham, but there has been nothing like a celebration of it in or about Philadelphia.[2] When the old hero is laid in the grave and can no longer hear the jubilee, then the world will do the day and the deed ample justice. . . .

2. In the Battle of New Orleans, 8 January 1815, Andrew Jackson had led American forces to a crushing defeat of the British, commanded by Sir Edward Pakenham.

11 January, Tuesday.

This evening I attended Doctor Sammis' lecture without any company. The house had only about thirty in, which number at six and a quarter cents each will not half pay expenses. Notwithstanding this discouraging account of empty benches, the lecturer was quite animated and interesting. Isaac Cole evinced a little dissatisfaction with examination of Charles Garrett's[3] head, and had something of a debate with the Doctor, during which he laid on the emphasis with his cane pretty strenuously. But the blindfold examination or rather reëxamination, of Joab Scull's cranium satisfied his doubts. The lecturer described him very much as he did last Tuesday evening when his eyes were open.

During the exploration of Charley Garrett's bumps Mr. Sammis remarked that he had weak perception faculties. "The audience" said he "can perceive the deficiency by comparing this forehead with Mr. Mickle's." I sat in a conspicuous place, and notwithstanding my respectable development of "approbativeness," must have blushed a little when all eyes were turned on me.

12 January, Wednesday.

J. Hall Bready Esq., being prevented by sickness from lecturing for us this evening, we procured Charles West Thompson to pronounce his poem on "The Love of home."[4] It took very well with the ladies, and some of the gentlemen, even, shed tears. Some passages of it were very fine. . . .

I supped this evening at Cole's palace with Mr. Thompson, and after the poem, drank a glass of wine with him at the same place. He is much less animated in the drawing-room than on the rostrum.

14 January, Friday.

Bob Ogden practised two hours with me this afternoon.

In the evening I escorted Miss Josephine to a temperance lecture at the Methodist Church. One Colonel Wallace was the orator. If he can do as much murder in the army of prince Alcohol as he does in the King of England's grammar he is an invaluable champion. The house was very full.

Although the night was unpleasant and the walking very bad, I shall never forget the pleasure of this promenade. The token was

3. Cole and Garrett were prominent citizens of Camden, the former a coachmaker and the latter a saddler. Both were active in city politics and held various local offices.

4. James Hall Bready, a Philadelphia attorney since 1832, would die later this year, at age 32. Charles West Thomson (1798–1879), a native of Philadelphia, was an Episcopal minister and poet.

slight—scarcely did my nerves perceive it. But I am sure—and Venus! how glad am I that I am sure!—that it was a token.

But stop! The reader has no business to know my secrets!

16 January, Sunday.

Miss Josephine, on last Friday evening, asked me why I did not often go to Ide's Church, and invited me to come into their pew near the eastern door, whenever I did go. I promised her I would attend this morning, but somehow-or-other I—I—did not get up in time.

In the evening I went to hear Smith, at the Camden Baptist Church.[5] When he read our notice for Mr. Thompson's lecture he paid a very fine compliment to our Society.

Misses Hannah and Josephine came in soon after I did, and took a pew just before me. I had some talk with them after the benediction, but did not offer them my company home.

17 January, Monday.

This morning at nine o'clock I started for Trenton to look up material for doctor Mulford's lecture on the history of West Jersey. I arrived there about eleven, and repaired to the office of the Secretary of State. Doctor McChesney[6] received me very politely indeed—thanks to the compliment in my letter to him—and ordered his clerk to bring me all the records I might want to refer to. . . .

I dined and supped at Snowden's with several members of the Legislature. They are a great set of asses. I called upon Mr. Sherman, the editor of the *Gazette* during the afternoon, and after tea I took a stroll out to the canal.

The cars having broken down between Princeton and Trenton, we did not leave the latter place until eleven o'clock, an hour after the time at which we ought to have been at Camden. I whiled away the tedium of our waiting by dropping into the Methodist protracted meeting, and by listening to a conversation between a clergyman, a farmer, and a drunken cobbler at the office. Their subject was Phrenology.

We arrived at Pennshawken about one o'clock; at which time we discovered a large light in the direction of Philadelphia. It lit the heavens far and wide; and in the quiet atmosphere a luminous column of smoke raised to a tremendous height, reminding us of the pillar of fire that guided Moses in his wanderings towards the promised land. As we approached it was made apparent that the conflagration was in Camden, and as we . . . were crossing the creek I feared that it was

---

5. William W. Smith was pastor of the church from 1841 to 1842.
6. Charles G. McChesney was secretary of state from 1840 to 1851.

very near our house. Oh, how badly I wanted to be on the spot to save my diaries! We landed a little before two o'clock and I found the fire to be in Vansciver's five-story coach manufactory, opposite the house in which my grandfather died, on Front Street. The walls had partly fallen in when I reached the ground, but the flames were still raging with great violence. This is the second time Vansciver has been burnt out upon the same spot. The Brownings owned the building, which was not insured.

I got asleep about four o'clock.

19 January, Wednesday.

Richard P. Thompson of Salem lectured this evening upon "The power of knowledge." As I had predicted to some of my friends his text was Lord Bacon's motto "Knowledge is power." The lecture was very good and the lecturer a fine looking man. To the last cause is to be attributed the close attention of the ladies.

One of my country cousins—a pretty girl too—called at our house this afternoon, and said to mother that if I were at home she would ask me to take her to the lecture. Acting upon this hint I waited upon her in the evening and gallanted her up to the church. I observed some scrutinizing looks from some of my Camden acquaintances.

After I had escorted Miss Champion home after the lecture, I went around to Doctor Harris', where Mr. Thompson, his sister, and two other ladies who accompanied him, had stopped. The Sheppards were there, and Meriam Clement. At ten o'clock the lecturer and his ladies went to Elwell's. Here we had a whiskey-punch party. They crossed the river in the mail-boat.

20 January, Thursday.

An advertisement in most of the city papers has been announcing for two or three days back that Orestes A. Brownson, the famous editor of the *Boston Quarterly Review* would deliver a course of four lectures on "civilization"—beginning this evening in the lecture-room of the Philadelphia Museum. I did not need much persuasion from Kelley to induce me to take a season ticket; for like *tout le monde et sa dame* I entertained a great curiosity to see and hear a man who, from a sordid apartment in an obscure street of Boston, fulminates doctrines that shake the hoary dogmas of antiquity, and finds able espousers from Maine to the Gulf of Mexico—disciples some of them, who would die in defence of their master's theories.

To gratify this curiosity I crossed in the last boat this evening, and was proceeding up Market St., when I met two of the Sheppards. I of course esquired them to the ferry, but "of courser" did not tell them when I left, where I was going to spend my time. I chose rather to leave them to their own suspicions. Presently I ran afoul of Cowper-thwait and Davis who were staying over to attend auction, and who tried their best to learn where I was bound. We agreed to meet at 11 o'clock at Bloodgood's,[7] and then I went my way.

I reached the lecture room about seven o'clock and found it filling up pretty fast with very respectable people. About half were very intelligent looking ladies—not Fanny Wrights nor Mary Woolstone-crafts, but modest, feminine women.[8] The men as a general thing, I thought, had low crowns—they lacked the organ of veneration; but this may have been mere fancy.

At half-past seven the lecturer appeared, escorted by my friend Kelley with whom he stays, and Doctor Patterson. When he took the stand he was greeted with a warm round of applause, which he acknowledged by a very slight bow. Having taken my seat on the front bench within a few feet of the lion, I had an excellent oppor-tunity of observing him. He is of a middling stature, with a large head and bust, and rather a spindle pair of legs. His hands show him to be, or to have been, a democrat in one sense of the word, that is a working man, while his forehead shows that his mind, too, has not been idle. His brow is high and commanding, and his head is altogether strongly marked. I should say that benevolence and veneration were full, while causality and comparison were very large. At least there is a huge hill in their neighborhood, but I may be mistaken in the organs. His per-ceptive faculties are I think quite as prominent as his reflective, and his slow, hesitating manner of speaking seems to show that his lan-guage is not extraordinary. He wears spectacles, so that I could not get the expression of his eyes, but it is said to be very brilliant. "His cheeks" says the editor of the *Times*, "are somewhat hollow, his nose small and straight; and a characteristic expression is given to his countenance by the slight protuberance of his nether lip, as well as the square and prominent form of his chin."

His manner of delivery is slow and distinct, and at first unpleasant. He frequently goes back after a better word and sometimes falters so long that his hearers begin to feel fidgetty. His voice at the end of a sentence falls a whole tone, sometimes with a very happy effect, and sometimes with a very bad one. He attempts but few gestures and makes them only tolerably. His favourite position is an erect posture, with his heels close together and his toes turned out, his left thumb

7. Bloodgood's Hotel, at the foot of Walnut Street in Philadelphia, was owned by the Camden and Philadelphia Steamboat Ferry Company.

8. Frances Wright (1795–1852), British abolitionist and socialist, and Mary Wollstonecraft (1759–97), British writer, were both ardent advocates of women's rights.

hanging in his trousers pocket, and his right fore finger raised demonstratively to his eye. Mr. Drew,[9] Brownson's agent in Philadelphia, informed me that he has seen him speak for an hour and a quarter at the Odeon in Boston, without moving his feet from the spot on which he first placed them.

He began this evening by saying that he did not hope to give the great subject before him a thorough discussion; he would be satisfied if he incited others to consider it as it deserves. Civilization embraces all the actions ever done by mankind. He described man to be a being capable of acting, knowing and feeling; and all he has effected in these three departments constitutes civilization. In some men action predominates, and they are of the industrial order; in others cognition, and they are scientific; and in others feeling, and they are artistic.

The chief feature of civilization is progress, and its beginnings, he said must be by inspiration. No savage tribe has ever per se advanced. The description of the barbarians whom Alexander saw in Asia will answer for the same people to day. A civilized people may polish the uncivilized nations of the earth, and that he called inspiration; but the origin of human progress must be traced up said he "to that great being whom I have learned to love as my God and the God of my fellows." Here there was great applause, in which the radicals did not join.

His remarks were chiefly upon the origin of civilization, and he convinced me that his theory in that respect is true. He expressed his belief in the inspiration of Moses and Isaiah and in the god-head of Christ. Indeed his strong professions of Christianity astonished his own disciples no less than his conservative hearers. If these be sincere he has been much belied, and that by his own writings. In politics he was far less radical than I expected. He contended that there was a very manifest superiority by nature in the aristocracy of England over the commons, and wisely argued from this fact that it ought to be the aim of philanthropists to put the system of aristocracy down. He even vindicated ancestral pride, at which there was a slight show of applause; and throughout his observations on politics he took vastly less levelling grounds than some of his followers. . . .

It is the lecturer's opinion that all nature is improving. He ridiculed the common idea that men retrograde physically or morally. This was the only thrust he made at sacred history, and he attempted to establish it by reference to facts in geology and human history; the first to prove advancement in the soil and atmosphere and the latter, advancement in man.

9. The agent was probably Thomas Drew, Jr., a publisher on South Third Street.

After speaking for about an hour and a quarter he took his seat amid the claps of the audience that came there to listen to an infidel, but which doubted if it had not been attending to a sermon by a Christian clergyman.

I crossed the river with Cowperthwait and Davis and several other Friends about midnight.

22 January, Saturday.

I went to hear Brownson again to-night. His house was very full, and his manner was more agreeable than on Thursday evening. His subject was Christian civilization, and he took unusual pains to make us think him orthodox in his faith. After the lecture I dropped into the Circus and looked at the performances along with Colonel Page.

The mail boat got over to Camden a little after eleven o'clock.

24 January, Monday.

The famous Brownson was at the office an hour or two to-day. A deliberate scanning of his outward mein gave me no reason to alter the description thereof which I wrote last Thursday. He dresses very well—but Kelley says he is in the depths of poverty, owing to the agents of the *Quarterly* carrying out the "repudiation system" with his funds.[10] His body-guard here in Philadelphia consists of Kelley, Patterson, Drew and one or two Hicksite Quakers,[11] who move about him as faithfully as satellites around a planet. He preached yesterday at Clarkson Hall, Cherry St.

This evening, according to arrangements made last night on our way from church, the Sheppards, Miss Clement and one or two other ladies—accompanied by Browning, Clement and myself as beaus, walked down to Kaighn's Point to see the operations in the new glass-factory which has been erected on the property of the late John Kaighn. . . .[12]

There were a great many of our acquaintances at the works, on the same errand as ourselves, and they all agreed that their trouble was amply repaid. We remained there until about nine o'clock, and then started by the upper road for home. The ladies were full of fun, and the gentlemen of course had to unite with them. In coming thro' Fetterville the **former** proposed a serenade, and **we** said of course. "O,

10. Brownson was editor of the financially troubled *Boston Quarterly Review* which issued its last number in October 1842. "Repudiation system," refers to the idea advocated by a few Americans at the time that governments might repudiate their debts as a means to escape financial difficulty.

11. Followers of American Quaker preacher Elias Hicks (1748–1830) had created a schism among the Friends in 1827–28 and were commonly known as Hicksites.

12. The Capewell Glass Works at Kaighn Avenue and Locust Street.

capital! capital!"—and accordingly we drew up under the window of the most respectable looking house we saw, and began the air of *What fairy-like music*. After it was finished, Phoebe asked me who lived there, and I told her "Drew the Shoemaker," whereupon they concluded to adjourn to Mr. Rhees'. Here they sang *Oft in the stilly night*, but Miss Rhees struck up *What a rumpus and a rioting* upon the piano, and we concluded to move again. Mr. Rhees came out and invited us to go in, but we declined. He did not recognize us. At Browning's we sang—or rather **they** sang, *Am I not fondly thine own*, and at Dr. Harris', after we had left Miss Meriam, *The Banks of the blue Moselle*. We got home a little after ten, having passed a fine evening in a merry manner.

26 January, Wednesday.

Morton McMichael and I. Hall Bready both disappointing us to night, we had no lecture. This is the second baulk, during the present course. "It is an ill wind"—the reader knows the rest; I will have no notice to write this week for Gray. By the by, there was a great wondering up at Sheppard's the other night, who was the author of the critiques, if I may so call them, upon the lectures delivered before our company. I of course kept mum.

My presence not being required in Camden, I went over to hear Brownson's third lecture. He was discussing in his usual able and original way, man's title to property, which he contends can only be based upon occupancy, production, or the enactments of the legislature. He thinks the law of inheritance has been wrongly called a result of natural principles, and that title by descent is derived altogether from civil enactments. These may be true positions; but certainly the political law which allows a son to take what his father possessed is only declaratory of nature's law in the premises. The lecturer was quite as conservative as when I heard him before.

28 January, Friday.

A Mr. Levin[13] from Philadelphia delivered an eloquent temperance lecture this evening in the Methodist Church, to which I went in preference to going over to hear Brownson's last discourse. I of course did not go alone, and "of courser" did not go astray; for how can a lamb wander when there is **a Sheppard** on either side of him?

Immediately after the lecture and before the orator had left the church, he was arrested by Bill Hugg, at the suit of one Williams, for

---

13. Lewis C. Levin (1808–60), a lawyer, arrived in Philadelphia in 1838 and edited the *Temperance Advocate* there for several years. Later he became prominent in the Native-American movement and served as a nativist congressman from 1845 to 1851.

debt. This made quite a stir among the Methodists, and something of a laugh among the Episcopalians, who are inimicable* to the temperance cause in general and to Mr. Levin, in particular, for his having dealt a pretty hard thrust at Bishop Doane's "drinking the health of the princess-royal of England in three times three of ruby wine."[14] Mr. Daugherty gave bail for the orator's appearance, and so the farce ended.

31 January, Monday.

Winter is now two thirds through, and as yet we have had less cold weather than the oldest men of my acquaintance remember ever to have witnessed before. A great part of the two past months has been of a mildness equal to October. There has only been one or two days of skating, and even then the ice was barely strong enough to sustain a small boy. The ice-merchants have almost despaired of filling their houses with summer's greatest luxury, and we the consumers may as well give over the idea of getting any ice-cream next August, without it is at a price that our pockets cannot afford. The Delaware is entirely clear, and navigation is going on without interruption.

This evening, influenced by my own convictions and several recent occurrences, I signed the total abstinence pledge of the Camden Temperance Society. The paper to which I put my name was in the hands of Miss Sarah Delacour; and it is a little singular that Lemuel H. Davis signed just after me. Our parents were married on the same day; we were born almost at the same hour; we entered into the business of life together; and now we both sign the temperance pledge with the same pen-ful of ink. I wonder if we will ever be hanged out of the same cart.

* If any grammarian object to the use of this world instead of "inimical" let me ask him why we say "amicable." [*Mickle's note.*]

14. George Washington Doane (1799–1859), the Episcopal bishop of New Jersey from 1832 until his death, was renowned, and sometimes disliked, for his advocacy of "high church" principles and his aristocratic air.

The Henry Institute was reorganized to-night under a Constitution reported by me. It was adopted without a single alteration.

2 February, Wednesday.

Stacy G. Potts Esq. from Trenton lectured before us this evening on "Scotland," the glorious home of my forefathers. . . .

Mr. Potts and a friend who was with him wishing to get back to the city as soon as possible after the lecture took a wherry and went over. Ballantine and I accompanied them, and although we had no over-coats had a very pleasant ride. The weather is as mild as spring.

4 February, Friday.

Mr. Levin delivered another eloquent lecture in the Methodist Church to-night. Hugg had given out that he had another *capias* which he intended to serve upon the speaker just as he served the other, and the Methodists declared that if Levin was taken out of the house it should be over their dead bodies. In consequence of this expected row there was an immense audience, some twelve hundred persons. Every thing however went off quietly. Mr. Levin said in alluding to "a certain individual" who had been liberal of abusive epithets towards him, that he "would not exchange situations with him, in birth, wealth, intellect or Christian love." The individual alluded to was Clement. He got a complete flaying for the part he took in the lecturer's arrest.

6 February, Sunday.

I was in the house all this forenoon attempting to compose some music, but my thoughts were running too much on other things to enable me to succeed.

Bob Ogden and John Weight spent the afternoon with me. I read them some extracts from my journal and put them both in the notion of beginning one themselves. We played two or three games of chess. . . .

After church Bob and I called at Stiver's a few minutes to see Mr. Weight.

7 February, Monday.

"The State Fencibles," the gallant Corps over which Colonel Page commands, gave a ball to night at the Musical Fund Hall.[15] No doubt it was a grand affair. The Colonel asked me to go several times, but I declined; because those ladies with whom I would attend such a fete are averse to going, and those who are not averse to going I would

15. Musical Fund Hall, erected by the Musical Fund Society in 1824, still stands at 808 Locust Street, Philadelphia.

not be seen with. So I staid at home, and in the evening met with some of my friends at the Library Room to form a musical Association. We had some pretty good harmony. John Weight was appointed Leader and Cowperthwait and I were placed upon the Committee to draw up rules.

8 February, Tuesday.

Johnny DuSolle[16] the Editor of the *Times* was invited to the ball last night upon condition that he would not serve it up to his readers a la Bennett, as he has done several times before. He promised the Colonel faithfully that he would have nothing of the kind, but this morning he says that to-morrow he will give the minutiae at large! This is a fair specimen of the man's acts.

9 February, Wednesday.

Doctor Mulford gave us an excellent lecture this evening on "The Settlements on the Delaware." I had not supposed that the subject could be made so interesting. At another time I will make some extracts from it for future reference.

Two of Benjamin Wilkins' daughters from Woodbury came up to hear the lecture. I walked with them from the Doctor's to the church, and observed a good many close looks from my Camden lady-acquaintances as I showed them up the aisle.

The tide in the Delaware was very low this morning at nine o'clock. The rocks at Cooper's Point and below were bare and Lem Davis walked out upon them nearly half way to the Bar. The ferry boats were aground in the docks so that I could not get over to market until nearly eleven o'clock. All this was caused by a severe northwester which continued all yesterday and last night.

11 February, Friday.

This evening I attended the annual meeting of the members of The Union Temperance Society of Camden, in the Methodist Church. There were about a hundred present, all males; among whom were a committee from South Camden or Fetterville with instructions to offer the resignations of some of the inhabitants of said South Camden, who intend to form a society among themselves. A warm debate arose upon their request, during which some of the queerest speeches were made that I ever listened to. One Williams,[17] a tool-maker undertook to treat the matter metaphysically—but shades of Plato!—what

16. John S. Du Solle (1811–76) edited Philadelphia's *The Spirit of the Times* from 1837 to 1849.

17. This may have been the Hampton Williams whose name first appears in the Camden city directory for 1844.

metaphysics! The malcontents were at last allowed to retire, and then we went into an election for officers. I was nominated as a Manager by three or four voices, but rose and in a short speech declined. The nominations however thickened and thickened, and the President put the question whether "brother Isaac Mickle" Should be one of the board of fifteen? The[y] hurraed me in, in a manner that could not but have gratified my pride. Immediately after my election Lemuel H. Davis who sat by my side was also elected. Another coincidence.

15 February, Tuesday.

The frigate *Mississippi* which was built at the Philadelphia navy yard, and has been lying at New Castle ever since her launch to receive her spars and engines came up this afternoon by steam and passed the city. I happened to be crossing from the office when she came around Gloucester point, and we induced Captain Roth[18] to run down past her. We went close under her quarter opposite the Navy Yard and gave her three cheers. She is a magnificent specimen of Philadelphia workmanship. She came from New Castle with tide in two hours and ten minutes. . . .

16 February, Wednesday.

My friend Harry Patterson lectured this evening on "The French Revolution." He ridiculed the idea of "horror" which some invariably connect with the mention of that event, and showed with an eloquence of description that I have rarely heard equalled, that the really "horrible" part of French history was that which immediately precedes the Revolution. It was a transcendental view of the matter that he took, but I am half inclined to think it was the true one. He supped at Clark's, and after the lecture he and two of his friends, two of the Sheppard's, Delacour and myself adjourned there and had a very agreeable evening. I walked down with Mary Sheppard and Mrs. Clark—the latter a lively little woman enough; she is all feeling, and as Doctor Sammis told us when her cranium was examined, is an excellent musician. Clement was also there, and engrossed Doctor Patterson in a conversation upon capital punishment. He did his best to astonish my friend, I have no doubt; like some merchants he puts all his wares in the window, and you see all at first; but Doctor Patterson could not be deceived. He reads human nature as he would the *Boston Quarterly*. When we were going down to the boat he asked me "what damned squirt that was who prevented him from talking to the ladies?" He said he appeared to be afraid to laugh lest he would disarrange his

---

18. William Roth, of Plum Street above Third, was captain of several Delaware River ferries.

curls, and the two friends who were with him had a hearty roar at the faces which Johnny made.

20 February, Sunday.

I was in the house all to-day writing a notice of Doctor Mulford's lecture for Gray. In the evening I went to Baptist church and heard one Mr. Walsh from Burlington. I walked home with Miss Josephine. As we were going along she pulled a letter out of her muff and asked me if I knew the writing of the superscription. I held it up in the moonlight and immediately recognized Sam Cowperthwait's hand. It was a valentine which he had sent to one of Josephine's acquaintances; having followed her home and seen her father's name on the door plate. I am promised a full account of the whole thing.

21 February, Monday.

This evening I took my box of coins and my likeness (by request) up to the Parsonage. After which I went down to Fetterville and heard Colonel Wallace deliver a Temperance address.

22 February, Tuesday.

. . . There was nothing like a celebration of this day in Philadelphia. Men have become too corrupt in that place to remember the great Washington. The temperance men had a convention at Norristown.

23 February, Wednesday.

Colonel Page introduced me this morning to Ex President Van Buren and James K. Paulding, who is better known as the Author of the *Dutchman's Fireside* than as the Secretary of the Navy under the last administration. These distinguished gentlemen are on their way to see the Hero of the Hermitage, and are staying at the house of Henry D. Gilpin, late Attorney General, next door to our office in Walnut Street. Mr. Van Buren looks very well, and he assured Colonel Page that he was a happier man than his successor. Mr. Gilpin remarked to me that raising cabbages appeared to agree with him. His hair is quite gray, but his whiskers are sandy. The likenesses published of him are pretty correct. There is that same affability mixed with an air of cunning which they contain, and which has caused the New York Courier and Enquirer to call him in one column "the politest man in America" while in another it pronounced him the most artful politician that ever breathed. The phrenological development of his head is fine. Paulding's on the contrary is contemptible. His sconce is shaped like a cocoa-nut lying horizontally. He looks very little like the eloquent limner of Kath'rina and uncle Auriel.[19]

19. Catalina and Uncle Ariel are characters in Paulding's *The Dutchman's Fireside* of 1831.

Although the coming of Mr. Van Buren was unexpected, he was soon overwhelmed with visitors. Who can tell what influence this trip may have upon the Baltimore Convention that is to nominate the candidate for the next Presidency?

I met Doctor Sammis this afternoon and was introduced to his little wife.

Our lecture this evening was by Mayor Fisler,[20] on "modern witch-craft." He told us that "witches and wizzards were of the same nature as the fairies, the haunts, the elfs, the nymphs and **The Druids** of the Olden time!" What an ass can become Mayor of a city about these times!

Gray's paper of to-day contains my notice of Doctor Mulford. It is a column and over long. The notice of Doct. Patterson is to appear next week.

24 February, Thursday.

Our Amateur's Association met as usual this evening, and had some pretty good music. Thomas Bender[21] came around. He plays negro-extravaganzas very well.

27 February, Sunday.

I went to Mr. Ide's church this morning, and by invitation took a seat in pew no. 21. Mrs. Sheppard and all the girls but Mary were in it. They seemed glad that I sat with them. The subject of the preacher's discourse was Paul on Mars'-hill, and he handled it very eloquently. I almost fancied I saw the Apostle and the Acropolis, the sneering philosophers and the careless populace. After Church I accompanied Miss Hannah over the river. I am almost certain that the affection between her and Clement exists altogether upon his side.

In the evening I went to Smith's church.

28 February, Monday.

A kind of mongrel town-meeting was held to night at the Court-house in Camden, to nominate a ticket for the township election. The Methodist temperance men formed a majority, and got their candidates taken up. Bill Hugg and one Jim Wilson,[22] a one-armed tavern keeper, made some disturbance. The first sang out in a loud voice "This is Jimmy Sloan's meeting and no body else's.[23] I go in for a little

20. Dr. Lorenzo F. Fisler (1797–1871) was a native of Cumberland County who moved to Camden in 1836 and became a successful physician and politician. A Whig, he was elected mayor of the city seven times between 1840 and 1855.
21. The Camden city directory for 1850 lists a Thomas Bender as a "market-man," at the corner of Berkley and Sixth Streets.
22. James H. Wilson was proprietor of the Washington Hotel in South Camden.
23. James W. Sloan was a long-time justice of the peace in Camden.

honesty!" There sat said Jimmy Sloan and took the compliment very coolly: But Hugg's slurring at his honesty reminds one of the pot and the kettle. There were some very droll speeches made on this occasion.

The winter which is just past has been a very extraordinary one. There has been very little ice and snow; and a great part of the time we have had a clear sky and May-like sun. My mother picked a jump-up-johnny [*pansy*] in full bloom from our garden to day, and Phoebe Sheppard told me she found one in theirs three weeks ago, that is about the seventh of February. The navigation of the Delaware has not been obstructed for a day. I have heard some say that the winter of 1815 and '16 was very much like that just past. The confectioners and ice-men in Philadelphia are bringing solid water from among the Alleghanies; and others are importing it at great expense from Boston and the north. The thermometer has scarcely stood for twenty-four consecutive hours below the freezing point.

But although this season has been physically mild, it has been metaphysically rough. I mean that the times have been very hard. Banks have been breaking daily, and the currency vascillating like a flitting breeze. Had not the weather been very favourable to the poor they would have suffered extremely.

4 March, Friday.

A year has now passed since the Harrison Administration came into power. Then how bright were the hopes of the Whig party—now how dark! They are split into factions, jealous of each other, and fearing their own clansmen more than their enemies. And what has the country gained by its change of rulers? The experience of a year has shown nothing. The Bankrupt Law is the only equivalent we have for the enormous expense of a year's legislation, and serious doubts are entertained as to **its** constitutionality. The Florida war is not yet ended; our affairs with England are not cleared up; our treasury is not in a way of being filled; our people have not improved, but deteriorated, in their morals. "*O tempora!*" I will not however moralize upon this theme. When Martin Van Buren, or Commodore Stewart or Jammie Buchanan takes the Presidential armchair in 1845, all things will come right.

I have not lost a day nor part of a day from the office, this week. The second of Coke upon Littleton will soon be returned to its shelf.

This evening I called at Sheppards with Bob Ogden. Misses Phoebe and Josephine were at home. The latter has been making some bracelets, which she was showing to us, when Bob remarked with far more candor than politeness, "This one is too tight for your wrist"—pointing to one I had just slipped over her hand and which slightly indented her plump round arm. She blushed scarlet, and exclaimed with much naiveté "Why you are complimentary! You ought to say it is too big by half!" Bob looked even more simple than he commonly does, and learned, I hope, to understand my maxim "Where there is nothing to be said, say nothing." The implication of his uncivil remark is altogether unwarranted; for I never beheld a more lovely hand and wrist than those which grace Miss Josephine's arm.

5 March, Saturday.

I see an extract from my notice of Richard P. Thompson's lecture going the rounds of the papers. It is headed "The Jersey Boy," and relates to John Henderson, Senator from Mississippi,[24] who was a shoe-maker apprentice in Cumberland County. Gray says it has been republished over and over again. It is quite an honor to my young pen, for the paragraph is almost entirely original; and what is a little odd it was written in more haste than any other part of the critiques which I have furnished the *Mail*.

This afternoon I went around to Wainwright's[25] to see young Mr. Wainwright operate in Mesmerism. The subject was a bound-girl in good health and about sixteen years old. She was put to sleep in about twenty five minutes, and her arms were retained in one position more than a half an hour. I tried in vain to bend them. They seemed to have the rigidity of iron. Her pulse, as she was going to sleep, increased from 78 to 105 beats per minutes. We pinched her, stuck pins in her, tickled her nostrils, and endeavored by various means to arouse her, but to no purpose. Mr. Wainwright succeeded after a while in getting her to speak. Some experiments were then made in clairvoyance, two of which were successful (with a possibility however of deception) and one a complete failure. This part of the thing is, I believe, all humbug. But I am not willing to disbelieve that some persons can be put into a kind of cataleptic state by the manipulations of others, in which they are insensible to physical impressions.

I will investigate this matter further. It is strange—very strange.

8 March, Tuesday.

I staid in town to-night to hear the famous Doctor Lardner[26] who is lecturing at the Chesnut Street Theater, *sed non audivi*. His house was crowded. The piece at the American was *The Surgeon of Paris*.[27] Ned Conner took the leading character.

24. Henderson (1795–1857) was born in Bridgeton, New Jersey, studied law in Ohio, and moved to Mississippi in 1820. He served in the United States Senate, as a Whig, from 1839 to 1845.

25. Probably the home of James Wainwright, which was on Federal Street below Third.

26. Probably British physicist Dionysius Lardner (1793–1859) who lectured widely in this country between 1840 and 1845.

27. Joseph S. Jones' *Surgeon of Paris* was first performed in Philadelphia in 1841.

The celebrated Dickens, or "Boz" is in town. Our republicans as usual are making a fool of him and dunces of themselves.

9 March, Wednesday.

Mr. McCalla lectured again this evening, on "Ruins." It was rather a sermon than a lecture. I accompanied the Sheppards.

10 March, Thursday.

To-day I opened the last volume of Co. Litt.

This evening three or four of our amateurs met and had some good music. After we adjourned I left my violin at Delacour's, and went down to the Methodist protracted meeting, where I met my pretty friend [*Josephine Sheppard*], and saw her home. She told me that we were performing *I remember, I remember,* when she passed the Musical Club Room, and that it sounded very sweetly. A little incident occurred during our walk, that would interest no one but ourselves.

11 March, Friday.

This evening I dropped in at Hugg's where I unexpectedly found a large company. Doctor Andrews[28] put Miss Anne into a magnetic sleep for the instruction of unbelievers, and created much amusement by his experiments in clairvoyance. They all failed.

12 March, Saturday.

This evening by invitation I went to Stiver's, where there were some fifteen or twenty young people assembled. We had a pleasant little soiree. I am invited to Vansciver's on Monday night, but cannot go.

13 March, Sunday.

As usual, I was busy to-day in copying music. My *"Liber Musarum"* is filling up fast, at the expense however, (the ministers would tell me) of one of the commandments.

This evening I went to Baptist Church and heard a dry sermon; and then adjourned to prayer-meeting at the Methodist Church. Here I met my beautiful friend—and, need I add?—saw her home. *Aujourd'hui elle prend mon bras tous les fois que nous rencontrons, sans hesitation, ou la semblance de repugnance.*

14 March, Monday.

There was a public debate before the Institute this evening at the Academy, on the question "Were our ancestors justifiable in dispossessing the Indians of their land?" Dudley and I on the affirmative won the decision.

The town-meeting took place to day in Camden. There are six dif-

28. Dr. John R. Andrews (1818–64) of Kaighn's Point.

ferent tickets out, and all politics seem to be merged in the question of reform or no reform in temperance. The temperance ticket has been elected in Burlington by a majority of thirty. This is a very good opportunity for an organization of the reform party; for since Tyler's elevation, old political land marks have been overthrown, and the ancient factions are all set afloat, so that a man scarcely knows how he stands.

16 March, Wednesday.

The Rev. Mr. Eustis, an Unitarian, lectured this evening on The "Influence of Associations." It was so transcendental that no one could get the head—or tail of it. Mr. Kelley came over with him, and went with the lecturer and committee down to Turner's, where we staid till the mail-boat crossed. "Dear" Mr. Smith declined my offer of an introduction to his fellow-ship. Ahem! Did he smell a rat?

17 March, Thursday.

Saint Paddy's day, for a wonder is clear. It has been remarked that it has generally been attended with rain or a violent wind. To-day is an exception.

This evening our Amateur's Association met and began our performances with the fine old air named after this day. Our meetings improve all who attend them very much. For my part I can play almost as well as I have any desire to.

18 March, Friday.

Mr. Levin, the Temperance lion lectured this evening in the Baptist Church on "the modern poets." The house, owing to the twenty-five cents admission, was rather, nay very, slim; which mortified him very much. I promised Gray I would write a notice of this affair if he would release me from saying any thing in reference to Mr. Eustis' lecture. I could not please both the editor and the orator in the case of the Rev. gentleman, and so prefer saying nothing.

I took two ladies with me to the above lecture—what two I can remember without writing it down.

19 March, Saturday.

This evening I went to the Hicksite meeting in the woods near Camden to hear one Treadwell,[29] a great teacher among that sect. His sermon was nothing short of deism. He considers the fall of man in Adam as mere moonshine, and the doctrine of salvation through the

29. Stephen Treadwell (1791–1843), a native of New York, was a frequent speaker at Quaker meetings in that state and Pennsylvania in the 1830s and early 1840s.

blood of Christ, as a fable. He measures revelation by human wisdom, and not human wisdom by revelation. Is he or is he not correct?

21 March, Monday.

This morning I submitted myself to Mr. Gilliams, dentist, in Ach St. to have my mouth overhauled.[30] He pulled one tooth that was entirely decomposed at the root. Very pleasant to think of—this suffering purgatory for an hour every other day for two weeks! very pleasant. . . .

22 March, Tuesday.

Mr. Martin, my office mate obtained my promise last week to join a class to take instruction in the German language of one Gustavus Remak, a teacher at Second and Willow Streets.[31] We commenced this afternoon. Our number is five, all lawyers or students at law. We got through our alphabet to-day. He offers to make us speak and write the tongue in six months. . . .

Feeling a little sad to-night I almost made up my mind to shut myself up in my room and go to hard study again. I must do this before long. I will however make no rash resolves. Let me consider the step well.

Morton McMichael Esq. lectured to night on "Education." He played us rather a scurvy trick in disappointing us on a former occasion, but he told Mr. Clark that he did not mean to do it; and so I waited upon him again. His lecture was admirable.

I was at my dentists again this morning.

25 March, Friday.

This evening I took Misses Hannah and Josephine to Wainwright's second exhibition in Mesmerism. They were much amused.

I had another tooth pulled this morning.

26 March, Saturday.

I took my third lesson in German this afternoon. I may as well say once for all, that "until further notice" I shall attend my class at Second and Willow Streets, on the afternoon of every Tuesday, Thursday and Saturday, at three o'clock. Mr. Remak is a good natured and good looking young Polander—of very considerable attainments as a linguist. He eases our labour considerably by showing us the analogies between the ancient languages and the German.

This evening I took Miss Josephine to Wainwright's third exhibition. The experiments in clairvoyance and sympathy were more successful than upon any former occasion; The success however was not com-

30. Jacob Gilliams' office was at 35 Arch Street. Mickle has probably misspelled the street name on purpose.
31. Remak lived at 264 North Second Street.

plete enough to convince me, although I will own that we should rather wonder that one succeeds than that ninety-nine fail. Miss Hannah (as the subject is called) is not very well calculated to carry on a scheme of collusion so deep: as, unfortunately, nature, in stocking her head, forgot the brains. No training I think can deaden the sensibilities of any one so that a needle can be run into her thigh an inch, without causing any symptoms of pain. This Doctor Burrough did to Hannah last night—for which he got a sound lecture when she awoke. The doctor is an unbeliever; and in his attempt to explode the humbug he made both the Mesmeriser and the Mesmerisee, angry. . . .

27 March, Sunday.

I went to Ide's Church this afternoon with Sam, and to the Camden Baptist church in the evening. From the latter I saw Miss Josephine home. Smith used the word "dear" just eighty one times in his sermon.

28 March, Monday.

I was at the dentist's again this morning. I have more gold now in my mouth than in my pocket.

This evening, instead of going to the meeting of the Institute, I went around to Sam's and played with him until after nine o'clock. We had some excellent music. Several persons stopped under the window to listen, and some came into the room.

30 March, Wednesday.

I had another sitting with Mr. Gilliams this morning. When will this horrid business be over?

Mr. Charles West Thompson repeated his Poem on Home this evening. I procured its redelivery to oblige (among others) Miss Mary Sheppard. The house was very well filled; but I did not go. I spent my time in looking at and listening to an exhibition by the black pupils in Mr. Holland's school in South Camden.[32] John Browning and Ned and several more of us went down, and got pretty good seats near the pulpit and stage. Richard Fetters and his lady were there. The performances opened by a prayer from Parson Wilson,[33] a decent old negro who does a good deal of ditching for my uncle. The dramatis personae then came out, *seriatim*, and bungled some of the finest pieces in the English language. We hissed Cowper's "O for a lodge in some vast wilderness," to the great discomfiture of Mr. Holland, who assured us that "Dis is de best ting you eber heerd." They acted the ghost-scene in the tragedy of Hamlet, in an original manner, intro-

---

32. Holland's first name is unknown. The school had opened in the Fettersville Methodist Episcopal Church in May 1840.
33. Benjamin Wilson had been one of the first residents of Fettersville.

ducing a clown with his goblinship, which last in all conscience was ridiculous enough in itself; with a face as black as the devil's pet raven, and a voice far more like a hod-carrier's than an entombed king's. The clown maintained his position on stage through tragedy as well as comedy, except for a few minutes when he descended into the green-room, to quell a riot that had been raised there. We staid till between ten and eleven o'clock, and enjoyed the burlesque very much.

Mrs. Finch stays with us to-night. I would be glad to see her if she would leave her squalling child behind.

31 March, Thursday.

This afternoon, after my return from the office I was seated in my study practising upon my violin, when the cry of fire reached my ears and made my blood course along my veins with a thrill that cannot be described. Sallying forth I soon found that "the Rail-road House" was all in flames aloft, while people were gathering thick and fast beneath, either to help rescue the goods, to look on, or to see what they could steal. Our Camden engines were already on the ground, doing their best; but it was impossible to save the Hotel. I assisted in carrying the furniture out, until the ferry boats arrived with several of the fire companies from Philadelphia, whom I then assisted in playing upon the extensive car-houses which, being to leeward, were in great danger of destruction. We succeeded in saving them, though the high wind carried a dense mass of sparks and flame over them and against them. The fire was discovered about half past five o'clock, and by nine the splendid hotel was a pile of smouldering ashes—four hours having ruined the fortunes of Mr. Elwell, and consumed the fruits of several years' industrious labour. The papers in the post-office were all rescued. Severe wounds were inflicted upon two or three of our citizens by the imprudence of some in tossing goods from the balcony among the crowd. One man having thrown four or five pitchers down from the windows, at least descended the ladder carrying a shovel and pair of tongs very carefully in his hands! The fire is supposed to have been communicated by a flake from the chimney of the Steam-boat *Phila-delphia*, plying to the north dock, though some, in view of the many enemies the Ferry Company has, think differently. . . .

The Banks of the Commonwealth of Pennsylvania resumed Specie payments about the First of the month just flown. The crisis in the monied affairs of the state is now considered to have passed.[34] Matters will soon come right, and business will soon prosper again. The next

34. The banks were forced to resume specie payments by a Pennsylvania law of early March 1842. The crisis was indeed over and prosperity was again beginning to build in the region.

generation may have to go through the same ordeal; but this one may clap its hands and be glad at the end of its trials in the particular of which we are speaking.

Our relations with England are again of a delicate nature. The opinion is gaining ground that we must have a war with her during the present administration.

News reached us a few days ago of the invasion of Texas by a Mexican army.[35]

3 April, Sunday.

This morning I went to a Sunday school examination in the Synagogue [*Mikveh Israel*] in Cherry Street; in the afternoon to old Christ's Church, and in the evening to brother Smith's in Camden.

4 April, Monday.

Clement is about leaving Camden for the west. To-night, by a fished-for invitation from the Institute, he read an address on Mental Discipline before us in Miss Turner's School room, as a valedictory. There were some fifteen or sixteen ladies present, and gentlemen to correspond. I took Miss Hannah. He came up to the Parsonage after the meeting, and I thought had something on his mind to dispirit him. Miss Josephine gave him a bracelet of her hair—a token, the like of which I mean to sue from Hannah, let her beau say what he will.

6 April, Wednesday.

Joseph R. Chandler, Esq. closed our course this evening by a lecture upon "The influence of the Christian religion upon the character and condition of women." Notwithstanding Bishop Doane's "vernal visitation"—and to night was the great confirmation—we had a very good house. By the by, Bishop Doane was walking about our city to-day with an Oxford hat, turned up in front, and covered with ribbons and cockades, stuck upon his head very differently from the manner in which he used to wear republican beaver before his visit to England. He was unpopular enough when he wore a common hat like common men; what must he be now, with such an outlandish pidgeon-box upon his cranium?

I saw "the empress" [*Josephine Sheppard*] home after Mr. Chandler's lecture, and then rejoined the committee at Gray's. Mr. Chandler, notwithstanding great bodily infirmities edits a daily paper, presides over the grand lodge of the city of Philadelphia, is an active member of the Councils, contributes to the periodicals very frequently, and writes and delivers more lectures on various subjects than any man between

35. A force of five hundred Mexican soldiers had captured San Antonio on 5 March and held it until 7 March.

the Shuylkill and Delaware, except perhaps my friend Kelley. He stands preëminent among his fellow citizens for industry.

I was at the dentists' again this morning. I missed Monday.

9 April, Saturday.

Our German class did not get together this afternoon. I was the only one that came. I had a long talk with Remak about poor Poland.

In the evening I was at Cowperthwait's, fiddling.

10 April, Sunday.

We had plenty of visiters at our house to-day. *Tout le monde et sa femme* seemed to have turned out to see us. Among others my Aunt Eliza from Philadelphia and my aunt Mary from West Chester came.

In the evening I went to Mr. Berg's[36] Church in Race Street Philadelphia, to hear that gentleman lecture against the Catholic mass. The house was very much crowded; and the audience in general seemed considerably tickled with the vituperation poured out upon their fellow Christians. I got across the river about midnight.

12 April, Tuesday.

This has been a memorable day for Temperance men! The anniversary of the Jefferson Society of Philadelphia was celebrated in that city by a procession which has rarely been equalled for splendor and dignity. About ten thousand temperance men, decorated with badges, and provided with banners and music, met and formed in the north of the city (Spring Garden Street) and at ten o'clock moved off in good order, and passed through the principal streets, amid dense crowds of admiring people. After marching until about two o'clock they entered Independence Square by the south gate, where they were addressed by my old dominie, Samuel Aaron, Mr. Levin, Mr. Chambers and some others. One of the speakers stated that the procession had passed by some six hundred grog shops!

The "Union" Society from Camden, "The Washington and Levin" from Fetterville, and the "Union" from Kaighn's Point, joined the Jeffersonians, each with a banner. Many other societies from New Jersey turned out. I marched with the Camden Unionists. We formed before the Methodist Church at half past six o'clock in the morning, and marched through Fetterville and Kaighn's Point, then back to Camden and through one or two of its streets; we then crossed the river at Market Street, and proceeded with the Fetterville Society, up to Spring Garden Street, where our position was assigned us near the centre. We had a good band of music. Our banner was the one used

---

36. Rev. Joseph Berg (1812–71) was pastor of the Race Street Church in Philadelphia.

at the great Whig convention at Trenton during the hard-cider campaign—having the arms of the state, and the altered inscription. "Our sovereignty shall be respected—Temperance is our security."

I marched with the company until twelve o'clock, when becoming tired, I dropped astern, and went home. I did not hear the speeches.

This evening I began to read *Telemachus*[37] in French, with Phoebe Sheppard and Master Ben. Browning. We translated half of the first book; after which I took up Ned King's violin (which he left at the parsonage last Friday night) and accompanied Miss Josephine in two or three simple airs.

After all this hard work of course I feel pretty tired.

13 April, Wednesday.

Mr. Plankinton the whig County Treasurer of Philadelphia[38] has been discovered to be a defaulter to the amount of about sixty thousand dollars. The Commissioners very promptly removed him and appointed my respected friend, the Colonel, in his place. This is a great compliment. . . .

17 April, Sunday.

After moping in the house all day, I turned out towards evening and went across the river with Sam, expecting to hear Doctor Moriarty reply to Berg's sermon this night week. His church was not open however; so we went in Race Street to hear Berg's second lecture, which was upon the Catholic baptism. We crossed the river through a terrible storm, about midnight, or a little before, in the mail-boat *State Rights.*

19 April, Tuesday.

This evening I went to Sheppard's to finish the first book of *Telemachus*. Ned Drayton, Ned King, Doctor Andrews and Benjamin Browning were likewise there—the last however, being the only classmate that Phoebe and I had. I am going to make my visits at this house more like those of the angels—I am not **quite** ready yet to say I will never enter it again. But of this more anon.

The second annual meeting of the members of the Library Company, in their incorporated capacity, was held to night to elect seven trustees. The old board with one exception was reëlected. The electees met immediately afterwards and did me the honor of making me President for the ensuing year. Samuel Cowperthwait was appointed to succeed me as Secretary.

37. François de Salignac de la Mothe Fenelon had written the romance *Les Aventures de Télémaque* in 1699.

38. Joseph Plankinton served as county treasurer from 1841 to 1842, when he was succeeded by James Page.

20 April, Wednesday.

This evening I staid in Philadelphia to call upon my friends Rufus Wilkins and Harry Edwards, at Mrs. Simmons' in Second Street. I had a pleasant time, especially as I met a large party of ladies and gentlemen from Camden on their way to see Miss Vandever, in Thirteenth Street. The company at Miss Lydia's was very numerous, and mirth and music filled the fleeting hours. They as well as myself and two or three other of my acquaintances got left by the mail-boat which arrived sooner than usual. We proceeded en masse up to Market Street ferry, where we took the liberty of unmooring one of the Company's wherries—it was done on my responsibility—and rowing across. The ladies sang some sweet airs as we skimmed the moonlit waters. We got to Camden about midnight.

21 April, Thursday.

A Yankee named Howe[39] called upon me to-day, to collect material for a book upon New Jersey which is to be published about a year hence somewhere down east. He was recommended to me by Mr. Gray and Doctor Mulford, and we soon became very well acquainted. I read him extracts from my journal concerning the battle of Red Bank, the settlement of Woodbury, the stabbing of Miles Sage, and so forth; and gave him all the information I could upon the wreck of the *Alliance*, the history and topography of Windmill Island, and the history of Wood's old house at Haddonfield which was burnt down on last Monday or Tuesday night.[40] This venerable mansion was built with materials brought from England by the Haddon family many, many years ago, when our now blooming country was a dreary wilderness. Mr. Howe is going to take a drawing of the ruins. He will be back to Camden in about ten days, when I am to have some extracts from my diary made for him, and if possible, a copy of Doctor Mulford's lecture. He was with me several hours, and I find him to be a true specimen of the Yankee character—shrewd, quick and observing. I recommended him to Benjamin Wilkins at Woodbury and to James S. Green, Esq. at Princeton. . . .[41]

22 April, Friday.

Mr. Howe leaves Camden this afternoon. He travels on foot, carrying his knapsack with him, and a little book in which he dots down all his gleanings. He says he wills the anecdotes which I furnished him

---

39. Henry Howe (1816–93) of New Haven, Connecticut, had already published several books and now was at work on his *Historical Collections of the State of New Jersey* (New York, 1847), of which John Warner Barber was a joint author.

40. This was the former residence of John and Elizabeth Haddon Estaugh.

41. Green (1792–1862) was a prominent attorney, later a professor at Princeton College.

inserted in their book verbatim as I gave them to him. Quite a compliment! . . .

23 April, Saturday.

I spent this evening at Stivers'. There was a good deal of company there, among the rest the facetious Ned King with his violin. Ned Drayton was also there, with—a remarkably red pair of eyes. My friend I fear does not belong to the Tee-total Society.

26 April, Tuesday.

I read the chief part of book second of *Telemachus* this evening with Phoebe. Mr. Browning was not with us. We now merely read the English—translating liberally, but faithfully and grammatically.

I went this noontime to St. Joseph's Church to see the remains of Bishop Conwell,[42] laid out in State. The house was densely filled with spectators of the impressive funeral service which the living priests were doing over the corpse of their dead brother. The procession moved from the church at one o'clock.

28 April, Thursday.

This evening I staid in Philadelphia to hear a debate between Rev. William S. McCalla and the somewhat famous Charles C. Burleigh, on The Capital Punishment question which is now agitating the good people of the Commonwealth of Penn.[43] McCalla is against the abolition of the punishment of death and Burleigh in favour of it. The latter gentleman got the best of the encounter to-night. He advanced some hard arguments. McCalla seems to be driving at a justification of war, upon which foundation he will base a justification of capital punishments. The whole debate was a brilliant display of mind. "Where Greek meets Greek, then comes the tug of war!" The audience, (near two thousand in number) seemed to incline towards my reverend friend's side. Kelley was on the committee of arrangements.

29 April, Friday.

Kelley spent the afternoon and took tea with me, to day. We visited Mr. Fetters hot-house, and called upon the Sheppards. We had a fine time. He crossed the river early, to be at the continuation of the debate on capital punishment. He is a Burleigh man—I go in for McCalla, or rather for McCalla's side. This evening I met the Baptist

42. Henry Conwell (1745–1842), a native of Ireland, was Roman Catholic bishop of Philadelphia from 1819 to his death. St. Joseph's, on Willings Alley, between Third and Fourth Streets, is the oldest Catholic church in Philadelphia.

43. Burleigh (1810–78), a native of Connecticut, was now a prominent antislavery editor in Philadelphia. Campaigns to limit or end capital punishment were agitating most of the northern states in the early 1840s. Pennsylvania legislators were being swamped by anti-capital punishment petitions in early 1842.

Choir, and helped them till near eleven o'clock. I can now play in three flats.

30 April, Saturday.

Edward Chandler showed me the Prospectus of a democratic paper, this afternoon, which he and Henry Buffington intend to start in Camden.[44] Now is the time for such an enterprize, but they will find a drawback I fear in the fact that they have both been whigs. Men never forget political somersets.

This evening I heard the concluding set-to of the controversy between McCalla and Burleigh. I must own the latter gentleman used the skilful debater by whom he was opposed, entirely up. I never met with Burleigh's equal for the keenness of his perception and the readiness with which he turns everything to his advantage. They had a trial last night. There is to be no express decision.

The Methodist Conference began its session in Camden on last Wednesday. There are a hundred and fifty reverends quartered upon our citizens.

1 May, Sunday.

May-day this year is exceedingly unpleasant. The wind is high, and every little while the clouds pour down rain in torrents.

I was at Conference a few minutes this afternoon, and saw some assinine-looking blockheads ordained for the ministry by the laying on of the hands of four of the brethren, and the palaver of the bishop. In the evening I took two of the Cooper Street ladies to hear Charles Pitman preach.[45] The house was densely crowded.

We made up a party at Sheppard's **this** evening to go to Philadelphia **to-morrow** evening to hear Levin and Samuel Aaron.

2 May, Monday.

I did not go to the office to-day, but staid a home fiddling, until six o'clock, when I dropped around to see Ben Browning. From there we proceeded to Sheppard's, got Miss Mary and Miss Josephine, and crossed the river; being safely arrived on the other side of which we sought the hall of the Chinese Museum, and entered the same. There was an assemblage of about two thousand people awaiting the appearance of the speakers. We got pretty good seats, though the pillars obstructed our view of the orators. Mr. Aaron presently came forth and taking as his text the proverb *"Obsta principiis"* (which he trans-

44. Chandler did publish Camden's *Hickory Club,* with Charles Hineline, for a time in 1844.

45. Pitman (1796–1854), a minister in many New Jersey and Philadelphia churches since 1818, was currently corresponding secretary of the Missionary Society of the Methodist Episcopal Church, with offices in New York City.

lated, "stick to your principles") he made some excellent points. After speaking near a half an hour, he turned to Lewis Charles Levin who was on the stand with him, and exhorted him to "stick to his principles" to the death, in an appeal that could not be surpassed for neat compliments and forcible considerations. Mr. Levin then rose, and read an address upon the life and character of John Howard.[46] It was about an hour long, and pretty good. We were then dismissed with a benediction. The affair was given as a complimentary benefit to Mr. Levin, by the Howard Temperance association, and passed off very well.

Our party stopped in at Hutchinson's and got some ice-cream, on our way to the ferry. We got over the river about eleven o'clock. Ned King was on board the mail-boat with us, and as usual, was full of his flummery. He continued his didoes with me until I exclaimed in rather a sharp tone, "Go away, will you?" I hope it has made him mad.

3 May, Tuesday.
A year is to-day completed since I entered upon the study of the law; and this afternoon I finished Coke upon Littleton at which I have been at work more than six months. I have read Blackstone in four volumes, De Lolme's *Constitution of England* in one volume, Kents *Commentaries* in four volumes, Montesquieu's *Spirit of Laws,* in two volumes, and Fergusson's *Civil Society,* in one volume, besides Coke's work, in three volumes. This is sufficient ground to have gone over, if I had properly digested all I swallowed: this unfortunately is not the case. I blush when I realize how little I know of the "*summa ratio*" (as Cicero calls it) in the acquiring of which I have spent my first year. The reason of my backwardness is evident. I know the disease, and that is the best half of the cure. Part of my freshman year has been spent in dissipation, and the balance in attentions to the ladies and to music. I stopped at the beginning of this year now current, the practice of playing billiards; but the reform has not helped me along in the law. The time I used to spend at Heyl's I have since passed with my female friends—and it may well be asked, which will the sooner make one a lawyer, to pass his time at billiards or to consume it in gallantries. The latter may—nay, undoubtedly does, improve the heart; but for cultivation of the head, it is quite as inadequate as the former. The truth is—I feel it—I cannot but confess it—I am in love. The girl [*Josephine Sheppard*] whom I loved as a child I love now that I begin to become a man. The first object of my affections is still mistress of my heart. She is now just budding into young womanhood. To an ele-

---

46. English philanthropist John Howard (1726?–90) was most famous for his efforts to reform prison conditions.

gant form she adds a brilliant eye, a rosy cheek, an exquisite pair of lips. The gentleness of her manners and the accomplishments of her yet unfinished education, admirable as they are, are insignificant when compared with her rigidity of virtue, and her strength of principle, her great prudence and unusual intelligence. How could I see such a being as this and not love her? Her voice for years has been the sweetest music that could greet my ears, her figure the brightest vision that could flit before my eyes. I have no reason to think that she knows aught of the feelings I entertain for her; for from considerations of our youth, I have never breathed my weakness (if such it be) upon her hearing. Other circumstances too have conspired to force me to silence. I knew that she had a wrong impression of my character, and I believed that her affections were centered elsewhere; and until I was convinced that both these obstacles were removed, I could not, I would not, hang my happiness upon a die, the chances of which were mostly against me; for uncertainty, alleviated by hope is better than certainty loaded with despair. For nearly a year back I have been in company with this lady very frequently—upon an average, as often as twice a week; but like the miser's avarice or the drunkard's thirst, my desire to be with her increases in proportion as I gratify it; and if I continue to slacken the curb to this inordinate passion my sergeantship will have expired, and I will enter upon the world, incompetent for the struggle of life, and unworthy to sue for her hand, or any body else's.

"*Censeo igetur Carthaginem esse delendam!*" My heart must be subverted, laid waste; and reason shall sit upon the ruins of my passion like the stern old Roman among the fallen grandeur of Dido's city—triumphant indeed, but with no sign of the joy of victory upon her countenance. The sacrifice must be made, be the struggle what it may. Fortune, reputation, happiness are at stake! Let these considerations then enable me to strangle the love which rages within me with the fury of the Nemean beast, and which seems to have the vitality of the hydra! Then will the law prosper. . . .

4 May, Wednesday.

I began to day to read Justinian's *Institutes* in Latin, having borrowed a copy of Ex-Attorney General Gilpin.[47]

This evening we had a musical soiree at our house. Bishop, Baxter and Cowperthwait attended. We played sacred music only, and kept it up until near eleven o'clock. . . .

5 May, Thursday.

The Methodist Conference rose to-night, after having done a good deal of business, among which was the trying of five ministers for improper behavior towards females! What are we coming to? Not a

47. Henry D. Gilpin (1801–60) had been Jackson's attorney general in 1840.

month passes without our hearing of some faux pas among our spiritual teachers. The church is affected by the general depravity of our times, and a white cravat is no longer the symbol of a pious man. There have been somewheres in the neighborhood of an hundred Methodist clergymen in attendance at this session of the conference, and some of them look as much like fools as others do like knaves. Take them all in all, however, they are a fair set of men. Bishop Waugh[48] presided over their deliberations. This evening I dropped in to hear the appointments read, and after the adjournment, ran afoul of Miss Josephine, and saw her home.

Colonel Page gave me a likeness of himself to-day, by Sartain.[49]

6 May, Friday.

We go upon the agrarian principle at our office, in all things relating to literary property. . . . Major George Cadwallader[50] is a candidate for the Brigadier Generalship, and all our folks go for him. There is to be a meeting to-night to promote his cause, somewhere down town. They sent to Colonel Page for a set of resolutions, but he not having time to write them, passed the matter over to me. Without the least assistance in this novel business, I drafted a preamble and four or five resolves, and gave them to the Colonel to read. He pronounced them good—said indeed they were excellent, as he of course was forced by politeness to do. Just then the committee came for them. "Here they are" said he "but I have not had time to copy them: take them along." And out went the gentlemen, highly gratified with what they supposed was my master's panegyrics of their favourite.

This evening I met the Baptist Choir again. I improve very much by our practisings.

7 May, Saturday.

The famous family of Rainers[51] gave a concert to-night in the Baptist basement. There was some delay on account of the compunctions of some of the elders, but after a time they got in and gave some excellent pieces. I was not present—being at a Concert and fair in the Museum in Philadelphia. Hazzard's band[52] made some sweet sounds—quite as agreeable to me as the Rainers' voices would have been.

48. Beverly Waugh (1789–1858) was bishop of the Methodist Episcopal Church from 1836 until his death.

49. John Sartain (1808–97), a London-born engraver, portraitist, and publisher, had moved to Philadelphia in 1830.

50. Cadwalader (1804–79) was a Philadelphia lawyer who saw military service in the Mexican and Civil Wars.

51. The Rainers were a group of Tyrolese singers who had made their New York debut in 1839.

52. Hazzard's band was a black organization which played for many Philadelphia balls and parties in the 1840s.

8 May, Sunday.

I went to Ide's church this morning at the invitation of Miss Josephine. Some of her schoolmates were baptized. She goes to school in Arch Street above the theatre, where Mr. Cushman used to teach;[53] and seems to be on very good terms with all her acquaintances, saving Miss Lambourne from Camden, who sometimes takes the liberty (as Sam Cowperthwait tells me) of using my name in a way that she does not like. I crossed the river and walked home with her—my resolution of Tuesday to the contrary notwithstanding.

9 May, Monday.

I called at the Parsonage this afternoon and spent a very agreeable hour. My French class-mate presented me with a watch-chain woven with her own fair hands—having taken pity upon the straits to which I was reduced, of using a twine string! I will wear this little gift in remembrance of Phoebe, until—it wears out.

This evening I went to a Ball in the Masonic-hall, given by the Hibernia Fire Company[54] of which Colonel Page is President. He was there, and showed himself to be a very graceful dancer. The company numbered about three hundred, and although it was rather promiscuous, behaved very well. I got down to Burr's ferry a little before daybreak, but did not sleep any.

As a specimen of Colonel Page's industry, I will record what he has done to-day. This morning he was in his law-office hearing clients until nine o'clock; he then went to the County Treasurer's office and superintended its affairs until ten; from there he went into Court and got a case through; from twelve to two he was at his profession; at two he dined and immediately afterwards formed his company of Fencibles and paraded them over the city until six; at seven he made a speech at the Rhode Island meeting in front of the State-house;[55] at nine he went to the Ball (of which he was floor manager,) and danced until three o'clock to-morrow morning!

10 May, Tuesday.

Notwithstanding my spree last night I was in the office betimes this morning. This evening I read the balance of the third book of *Telemachus*, with Miss Phoebe—Mr. Browning being absent—and got to bed about eleven o'clock. I had a nap or two through the day.

53. Robert W. Cushman had operated a "college for young ladies" at 229-231 Arch Street as recently as 1841. Camden city directories make no mention of the name Lambourne.

54. One of the oldest of the many private fire companies in Philadelphia, the Hibernia occupied quarters on Dock Street.

55. The Rhode Island meeting supported "Governor" Thomas L. Dorr of Rhode Island. See entry of 11 May 1842.

My Cadwallader resolutions are in the *Ledger* of this morning with one or two typographical errors—just as I wrote them. They were "adopted by acclamation." What a deal of humbug there is in this world!

11 May, Wednesday.

In addition to the many other advantages which my situation in the office of Colonel Page gives me, I have an opportunity of seeing and hearing most of the great men of the day, at least most of the great men of the Democratic party. This afternoon the famous Governor Dorr of Rhode Island called upon the Colonel and introduced himself. That little state has two governments at the present time, each contending that it is the true one. One King[56] has been elected Governor under the charter of Charles II, and this Dorr has been elected by the people under a Constitution which they hold has been legally adopted. The question then, who is governor and who is traitor, depends upon whether the Charter or the Constitution is the supreme law of the land. By the technicalities of the courts perhaps the former is still in force; by an acknowledgement however of the great truth, of the axiom of democracies, we acknowledge the validity of the latter. Let future historians settle this mooted point—we who live in the smoke and dust of the conflict cannot do it impartially. Governor King (if Governor he be) sent a message to President Tyler, saying that the state was in the midst of an insurrection, and calling for the aid of the United States to bring things right. Tyler wrote back one of his peculiar letters which say Yes and No both at once; but the Yes being rather the most predominant in this case, Governor Dorr hastened off to Washington to represent **his** side of the question. By his looks to-day I should suppose Tyler has given him a cool reception. His object probably in calling upon Page was to learn the inclination of the volunteers, should they be called into action; these, who are the people, are with him. The sympathy with the suffrage party is very general, especially among the democrats—I might say, indeed, it is universal with them. They are always found on the liberal side. Governor Dorr is a fine looking man, of middle stature and rather corpulent. There are no indications of firmness in his countenance, and the Colonel says there is not much show of it in his conversation. If he has not some of that attribute and a good deal of what is quite as valuable, tact, he may yet be swung for a traitor. Some of his friends have been arrested on the charge of treason already.

This evening Ned Drayton and I called upon Edwards and Wilkins,

56. Samuel Ward King (1786–1851), a physician, businessman, and politician, was governor of Rhode Island from 1840 to 1843.

but they were neither of them at home. We then went to Arch Street Theatre and saw part of a play. Colonel Page was there.

13 May, Friday.

My friend William D. Kelley delivered a Temperance lecture this evening in the Camden Methodist church. The house was not so full as I could have hoped, but the lecture was admirable. It was a political view of the evils of intemperance—an original way of handling the matter, and a very effective one. The orator supped with me. He went over in the mail-boat.

16 May, Monday.

I was at the Institute meeting to-night for a wonder. After it was over I stopped at Stiver's a while.

Ned Drayton has begun to read law with Mr. Howell!

When I have more time I must narrate a little affair between Ned King and Mrs. Clark which is making some noise at the present time. I saw the correspondence to night between King and the lady's husband. Things look bad.

19 May, Thursday.

Sam Cowperthwait and Bob Ogden were *chez-moi* to-night fiddling and fluting; we had some pretty good music, all things considered.

20 May, Friday.

Last evening's company were in my study to-night for the same purpose. I find myself going deeper and deeper into my infatuation.

21 May, Saturday.

This morning, John Weight, Ned Drayton and myself took a sail in my skiff around to the creek. We got some gingerbread at the bridge-cake shop and made our dinner thereupon. . . .

25 May, Wednesday.

The frigate *Raritan* was to have been launched to-day from the Philadelphia Navy-yard, and every thing was in readiness; but the morning mail from Washington brought a countermand from the commissioners, in consequence of which it is put off *sine die*. This was a great disappointment to the steam-boat men, the public in general, and Hannah Sheppard and myself in particular, for we were calculating on a pleasant excursion in the *Fitch* to see it. The reason of this tack about in the intentions of the powers that be is, want of funds in the Treasury.

This evening I took the lady above named to a lecture in the Baptist church on India. It was rather a lame affair. I found Ned King with his fiddle in the parlour when we got back to the Parsonage.

28 May, Saturday.

. . . I was sailing several hours to-day. My skiff is launched, rigged, and in fine trim. Colonel Page, who read the first volume of my diary this week, says he sees that a boat is my hobby.

29 May, Sunday.

Buffington, Charles Garrett and I had an interview this morning about the establishment of a democratic paper in Camden. Charley and I are to ride the county to fix the monetary affairs.

This afternoon I went to Ide's church and shared the Sheppard pew with Miss Phoebe. It commenced raining just after we got over home.

30 May, Monday.

There is to be a meeting at the State House to-morrow in reference to the Navy. Colonel Page requested me to write some resolutions to be laid before it, and I began the task this afternoon, but did not get done.

In the evening I was in Charley Bontemp's shop fiddling with him.

31 May, Tuesday.

I arose before five o'clock this morning and went over to the office to finish my resolutions. I got them done before the Colonel was up, and went back to breakfast. A little after eight my mother, my aunt Eliza and myself started in a one-horse wagon for Richard Hugg's, where we are in the habit of paying an annual visit in this month. We arrived in about two hours, and had a very pleasant time. Old Joseph Hugg entertained me a good deal by his well-told stories of **other** days, and young Joseph by his merry pranks, and his hearty enjoyment of the happy days that **are**. The former knew Lawrence and Decatur well when they went to school in Woodbury.[57] He rowed Lawrence up to Philadelphia when he first embarked in the service; and once, when it was feared that the passengers of a West India ship lying down by the Fort with the Yellow fever, intended to land and get into Philadelphia by way of Jersey, he was an officer in a company of minute-volunteers in which Decatur served, whose object was to guard the shore. Mr. Hugg was entrusted with the stationing of the guards, and forgot to relieve Decatur, who was on the north side of Woodbury creek. He remained on duty all night, but damned his superior for forgetting him when relief-time came, as he believed it had been done on purpose. This little incident occurred in 1799. The last time he saw Lawrence, he says, was at the ferry in Camden now occupied by Israel English. He told him he "burned to wipe out the stain of the Chesapeake"—little thinking as the old man continued, that his blood

57. See entry of 19 February 1838.

was so soon to die her deck.[58] The gallant Captain fell not a great while afterwards. The John Hugg mentioned in Smith's History of New Jersey was this Joseph's great grandfather.[59] His family is one of the oldest in the state.

This evening after we got home (which was about seven o'clock) I took my violin around to Turner's and played with Miss Angeline until after ten. We got along much better than I expected or even hoped.

1 June, Wednesday.

My resolutions were adopted at the Naval Meeting in the State House yard yesterday afternoon, "amid loud and continued cheering" as the *Chronicle* has it. Colonel Page added two resolutions to the set, containing some statistics, of which I was not in possession; with which exception every syllable of them is mine. I consider it quite an honor to have given the tone to a meeting over which George M. Dallas presided, and in which his kindred spirits took a part. The proceedings and resolutions are published in all the morning papers. The assemblage was large and very respectable.

This evening I was at Hugg's. The house was full of company.

2 June, Thursday.

The papers speak favourably of my resolutions. One of the sixpennies says "the language though respectful is strong," and *The Times* and the other pennies have no objection to make. This is singular.

Sam and I went to the city this evening to hear a complimentary Concert, given to Mrs. Watson the singer. The Rainers sang the Laughing Chorus, and some other fine pieces, Signor Begnis also sang in Italian and English—Mrs. Watson warbled some delicious songs, and one Hupfeldt performed an admirable solo on the violin.[60] Ned King played double bass. There were about thirty performers and a thousand auditors. We had an agreeable time. The mail-boat was full of Jerseymen on our return.

58. Lawrence was killed in 1813, when his ship the *Chesapeake* was devastated by H.M.S. *Shannon*. The *Chesapeake's* record had been stained in 1807, when H.M.S. *Leopard*, searching for deserters, opened fire on and crippled the American ship.

59. Samuel Smith's *The History of the Colony of Nova-Caesaria, or New Jersey* (Burlington, 1765) speaks of Hugg's presence at a meeting of the West Jersey Council of Proprietors in 1703 and records his death in 1730.

60. Mrs. Watson (formerly Miss Wells) was a popular English soprano who had made her New York debut in 1835. Giuseppi de Begnis was a renowned singer of Italian buffo roles. "Hupfeldt" was one of the three violinists in Philadelphia's Hupfeld family: Charles Frederick (1788–1864) and his sons, Charles and John.

3 June, Friday.

The Colonel transferred to me the task of drafting another batch of Cadwallader resolutions this afternoon. Well, as Mr. Kelley says, this may be "like bread cast upon the waters." At all events I will write them.

The *Times* says to day that the resolutions of last Tuesday "were drafted by a celebrated democrat of Philadelphia." Isaac Mickle Esq. is a democrat, undoubtedly, but neither a Philadelphian, nor celebrated! By the by I saw my notice of Senator Henderson to-day in a Massachusetts paper credited to some gazette in Maryland. Fair play is a jewel.

Sam, Josiah Atkinson and I had some music to night, after which I call'd at Hugg's.

4 June, Saturday.

The Philadelphia correspondent of the Trenton paper says the resolutions adopted by the Naval meeting the other day "were very pointed but just." That is exactly what I aimed at.

This afternoon I attended the funeral of General Goodwin, up in the Liberties.[61] He was buried with all the honors of war. The volunteer-escort which was under the command of Colonel Page, was very numerous, and looked very fine. It was upon the whole an impressive sight. By some default on the part of the undertaker no guide was sent to conduct the Colonel to the grave-yard, and he was in a great dilemma thereupon, when he saw me fortunately and got me to procure him a pilot.

This evening I called upon Ned King and went with him to Ackley's.[62]

I got my Cadwallader resolutions done this morning. The meeting is to be this evening in front of the State House.

6 June, Monday.

The election for Brigadier General and other officers comes off to-day. There is a good deal of excitement about it. Banners are flying and music playing in every direction. About four o'clock this afternoon two wagons covered with Cadwallader placards, and filled with musicians hauled up before our office, and gave us a march. Kelley and I will divide the honor of this day-light serenade between us. There will be a warm contest between Cadwallader, Lee and Fritz,

61. Gen. John D. Goodwin, Northern Liberties businessman and an officer in the Pennsylvania militia, had died on June 2.
62. Thomas Ackley (1802–63) was a Camden dry-goods merchant.

but it is believed the first will be successful.[63] My second batch of resolutions is published in all the papers except the *Times* and *Sentinel*. I hope they may aid Cadwallader's cause in some degree.

This evening I met the Town clerk of Camden, Josiah Atkinson, Jr. Esquire, and invited him around to my room to help me make music. This was after the last meeting of the Institute, which is adjourned until September. We played until eleven o'clock.

I spent an hour or two at Sheppard's this afternoon. There was one Doctor Ward[64] there, a very clever man but a very affected singer.

7 June, Tuesday.

Major Cadwallader was triumphantly elected yesterday. The following is the number of votes received by each candidate, as reported in the papers: Cadwallader 3560, Fritz 3050, Lee 1216.

Upon the strength of the above glorious victory I thought I could afford to take a holy-day, and so I did it. Having got Robert Ogden, James Ballantine, John Weight and a young man named Sam, we went over to the island on a fishing party in my skiff. I took my fiddle along and we had a flute. We had some good music, though the fishing-luck was bad. We returned towards evening.

Abraham Browning married Elizabeth Matlack about a fortnight ago. The match made a good deal of noise, owing to the singular remarks passed by Miss Matlack on the Camden people in general, and some of the inhabitants in particular. She said for instance that "Sausageberg,"[65] that is, Camden, "contained no ladies with whom she cared to associate," and that she did not want to reside too near this one or the other. Some of these reflections of the blacksmith's daughter did not go down well with our young gentlemen who have sisters, who think themselves equally as good as she. So they resolved to give her arrogance a rebuke by a mock concert. I was invited to go along, and being fond of fun could not decline.

We met at midnight at Heyl's. The following are the performers, and the instruments performed on.

Edward King, an old cow-bell and door key, quasi drum and drum stick.

John J. Weight, a sheet of copper to imitate thunder.

John Burr, a tavern dinner-bell, half as big as that in the tower of our St. Paul.

James Carman, a string of sleigh-bells.

James George, the half of an old flute.

63. Cadwalader's opponents in the election for the brigadier generalship of Philadelphia's militia were Major Peter Fritz and Colonel Robert M. Lee.
64. Ward was music director at Philadelphia's Second Baptist Church.
65. Camden sausage had been popular in Philadelphia for many years.

John Humphreys, the mouth-piece of a clarionet.

William Heyl, a tin waiter and stick.[66]

Myself, with a tenor-bell.

About half past twelve we drew up along the fence below Abraham's dwelling, and struck up the Battle chorus from the opera of *Norma*. Every instrument bore its part nobly. Such a noise was never heard before. The windows in the neighborhood flew up and heads popped (with eyes expecting to see half the town in flames) two or three feet out of them, but perceiving the state of the game they quietly looked on and enjoyed the joke. The city patrol (for the city has had a patrol for a week back, on account of the numerous burglaries which have been committed of late) gathered under the trees on the opposite side, and laughed heartily; and every thing went off well. After the chorus King struck up a song, the burden of which was "Sausage! Sausage, Sausage ho! I'm going among the sausage-makers o'er in the Jarsies!" All the instruments joined in and did their part; and this too went off well. We gave them two other select pieces, and then adjourned with a grand instrumental overture. King was afraid of getting shot, or we would have given another evidence of our skill. I got home about one o'clock.

The newly married pair only returned from their bridal tour yesterday. I wonder how Mrs. Browning will like her reception in Sausage-berg?

I had an introduction this evening to Miss Caroline Cole who has returned within a few days from boarding school at Lititz, full of accomplishments and loveliness.

8 June, Wednesday.

I dropped in at the parsonage this evening and found the ladies alone. I stopped for Bob Ogden who was to have gone along and taken a boquet, but they did not hear the bell, and so I went by myself. The girls set me at work on some articles for The Fair which begins next Tuesday.

11 June, Saturday.

For some time past it has been a fixed thing among some of my companions that we should have a fishing party to-day—and so to-day we had our fishing party.

At nine o'clock this morning we started in two boats, my skiff *Poms* as uncle has named her, being one, and a wherry the other. I com-

66. John Burr was probably the son of Joseph Burr whom city directories list as a "gentleman." James Carman may have been the son of entrepreneur William Carman, and William Heyl the child of Elizabeth Heyl, owner of the Columbia Pleasure Garden. John C. Humphreys was a Camden coachmaker in later years.

manded the skiff and had with me, Ned Drayton, James Ballantine and one of his friends from Philadelphia and Lemuel Davis. Bob Ogden was captain of the wherry, and had with him John Weight, Joseph Simpson and Charles Apple, the two last from Philadelphia.[67] Each one took a basket of provisions, I had my fiddle, and two or three had flutes.

The wind blew tremendously, so that we could not carry sail on the skiff at all. The wherry did better. She got started first and stopped at Kaighn's Point to get the net. We passed them here, scudding under bare poles, and proceeded down to our fish-cabin in Newton. At this place we stopped and went into the cabin and had a dance. In about an hour we saw the wherry rounding into Newton Creek, and Ned Drayton dropped the skiff down there too. Very fortunately we met another fishing party with light batteaux, one of which we made arrangements to borrow, and hauling her over the dam, fixed the net and proceeded to the amusement of the day. We made eight or ten hauls with the seine and caught about a bushel of fish, which we gave to the owner of the batteau we had loaned. Between each haul we adjourned down to the dam to have music and refreshments. Some of the young gentlemen went in pretty deep for the brandy, but Lem and I being temperance men, had to be content with lemonade.

We stopped fishing about four o'clock, and were enjoying ourselves at the dam by dancing in our wet and muddy breeches, when whom should we see coming up the causeway from towards Woodbury, but Ned King? He had started a little after us in his gunning skiff, and as we had expected to go to Red Bank, he kept on to that place, not seeing our fleet in the mouth of Newton Creek. Being unable to spy us, and the wind blowing too hard to allow him to return, he left his boat in the charge of an old woman in Woodbury Creek, and started off to walk back to Camden. He saw us at Newton Bridge and joined us, hungry and tired enough.

Having got the batteau hauled into the river again, and the net and other articles put into our boats, we waded them up to the cabin, and the whole party entered the same and built a large fire to dry our clothes. We staid here, dancing, singing, eating and drinking until sun-set, when as the wind began to lull, we made sail and beat up against the ebb to Kaighn's Point. The breeze failed us at this place and we were obliged to row the balance of the distance. King played two or three operas on my fiddle and made the task of rowing very light and agreeable. The wherry came along side of us at Fettersville,

67. Philadelphia city directories list Simpson as a bookbinder at 304 Pine Street, but do not mention Apple.

and we found Weight shaking with an ague-fit and writhing under a violent tooth-ach. This was the only thing that marred our pleasure.

I got home about nine o'clock, dressed myself, took tea, and went around to Captain Manly's where the Sewing Society met, to arrange things for the fair that is to be next week. A little after ten o'clock I accompanied two of the constellation to their door, and pretty soon afterwards went to bed, pleased with the manner in which I had passed (might I not say, wasted?) the day.

12 June, Sunday.

I crossed the river this morning and took a walk. On my return I met the Cooper street ladies, and saw them home. In the afternoon I went out to Fairmount with Sam to see the Wire Bridge—It is a master-piece of art.[68] In the evening I went both to Baptist and Methodist Church, but profited little at either.

13 June, Monday.

Colonel Page introduced me to day to Brigadier General Cadwallader. He is a military looking man, and I have no doubt inherits the valor of his ancestors.

In the evening I accompanied Misses Mary and Josephine Sheppard down to the Fair Room. Mary took an elegant castle which she had wrought of shells, and Jo went for fun. There were a good many ladies there arranging the articles. The room used is Scull's Coach Shop on Front Street near Cole's large Mansion. During the evening I got dry, and went with Jim Ballantine back to their pump to get a drink—in the performance of which act I had the pleasure of having a chat with Miss Caddy Cole. She came out to take a look at the Fair Room, and did not see me until it was too late to retreat.

My mother hurt her foot this afternoon and is so lame that she had to call in one of her neighbors' little girls to help her.

14 June, Tuesday.

The long-talked-of Fair (or Sale as the Rev. Mr. Burroughs will have it called) begins to-day. I was in, this evening, and could not tell which to admire the most, the taste of the ladies in making the articles or their tact in selling them. It was with the greatest difficulty that I got off with one or two slight purchases. Among other means of turning a penny, they have a mock post-office, where they receive and deliver mock letters. The postage is the only reality about it. I wrote three letters at Phoebe Sheppard's request and put them in to be delivered to somebody. . . .

68. The wire suspension bridge across the Schuylkill River was opened to traffic on 2 January 1842.

I went to Cole's pump again to-night for a drink, and strange to say, met Caddy again. Josephine—but never mind.

Ned Drayton's papa who has been out with the Exploring Expedition since August 1838 returned to Camden to-day.[69] He arrived at New York on Friday. He was at the Fair to-night, but I had not time to talk with him. I wonder if he has any coin?

I walked home with the empress and one of her sisters from the Sale, after having passed a rainy evening in a pleasant manner.

My mother's lameness is much better to-night.

15 June, Wednesday.

I was at the fair this evening of course, and saw two of the constellation home. This is the fifth day handrunning I have had the pleasure of their company. They must certainly be tired of seeing me, but they conceal their feelings very adroitly if such is the case. . . .

16 June, Thursday.

This evening Sam, Bob and I met at the Library room, and had some music. Everything went off smoothly until the conversation happened to turn upon the ladies, when Sam made some remarks about Josephine which I was bound to resent. I told him he was a liar, and laying my fiddle down upon the table, added, "and you are a coward if you do not repel the epithet upon the spot." This he did not chose to do. He afterwards swallowed his words, and we parted pretty good friends. I must confess I was angry. I owe Sam fifty cents; but if I owed him my life he should not breathe the name of any of my lady acquaintances in connection with any thing improper.

17 June, Friday.

I drafted a Circular to-day for the Colonel, to be addressed to Martin Van Buren and other great democrats inviting them to participate in the celebration of the Fourth of July, in Independence Square, by the democracy of Philadelphia. . . .

20 June, Monday.

This evening there was a meeting at Captain Manley's of "The Sewing Society of St. Paul's Church" in reference to continuing the fair. The Rev. Mr. Burroughs was Chairman, and all the ladies not *seriatim sed conjunctim*, were speakers. They decided upon a measure first and debated it afterwards, as ladies usually do. Phoebe and Mary came in about nine o'clock, and I had the extreme pleasure, and so forth—

69. Drayton had been on the famous Wilkes Expedition, led by naval officer Charles Wilkes (1798–1877). This first national marine exploration effort surveyed the Pacific Ocean and South Sea waters and claimed to have discovered Antarctica.

21 June, Tuesday.

I drafted a letter to the "old Chief"[70] to day, at the request of the Colonel, inviting him to participate in the celebration of the Fourth of July in the State House Yard. . . . I have a good deal of this kind of work to do, but I do it with pleasure. It may "like bread on the waters," return some of these days. . . .

25 June, Saturday.

Our *partie à peché* on the 11th inst. gave so much satisfaction, that we resolved on having another to-day, and we carried our designs into execution with the same boats, and nearly the same crews, that we had before. We started at nine o'clock, and went into Timber Creek; made a dozen hauls and caught about that many fish; had plenty of music and dancing in the fish-cabin at our farm, on our return; enjoyed a good breeze, and good appetites; kept in good health and spirits; and lastly returned about seven o'clock, gratified with the manner in which we had spent the day.

In the evening I went to the Fair. Mary and Josephine were there. I had a little talk with them, but pretty soon sheered off, left them, and went in to see Caddy Cole. That is very, very, exceedingly, well. I like to keep accounts of all kinds square.

26 June, Sunday.

This evening I called upon the Sheppards to accompany them to hear one Mr. Osbourne preach at the Baptist church.[71] Phoebe and Josephine went. I observed on the road to Phoebe that if it were possible I was going to sit in the same pew with them, and sure enough I was just entering one after them when an old lady came along and lo! I had to back out to make room for her. Phoebe had a hearty laugh at my disappointment, and vexed as I was, I had to laugh too. By the by, Josephine asked me this evening where I went to from the fair last night. Enough—my point is carried.

30 June, Thursday.

I have read more law within a week back, and understood it better than in any other equal period of my scholarship.

This evening I went to Sheppards with my violin, to play airs to be accompanied by Ned Drayton on the piano. The plan worked very well. I introduced a piece which I had composed, as a "Thema and Variations by Gustavus Schwogel." I played it amidst a shower of "O, beautifuls" "how lovelys" and such like droppings. The girls encored

70. The "old Chief" was ex-president Andrew Jackson.
71. Camden newspapers reveal that Osbourne lectured on the "millennial state," but do not give his first name or pastorate.

it, and really seemed to admire it. More of this hereafter. Ned made some very sweet accompaniments. He certainly has an extraordinary ear for music, but he does not like Mrs. Sheppard's telling him that he had better study music than the law. Ha! ha!

1 July, Friday.
This day will be remembered for many a year on account of the violent thundergust which it brought forth. The oldest inhabitants of this city say that they never saw but one equal to it, and that was during the last war. Some fool had prophecied that the world was to come to an end on that particular day, and the terrible storm that happened seemed for a while to make the prophecy triumphant. Some people went so far as to get into the river to keep cool a few minutes longer, and very many who never prayed before, began to pray then in earnest. . . .

A little before six o'clock, I was in John Baxter's tailor shop, tuning a tenor violin in order to play some hymns with him, when suddenly our eyes were almost seared with a flash of lightning to the south east. In two or three seconds a tremendous clap of thunder succeeded and put an end to our music. A tree in a field just below the rail-road had been struck and shivered into a thousand pieces. One Elfreth,[72] as I have since learned, was so near that he was knocked down and much stunned.

So sudden and so severe a beginning alarmed every one. All who were in the tailor-shop hastened to Delacour's, and Baxter was so undone that by the time we got there he was as weak as a rag and seemed to be in a way of needing some of the medicine with which he was surrounded. He got back into the darkest place and reclined his head upon a desk, from which position he hardly moved until ten o'clock.

The gust was now fairly advancing upon us, red and gloated, as it were, with fury. I never before saw, though I have read in the Bible, of a cloud—No,—I believe it is, "a pillar of fire." The rain began to patter down in huge drops, and in a few minutes it seemed as if heaven's artillery were firing in platoons at the earth. The lightning came sometimes in balls which as they got near the earth, burst and flew in different directions like rockets, and sometimes in snaky spirals or zig-zag flashes, which were heard to hiss through the air like red hot iron plunged into water—a sound more terrible than even the ear-splitting thunder which rolled almost incessantly.

72. Probably Samuel D. Elfreth who ran a smithery on Front Street above Market, Camden.

Among the party at Delacour's was Mr. Lenhart,[73] the Methodist minister, a fat, merry kind of man, who may fear God, but who certainly does not fear God's work in the way of *donner und blitzen* a whit. He and I were discussing the Rhode Island war and the cowardly conduct of Dorr, when a very vivid gleam of lightning accompanied almost instantly with a terriffic peal of thunder brought even Baxter to his feet. "I think that struck in Fetterville" said I: "I think it struck our church" said the clergyman; and we commenced our conversation again. In a few minutes in came John Morgan out of breath, and cried "The church is on fire—where's the key?—Fire! Fire" and off he went, and some of the rest followed. I borrowed an old hat and was about going too, when a boy came back and told us that the Methodist church had been struck, but the rain had put out the fire. This building stands about a hundred yards from our dwelling, and about three hundred from the tree that had been struck before. The stroke shattered the cornice a good deal, knocked off the rain conductor, and did some other damage. This was at nine o'clock.

The storm continued with unabated fury for an hour longer, during which time I was reading an account of the settlement of Bethlehem, Pennsylvania. At ten o'clock however it had so far cleared off that Baxter went home to his supper, and I to-bed. On my way I found the water knee-deep in the streets in several places. It had rained for three or four hours in torrents.

How much damage has been done I cannot guess. There were two or three lights of fires in Philadelphia visible at ten o'clock. An awful evening has this been for the wicked!

4 July, Monday.   Columbia's Sixty Sixth Birth-day.

In beginning a new volume of my diary, now that I am entering upon the third year of my experiment, I have resolved to pay less attention to those small things in my own history for which nobody but myself will care, and to devote more space to those great public concerns in which all posterity will feel an interest; in other words, to make it a diary of my times rather than of my life. The day is approaching when I may assume the *"toga virilis,"* and mingle in the affairs of men. It is proper therefore that I should begin to observe the incidents of the great drama that is going on around me, to learn my part, and prepare myself to act it becomingly. . . . But while I shall note down the acts of others I neither assume the province of the historian, nor look for praise from anybody but myself. I do however

73. John L. Lenhart was pastor of the Third Street Methodist Episcopal Church from 1842 to 1843.

flatter myself that should my book fall into the hands of any young politician it may in a measure answer the purposes for which I design it.

Perhaps I could make some improvement in the present volume in the point of execution; but I have promised a reformation of my hasty composition and bad penmanship so often, that it would be almost absurd to revive the resolution. Like its predecessors, much of the tome in which I am now writing will be thrown together late at night, when I am sleepy or tired, and illy qualified to compose carefully. This general apology must answer for every thing but blots and bad grammar—for which nothing can apologize.

So much for an introduction: now how did I celebrate the present glorious day?

This morning I arose at the usual hour, about eight o'clock, and after breakfast went into my room tuned up my violin, and played *Hail Columbia, Yankee Doodle* and *The Star Spangled Banner*. After this patriotic beginning I took a walk in the woods, and saw that the Philadelphians were beginning to come over.

In the afternoon I casually met Ned King, James George[74] and Ned Drayton, and a sail being proposed, we went down to Fort Mifflin and Red Bank in my skiff. At the former place there is a garrison of about an hundred United States troops; the guns are all mounted and every thing is in order. At Red Bank we met some friends who took us up to a farm house near by and treated us to apple-pie, spruce-beer and cigars. They were making arrangement for a party on the Bank to-morrow. We left for home at about five o'clock and had a tight race with a boat load of Frenchmen—we beat them however at last. There was a fine breeze, sufficiently strong to break our mast short off although we were reefed.

In the evening I called at Sheppard's where I found Ned King. Ned Drayton came in after me. The time was very agreeably passed in music, conversation, and looking at fire-works which were being displayed all around us. The Empress and I talked over the days when we used to play Copenhagen together, and—I wished those days could return![75]

5 July, Tuesday.

I was at the office to-day, although it was so near "the fourth" that I could not do much in the way of business. Ned Drayton appeared to be in the same dilemma, for he borrowed my boat to go a-sailing.

74. The Camden city directory for 1850 lists George as a broker on Market Street above Third.
75. Copenhagen was a children's kissing game.

This afternoon I was introduced to a Mr. Mulford,[76] the sixth student at law in Camden! He is with Mr. Jeffers, looks like a Methodist class-leader, and appears to be intelligent and well educated.

In the evening I stopped at Sheppard's to borrow the *Ivy Green,* a piece of music, but contrived to spend an hour with the girls. Mary and Phoebe and I went to see Mrs. Clark, but she was not at home. I arranged it with Miss Josephine that I should take her into the country next week to see Caddy Cole, who is staying with her grandmother.

7 July, Thursday.

It is I believe a year to-night since I was introduced by James Ballantine at Sheppard's. I first entered their parlour under very unfavourable circumstances. I was placed by the misrepresentations of others in an embarrassing situation, and for months I never went there without being under extreme restraint, and showing the greatest stiffness in my deportment. Now I hardly know any difference between visiting the "parsonage" as we call it, and dropping in to see my aunt or any other relative. I flatter myself that I am "a welcome guest" at this house, and I will strive to do nothing that will impair my good standing. I may safely pronounce the past twelve months the happiest year of my life, though I cannot but own it has been a profitless one, so far as mental improvement is concerned. . . .

8 July, Friday.

There was a Prussian lectured this evening in the City Hall on Arithmetic. He professes to have discovered a new method by which all problems can be wrought in a short time and with great accuracy; and from the examples he gave us of his theory, I am inclined to become a convert. . . .

9 July, Saturday.

I was not at the office to-day as I usually am not on Saturdays. There is marketing to be done, and a good many things to be seen to which keep me from my studies.

This evening I called at Hugg's. I am getting to be too intimate there, and from henceforth I will make myself more scarce. Perhaps if I were only to go once a month they would call me **Mr.** Mickle.

10 July, Sunday.

This evening I called at the Parsonage and accompanied Misses Phoebe and Josephine to Methodist Church. The visit to see Caddy

---

76. Thomas W. Mulford (no relation to Camden's Dr. Isaac Mulford) was a native of Salem County who had recently arrived in Camden to study law with William N. Jeffers. He would serve in the state senate in 1851.

Cole which I am to make with the latter, is to take place to-morrow. May the day be pleasant!

11 July, Monday.

My wish was granted! When I arose this morning the sun was shining in unclouded splendour—the air was delightfully cool—all nature was smiling. A finer day for our rural jaunt could not have been found for a month past, the old saying that the "wishes of the wicked avail not" to the contrary notwithstanding.

About eight o'clock I went over to Fullerton's and Claxton's[77] in Market Street, as I promised Edward Cole yesterday, to get a package of letters for his sister. Returning to Camden as soon as I could, I ordered the horse and carriage and stopped for Josephine at or very near the time appointed. I like punctuality, especially in appointments with the ladies. The Empress was all ready, and in a few minutes we started off amidst the smiles of her sisters who bade us "good by" and "take care" from the steps of their house.

Mrs. Rowand, Caddy Cole's grandmother, lives near a place called Fellowship, a mile and a half from Moorestown, and about a half a mile from my uncle Richard Hugg's. She is famous throughout the neighborhood for her benevolence and kindness, qualities which her grandchild seems to possess in an eminent degree. The old lady is at present much indisposed and the young one prompted by an affection that does honor to her character, has repaired to her bed-side; leaving the most splendid home that Camden contains, to pass the summer in an irksome duty in a little cottage almost hid in the woods of Burlington county. This however is only of a piece with the rest of Caroline's conduct. She is a lovely girl; and the more I see of her the more I admire her loveliness. I know not to what this admiration may come.

It might be expected that during a ride of two hours with the girl of whom I have so often and so warmly spoken, and that, too, when the time, the occasion, and all things conspired to unbind the fountains of the heart, I should have made a fool of myself as most lovers do as soon as an opportunity for a *tete-a-tete* is offered. This was not the case, however. We conversed of days gone-by, 'tis true—of those happy days when we used to meet at little birth-day parties, and romp in all the thoughtfulness of childhood; we spoke of more recent occurrences, such as the gallantry of Master Sam Cowperthwait and his adventures with the young ladies of Ide's church; we touched upon other subjects calculated to pave the way for the introduction of our own feelings;

77. Alexander Fullerton operated a drug store in Market Street. John W. Claxton was formerly associated with the business.

and in all our dialogue we were perhaps more unreserved than ever before. But, for my part, I felt a strange indisposition to commit myself; and for hers, she would have had too much modesty to make even the slightest advances if she had felt anything more than friendship for me—which I have begun very decidedly to doubt, and as to which, I must confess, I am much more indifferent than I was some time ago. I have observed certain things in her conduct towards my long-haired friend, Ned Drayton, which sprang either from a particular liking for him, or what I would regard still more, a disposition to coquet. In addition to this, she placed a bracelet of her hair upon the wrist of my enemy Clement, and wore a ring made of his, for several weeks. . . .

Although I do not claim to be a Platonic lover, I **do** presume that I always submit my passion to reason. I have come to the above unwelcome conclusions deliberately and cooly. . . . I feel it due to myself, my pride is imperative in its commands, to be blinded no longer. And my pride shall be obeyed, be the price what it may. Self should be respected, though the sacrifice required were to tear my heart from my bosom.

In thus renouncing a relation with this girl which I have occupied for five years and in which I have found an exalted pleasure, I disclaim being actuated by anything but reason and prudence. To the feeling of jealousy I am a perfect stranger. . . .

A contest between Pride and Love has been raging within me for some time. It has been evident to me for months that one or the other must prevail at the expense of the other. Reason and prudence decide for the former, and to the former therefore I yield. To assure myself that I was actuated by nothing momentary and transient, I have used the greatest deliberation. I have visited the Parsonage more frequently than ever, in order to observe Josephine's behaviour under different circumstances. I have assumed various phases, the better to test her. The result of all has been to hasten the resolution I have just recorded. If I have been deceived, this long episode shall be cancelled; if not, it shall be as binding as my bond.

We arrived at Mrs. Rowand's about eleven o'clock; not however until we had passed the cottage a mile or so without finding out our mistake. The dwelling appears to be a century old. The windows are patched up; the doors are swayed and crooked; the weatherboards loosened and black with the wear of time; the chimney seemingly ready to fall; and everything else in a like plight. We could not believe that that house, although it answered the description we had obtained as a guide, could contain the charming Miss Cole. Yet there we found her—and she seemed to me the more charming from that very fact.

She welcomed us with a heartiness that made me feel at home immediately, and without any apology for the humble mansion in which she was found, proceeded to converse with a sprightliness and frankness that delighted me. Her countenance only lost its mirth when she spoke of her grandmother, whose health continues very feeble, and whose indisposition will probably confine her to her bed and her grandchild to her bed-side for the chief part of the summer.

I pretty soon jumped into my buggie and drove around to my uncle's where I dined. I told them a fib about my company—to wit that James Ballantine came up with me, which makes me feel very uneasy. I did it through mere inadvertence, without any motive at all—a very foolish thing indeed. . . .

About two o'clock I drove into Moorestown, rode through it, and undertook to return to Rowand's by the Medford road, but got lost, among the woods and barrens. After a good deal of trouble however in inquiring my way of the half civilized natives, no two of whom could agree, I came out by Hugg's again, and knowing the coast from there, soon rejoined my girls. I had been riding about two hours pretty fast, and must have travelled some ten or twelve miles, a part of the distance, as I knew by my horse's shadow, directly from the point I wished to go to.

The balance of the afternoon was spent in pleasant chit-chat. At seven the three of us sat down to tea, and I did a considerable deal of eating. The ladies not having had my ride through the woods had not my appetite. Pretty soon afterwards we started for home, leaving Caddy to return again to her sick grandmother. We came through Ellisburg and Haddonfield and had a delightful ride, reaching home about nine.

My friend seemed inclined to make me believe that she would like me to visit Doctor Smalley's[78] next week, when she and her sister Hannah will be there. She observed also in reply to a remark of mine, that I thought she and her sisters must be tired of seeing me so often, that such was only my own fancy. And on the whole she was more loquacious on our return than in the morning, while I was less so. I would have felt gratified at some of the words she let fall to-night if spoken some time ago. I fear I was too indifferent, and I fear still some more she will attribute my indifference to the wrong cause.

Notwithstanding the circumstances upon which I have dwelt so tediously I enjoyed the whole visit highly, and Josephine says she did too. During the remainder of the evening (which I passed at the Parsonage) she was in excellent spirits, and I appeared to be, too;

78. Dr. Joseph B. Smalley, father of Mickle's friend of the same name, resided on a farm three miles east of Mount Holly.

but who can describe the difference between my semblance and my reality? It is no light matter to relapse from the character of lover to that of merely a friend.

12 July, Tuesday.
The transactions of yesterday and the resolutions of last night have been uppermost in my mind ever since morning. I sometimes fear I have wronged an innocent creature, and sometimes wounded pride impels me onward in the course I have undertaken. A few weeks will decide. *"Festina lente"* shall be my motto.

I was walking up in the Woodlands this afternoon to hear the music when I met the Prussian mathematician spoken of last Friday. I had quite a talk with him. He had the proof-sheet of a work called the *Plain Calculator* in his hat, and says it will be published in a month or so. I must get a copy and investigate the new system of arithmetic.

Sam Cowperthwait and I were playing together this evening. He has almost given up the violin for his flute.

13 July, Wednesday.
. . . I was at the office to-day from nine o'clock to four, with very few minutes intermission. This evening I spent at home with my aunt Mary from West-chester. Thus have two days passed without my being at the Parsonage.

15 July, Friday.
I was at the office for six hours to-day and studied for the chief part of the time very industriously. The chaotic mass of knowledge of the laws which I have thrown into my head is just beginning to assume some order.

In the evening Ned Drayton and I visited Stivers'. Ned presided at the piano, John Weight played upon the flute and myself upon the violin, making together some pretty good music.

16 July, Saturday.
My aunt Haines is still with us.

This evening Sam Cowperthwait came around to my room with his violin, and we had some sweet duetts. His little sister has been so ill for nearly three months that he has been obliged to suspend practising. I have in consequence got a good way ahead of him—indeed I could now give him lessons, as he gave me one year ago. I can make out to go into the third position with a good deal of correctness and with some degree of celerity, at least in the more common keys of one and two sharps. Ned King says it was more than a year before he could do this; and he had a good teacher, whereas I have had none; so that I begin to hope I may become a fiddler yet. *"Nil desperandum."*

17 July, Sunday.

This morning (and a delightful one it was!) I rode out to Heulings Haines' farm[79] to dun him for my mother's interest money which he is very slow this year in paying. He was not at home.

In the afternoon I took a long walk with Ned King. We went through the woods in search of huckleberries, as far as Newton Creek, then visited the farm house and returned by the river-side to Kaighn's Point. Here we refreshed ourselves with ice-cream and so forth, and then started for home. Along the causeway below South Camden we saw a grand row, occasioned by Constable Sawns'[80] attempting to arrest a negro who had been acting against the peace and dignity of our town, and whose friends resisted the officer in a very spirited manner. Pistols, canes and loaded handkerchiefs, to say nothing of fists and feet, came in great requisition. At last the first negro was secured, and the Constable then proceeded to seize one of the worst of those who attempted to make "rescous." He jumped into the river and was going to swim across, but they got a boat and drove him ashore at Camden, where he was nabbed and put in "the stone jug."

This evening Ned aforesaid and I called at Sheppard's and took the girls out to church. I got into the pew with Hannah and Josephine, Ned along with Phoebe. This is the first time I have seen these folks since Monday last. Josephine seemed this evening more open and sincere than usual. What shall I **do**? What **shall** I do? **What** shall I do?

18 July, Monday.

I was at the office to-day and read pretty industriously.

This evening I went up to Burlington on an excursion in the steamer *New Philadelphia*. We left Chesnut Street wharf at eight o'clock with about five hundred passengers. My uncle and I went together—no ladies were along with me. They had a very ordinary band of music which played for the cotillions on the after-deck, while the "hard cases," the wild young men who came aboard without any girls, had the Scotch bagpipes and an old fiddle, on the forecastle, to the music of which they performed a certain dance called a "hoe-down." Some of them danced all the way up and down.

We got into Burlington a little after nine, where I and Dudley and a good many others went ashore and promenaded about in the moonlight and sipped ice-cream. The boat took the others over to Bristol where they stayed until between ten and eleven o'clock. She then came

79. Heulings (or Hewlings) Haines' farm lay north of Cooper's Creek, just east of Browning Road.
80. Josiah Sawn, of Fettersville, had been one of Camden's two constables since 1841.

back, and we reëmbarked; we arrived in Philadelphia before one o'clock, and before two I was sound asleep at home.

19 July, Tuesday.

I took a walk this evening into the woods with Turner's girls and Browning's. They wanted to select a spot for a school pic nic to-morrow. Hollingshead[81] and Ned Drayton were along. I had a slight misunderstanding with the latter which resulted in a dissolution of our friendship. So be it! I only regret not having slapped my long haired chum in the mouth for some of his impudence.

President Dougherty invited me to-day to deliver a Temperance address some time soon.

20 July, Wednesday.

This evening I walked out with the four Sheppard's girls. We went around by Cooper's Point; dropped in a friend's; returned by the river; stopped to see Abby Wilkins;[82] and arrived at the Parsonage about ten o'clock, where we found Ned King. I had a great deal of gratification from the promenade; but as for Miss Josephine, what shall I do? What shall I do?

21 July, Thursday.

My aunt Haines, Doctor Mulford, wife and children, my mother and myself took tea this evening down at the farm-house. "Poplar Hill" looks so pleasant that whenever I get there I wish to stay.

After our return I met Ned King at the Parsonage. He took Phoebe to some exhibition of fire-works at Cake's garden where Mary and I joined them after having heard one Mr. Appleton[83] deliver a Temperance lecture at the Methodist church. The lecture was good, but the pyrotechnics were excellent. I am getting into my old habits again. Can it be true that—I love the Empress yet?

22 July, Friday.

. . . This evening Ned King and I called at . . . the Parsonage, and took the girls out a-walking. I prevailed on Phoebe to go down to see a menagerie that was exhibiting in our part of the town. The famous Herr Driesbach,[84] a German, was there with his lions. He has brought the savages of the desert to more complete subjection than any other

81. Mickle's young friend, Charles Hollingshead, was currently studying law in Camden. He was admitted to the bar in April 1846.

82. Abby Wilkens was probably a daughter of Isaac Wilkins, lumber merchant of Market Street near Front.

83. James Appleton (1785–1862) was one of the country's leading temperance advocates, especially in efforts to secure state prohibition.

84. Driesbach's Menagerie toured the United States for many years, after 1853 with "Mabie's United States Circus."

man that ever lived, and plays with them the same as I would with a cat or dog. Besides a fine, noble lion, he has a leopard, a tiger or two, and some others. When he was exhibiting in Philadelphia his mode of advertising was to ride around the town in a barouch with his tiger unconfined alongside of him.

23 July, Saturday.
I was practising pretty industriously to-day on the violin.

This evening I called at Stivers' to see Elizabeth, who has just returned from a visit at New York. She saw her brother Gideon, who lives in Brooklyn and follows his trade of carpentering. She says he inquires particularly after me and the Library. The house beginning to fill up with company, and Angeline Turner starting to go home, the former was the cause and the latter the occasion of my withdrawing.

24 July, Sunday.
William Shaw spent the day with me. We walked down to Kaighn's Point to see old Sally Boggs, but she was not at home. Bill is better as a man than he was as a boy.

This evening I called at Sheppard's and found Ned King there. I asked Phoebe some days ago to go on an excursion to-morrow night. King was present and offered to accompany Mary, but the girls declined giving an answer until this evening, when, as I began to broach the subject, Phoebe took me into the next room and told me that she did not like to go with King, since from his character and disposition she feared he might have too many roué acquaintances, especially as he had played in the theatres. She asked my opinion, but I declined giving it; and so the matter now rests.

25 July, Monday.
I staid in the city this evening until the mail-boat crossed, when of course I ran afoul of King. Baxter and Sam Cowperthwait are some where in the city of brotherly love to-night with their fiddles. They had better stay at home and save their credit.

26 July, Tuesday.
While I was at tea this evening Ned King called upon me to go with him to Walnut Street Theatre, to see Fanny Fitzwilliams and Buckstone the famous comedy-maker.[85] He borrowed my violin to play with, and as a kind of *quid pro quo*, I suppose, took me into the orchestra along with him. We staid until the second piece—called

---

85. Fanny Fitzwilliam (1802–54), a popular English actress who had made her American debut in 1839, and John Baldwin Buckstone (1802–79), English actor, playwright, and theatre manager, were performing in Mark Lemon's *The Ladies' Club* and Buckstone's own *The Widow Wiggins*.

Widow Wiggins, I think—was over, and just got down to the boat in time. Our mayor, Doctor Fisler was also in the house. Ned King knows every body and every body knows him; so he must have some roué acquaintances. This Buckstone is the author of more than an hundred popular farces.

27 July, Wednesday.

This evening Sam Cowperthwait and Charley Hollingshead called upon me, the former to make music and the latter to listen to it. We played until about nine o'clock, when in came King, who occupied the balance of the evening in performing solos. He seems to be perfectly master of the whole finger-board.

Mr. Appleton lectured again this evening in the usual place. I invited Phoebe to go, but forgot to call for her.

There was a horrid murder in Third Street near Chesnut this morning about six o'clock. A man just arrived from the West, and calling himself Smith,[86] in other words having no name at all, went into the office of a broker named Lougee and asked him to change a Missouri note. The broker told him it was a counterfeit, which he denied. Words ensued, and at last Lougee called Smith a liar. Hereupon the latter drew a dirk and stabbed the other across the counter, the blade entering very near the left nipple. He staggered to the door, gave the alarm, and fell dead. The murderer ran down Chesnut Street crying "stop thief," but was not successful in getting off. He was arrested and committed but our jurors have too much of the woman in their composition to find him guilty of any thing that would hurt his neck. As an instance of the smothering of all the finer feelings of humanity in these hard times I will mention the fact that before ten o'clock a dispute had arisen as to the property of the murdered man, and Colonel Page had been feed as a counsel by one of his relatives.

28 July, Thursday.

This evening I went to the Parsonage and found Ned King and the Rev. Mr. Ide there. The latter gentleman may be what his profession requires, but—but—

Phoebe and I had another *tete-a-tete* to-night. I feel quite honored by the confidence she reposes in me. Cousin Phoebe is a lovely girl.

29 July, Friday.

Last evening at the Parsonage it was half agreed that cousin Phoebe and myself should go up to Mount Holly on Saturday to see the girls,

---

86. The Camden *Mail* of 3 August 1842 reports that Noah Lougee was murdered by a man calling himself Smith, but actually named Fulton Alexander. See entry for 30 November 1842.

and this evening our inchoate resolution was confirmed. Ned King was present, and unless he is more stupid than I think he is he will take his cue from this circumstance, for after the abandonment of the river excursion it speaks very emphatically. Poor Ned! I suspect he thinks more of Phoebe than he expresses, and it is too bad for him to have the cold shoulder given thus. He deserves as much, however, for not having kept better company.

I forgot to mention last night that Mrs. Sheppard in speaking of John Clement, observed that his uncle Doctor Harris had a very poor opinion of him, that indeed he freely denied his nephew the possession of honest principles! I was surprised at this, but concluded it was most prudent not to tell all I knew.

30 July, Saturday.

Having done all the little matters which appertain to a Saturday morning and brushed up my go-ashore clothes, I put a few dollars and three dickies into my pocket, bade our folks good-bye and started off on my tour to Mount Holly. I called at the Parsonage at one o'clock as per appointment and found my pretty cousin all ready. We immediately crossed the river and went on board the *Trenton* which started at two for Burlington. Owing to the cheapness of the fare, six and a quarter cents, and to there being a temperance festival in the old metropolis of West Jersey, there were near six hundred people on the boat bound up, the opposition boat being also well filled. But I will venture to say with all the positiveness of a feudal knight in days gone by, that there was not a lovelier being among the ladies than she who hung upon my arm, nor a happier man among the gentlemen than himself. I was conscious that the young chaps envied me as they stole furtive glances at Phoebe's sweet expressive face and mild but brilliant eyes, as well they might—for she never looked better than to-day, when, her cheeks glowing with the roses of health heightened by the pencil of modesty, and her glossy ringlets waving to the gentle zephyrs of Delaware, to say nothing of those lips which seemed at once to woo and repulse a kiss, she presented a *tout ensemble* that might subvert another Troy!

We arrived in Burlington about three o'clock and in a few minutes took stage for Mount Holly. We had a merry ride of it, cousin Phoebe seeming altogether to lose the tinge of seriousness which usually characterizes her. In going along she wrote a note, upon the crown of my hat for a writing desk, to the Smalleys, saying that she had arrived in Mount Holly with Joseph's old schoolmate Isaac Mickle, and that she should stay at John Cox's until Monday morning when they must send in for us. This queer specimen of penmanship was forwarded on our arrival, and we proceeded to Cox's aforesaid, where I was introduced and pretty soon felt myself at home. The family are no connections of Phoebe's, but friends; and very sociable people they are. They have a son about fourteen years of age, who can do all kinds of needlework equal to a lady—he is very curious in all matters of dress, and I observed him looking very closely at the construction of my friend's boddice—frock as she says, for the purpose of dressing a doll in the same manner. This gumpey[87] was the first lion I saw to-day.

After tea Phoebe and I took a walk out to the new cemetery on the Mount.[88] It is a lovely spot admirably laid out in avenues named according to the different trees with which they are edged. It slopes down gradually from the top of the hill to the road at the bottom, and in the middle there is a tasty monument which can be seen far and near. From this garden of the gone a beautiful prospect of the town with its churches, court-house, cottage *a la mode de l'orient* and masts singularly in contrast with the distant woods and cornfields, extends to the southward. In other directions neat country seats enter into the panorama and make the picture complete. What a place is this to talk of love!

From the cemetery we returned to the town by Dunn's Chinese cottage[89] and took a view of its picturesque grounds and castellated walls. From here we went to call on some of Phoebe's friends, and en route she pointed out to me an old venerable looking quaker lady sitting at a window knitting, I believe who was a first cousin to the celebrated painter Benjamin West.[90] This was the second lion, or rather the first lioness, of to day.

Leaving Phoebe at one of her acquaintances I called upon Charley Lanning and talked over old times for an hour. When I returned I found William Holmes at the visitees, and accepted an invitation to stay with him all night. He is a great phrenologist and is very intimate with the Sheppards. I have met him there frequently. Having gallanted Phoebe to Cox's, we bade her good night, and had just got to Stryker's tavern[91] where Holmes boards when we heard the cry of fire. I went of course to see it out. The subject of combustion was a coach-maker shop which burned to ashes. The court-house which was about a hundred yards to leeward caught in several places, without suffering

87. "Gumpey" is apparently Mickle's variation of "gump," meaning a foolish person or a dolt.

88. The Mount Holly Cemetery had been laid out in 1840.

89. Nathan Dunn, proprietor of the Chinese Museum in Philadelphia, had built a Chinese-style home on Mount Holly's High Street in about 1832.

90. West (1738–1820), a native of Springfield, Pennsylvania, had worked in Philadelphia and New York City before moving to Europe in 1760.

91. Peter C. Stryker was proprietor of Mount Holly's Black Horse Tavern.

any considerable damage however. I saw several acquaintances by the glare of the fire and spoke to them. They will bear testimony to my having worked as industriously as though I had been a burgher of Mount Holly.

I got to sleep about one o'clock.

31 July, Sunday.

I awoke this morning after a doze of three hours, and philosophicated just twice sixty minutes on divers subjects, when I bounced up and dressed for breakfast. This was over by seven o'clock, and I then took a walk with Holmes up to the scene of the fire. At eight I called for Phoebe and took a more agreeable promenade with her to the old grave yard where her maternal ancestors lie. If tomb stones are to be believed, they lived to a good old age and died respected and regretted by all the neighborhood. We returned across some meadows and through some "tangled brakes" in time to go to Baptist Church, and hear an awfully stupid sermon. In the afternoon we went to Episcopal Church and in the evening to Methodist. Mr. Cox's son Benjamin had arrived home in the afternoon and accompanied us to night with a Miss ——— I don't know what her name was. He is a hard colt, as the saying is, one of Sammy Aaron's scholars and a real jockey.

Mr. Shaw[92] lately of Camden is stationed at this place. He preached one of his real thunder and lightning sermons to-night, notwithstanding which I fell asleep twice. After the meeting let out I spoke to the pastor, and got an introduction to a nephew of Samuel Drew, the great English metaphysician.[93] He is a shoemaker as his illustrious uncle was, and is said to be an excellent mathematician and musician. Euclid combined in his person these two characters, and so have many other persons done. There seems to be some affinity between the science of sound and that of figures. This man has a brother I think in Mount Holly. They are named Kingdon. The people of the town appear to know them as "good citizens," and that is all. I expressed my desire to follow up the introduction to acquaintance, and he affirmed his pleasure at the proposition. I will set this man down as the third lion.

I staid to-night at Cox's.

1 August, Monday.   Doctor Smalley's Farm; Burlington County, N.J.

Mr. Holmes and a friend of his saved Joseph Smalley the trouble of coming into the town for us this morning by taking us out to the farm

92. John K. Shaw was pastor of the Third Street Methodist Church in Camden from 1840 to 1842.
93. Jabez Kingdon of Mount Holly was a nephew of English author and preacher Samuel Drew (1765–1833).

in their conveyance. The place is about three miles from Mount-Holly on the road to Pemberton just at the junction and crossing of the Vincentown and Columbus highway. It might be called the Four Points. When we arrived the best carriage was ready to come in for us and the girls were dressing to come along with it. Josephine was really glad to see me, and Hannah too. I may say the same of the family of Smalleys without any undue indulgence of my self esteem.

We spent the morning in talking over the news. In the afternoon Josephine and Hannah went to see some of their country cousins, Phoebe and I preferring to remain. Towards evening Joseph geared up his horse and took me into Vincentown to call on Mr. Cox, A.B. my old domine. He had gone a-fishing on the mill-pond, but I saw his wife and step-daughters, who began to quiz me about Miss Sheppard. After looking at the town, (which by the by, is only famous for its always having been a place of great dissipation on the way of balls and dances) we returned—shall I say home? Yea, for such I felt it to be as soon as I alighted there.

After tea Phoebe, her cousin and myself took a walk to a romantic little mill-stream, about a mile from the house, where she favoured us with two or three songs. We returned before the dew had begun to fall, and before I got back I was fully convinced that one or two more promenades with my lovely companion would be attended with consequences imminently dangerous to my heart. I must beware.

Doctor Smalley reached home from Philadelphia about eight o'clock and brought news of a grand celebration by the blacks in the woods near Camden. It is I suppose the anniversary of the emancipation of the West India slaves.[94] Mr. Smalley is a man of quiet manners, of great affability, and considerable science. To the blandness and polish of the physician he adds the heartiness and hospitality of the farmer. He seems perfectly contented in the possession of an excellent farm, a lively wife, and two obedient children, Joseph and John.

The girls got back about nine and we pretty soon went to bed, mutually exhorting one another to throw off our city laziness and rise in the morning in time for the grand party out at Brown's Mills to-morrow.

The weather is almost as cool as November. Yesterday at twelve o'clock the thermometer stood at ninety degrees, but a rain coming up, it fell before two, to sixty six—twenty four degrees in two hours, and ever since the air has been unpleasantly cold and raw.

2 August, Tuesday.
Phoebe and I having been invited to join a party in the pines to-day, of course accepted the offer. I only slept an hour or two last night

94. Slavery had been terminated in British possessions on 1 August 1834.

owing to the cholic, and was so unwell in consequence this morning that I was obliged to leave the breakfast table without having eaten any thing. I was resolved however not to stay behind, so assuming a gay face I embarked with Hannah, Josephine and Joseph in one carriage, John Smalley following in another with his mother and cousin Phoebe. We started at eight o'clock, and were joined by two or three other waggons at Pemberton. From here we proceeded to Brown's Mills, several miles in the pines, where we arrived after a delightful ride of three hours.

From the fact of the late Doctor Parrish[95] having recommended Brown's Mills as a proper resort for some of his patients, it has become quite a fashionable watering place. The homely diet which then might have been a benefit to the dyspeptic has given way to the indigestible messes of the city, and the serenity which then might have soothed the nervous subject is now disturbed by the violin and the crazy feet which it animates. There are at present forty or fifty fashionable people boarding there. The natural attractions of the place are not of a very high order. It is embosomed in the pines, and of course abounds in musquitoes. The house stands near a mill-pond, (quasi "lake") and near by is a mossy old mill, whose ponderous wheels have perhaps kept up their clattering for the last half century. Below is the race, in which amateur invalids bathe; several of them were in during the day and seemed to enjoy it very much. Phoebe wanted to go in, but she feared I was too unwell to accompany her, and I did not demur to her apprehensions, although I now felt entirely recovered from my slight indisposition.

Several other wagons arriving shortly after our caravan, we crossed the dam and procured the grant of a cottage-yard on the other side

95. Dr. Joseph Parrish (1779–1840) was a Philadelphia physician, educator, writer, and reformer.

for our dinner, which while the old ladies were preparing the young ones separated for enjoyment, some to swing, some to walk in the woods, and some to boat on the pond. With Phoebe and Josephine for my "guardian shepherds" I participated in all these pastimes, and really felt in their smiles, the happiness of an earthly paradise. The ghosts of my neglected law-books never once rose before my mind; these, together with ambition and other vanities, even my fiddle and my debts, were forgotten in enjoyment.

About one our party, numbering not quite fifty, sat down to a repast excellent in quantity and quality. We all ate heartily, and one old gentleman named Woodward appeared to drink heartily too. All the rest with one or two exceptions were temperance folks.

After dinner we young ones squandered through the groves again and amused ourselves in various ways until five o'clock. We then got under weigh and passed on through Greenwood where Mrs. Clark was last summer, and where we only tarried a half an hour, to the County house of Burlington County.[96] Here we all alighted and were shown through the wards by the very polite stewardess. Phoebe did me the honor to take my arm, *me solicitare oblito*, and shew me some poor beings with whose history she was acquainted. There was one, named Robert Love, lying in stupid insensibility upon his pallet, who, she informed me, was crossed in his affections thirty years ago, and has ever since been a madman. Some of the idiots were the most disgusting objects I have been so unfortunate as to meet. Others were very amusing—especially one whom we saw in the yard. To a very comical look he added a very good nature—but the veriest ridiculosity in his composition is his love for military display, "the pomp and circumstance of glorious war." Phoebe told me that one of her relatives named Frick, a revolutionary character, gave him a sword and cap, which he mounts every spring after corn-planting time, to keep the crows out of the County house corn-fields. "Lord" said he in perfect ecstacy "Gin'ral Issac's sword shines so the crows daren't come near me." He parades up and down the fields they say as regularly as any sentinel on the *campus Martii*. Is not this man the fourth, and the most lion-like, lion of my trip?

Having seen all the curiosities of the Pauper's Palace we left it, and got home in good time, highly delighted.

Miss Josephine conducted herself during this party in a manner that satisfied me that her heart is at least ungiven to any one beside myself. That she returns my old passion, that she ever will return it,

96. The "Old Alms House" of Burlington County was located a short distance north of Pemberton at the intersection unkindly called Comical Corner.

are still doubtful points. Her coldness heretofore is explained, and that honorably to herself and agreeably to me. Shall I put all upon the hazard of a question; or shall I do like a wise man, forget this foolish affair in my studies?

3 August, Wednesday.

This morning Joseph Smalley brought all the girls and myself into Mount Holly and at seven o'clock Phoebe and I bade them farewell and started in the land mail-stage for home. The other girls had a great mind to follow, but concluded to stay until Friday which will complete their two weeks.

We passed through Centerton and Moorestown and after a very pleasant ride reached home at eleven o'clock. . . .

Just below the Spread Eagle Tavern[97] we met a man footing it up the road with his pack on his back, as if he were in great haste. He hailed us with "Dont go into town for God's sake! They're killing every body off there." We heard indistinct rumours yesterday of there having been great riots in Philadelphia on Monday between the whites and the negroes. The latter were celebrating the emancipation of their fellows in Jamaica, by a procession in which was carried a banner inscribed "Liberty or death". As they were passing through Moyamensing some boys began teasing them and scouting their abolition motto. This resulted in a row which broke up the procession and terminated in a bloody riot which raged all Monday and Tuesday. Two or three public buildings belonging to the blacks were burned, their houses stoned and many of them shamefully beaten with clubs. On Tuesday afternoon the First Division was ordered out and was under arms all night. This intimidated the mob and prevented the further commission of outrage.[98]

4 August, Thursday.

I was at the office to-day reading and writing for seven hours with only twenty minutes' intermission. In the evening Mr. Atkinson and I had some pretty good music.

5 August, Friday.

This evening I spent an hour at the Parsonage. The young ladies got home this afternoon, in company with Mr. Holmes. After this call I went to a meeting of our Temperance Society, under the church; where they were making arrangements for a grand festival on next

97. The Spread Eagle Tavern was on the Moorestown Road about five miles east of Camden.

98. Mickle's report of the riots of 1 and 2 August is basically accurate. Some of the brutality he mentions occurred along Lombard Street, from Fifth to Eighth.

Thursday. I had a slight sparring match with one Sam Lummis, a gabby, saucy shoemaker.

6 August, Saturday.

Up at Smalley's the other day I asked Josephine if I might come to see her on Friday night after she got home. "Yes," said she "and on Saturday, Sunday, Monday night too, if you wish." She said this with such naivité that I know she was sincere; accordingly I not only went last evening, but this also. Ned Drayton, Ned King and one of his cronies from the city were there to-night—the latter an excellent piano-player. Ned Drayton and I did not speak. The conduct of Josephine during the visit satisfied me of a fact of which I feel proud and happy.

7 August, Sunday.

This afternoon I took a walk with Sam Cowperthwaite over the scene of the late riots, and afterwards dropped in at Ide's Church. I sat in "our pew," and after the services walked home with Phoebe.

This evening I went to Baptist church in Camden, and as I was waiting in the vestibule for the prayer to be ended, in came Ned Drayton with Annie Hugg; he spoke to me and offered me his lump of tobacco. A queer fellow is this!

By the by, there has been a fandango cut up in the Baptist choir by reason whereof several of the singers have come below stairs. It is said that Harry Samuels, the "smart carpenter boy" mentioned somewhere in the first part . . . of my diary, and for a year back the leader of this choir, has been kissing a married singer, named Pine. Baxter thinks the matter has gone quite as far as kissing! Ahem—More of this scandal anon. The music was pretty good to-night notwithstanding the defection of the leader and some of the best followers. I recognized Mrs. Pine's strong voice in the alto—she sings pretty well, though she is as ugly as the devil.

8 August, Monday.

I have resolved upon two of three occasions heretofore, to go about my studies in earnest; but those resolutions have been followed by little or no execution. To-day, however, I begin at the right end, and set upon the execution without any pompous boastings beforehand. Hitherto I have been at the office only four or five hours a day, and hardly four days a week—so deeply have I been engaged about the ladies and similar toys! This morning I reached my seat at nine o'clock, and only left it a quarter of an hour to dine at Simmons', until six in the evening. My law book is Read's Blackstone; my miscellaneous works, Plutarch's *Lives*, Goldsmith's little *History of Rome*, and Fergusson's attenuated, non-sensical treatise on *Civil Society*. I continue to wade through the polished but flat and idealess sentences of the last work only because I dislike to quit a thing that I have begun without going through it.

This evening, after practising a while with Atkinson and Weight, I went up to Bates' with the latter, and staid an hour among the girls.

9 August, Tuesday.

I read nine hours again to-day, and already begin to forget the girls, and to feel the enthusiasm of study.

This evening two or three of us met for music at the Library room, and inflicted several airs on the neighborhood. After the assembly broke up I left my fiddle at Delacour's, and went to Hess's by invitation.

10 August, Wednesday.

So far my resolution to be industrious holds out admirably. I reach the office about nine o'clock, and stay until the bell at St. Joseph's rings for mass, at six o'clock in the evening. I read law until I begin to feel wearied, and then begin to write, and read Plutarch. I am also making some little progress in Sallust's *Jugurthine war*—about a section a-day. There is happiness in studying, a pleasure in the reflection that one has well improved his time, that I cannot describe—with me it may be called an enthusiasm, strange as the confession may appear after the grievous indolence which my diary for a year or so back attests.

This afternoon I finished Doctor Mulford's lecture for Howe.

This evening I was at the Parsonage, and met Ned Drayton. The conduct of the Empress was flattering and gratifying to me, though how it affected Ned I cannot say. She promised me another and a better guard chain than the one I now wear. This and other, to disinterested persons, trifling partialities, to us are important. Ned King accompanied Hannah down to Bridgeton to day to see her sister Mary. Mrs. Sheppard signified to me this evening that perhaps Mr. King would have no acquaintances on the route! . . .

The news-boys were hawking another "veto-message" about the streets this morning.[99] These have become so common under Tyler's administration that they attract but little notice.

11 August, Thursday.

For some weeks back Mr. Dougherty the blustering, stirring president of our Temperance Society and Charley Delacour, vivacious, head over heel, Charley, have been busy in getting ready for a Grand Harvest Home in Camden to day. All our temperance public have been on

99. Tyler, on 9 August, had vetoed a second tariff bill, which included a provision that proceeds of land sales would be distributed to the states.

the *qui vive* as to this important affair, which I must as a faithful chronicler, record.

An invitation had been extended by Delacour in a very awkward advertisement to "all the temperance societies of Philadelphia, to partake of the exercises" and a general coöperation of the Gloucester associations was expected. It was, indeed, instead of a "celebration" as Delacour called it, a County Convention, conducted under the auspices of our Camden Society, in which the others only "partook."

The morning was rather unpromising, but by ten o'clock the muster began in Third Street below the Railroad, which portion of that important road, by the way, was opened by the Councils only last Spring and is now one of the finest promenades we have—grassy and level, with no houses, pavements nor gutters, to mar its romance. Here our men were joined by the Jefferson and Delaware Societies from Philadelphia, the Fetterville, Kaighn's Point and Gloucester Societies, and the Camden Boy's association, with two or three bands. About eleven o'clock the procession began to move under the command of old Jimmy Sloan who looked quite as unsoldier like as he did when he ran away from the British during the last war, on the northern frontier. . . . Along with him were President Dougherty, Charley Delacour and other chief men. Then followed our Jersey Societies, and afterwards the Pennsylvanians, numbering together perhaps five or six hundred, with banners and other paraphernalia. They marched through Camden, Fetterville and Kaighn's Point, and reached the site of the Whig celebration about one o'clock.

My cousin Mary Hogeland[100] and one of her friends named Graeff having come over to see the pageant, I got a wagon, and calling for Josephine Sheppard, got her in, introduced her to my visitors, and drove off to the ground. We arrived in time to see the procession pass in array, and to hear the beginning of the exercises. First a prayer was made—then a temperance song was sung, and then Mr. Levin arose and made an excellent speech, though somewhat like his other efforts, tautological. He concluded by soliciting subscriptions to his paper in a very insolent manner, as he usually does. After this they adjourned for dinner, and I brought my girls home for the same purpose. "Our worthy citizen Joseph Sharp"[101] as the advertisement calls him, prepared a banquet in the woods for five hundred people, but only one hundred and fifty sat down. We preferred to eat at home, where there would be no grand-daddy long-legs dropping down into our broth. . . .

100. Mary Hogeland's friend was probably the daughter of Daniel Graeff, a merchant on Market Street.

101. Joseph Sharp was a Philadelphia dry goods merchant of South Second Street.

After dinner I got all my girls in again, and returned to the scene of action, which looked, as we approached it, very much like a camp meeting. There were now perhaps three thousand persons assembled; for the weather had cleared up and many citizens had come over. There were numberless booths interspersed among the trees, where every thing but rum might be procured. Two long tables invited the apetite, a little way off, and in the lowest part of the hollow was the speaker's rostrum, with auditors' seats rising, like the benches in a theatre pit, from the centre. This was already occupied by the orators, marshals and invited guests, and Mr. Appleton, had begun his speech.

After one or two "smaller guns" went off in Mr. Appleton's suit, the girls concluded they would take a ride;[102] so we embarked and rode down to Gloucester, and returned by the Farms and Kaighn's Point, through a little shower which came up just as the convention had adjourned. My cousin and her friend supped with me, and returned to the city about sunset, gratified with their trip, and delighted with Josephine's vivacity.

Upon the whole the day passed off very well. Some of the temperance men expected more than they saw, but I looked for less. It is best to be disappointed agreeably, and the only way to secure such a disappointment is to expect but little.

This evening Ogden, Atkinson and myself met at the Library room and made some pretty tolerable music.

12 August, Friday.

At the convention yesterday (which cost me by the by, three dollars) it appears they formed a County Society, of which I was told to-night they made me one of the Vice Presidents. Honors thicken on my brow!

I was at the office very assiduously to-day.

This evening Atkinson and I had some music.

Ned King and Hannah Sheppard returned this afternoon.

13 August, Saturday.

I was at the office until noon to-day, after which I kept up the good old school plan, of a half holy-day to prepare for to-morrow.

In the evening I was—where I so often am o'nights—in excellent company. Josephine and I are to go to church to-morrow to hear Mr. Cushman, her sisters' educationist.

I forwarded Doctor Mulford's lecture to Howe to-day, with a note.

14 August, Sunday.

This morning Hannah, Josephine and I went to church in Spruce

102. Mickle means that he and the girls left after Mr. Appleton had made one or two minor points.

Street, in Philadelphia, to hear Mr. Cushman, who is mentioned yesterday. I was introduced to him by Mrs. Sheppard on the day of the
Temperance Harvest Home, at her house. He is an excellent scholar,
and a good preacher, and decidedly the finest-looking man I ever saw
in a pulpit. Like so many others, he lost a fortune in stocks after he
had returned to live in *otio cum dignitate* at Boston, whereat he is so
downcast that he told Mrs. Sheppard the other day he would not care
if Miller's predictions were true that 1843 would witness the end of all
human things. His sermon this morning was in a measure tinted with
Millerism.

15 August, Monday.

There is nothing particular to be recorded to-day. I was at my
studies for eight or nine hours very industriously. This hard work is
already beginning to drive the hair from my head, and in three months,
at the rate at which it is now shedding my temples will be bald
enough. . . .

16 August, Tuesday.

Having been up late last evening I slept so long this morning that
before I could go to market and return the day was too far advanced
for me to get to the office before dinner. In the afternoon however I
went, and studied until St. Joseph's mass bell rang my release.

This evening I began to take lessons of Ned King on the violin. He
has hired a little room at Knave's corner, and fitted it up with carpet,
chairs, music-stands, instruments and books. This he calls "The Conservatorio." He has three pupils beside myself. We were employed two
hours to-night, in playing Pleyel's duetts. I got through the first violin
part at sight, although the key was three flats, and required the third
position. He will make me a player, if I do my portion.

17 August, Wednesday.

This evening I was at Stivers' a few minutes. There is nothing new
except a little flare up which James George has had with the girls.
Hugg's folks were there, and from what I observed I think going to
Camp Meeting does not improve them much! Harry Samuels also
obtruded himself into the parlour and took more liberties with Eliz's
pretty hand than I would allow my father's apprentice to take with
my sister's.

19 August, Friday.

This evening Atkinson and I played together a while for the amusement of my aunt[103] and some of her friends who had called in to see
our folks. I hope our harmony may have the effect to arouse her spirits

103. Mickle refers to his Aunt Rachel Mulford.

from their present excessively low condition. She caught cold on the evening that Elwell's house was burnt, was sick some time afterwards, and has since been deplorably unlike herself. This is a thing to which the Mickles are somewhat liable by constitution. I must beware and strangle the monster in his infancy—the best way of doing which is to visit the ladies frequently; so—

After our concert I stopped around to Hugg's, where I have not been before for several weeks.

20 August, Saturday.

I was at the office to-day until noon. The afternoon I spent in calling upon my friends and practising upon the violin.

In the evening, I took my third lesson and got along to my own amazement, which is saying a great deal, for I am not easily amazed. After the lesson my tutor and his pupil went to the Parsonage and spent the balance of the time until the mail-line came rattling over Cooper's Creek bridge, which is generally our Signal for beating a retreat.

22 August, Monday.

This evening by arrangement Hollingshead and I called on the Cooper street girls to take a moonlight walk down to Kaighn's Point. We started about eight, Phoebe and Hannah with me, and Josephine with Charley, and went down Third street, a new and delightful promenade. . . .

23 August, Tuesday.

I took my fourth lesson this evening, and I flatter myself that I make some improvement.

25 August, Thursday.

There was a grand fandango this morning at ten o'clock in St. John's church, because, forsooth, the Duc d'Orleans the heir apparent of the French throne killed himself, or rather was killed, some time ago by falling from a carriage.[104] What nonsense to observe the obsequies of monarchy in a republican country! Colonel Page went in uniform, by special invitation. I also tried to go, but I was too late; but let not the reader from this fact suggest the old fable of "sour grapes." I started with the intention of scoffing such ridiculous mummeries on such a ridiculous occasion, and if I could have got in it would not have been, I fear, to pray.

This evening I took another lesson, after which I went up to Heyl's on an errand. I saw Charley Bontemps in the Billiard room, and when

104. King Louis Philippe's eldest son, Ferdinand Philippe, had been killed in July.

I began to quiz him about breaking his resolution not to play that game any more, he looked very sheepish. He confessed that I must feel happier after having been fiddling during the evening, than himself after having spent his time in pushing ivory balls into twine pockets. John Weight was also there, and he insists stoutly that the story is false about Harry Samuels and Mrs. Pine. It may be, but it appears that he confessed before the church-meeting that he had kissed her!

26 August, Friday.

Truly hath it been said "We know not what a day will bring forth." At ten o'clock to-night I left the Parsonage after a visit which seemed to promise an enduring acquaintance with its lovely inmate—at half past ten, I had heard that which makes the dissolution of that acquaintance inevitable. During the evening we were laughing and talking and even romping with more than usual unreservedness. Having occasion for a pin I asked Josephine to lend me one, and she replied, extending the desired article in her plump hand, "Here take it dearie!"—a freedom she never used before. When I went home I copied the *Farewell to Banff* which I had borrowed of Hannah, and went down into the dining room where my mother was sitting. She asked me if I had been to Sheppard's, and I told her I had. She then informed me that uncle told her at supper that some lady who crosses the river a great deal told him on the steam-boat the other day that some of the Sheppards had said to her that I was at their house every day, and that they knew not how to make my visits less frequent. This I believe to be a lie coined by Meriam Clement, an envious little devil that has no particular liking to me; but lie or not, my mind was made up in a minute to visit the Parsonage no more. . . .

27 August, Saturday.

This evening I took an other lesson of King, who afterwards went to the parsonage. I sent home *Love is the Theme* and Miss Forbe's *Farewell to Banff*, with many thanks and so forth, by this obliging messenger.

I wrote a letter to Phoebe Sheppard to day, reviewing our acquaintance and announcing its dissolution; but concluded not to send it at present. I will copy it some of these days, as evidence of my feelings in my predicament. When I came to allude to Josephine's guard-chain I was a little affected, but nothing like weakness appears I trust in any part of the billet.

28 August, Sunday.

I spent the chief part of to-day in fixing my studio and reading. In the evening I went to Baptist meeting, not however as in days "lang syne" well armed, but alone.

29 August, Monday.

Yesterday Samuel Lanning the oldest inhabitant of Camden township died, and this morning John Ward the eldest man in Newton [*Newton Township*] fell upon the protruding round of a broken chair, and broke one of his ribs, which resulted in his death. The lives and exits of such venerable citizens as these ought to form a part of our country's history.

Mr. Kelley and his friend, Christopher List,[105] drank tea with me this evening. We called upon Turner's girls, where List edified us by an account of my old German master Remak, who with a friend has walked to Niagara and back during the holy-days—a Quixottic feat!

An encampment at Easton begins to-day. The Colonel's Fencibles and the Colonel's self participate.

Somebody has been robbing money from Kelley's drawer at the office—either the black servants or a white hanger-on. It makes me feel damme'd bad; but *"Mens conscia"* and so forth.

30 August, Tuesday.

For a day or two back I have been busily engaged on my temperance address. President Daugherty wants it delivered on the fourth Friday night in next month.

All is wonder at the office about the missing money. The servants in the kitchen say that so far from their having taken any that did not belong to them, they have lost fifty cents that did. There is a young man, now at Easton, who forms a part of Page's family, and who is without any support but Mr. Washington's bounties—but God forbid me to suspect him unjustly.[106] For myself I know that whoever the thief may be, his knavery makes me feel very uneasy—not that I am not perfectly conscious that I am not suspected, but that I dislike to be in a situation where suspicion is possible. Time will trap the rat, be of what gender or color it may.

This evening after playing my exercises with King I went around to Cowperthwaites and helped him to make music until after ten o'clock.

31 August, Wednesday.

I was at the office as usual for nine hours to-day, and employed my time chiefly in writing my address. The Colonel and Bill Vanarsdale, and a good many of the loafers that generally hang around the office, are off to Easton this week,[107] and I got along, in consequence, without any interruption.

105. List, an attorney, had joined the Philadelphia bar in June 1842.
106. Mickle probably refers to William Vanarsdale; see entries of 31 August 1842 and 2 May 1844.
107. Page and Vanarsdale were in Easton for militia exercises.

How long the evenings seem since I have exiled myself from the Parsonage! I would to God pride had no place in the human character. I am obliged now to pass my nights at Delacour's, or at Heyl's, among roués that I despise. King begins to wonder what is the matter.

Clement got back from Pottsville a day or two ago. He has raised a moustache since he has been among the mountains. He applies, on the ground of said moustache perhaps, to be admitted at the next term of the Supreme Court.

1 September, Thursday.

I made a good deal of progress with my address to-day. It will advocate an unpopular course, but I guess it will not be damned on that account.

This evening I undertook to take another music lesson; but I felt so really depressed on account of the recent revolution in my social prospects, that I could not distinguish between a flat and a sharp. After the bungling over some of Pleyel's peices I went around to Delacour's, and had a warm discussion with Lenhart the minister, on politics; after this I walked about town with John Weight until near eleven o'clock. What a vagabond I am becoming!

2 September, Friday.

This evening the Baptist choir resumed its meetings. They muster rather slimly since the affair of Mrs. Pine—none of the implicated parties nor their friends deigning to assemble anymore. Baxter leads, and plays bass; Cowperthwait carries the air, and I the tenor. There were four girls and one gentleman present to night in addition to the instrumental performers. We made some excellent music.

I rode out to Doctor Smith's, near Laurel Hill Cemetery, this afternoon, to accompany my aunt and cousin, (who have been staying there a day or two) into the city. They concluded to stay until to-morrow, and so I returned immediately by the Manayunk rail-road.[108]

Kelley went to Baltimore this morning—so I am no longer the miller's man, but the miller's self. I have got a precipe to issue to morrow for the District Court, in a case of debt.[109]

3 September, Saturday.

The Easton encampment broke up last night, and the Fencibles and other Philadelphia companies returned to-day. The ladies of the town presented Colonel Page with a tremendous pound-cake as a token of their regard for him and his company. They had a fine time. I learn

108. Reading Railroad trains ran between Philadelphia and Manayunk, a new factory town on the Schuylkill River, which became part of Philadelphia in 1854.
109. A precipe is a written order requesting a clerk or prothonotary of a court to issue a writ.

that the number of troops in all was about nine hundred. Their pastimes were mock duels, and fights, circus-shows, balls, and the like.

Being tired of loafing away my evenings in Camden, I crossed for that ilk reason, to the city, this afternoon and staid there until the mail-boat returned to Camden. I met Jim Martin and some of his friends at Harboard's[110] in Decatur Street, where there was a kind of a concert.

4 September, Sunday.

A young man named Hineline[111] is attempting to start a Democratic paper in Camden, to be called the *American Eagle*. Buffington got the cold shoulder on account of his suspicious democracy. Hineline and I have had several interviews about the project.

This evening I went to Baptist Church in Camden and sat up-stairs. I saw no one I cared for—no one that cared for me. Alas! what a change!

5 September, Monday.

Everything is bustle at the office again. I did not make much progress in my address.

This evening I called on my cousin Mary Hogeland and went to see Miss Graeff who was at the Temperance Celebration with me on the eleventh of August. We did not stay long. After I saw my cousin home again, I went up to Harboard's, where I met Jim Martin the second time. The mail-boat got back to Camden about half-past-eleven o'clock.

Having finished Read's Blackstone last week, I this morning began Starkie on Evidence.

6 September, Tuesday.

I was at the office as usual to-day, writing my address.

In the evening I took my fiddling lesson, and got along very well, though I say it myself.

7 September, Wednesday.

The democratic Convention was held to-day at Trenton and there were several hundred delegates in attendance. On account of the new law of Congress ordering the election for members of that body to be held by districts, and in order to prevent the whig cry of nullification, which has already been raised, from being urged to the disadvantage of their party, the convention resolved that it was inexpedient to make

110. Richard Harbord operated the Decatur Coffee House.
111. Charles D. Hineline (1818–62), a native of Pennsylvania, had just arrived in Camden. During his intermittent residence in the city he would be a newspaper editor, reform advocate, and a Democratic politician, serving as mayor from 1852 to 1853.

a general ticket.[112] They also passed resolutions in favor of a proper tariff. Thompson, of Salem, was the orator of the day.

It had been agreed between Hineline and myself that we were to go up together at six o'clock in the morning; I was to introduce him to some of the Loco-focos. But unfortunately I overslept myself and did not go until three o'clock—he never came at all. . . .

The mail-line came along about nine o'clock and Atkinson and I jumped into the last car and had a merry ride with some musical companions, down to Camden.

"This" as the paper will say "was a proud day for the democracy."

8 September, Thursday.

This evening after my lesson at the "Conservatorio," I went around to Cowperthwait's and fiddled a little while. My evenings drag out very slowly since my pride has debarred me from the society of the Sheppards—By the by, I was going up Third St. in Camden, a day or two ago, and ran across Josephine. We had a very short talk, and she looked as if she had something more to say when I was obliged to go.

9 September, Friday.

. . . The Baptist Choir did not meet to-night, so I went to the Methodist Meeting, to hear Burroughs deliver a temperance lecture. Sam Cowperthwait took one of his Quaker cousins and I took another. The lecturer expected not coming, they called on me for an address—but I declined, and afterwards Sam Lummis took the stand.

10 September, Saturday.

I wrote a letter of thanks to-day for the Colonel, for which see *postea*. Sam and I were fiddling to-night after my lesson.

I paid Joseph B. Cooper fifteen dollars to-day on account of some coins and medals which he had the kindness to sell to me at about a double price. . . .

11 September, Sunday.

Mr. Hineline, the young man who wants to get up a paper in Camden, is unfortunately without the necessary means. He therefore wishes the party to pay enough in advance to enable him to pay the first instalment on Irvin's establishment, one hundred dollars. . . .

12 September, Monday.

This has been a very warm day. It is said the thermometer stood in Philadelphia at 94°.

112. A New Jersey law of 10 November 1842, created five congressional election districts. Cape May, Cumberland, Salem, Gloucester, and Atlantic Counties were grouped in the First Congressional District.

The "Henry Institute" was awakened to-night after its long summer nap. We had a good meeting, and plenty of talking as a matter of course when the following law-students were present: Mulford, Dudley, Drayton, Hollingshead, Mickle and Clement. The last named person broached the subject of his indebtedness to the Library to me in a confidential matter, put in a plea of poverty, and said he would make me his friend in the matter. Curious!

13 September, Tuesday.

There was a brilliant rain-bow in the west this morning, which my good mother saw. I was not up in time. This is a rare phenomenon— the rainbow I mean!

In the Criminal Court yesterday they were trying one of the rioters of Moyamensing—the room was full, and among the spectators was the wife of the arraigned. She had watched the progress of the trial with intense interest until the testimony of one of the witnesses, closely questioned by the Attorney General, seemed to turn the scale and fasten conviction on her husband. It might be called the crisis of the case; just at the height of the stillness and excitement of which, a report rang through the hall, and startled their honors from their seats and brought all to their feet. The woman of whom we have been speaking was seen falling backward, and from her bosom, the ruby current of life flowed profusely and stained the very tribunal of equity. All were horrified at the heroism of the Second Artemesia[113]—the weak began to flee, and even the strong began to quake. At last they mustered courage to surround the prostrate woman—they tore the clothes from her devoted breast; but instead of finding a horrid hole bored therein by a bullet, they discovered a—a—porter-bottle, which the "gude wife" had brought to cheer her dearie on his way to the Palace, and which the heat of her excited bosom had caused to explode! In about an hour, gravity was so far restored as to allow the administration of justice to go on again.

I was in conclave with Irwin and Hineline to-day for an hour. The prospects of effecting an arrangement are dim.

14 September, Wednesday.

I was busy to-day about my address. In the evening I met some musicians at my friend Sam's.

15 September, Thursday.

This evening I called on some acquaintances made by dint of Sam's impudence in Sansom Street. He introduced me, though he was never

113. Artemisia, queen of Caria, 353–352 B.C., and builder of the great Mausoleum of Halicarnassus, is renowned for the grief she showed at her husband's death.

introduced himself. They are neither pretty nor intelligent, but they just suit him. We got to bed at Burr's about one o'clock.

16 September, Friday.

This evening I met the Baptist Choir. Baxter, Rogers, Sam, and myself were the gentlemen—Mrs Rogers and Miss Bates, the ladies. A queer *lapsus linguae* occurred; to wit:

Says Sam "This music stand is good for nothing—its top has got a crack in."

Now said music stand was made by one Ben Toms, which said Toms Baxter hates as he does the devil. Making it a point to let no opportunity of abusing his enemy pass unimproved, Baxter aforesaid replied to Sam's remark—

"Yes, and the bottom of it is like the Maker's too."

Sam blushed as red as the fiddle under his chin—the girls were of a Tyrian scarlet—the gentlemen roared out a-laughing, and Baxter was so confused that he could not get through with Old Hundred.

17 September, Saturday.

This evening I took another fiddling lesson. King says I dont improve as fast as he desires me to. By the by he told me yesterday that he had got a hint that he went to the Parsonage too frequently.

I finished my address this afternoon and gave it to Doctor Mulford for his comment.

18 September, Sunday.

Verily, verily, we "know not what a day may bring forth!" This morning it was apparently impossible that I could ever resume my former relation with the Sheppards—This evening Josephine was hanging upon my arm with all the cordiality of other times, and conversing with me with even more than former unreservedness. It may be worth while to record how this revolution took place. . . .

[*This evening,*] after the dismission of Church, I invited Josephine to take a walk. We . . . had a long talk about my absence from their house for nearly a month. I opened the matter candidly, told her that I had been informed that some of their family had spoken lightly of me, and assured her that if such were the case my visiting them any more was impossible. I told her that politeness alone had induced me to depart from my resolution in entering their door this evening; but assured her that whatever my conduct may be hereafter, my feelings will remain unaltered. She replied that to the best of her knowledge, none of the family had ever spoken of me but with respect—that they always really felt that they extended to my visits a hearty welcome, and that the report of which I complained must have been put into circulation by some one who knew my pride, and who assaulted it with no good intentions either to them or me. She seemed to be sincere in what she said—assured me, and reassured me that I would always be welcome—and invited me pressingly to come up soon and talk the thing over with the others. In the conduct of this delicate matter I trust I have neither forfeited the respect of the Sheppards or of myself. It is not yet ended, and I care not a tinker's damn where it may end. If they have not been playing double I can still visit them with pleasure; if they have I would sooner be bastinadoed than cross their threshhold again. I do not believe that Jo, lovely girl! has ever wronged me. . . .

19 September, Monday.

This evening a public debate came off before the Institute, upon the following question: Should the right of search on the coast of Africa, for the suppression of the slave trade, be tolerated? . . .[114]

The audience numbered about twenty-five. The Sheppards were there with Ned Drayton. Charley Hollingshead and I went home with them, and as we were coming away says Phoebe in a half-whisper:

"You must come and see us again right soon."

"That" said I "I shall certainly do"—

And so ended to-day.

20 September, Tuesday.

The old College near Bristol was opened to-day as a Military Academy by Capt. Partrige[115] formerly of West Point. The military of Philadelphia were invited to attend—and six companies went up in the *Trenton.* Two or three other boats also carried passengers, and in all there were over two thousand people there. Ned Drayton and I went in company—he having borrowed a dollar to pay his way, of a friend on the wharf.

We got up about eleven o'clock, and after some evolutions the military were drawn up in solid column and addressed from the portico of the College by Ovid J. Johnson, the Attorney General,[116] and Capt. Partrige. The former defended the military spirit in a long speech. He advocated duelling in an unblushing manner, and longed to see the return of the day when slanders should be wiped out with "the blood

114. The Webster-Ashburton Treaty with England, of August 1842, had authorized the formation of joint naval squadrons to suppress the slave trade along the African coast.

115. Alden Partridge (1785–1854) founded a number of military schools in the eastern states in order to bolster the nation's defense.

116. Johnson (1807–54), a Wilkes-Barre, Pennsylvania, lawyer, was attorney general of that state from 1833 to 1845.

of one or the other of the parties." Comfortable logic, this! to be slandered first and then shot!

The balance of the day was spent in eating, promenading and target-firing. On our return—we left at half past five—on our return I was going to say, all who were sober enough, officers excepted, employed their time in dancing to the fife.

General Cadwallader was on the ground and looked very well in his uniform; Colonel Page commanded the volunteers, who numbered about two hundred.

I got no music lesson to-night.

21 September, Wednesday.

Mr. Hineline has at last got a printing establishment. I am glad of it.

This evening Bob Ogden and I met at the Library room to have some music; but not having candle enough we adjourned to Sheppard's where I accompanied the girls in a few airs on the piano.

22 September, Thursday.

This evening being music-night, I went around as usual to the Conservatorio to take my lesson; but when I got there King told me that he was going to New Orleans on Saturday morning, and so we concluded to devote the balance of the time we had to visiting, and clearing out the furniture of the room. I am to pay him five dollars to morrow—and he leaves in deposit with me a violin and a music stand. We took these around to our house after returning from Sheppard's where we went to bid them good-by: I say "we," for I helped him do it. The old lady during my visit took occasion to assure me that my recent coolness was altogether without cause on their part. She had always respected me, and had always behaved in action and thought as she felt; and much more of a like nature was said.

23 September, Friday.

. . . King went up to Sheppard's again to-night to bid them adieu. He makes almost as many farewells as Fanny Ellsler, who "appeared positively for the last time before the American public," just sixteen evenings.

24 September, Saturday.

King got off sure enough this morning. He started for New Castle at half past ten o'clock. This movement is so sudden that I suspect his creditors have not been consulted.

I met with Ivins, Baxter and Sam to-night to play sacred music. Since Ned King is gone I can perform much better. "First in a village rather than second in Rome." A consciousness of inferiority in any thing is to me killing.

25 September, Sunday.

Mr. Hineline is in a hurry to get the first number of his paper out by next Thursday for the County meeting. He was at work to-day very industriously, and I went down to help him. I set up one of my own articles nearly a half a column long, and he says I am quite a practical printer.

I see plainly enough that I will have to be in reality the editor of this paper. Mr. Mulford may help me—Mulford our debator I mean; but Mr. Hineline, and I may add, some of the party, will look to me for the leading articles for some time, at least. This is a responsible duty for one not yet out of his teens, but I will try to acquit myself without disgrace. I have already written several little squibs for the first number—one concerning my old friend Gray, at which, however, he can not complain.

I was right in my suspicion about King. Atkinson heard in town to-day that his creditors attempted to stop him at New Castle.

This evening Hollingshead and I took the Sheppard's to Baptist Meeting, to hear Mr. Smith deliver his farewell sermon. The congregation have starved him out. He made a very pretty allusion to our ladies—"The consort and daughters of one of his predecessors in that pulpit." All eyes were fixed upon our pew. He also announced that Mr. Mickle, to wit myself, would deliver a Temperance lecture in the lecture-room of the church in which he was speaking, on next Friday evening; and he hoped the "dear youth" of Camden would fill it well. The "dear youth" would expect to hear something less barren than my address will be.

26 September, Monday.

The debate on the right of search was continued to-night in the Court-house; and decided in our favour. The elite of Camden were out to the number of thirty or forty. Mulford made an excellent speech against Slavery as a moral wrong. Hollingshead too did pretty well.

I took the Sheppards, and they are much pleased with the good nature with which our sparring is carried on. We had a good deal of it to night.

27 September, Tuesday.

I was at the office to day, more busy however in writing editorial for the first number of the *American Eagle,* than in reading law. I wrote an article on Gray's inconsistency, one on the politics of New Jersey, one touching up the stupidity of the Gloucester papers, and two or three short squibs on other subjects. Mr. Mulford is to contribute also, but his communications shall be under my supervision. An editor before I'm out of my nineteenth year! Precocious!

This evening Ned Drayton and I went up to the Parsonage to make music. The piano, guitar and violin conspired to bring forth sweet sounds.

28 September, Wednesday.

Gray's paper of this morning gives me quite a puff. . . . I wonder what he will think of the doctrine of my lecture, after next Friday night.[117]

My aunt Rachel was unable to sleep any last night, and in consequence is to day much worse. Her mind is very wandering—so much so that it was deemed best to go for my aunt Mary. I volunteered my services and went over to town this evening to start early to-morrow for West-Chester.

I spent an hour or two in Thirteenth Street, at Vandeveer's;[118] on my way whither I met Miss Hannah Sheppard and two of her cousins. Jim George and Annie Hugg were up there, and crossed over home in the mail-boat. I went down with them, and staid all night at Bloodgood's.

29 September, Thursday.

I started for West Chester this morning, and would have had a very pleasant excursion if I had been on any other errand. The two most interesting places which we passed were Paoli, the residence once of old Wayne,[119] and the romantic valley, a few miles east of West Chester.

Horses are slow means of travelling even on Rail roads.[120] It took me from seven to twelve to got out, and from two to seven to come in. I had a pretty good look at the town of West Chester in company with my aunt. She will come up to-morrow.

Hineline got his paper out to-day, in time for the County Convention which met at Woodbury to form a democratic ticket. It looks very well—but it puffs me!

I found my aunt about the same on my return.

30 September, Friday.

My aunt not having got worse I consulted the Doctor as to delivering my lecture which had been announced for to-night. He said he would rather I should go ahead, since the public would begin to

117. The *Mail* merely announced that Mickle would address the Camden Union Temperance Society on 30 September.

118. Mickle probably refers to William Vandever's bookbindery.

119. "Old Wayne" was General Anthony Wayne (1745–96), who had conducted foraging raids through South Jersey during the Revolution.

120. Some railroads of the period used horses, rather than steam engines, to pull cars along the tracks.

investigate the cause of a disappointment, which would be unpleasant to him. Notwithstanding there was a circus-exhibition conflicting with my house, the lower part of the Methodist church was well filled by the elite of our town. I read my address from the pulpit, and occupied about an hour. Mr. Lenhart moved a vote of thanks, and the rising was unanimous. I acknowledged the compliment in a very few words, and really felt what I said, that I was unworthy of so flattering a return for doing only what was my duty. I felt no embarrassment whatever, after I had begun, although I did not feel quite at home when I first went into the pulpit.

In coming out of the house I met Esquire Cowperthwait, and he told me that I had delivered the best Temperance address he had ever heard. I mention this not to gratify my vanity, but to show that my argument in favour of a law against drinking rum was approved by a rank Loco-foco. I was apprehensive that they could not go it. Josiah Atkinson says I was at least original.

After the lecture I went to the Parsonage, and received the most agreeable congratulations of all from Miss Josephine, who had not been out to hear me. She said nothing, but expressed a great deal.

My aunt Haines and the girls arrived to day. She is at our house, they at Poplar Hill.

1 October, Saturday.

On account of my aunt's sickness I did not go to the office to-day. In running about town I received numberless congratulations for my address last night—some sincere, but the most hypocritical of course.

Yesterday when the carrier of the *Eagle* gave Gray a copy of that paper, he says he opened it, read the name, and then tore it in two and threw it on the floor!

There was a Temperance meeting to night in the Court-house.

3 October, Monday.

The debate at the Institute to-night was upon the question "Should the veto power be restricted?" Affirmative Dudley and Davis, Negative Mulford and Drayton. I took our girls to hear Ned's speech, and a comical one it was. Jo said she could oppose such a dough-head as he is, herself; and I think so too. There was no decision to-night.

4 October, Tuesday.

There was a meeting of The Young Men of our town to-night to form a Temperance Society. I was made Secretary, and put on the Constitution-Committee. Nineteen names were procured on the member list.

My aunt is much better to-day.

5 October, Wednesday.

This evening I introduced Mulford at the Parsonage, and we took the ladies down to the Methodist Church to hear a lecture on education. It was by a Western minister, and was the drollest affair I ever listened to. There was a great deal of good sense in it.

6 October, Thursday.

Bob and I were playing at the Library room a while this evening. The other evening the gentleman just named, Mr. Mulford, Constable Morgan,[121] Ned Drayton, Charley Hugg, one or two others and myself met at Delacour's and resolved to go down to English's to set the coalmen to dancing. We had a fiddle along with us, but the coalies would'nt dance; so we gave Sculls a serenade, and then returned to Delacours just after he had shut up, and played him two or three tunes. Such frolicks are harmless, though undignified.

I was busy writing editorial to-day.

7 October, Friday.

This evening I took Miss Josephine to the meeting of the Baptist Choir. We had a pretty good time. I left her there in charge of Ned Drayton, and went down to the *Eagle* office to read the proof for to-morrow's paper.

8 October, Saturday.

Ned Drayton and I were at the Parsonage this evening on a musical errand. Phoebe and Josephine only are at home. When my hands are cold again I will get the latter to warm them:

The *Eagle* appeared in due time this morning, and looks very well. It receives showers of compliments from its cotemporaries. I wrote about three columns of editorial for this number. It puffs my lecture—for which my thanks are due to Mulford.

10 October, Monday.

This evening I went over with Sam to a musical party which his Philadelphia acquaintances have got up. We two played first violins, and had also the satisfaction of knowing that other people had made much worse harmony. The house at which our soiree took place was in Seventh Street above Arch; there were fifteen or sixteen present. I crossed over in the Mail boat, but Sam staid all night.

The political spirit waxes pretty warm in Camden. I expect a warm contest to-morrow. There was a Loco-foco meeting in the city-hall, and of course the Institute had to give ground this evening.

121. Edward Morgan was Camden Township constable from 1842 to 1844.

11 October, Tuesday.

The election begins to-day. It has taken up my time for some weeks back pretty exclusively, in writing editorial squibs and so forth. I'm a young editor, eh?

12 October, Wednesday.

The election in Philadelphia yesterday was hotly fought. The Whigs have carried the city and the democrats the county. Colonel Richard M. Johnson was in town and made two or three speeches in the county districts.

The box closed in Camden township to-night with Three hundred and ninety nine votes in it. They were counted off at Elwell's, and we had a majority of one hundred and twenty nine. Camden always does her duty. There was one democratic ticket scratched so as to present the names of Wm. D. Cooper Esq. Willm. H. Ogden, and John W. Peterson, the bank defaulter for coroners.[122] Cooper was present when this ballot was read, and must have been exceedingly mortified at the joke.

13 October, Thursday.

"Gloucester County has gone for the Whigs" was the unpleasant news I took over to the office this morning. I fear for the State.

This evening the following gentlemen met at the Library room either by person or proxy to form a musical society:

Samuel Spicer Eastlack Cowperthwait ⎫ Isaac Mickle, ⎭	First Violins.
John H. Baxter,	Violincello.
Josiah R. Atkinson ⎫ Robert W. Ogden, ⎬ Mr. Mulford ⎭	Flutes
Mr. Gerhard	Second Violin
Edward Drayton	Clarionet.

I was called to the chair and Mulford appointed Secretary. It was resolved to name the Society "The Amateur's Musical Association" of Camden; and to meet once a week in the city hall, after a few rehearsals in the Library room. We then selected some pieces for rehearsal on next Thursday evening, and adjourned, after a few flourishes from the violin of Mr. Mickle aforesaid.[123]

122. Cooper (1816–75), a leading citizen of Camden, had recently been admitted to the Pennsylvania and New Jersey bars. Ogden was owner of a coach factory on Front Street. Peterson had served as the bank's notary from 1839 to 1841.

123. The group did not function as Mickle wished, for he was still trying to organize it properly during the following spring. See entry of 5 April 1843.

The delegates of the first ward in Southwark have read Kelly out of the party. Their card appeared in the *Times* of last Monday. I wrote an article thereupon to-day for the *Eagle*. . . .

14 October, Friday.

The rumor is to-day that there is a tie in the legislature of New Jersey. Hardly. If Morris has gone for us there may be a tie, but that is very doubtful.

I was at the Parsonage this evening, and so was Dr. Ward with his violin. He plays very sweetly. Mary has got home from Bridgeton.

15 October, Saturday.

Morris County has gone for the Whigs, giving them ten majority on joint ballot. The popular majority for the Democrats will be very heavy.

The *Eagle* appeared to-day in due time. Our war with Gray goes bravely on!

I was at the parsonage again to night. We were to have had a walk, but the rain!

16 October, Sunday.

There was a little rain yesterday and day before—the first for twenty eight days! This is an unusual drought for this climate and season.

I was in town to-night and went to Stockton's church[24] with Lydia Vandeveer. In passing the *Ledger Bulletin* I observed by a slip, that the democrats are carrying every thing in Ohio. Clay had great hopes for that state, and may now consider himself used up. Truth must prevail.

There was a merry party in the mail line.

17 October, Monday.

The debate before the Institute this evening was on the question, "is there such a thing as natural genius?" Ned Drayton was one of the speakers on the negative side. He brought Josephine, probably to witness a demonstration in his own case, of the truth of the affirmative! She and I sat together and had a great deal of fun over Ned's dumpy oration.

18 October, Tuesday.

This evening I took my fiddle and went to Hugg's with Ned. Their piano is so out of tune that good music is impossible.

I wrote the first number of a series of letters for the *Eagle*, to day,

---

124. Thomas H. Stockton was pastor of the "Methodist Protestant Church" at Eleventh and Wood Streets, Philadelphia.

and signed it "A Gloucester Farmer." I intend that these shall excite some notice in this state. The times are propitious for denunciation.

Let me not forget to mention, to-day I am twenty years old! How time flies. "*Anni fugaces*"—but I am too busy to preach a sermon.

19 October, Wednesday.

Gray's paper of this morning is "mum" as to tearing up the first number of the *Eagle*.

This evening Mulford and I walked down to Kaighn's Point with Sheppard's girls. It was moonlight, and we had a very pleasant time.

21 October, Friday.

According to arrangement Josephine and I called on Miss Gray this evening. She had gone to the Rev. Mr. Osbourne's lecture in the Baptist Church, and so we went too.

I read the proof of the *Eagle* this afternoon. Hard work, this being an editor!

23 October, Sunday.

This evening I went to church with Annie Hugg, and woful to relate, had my old coat on! I saw Josephine, and had a great mind to go home with her instead of the lady with whom I came. I resolved to-night as I sat in meeting to drop my acquaintance with the Hugg's—I am tired of it.

24 October, Monday.

This evening Sam, Atkinson, Baxter and myself took our instruments over to Philadelphia, to play for a Sacred Music Society, which met in Eleventh below Chesnut. We had excellent harmony. The mail-boat was full of Jerseymen.

25 October, Tuesday.

I wrote No. II of "the Farmer's letters" to-day, and a good deal of editorial. In the evening I called at the Parsonage.

27 October, Thursday.

This evening Browning, Mulford and I took three of the Sheppards over to the exhibition of the Franklin Institute. We had a very pleasant trip—Jo and I, in particular.

28 October, Friday.

The Amateurs met to-night, and among other peices played one of Napoleon's marches which I arranged in five parts. All allowed that it went very well. This is my first attempt in harmony.

29 October, Saturday.

Mr. Hineline of the *Eagle* has taken Curts from Woodbury into partnership with him.[125] This last gentleman's capital consists of money and not of talent. So Mulford and I will still have to edit the paper. No. 5, issued to day has my second letter in, addressed to Samuel R. Gummere.[126] These epistles already begin to make a little noise.

There was a meeting at Sheppard's to-night to organize a Reading Society. I was called to the chair pro tem.

31 October, Monday.

The debate at the Institute to-night was upon the following question: Have the states a right to secede from the Union?

In the affirmative were myself and Atkinson; in the negative Hollingshead and Davis. On the bench, President Dudley, Mr. Mulford and Mr. Flowers. . . .

1 November, Tuesday.

I was introduced to-day by Colonel Page to Hon. James Buchanan, Senator from Pennsylvania, and to Mr. Rives,[127] one of the editors of the *Globe* newspaper. This is "glory enough for one day" to the rankest Loco-foco.

2 November, Wednesday.

I wrote my third letter to-day, "to Philip J. Gray, Esq." and also a leader for the *Eagle*, nominating Johnson for the Presidency. I did this last at the request of Hineline.

4 November, Friday.

Joseph Smalley and his brother dined with me to-day. They left Camden early in the afternoon.

This evening I took Josephine to hear Mr. Osbourne and an Indian deliver lectures in the Baptist Church. I sat along side of Gray—rather queer, considering I had just been reading the proof of a violent letter addressed by me to him. He was delegated by Mr. Osbourne to read a couple of essays by members of the "Evangelical Union" (of which he is Secretary)—but he read so low that nobody heard the nonsense.

5 November, Saturday.

The letter to Gray in this morning's *Eagle* makes a good deal of

125. Henry Curts, an experienced printer ran the *American Eagle* with Hineline, and later with Henry Bosse, until August 1844, when he became sole owner. Soon thereafter he changed the paper's name to *Phoenix and Farmers' and Mechanics' Advertiser*. The paper appeared under variations of this name until about 1860 when it discontinued.

126. Gummere (1789–1865), best known as an educator, headed a girls' school in Burlington from 1821 to 1837 and was clerk of the Chancery Court of New Jersey from 1840 to 1850.

127. John Cook Rives (1795–1864), one of America's leading journalists, was part owner of the Washington *Daily Globe* from 1833 to 1849 and publisher of the *Congressional Globe*, which reported congressional debates, from 1833 to 1864.

noise. I have been asked about it by half a dozen, but none of them suspect the authorship. Cowperthwait, (the old gentleman) thinks it is Mr. Jeffers, and says Mr. Gray is "essentially used up."

7 November, Monday.

The debate before the Institute this evening was on the question, "Would the increase of intelligence among the people of this country bring an increase of happiness?" I was on the affrmative and Mr. Mulford on the negative. They beat us and got the decision; Whereupon I challenged them to debate the point next night, and was taken up. The question is like the handle of a jug, all on one side.

8 November, Tuesday.

Being desirous of making "the Farmer's Letters" as authentic as possible, I wrote to Stacy G. Potts to-day to get some material for my next number, which is to be to Pennington. I used the name of Mr. Hineline.

In the evening I was playing with Angeline Turner.

11 November, Friday.

I read the proof of the paper this evening and then called at the Parsonage. After this I dropped around to the church, met our fiddlers, and went out with them on another serenade. Two nights handrunning! We had a minister with us however.

12 November, Saturday.

The *Eagle* appears to-day with my fourth number in. It is full of treason! Strange that these letters have attracted no notice yet. They shall before long—that's flat. In addition to my contributions to the *Eagle* over signatures, I wrote the chief part of the editorial. Mulford also assists.

13 November, Sunday.

I went to the Baptist Church this evening. It was full, and yet to me empty—Josephine was not there. O the misery of being in love!

14 November, Monday.

This evening the challenge debate came off, and was attended with some sharp shooting between Mulford and myself. In the course of my remarks I had defined man to be "a rising animal" at which he made light, joking at the description as if it were no description at all. When my return came, I repeated that as a general rule "man is a rising animal, but of course there are and have been exceptions." I then alluded to Judas Iscariot and Benedict Arnold as departures from the axiom, and said that in more recent times, we have seen falls quite similar. "We have seen" I remarked, "that a man can to-day stand behind the sacred desk and dispense the blessings of religious instruction, and to morrow shoulder the green-bag and live upon the exercise of his ability to mystify and deceive." Mulford has been a preacher and is now a student at law. Davis says he looked rattled while I was speaking, and whether he felt my words or not—he seemed willing when it was his return to reply to let my language pass without criticism. We will get along hereafter in peace. We got the decision to night triumphantly—more triumphantly because *ma chere amie* witnessed the tournament. To conquer in her presence is doubly victorious.

15 November, Tuesday.

This evening I took Miss Josephine to the "Evangelical Union" which a Mr. Osbourne has got up here in Camden to prepare for the coming of the world's end. By the by, World-End-Miller is at Newark in this State, carrying on his devout purpose of terrifying the weak brethren, and driving old women mad.

16 November, Wednesday.

Mulford spent the evening with me in musical exercises. The affair of Monday evening does not mar the harmony of our intercourse.

18 November, Friday.

This evening the members of the Choir resolved to have a serenade. Every thing was arranged, and the six of us were holding a consultation at the corner of Fourth and Market Street, when along came some of Sheppard's girls and some gentlemen. Bob Ogden and I stood our ground, but the rest ran away. It was infinitely comical to see them streaking in every direction through the moonlight, especially Baxter and his big fiddle! This was about eleven o'clock, and of course upset our serenade for Camden. We went down to Fetterville and played a tune or two, and got back about midnight. It was freezing very fast all the time. Our fingers were clumsy enough.

19 November, Saturday.

For some time past there has been a great movement in progress in Philadelphia, to convert the firemen into sober men. They have had immense meetings every week at the Museum, and the excitement, Kelly says, has been tremendous. It is their plan to set the women and music both at work for the cause of temperance, and a good one it is; for who can resist the two combined?

These remarks very naturally lead to what I was going to say—to wit, that this evening I took Josephine over the river to attend one of these nondescript meetings. It was held in the Museum. and the occasion was the presentation of a silver horn to one of the Fire Companies. It was ballotted for, and drawn by the "Reliance" Engine. My friend Kelley presented it to the delegate, both of them being in fireman's equipment. About forty delegates were in attendance in their different uniforms. The museum was well filled. Mr. Slicer, Chaplain to Congress, Rev. Mr. Chambers and Rev. Mr. Burrows made speeches.[128] A brass band also officiated, and in addition to this there were several tunes sung. So the evening passed very agreeably.

On my return, my fair companion was somewhat more communicative and unreserved than commonly. My prudence was hardly equal to the emergency—nay, it was inferior to it. I told her more than I meant to, and more perhaps than I ought. The effects of the accident are yet to be seen. Tom Gray crossed the river with us; and we got safely home about midnight.

The *Emporium* of to-day contains a reprint of the Farmer's letter to Pennington.[129] Quite a compliment!

Colt, who was to have been hung for murder, yesterday, at New York, killed himself a little before the hour arrived. This event makes some noise—why it should I do not see.[130]

20 November, Sunday.

I went home with Mary Sheppard this evening from church. I did not see Josephine, or I could have read in her face the answer to an important quere.

21 November, Monday.

The debate before the Institute to night resulted again in the triumph of our side! Mulford has the luck of it. The question was "Has the character of the Indian been improved by contact with the white race?" Davis and I were on the negative—and two of Sheppards girls were on the bench near the stove. I went home with them and saw Josephine. Her eye told me what I hoped for, but I beheld it with an unaccountable indifference. Strange indeed is the human heart!

22 November, Tuesday.

I spent this evening in town—in Sansom Street, with Sam and Atkinson. We had plenty of fun, such as it was.

23 November, Wednesday.

To-day I composed and arranged a little march for our Amateurs. I

128. Rev. Henry Slicer (1801–74) was chaplain of the United States Senate on three occasions between 1837 and 1862. J. L. Burrows was the minister of Philadelphia's Broad Street Baptist Church, at Broad and Brown Streets.

129. This was Mickle's letter which he had signed "A Gloucester Farmer" and published in the *Eagle* on 22 October.

130. John C. Colt's suicide created a sensation, partly because a prison fire broke out at almost the same time. The coincidence was too great for some New Yorkers, who insisted, contrary to all evidence, that Colt had escaped in the confusion.

must collect my musical efforts together. They may yet become famous—who knows?

24 November, Thursday.

I have not had much editorial work to do this week. The next number of the *Eagle* will be full of Sheriff's advertisements.

This evening our Club met and among other things practised my march. It is a simple, unadorned little thing; but they liked it, or at least said so.

26 November, Saturday.

The *Emporium* republishes another of my letters to-day. I wonder if the printer suspects the age of the author of these things. I guess not or they would not excite so much attention from him.

I was in Philadelphia to night again, and went with Sam and Atkinson to the Walnut Street Theatre to hear the opera of the *Bayadere*.[131] Three evenings in a week! Gracious, the people will think I am given to dissipation.

27 November, Sunday.

Miss Phoebe Sheppard some time ago gave me her album to receive a bagatelle from my pen. I to-day wrote [*one*] . . . and in the evening took it home, and gallanted the owner to Methodist Church, where they are acting a burlesque on all common sense, or in other language holding "a protracted effort." It is well I did my poetry before hearing the awful yells put forth by these fools, for my mind will not recover its composure, much less its inspiration, for a month. . . .

29 November, Tuesday.

I wrote the Sixth of the Farmer's series to-day, and a leader on the Presidency. It is unnecessary to say that I gave more light to the public than I acquired for myself from my law-books.

This evening some of our Amateurs had a rehearsal at the Library room.

30 November, Wednesday.

It has been snowing all day, and I have been setting type for my own amusement at the *Eagle* office. It was too unpleasant to cross the river.

Fulton I. Alexander is on trial before the Criminal Sessions of Philadelphia, for the murder of Lougee in Third Street. See the entry for July 27th last past. May he be hung, as he deserves.

---

131. Daniel François Esprit Auber's *Le Dieu et la Bayadère* was first performed in Philadelphia in 1838.

3 December, Saturday.

My letter on the Treasurer's accounts is going the rounds.[132] I saw it in three or four papers at the *Eagle* office this morning.

5 December, Monday.

There was a debate at the Institute this evening on the question "Have legislatures the right to prohibit the drinking of intoxicating liquors by direct legislation?" On the affirmative were myself and Mr. Hollingshead, on the negative Mr. Mulford and Mr. Dudley. On the council were Mr. Davis and two of the audience Messrs. Gregory and Jacobs. After a warm discussion of three hours the decision was given to the negative, Mr. Davis dissenting in our favor. On this we appealed to the house and reversed the decree; but wanting a complete victory, one about which there could be no doubt, we challenged them to go over the same question next Monday night—they to open, as if they were the affirmative. This offer was agreed to.

6 December, Tuesday.

This evening I was at Sheppard's. They have all got a good color this cold weather.

8 December, Thursday.

President Tyler's Message reached town to-day, but it causes very little excitement. It is rumored that the Bankrupt-law will be repealed early this session.

It has been a rainy Thursday, this.

11 December, Sunday.

I took some girls to Methodist Church to-night. That place is the scene of great attraction now, during the excitement of a protracted meeting.

12 December, Monday.

The challenge-debate came off to-night, before a crowded house. Davis, John Clement and Rogers were in the chairs, and all of them prejudiced against us; two of them avowedly so. We had an animated time. There was some sparring between Mr. Mulford and myself, all however in good humor. Every inch of ground was manfully contested, but we got the decision unanimously, so there could be no appeal. This is indeed a compliment to us, and we feel it properly. To get so unpopular a decision from prejudiced judges and against able opponents, and that before so many ladies, is, and ought to be, a source of pride. I made an awful bungle in quoting St. Jame's remark

132. This was another of Mickle's published letters, signed "A Gloucester Farmer."

about the "perfect law of liberty,"[133] but I got out of the scrape very well. It will mortify me, however, into reading the bible through. I have blundered into what little I know of other things, and why not blunder into a knowledge of the Scriptures?

I got a letter from Ned King to-day enclosing some petrafactions and arrow-heads from the banks of the Mississippi. All Sheppard's girls got billets too.

14 December, Wednesday.

Mulford and I were at Sheppard's to-night with our musical instruments. The girls play so wretchedly that it is impossible to accompany them.

For some time back I have felt a strange indifference to the younger sister of this agreeable family. She has observed this in my conduct, and after what has taken place between us, has a right to wonder at it. To night while the rest were talking she hinted to me that a promenade on some of these moonlight evenings would be a great enjoyment. I agreed, and so I suppose we must trudge down to the Glass-house again.[134] This much I am sure, the next step of our adventure must be made by herself.

15 December, Thursday.

Our Club met to night, but some of the sacreligious devils, beginning to dance, Baxter made tracks as fast as possible. His piety revolted at such shocking doings, but it does not revolt at retaining twenty dollars of the Library's money. Like the Pharisees, "he strains at a gnat and swallows a camel." That text is found in St. Matthew—I read it there last night.

17 December, Saturday.

No. seven of my letters appears to-day. It is the weakest one yet.

18 December, Sunday.

At home as usual, arranging music. In the evening I went to Methodist Church, ran afoul of Sheppard's girls and saw them home.

News reached town to-day of a mutiny on board the United States Brig *Somers*—headed by Philip Spencer, the son of the present Secretary of War, who with some others was hung to the yard arm by Capt. McKenzie.[135] The brig arrived at New York a day or two ago from the Coast of Africa.

133. James 1:25.
134. See entry of 24 January 1842.
135. Captain Alexander Slidell Mackenzie (1803–48), commanding officer of the *Somers*, had discovered plans for a mutiny and had executed three crew members in what some observers thought was unseemly haste. Worse, one of the victims was Philip Spencer, nephew of Secretary of War John C. Spencer. Mackenzie was exonerated by military and civilian courts.

19 December, Monday.

Atkinson and I went to Chesnut Street, to night, to see the opera of *Moses in Egypt*. The music is fine—but one of the Jewish women had a bustle on! Cowperthwait was there, with Miss Richards.

20 December, Tuesday.

Colonel Page gave me a Circus ticket to-night, which I made use of, and enjoyed a hearty laugh. The clown's freaks are irresistable.

23 December, Friday.

This evening, knowing that the elder Misses Sheppard would be at the sewing meeting or the reading circle, I called at their house to see Jo. Somehoworother (what an adverb!) my flame in this direction begins to wane. She wonders at it, and so do I! We called on Annie Hugg together. They live near by each other.

24 December, Saturday.

After the Library meeting this evening (at which we had a warm time about publishing the delinquents) I went home with Ned Cole. He showed me a letter from his sister Cad, who is now up Jersey, addressed to himself. It was well written and just like the amiable Caddy.

I forgot to mention that the historian Bancroft[136] was at the office yesterday. He is a fine looking man, but wears spectacles!

25 December, Sunday.

Christmas-day—which I celebrated by reading five hours and sitting in Methodist meeting two. I saw Sheppard's girls there, but concluded not to go home with them this evening. I'm getting wofully ungallant!

26 December, Monday.

Since I am to turn over a new leaf in industry next year, I thought I would take a foretaste to-day. So this morning I resumed my cross-legged chair, and Sallusts' *Jugurthine War*, and read several paragraphs of the same. After which,

I crossed over to Philadelphia and walked up and down Chesnut Street with some friends. I never saw so many people turned out to celebrate Christmas. The main streets were literally jammed. One centre of attraction was Parkinson's Confectionary in Chesnut St. opposite the Masonic-hall, where in front of their house they had an admirable representation of old Kris-Kringle just descending a chimney with baskets full of toys for the young ones.

136. George Bancroft (1800–91), of Massachusetts, was currently writing his monumental *History of the United States*.

28 December, Wednesday.

It has recently been discovered that the graves in the Camden Cemetery have been broken open and robbed. A negro named Henry Thomas, residing in that miserable place called South Camden, was yesterday arrested on suspicion, and examined before Justice P. J. Gray. Nothing conclusive appeared and he was discharged. A cloud still hovers over this fellow. The cause of his arrest was somewhat singular: on examining one of the violated graves, two or three feet from the coffin they found a fireman's cape, very like one which Thomas has been seen to wear on rainy days. Several witnesses swore to this much, though none of them were willing to swear positively that it was the same article. He was charged by the Cemetery Committee with petit larceny for stealing the grave clothes—there being an odd oversight in the English law, the law of New Jersey in the premises, in regard to the criminality of stealing a dead body.

To-day this same Thomas and two other negroes were brought before Justice Harrison,[137] and one of them confessed that the trio on the night of the first of this month stole a man and woman, stripped them in the yard, and carried them down to Kaighn's Point, whence two of them rowed them over to the Navy Yard, a little below which a waggon was in wait to take them to the dissecting room. Thomas stoutly denies his guilt, and he is certainly a better looking fellow than the rest; his apparent innocence however could not withstand all the law students in Camden. Mulford, Dudley, Hollingshead and myself volunteered on the part of the republic, and having stumbled upon the case of *King* vs. *Lyn*,[138] we got the Justice to bind them over.

The state's evidence is said to have declared (not at the examination) that while he was taking the girl across Kaighn's fields her tresses caught in the fence, and were jerked out by the roots! Horrid. He says also that they sold the two bodies for six dollars.

29 December, Thursday.

We had another Library meeting to-night and finally resolved to publish the delinquents. Cole showed me another letter from Caddy. I would give a million of dollars for such a sister as she.

30 December, Friday.

This evening I spent at Delacour's in edifying conversation with

---

137. Josiah Harrison (1776–1865), formerly of Salem, was now a Camden lawyer and justice of the peace.

138. *R. v. Lynn*, 2 T.R. 733, 100 Eng. Rep. 394 (1788), held that exhumation of bodies was an indictable offense under English common law.

the loungers who resort there. There is really a good deal to be learned in "the intellectual conflict" of such places and such men.

I have not been at the office during the holy-days.

31 December, Saturday.

The *Eagle* does not appear to-day. The reason is, they are enlarging it. My last letter (I see by the exchanges received at the printing office) is too denunciatory. None of the papers have dared to copy it. The Mount-Holly *Herald* however has copied my leading article on "The Revision of the Constitution," and referred its readers to it.[139]

This evening I called on Jo—and so

Farewell, old Forty-Two!

---

139. Mickle had already begun advocating changes in the New Jersey Constitution and would soon become a prime mover in the campaign for a new constitutional convention.

Southwest View of Mount Holly

1843

1 January, Sunday.

Now that I am beginning the sixth book of my Journal, it is a proper
time to adopt certain improvements in keeping it, which the experience
of five volumes has suggested.

I. In matter. Hitherto I have paid too much attention to small things.
These may perhaps interest me—but my labor will be idle indeed if my
records do not also interest and tend to instruct others. The present
age is replete with grand topics of political, religious and scientific
animadversion; and these are certainly more worthy of my notice than
the coquetries of a mischievous girl. It is said that in general one third
of a man's life is given to love, one third to fame, and one third to
money. I have chased the first butterfly for two years, with a most
laudable industry, and with quite as much success as I anticipated. I
have no longer a propensity to talk about it by day and to dream of it
by night.

As I have said on a former occasion my situation in the office of
Colonel Page brings me into contact with some of the principal republican politicians of the times, and into an acquaintance with the politics

of our whole country. The knowledge thus picked up finds its way to the public on the wings of the *Eagle*, of which the people of Camden are pleased to call me the editor. By preserving in my diary memoranda of public affairs, therefore, I will be enabled to discharge the duty thrown upon me by the want of education in Hineline and Curts, with readiness and correctness.

There are many things, such as meteorological phenomena, personal anecdotes and reflections on what I read, which may be profitably recorded. When there is nothing to be said hereafter I will endeavor to say nothing; for a neglect of this silver rule has infused a good deal of stupid stuff into my past volumes much to my regret and mortification.

II. In manner. I will strive to acquire a perspicuous style, by never using a redundant, or omitting an essential, word. Sir William Jones' little *Treatise on Bailments* is perhaps the best model for clearness now extant in the English language. I have heard Johnson's *Rasselas* also recommended; but he had too hearty a contempt for Saxon words ever to become my preceptor. I shall also try to write a more legible hand. Since I have been engaged in fiddling and similar amusements my diary has suffered a good deal in appearance as well as in substance. This shameful carelessness must be reformed.

Heretofore I have been in the habit of writing the day of the month as well as of the week over each entry. I will stop this, and thereby save ink and time. It was Stephen Girard,[1] I think who calculated that he had saved a thousand dollars by not crossing his t's or dotting his i's. And Noah Webster, who put forth an edition of the Bible,[2] says he saves no less than twenty five closely printed octavo pages by substituting "to" for "unto," throughout the book. Small matters are not always to be dispised. . . .

After having set upon this laborious but instructive and improving amusement, and persevered for two years and a half without omitting a single day, I think I may justly claim to have some industry.

In conclusion, I may say that from the manner in which the five preceeding volumes are composed they are proper to be shown only to my most intimate friends. The present series I intend to guard less securely from the eyes of my acquaintances, and I must therefore exercise upon it more discrimination in style as well as substance.

I employed the first day of the year in propitious industry; having read several paragraphs of Sallust's *Jugurthine War*, and the whole of

1. Girard (1750–1831) was a Philadelphia merchant, banker, and philanthropist.
2. Webster (1758–1843), most famous for his dictionaries, was author or publisher of a wide variety of books.

the Gospel according to St. Mark. I call this a propitious industry because, as the old saying goes, the birth-day of the year rules all the rest.

2 January, Monday.
Busy to-day in reviewing the II Blackstone, and reading Jones on Bailment.

3 January, Tuesday.
Employed in my legal studies with some zeal. I am often obliged to go over and over a passage before I can get an understanding of it. This may be owing to my stupidity or to the incessant clatter that is going on around me. Our office-door is continually swinging to and fro to give ingress or egress to a parcel of bores who have nothing to say but much to talk about. This is a great pest to me, but I suppose I must bear it.

Miss Caroline Cole is up at Cranberry. Her brother goes after her in a few days, and he invited me to accompany him. I should like to accept, but cannot.

4 January, Wednesday.
I wrote a queer leading article for the *Eagle* to-day on "Common law and Common sense." This was instigated by the recent outrages upon the dead in Camden.

8 January, Sunday.
This day, the anniversary of Jackson's victory at New Orleans, I spent in fighting the war of Jugurtha over on Sallust's brilliant pages.

9 January, Monday.
There was no debate before the Institute to-night. I was not sorry, for it is always repugnant to my feelings to talk in public.

10 January, Tuesday.
Edward Cole has got home, but did not bring his sister with him. Since I must yet talk of the girls a little, I will say that I met Josephine Sheppard this evening on her way home from the Post-Office. We shook hands very heartily, and she wished me a happy New Year. It was rather late for this compliment, but she was excusable, since she has not seen me before since the last day of December.

The Amateurs met this evening by accident.

11 January, Wednesday.
Baxter, Cowperthwait and myself officiated by invitation at a Concert held this evening at Gilett's Church in Twelfth Street, Philadelphia.[3]

3. Abraham D. Gillett was pastor of Philadelphia's Eleventh Baptist Church on Twelfth above Sassafras.

I played tenor, standing very prominently, and therefore very uneasily, in the pulpit. We had a good house, and good music and all returned in the Mail Line—not the house and the music, I mean, but we aforesaid persons!

There have been for a day and night back some serious riots among the weavers in the north and north-western parts of the city.[4] The military were called out by General Cadwallader this afternoon, and we saw many soldiers flying about to-night, in various directions. Every thing was quiet at midnight when we left Philadelphia. This city is no longer one of "brotherly love." It has more tumults and lawless proceedings now, than any town in the savage West.

I met Cole tonight. Caddy has returned.

12 January, Thursday.

The riots in Philadelphia are not yet entirely quelled. The military (I heard General Cadwallader say in our office this afternoon) would be called out again to-night.

I spent the evening quite pleasantly at Sheppard's. I returned from the office rather before dark this afternoon on account of the *Eagle's* business. Mr. Mulford is down at Salem, and I am obliged to edit the paper this week entirely by myself.

14 January, Saturday.

This evening I called on Caroline. She is a lovely girl—a very lovely girl—so accomplished, yet so unassuming, so kind and affectionate, yet so prudent and dignified! I could not stay so long as I wished, on account of a Temperance meeting at the Court-House which I had promised Mr. Levin to attend. That gentleman addressed us very ably—though he was a little vexed that no one but our Mayor, Dr. Fisler, could be prevailed upon by his eloquence to sign the pledge. I accompanied him down to the boat, along with Jim Cassidy who fell asleep at Elwell's much to Levins amusement.

I was appointed a delegate to-night to attend the Convention on next Wednesday.

16 January, Monday.

The well-known Indian question was discussed to-night in a tolerable manner before the Institute. I chanced to be on the lucky side again— the negative, that it was not wrong to dispossess the red man of his lands.

---

4. The weavers' riots in the Kensington section of Philadelphia arose out of fights between striking and non-striking workers. Eight companies of troops were called out to quell the disturbance.

18 January, Wednesday.

This morning I went to Trenton to the Temperance Convention. My uncle also went up to oppose some alteration in the law relating to Fisheries.

The Convention was pretty well attended. Stacy G. Potts Esq. presided. Dr. Appleton read a report (prior to resigning his agency) showing the number of Temperance people in New Jersey to be fifty seven thousand. This must be an exaggeration—I know that he magnified the returns of our Camden Society. No business of much importance was done. . . .

In the evening Levin addressed the Convention of delegates and the public in a very good and effective manner. Governor Pennington and many of the members of the Legislature were present by invitation, and the speaker's remarks were levelled directly at them. At the close of the harangue some twenty of the law makers formed a Legislative Temperance Society. A lady of the society of Friends rose in her seat and appealed very pointedly to Pennington to throw his influence into the scale of good. He began to excuse himself—he had not had time to weigh so important a matter, and so forth. When he had done he was hissed by some persons unknown! Very fortunately for the Gloucester Farmer he was not then in the room, but was waiting at the depot along with 'Squire Cowperthwait for the cars.

I spent part of the day in the Council Chambers, where the Council was sitting as a Court of Appeals. There was a lively passage between the blunt Mr. Patterson of Monmouth and the polished Moffat of Burlington.[5]

19 January, Thursday.

There was a party this evening at Sheppards. The seal on my note of invitation bore the inscription "Do Come"—and I did go. Caddy Cole was there, and I may say without incurring the imputation of fickleness, that she was the loveliest creature in the room.

20 January, Friday.

I was engaged at home to day in reading Anthon's *Abridgement of Blackstone.* Sam Cowperthwait examined me when crossing the river sometime ago, on the three first chapters and I passed without missing a question.

The Church Choir met tonight. I played alto for a change.

23 January, Monday.

There was a debate this evening on the comparative destructiveness

5. The two legislators were James Patterson, vice-president of the legislative council, and Craig Moffett, Mount Holly attorney.

of ambition and superstition. I did not attend, until nearly at the close, having chosen rather to chat the time away with Caddy.

25 January, Wednesday.

I was at the office to-day reading—not a law-book, but the history of New Jersey preparatory to writing a series of letters for the *Eagle*, in favor of a reform of the constitution. The Gloucester Farmer letters are concluded, by announcing editorially in the paper "that they emenated from us." There is not really material enough to sustain the strife in which I had begun to write, and I thought a termination would be better than a transition. Those letters made a good deal of noise, and I intend that those forthcoming, shall make still more.

28 January, Saturday.

Since Miss Cole's return to Camden I have been in company but very little. The fact is I am placed in something of a dilemma between my two old playmates—just at present I am suspended like Mahomet's coffin; but a little communion with Caddy will extricate me. She has a thousand sterling virtues which it were foolish to undervalue.

30 January, Monday.

The Institute question to-night was: "Which is the greater blessing, hope or remembrance?" I was on the negative, which side was victorious. After the discussion the first number of a collection of essays by the members, in newspaper style was read, and caused a good deal of amusement. The idea is Mulford's. The name of the paper is The Literary Hotch Potch.

1 February, Wednesday.

I resolved at the beginning of the present year, not to spend so many of my evenings with the ladies; and thus far I have abstained wonderfully. The habit of dropping in here and there (and especially at the Parsonage) had grown on me so much within a twelvemonth past that I could hardly leave home upon an errand, without bringing up somewhere and staying an hour or so, on a visit. Thank fortune, my habits never master me. I can change them when I wish and assume what others I like. The habit of going to the Parsonage I intend to drop entirely. It must be done gradually, however. The Sheppards are agreeable companions; but I must stop wasting so much of my time in their company.

2 February, Thursday.

The Amateurs met this evening and played until their fingers got so cold they were obliged to stop. We had no fire. "Music hath the power to soothe the savage breast"—but I know it hasn't power to warm frosted hands!

3 February, Friday.

Ralph Waldo Emerson the famous Massachusetts Transcendental philosopher, has been in the city for a week or two back delivering lectures in the Museum.[6] Kelley has proffered me a ticket for each occasion, but I could never find it convenient to attend. This afternoon however I went with him to the United States Hotel,[7] to make a sociable call on "the lion," and we spent an hour with him very agreeably. He is a tall, gaunt, man, with an expressive but not very agreeable face. His nose is sharp, and his forehead by no means, remarkable. This last may be owing to the manner in which he wears his hair—his "developments" may be covered up. He dresses very plainly, and wears a tremendous big shirt-collar, something *a la mode de* Byron. I objected at first to going with Kelley, because my boots were not blacked as they should have been to receive an introduction into such distinguished presence. I felt quite easy however when I found that Emerson's shoes were more rusty even than my own. We literati do not care much for such small things! Mr. Emerson has been pretty much over Europe, and his conversation, which is easy and unadorned, abounds with personal anecdotes of the literary men whom he saw. He says Thomas Carlyle told him that he once had got his duds packed up to start for America on a tour of observation, when his bookseller sent down word that his last work was "no go." The consequence was he consulted his purse, and unpacked again.[8] It amused me not a little to hear Kelley trying to keep up with his host—for my part I only listened. . . .

4 February, Saturday.

My leader in the *Eagle* to-day is on the Constitution again. I intend as soon as the Legislature adjourns, to commence a series of epistles on this subject. The public, I observe, are more easily aroused by the letter than the essay. Clement, by the by, who is living with Gray, edits the *Mail*. Mulford writes in the *Republican*. So we young ones have the whole duty of edifying the public, upon our shoulders.

6 February, Monday.

The debate of the Institute this evening was on the question: "Should the Constitution of New Jersey be altered?" On the affirmative were Mulford and myself, on the negative, Dudley and Davis. We got the decision of course.

6. Emerson (1803–82), who had recently published the first series of his *Essays*, was one of the most respected lecturers in the country.

7. One of Philadelphia's best hotels, the United States was located on Chestnut Street above Fourth.

8. Carlyle (1795–1881), British philosopher and essayist, never lectured in the United States.

The weather has been very cold to-day. Up to yesterday the winter has been quite mild.

7 February, Tuesday.

The ice in the river was "standing" as the shore-men say, all over, when I crossed this morning. This is the first time the Delaware has been bridged opposite Philadelphia for a year or two. There were a few persons on the ice in the Pennsylvania Channel this forenoon— but the venture was rather imprudent. There is said to be a heavy fall of snow off to the northward. The travelling is very much impeded on that account, even between here and New York. There is a little snow on the ground here.

I called on Caddy this evening.

8 February, Wednesday.

Kelley within a day or two back has taken a student. He is from Boston, named Wiley, is a free-thinker, but a very clever office-mate. He is aged about twenty-two.

10 February, Friday.

An eventful day! To wit:

I. Colonel Page introduced me this morning to Eli K. Moore, of New York.[9] This person is a member of the firm of "Slamm, Bang and Company" of whom Bennett so often speaks.[10] He is one of the leaders of the radical democrats of the Empire State; and I find that like too many of the head men in the ranks of all political parties, he believes just as much of the Bible as he sees fit. He is a very fine looking man, and loves a little to talk of himself. He told the following anecdote of Martin Van Buren, which is certainly worthy of preservation: When the President sent his extra message to Congress in 1837,[11] declaring war upon the Banks, he said to Moore, "Mark my words, dear sir, this message will defeat me and my party in 1840. Here is one man who will join the opposition in two weeks—there is another who will follow in a month. The fact is too many of our friends are beholden to the paper system—this will be a test; this message, sir, will separate the alloy from the pure metal, and though temporary defeat be the first result, we will come up again refined, and triumph permanently." Moore says that every man whom Van Buren thus pointed out, did go

9. Ely Moore (1798–1861), a printer and later a newspaper editor, was a New York congressman from 1835 to 1839. He was president of New York City's board of trade and surveyor of the port of New York.

10. James Gordon Bennett, editor of the New York *Herald,* thus derided the radical Democrats associated with union leader Levi D. Slamm.

11. The presidential message was Van Buren's call for a specie currency, issued on 5 September 1837.

over to the enemy. His reply to the President was "Sir, I respect you now, but if this prophecy come true, I shall adore you." I cannot believe that there is any exaggeration in this: Moore prefers Johnson I believe for the next Presidency; but how he can tell that anecdote and at the same time postpone Van Buren to any other man, is what I cannot see.

II. I went this afternoon with Edward Cole to see the dwarf now exhibiting at the Masonic Hall. His name is Charles Stratton, and he was born eleven years ago, in Lancastershire in England.[12] He weighs fourteen pounds, talks very plainly, takes notice of everything around him, and especially the ladies jewelry, and seems to be full of fight. He hit a little boy in the mouth for catching hold of his leg as he was running along the table. He is but twenty two inches high—less than some babies of four months old. He measures and weighs just what he did when he was six months old. When we went in, he was standing on the mantel peice, less than six inches wide, and he could stoop without trouble or danger, and pick up an object at his feet, with his back to the wall. His muscles appear very firm, and his strength unusual in proportion to his size. He kissed one of the girls. "There" said the keeper "I'll tell Celeste!" "Go do," said Tom Thumb quizzically—"You do if you dare." His head is shaped badly, however, notwithstanding the little replies that he has been taught, it is evident that he is nearly an idiot.

III. The second murder, and third violent death happened on board our steam-boat the *John Fitch*, about six o'clock this evening under the following circumstances. A profligate young man named Heberton some days ago seduced the daughter of a Mr. Mercer, a rich and respectable gentleman in Southwark. He took her to a bed-house in Pine Street and kept her for some days away from her parents. When they ascertained how the affair stood, the injured family sought redress by the law, but the law is strangely imperfect in this respect, and they were obliged to desist. Miss Mercer's brother, Singleton Mercer, in obedience to orders it is said from his father, waited on Heberton, and gave him the alternatives of Marriage or Combat. He declined both, saying as to the first that he could enjoy the girl whenever he wished. No retreat was left for the brother—he resolved on the death of one who had added the greatest insult to the greatest injury. Heberton, fearing the wrath of the indignant boy secreted himself. A friend, a lawyer by the name of Vandyke, took him into his house and hid him for a day or two. Young Mercer and some friends were on the lookout.

12. Stratton (1838–83), of course, was P. T. Barnum's famous "Tom Thumb." Despite Barnum's claims, Stratton was a five-year-old midget from Bridgeport, Connecticut.

This afternoon Vandyke ordered a carriage, and after several ingenious manoeuvers to deceive the spies as to his intentions, got Heberton in at an obscure alley-entrance, and drove off to Market St. Ferry. The *John Fitch* was in the dock. Vandyke looked through all the cabins to be sure that matters were right. He saw no body, and drove aboard. Vandyke himself was helping his negro hold his horses by the bridles, and no one was in the carriage but Heberton. Just as the boat got into the dock on this side, four pistol shots were fired into the carriage from behind, by young Mercer, who it is supposed had followed his enemy on the boat, and secreted himself behind a coal-team. The first ball passed through the shoulder blade, shattered a rib, perforated the lungs and lodged finally in the heart of the guilty profligate. He died before he reached the hotel nearby. Mercer was immediately arrested, and feigned to be crazy. He asked for a fiddle, and wanted to dance.

The Coroner held an inquest to-night, but adjourned without a verdict, till tomorrow morning. The dead man and all the parties were kept at Cake's hotel. I was in about midnight, and Mercer then seemed insensible, like a man arousing from a drunken frolic. It is the general opinion that he will be hung, but the general sentiment that he ought not to be.

We stopped the press of the *Eagle* on the occurrence of the murder, to get in an account of it.

11 February, Saturday.
The Coroner's jury returned a verdict in accordance with the facts set forth above, about noon to-day; my uncle Dr. Mulford and several other physicians having concluded the post mortem examination of Heberton's body. Mercer was committed to Woodbury jail and the murdered man taken over the river. The affair has caused a great sensation in both states; the majority appear however to go for letting Mercer off.

12 February, Sunday.
Public opinion sets stronger and stronger in favor of Mercer.

13 February, Monday.
This was Hotch-potch night at the Institute. We had a very agreeable time. I went home with Hannah Sheppard. Jo has not yet returned.

14 February, Tuesday.
The Camden Baptist Choir have been invited to go to Haddonfield on next Thursday night week.

I spent this evening at Cole's. It is arranged that I am to gallant Caroline to a Concert in Philadelphia next Saturday night. By the by, I obtruded this evening on the vesper devotions of this family. Hereafter, I must not go so soon.

15 February, Wednesday.
The opinion seems to be, especially in Philadelphia, that Mercer will not be hanged.

17 February, Friday.
I am still quite indisposed. I have been in general blessed with pretty good health, however, and I will not complain of a trifling sickness. Music is the only amusement for which I do not seem for a few days past to have lost all taste.

18 February, Saturday.
The *Eagle* issues to-day for the first time without containing something of mine. The reason of this is two-fold: my late indisposition, and the fact that the editors are getting rather too independent. I will hold off until they are reduced to terms, because I have a right, and am firmly determined to control their establishment, or to have nothing to do with it. I fancy they do not desire the latter.

This evening I took Caddy to a splendid concert in the Museum. Ned, her brother took his Dulcinea, a Miss Susan Wilson.[13] It was a singular coincidence that a few minutes after Caddy and I had taken our seats, my old music teacher came in with her old music teacher, and sat down just before us. Mr. Osborn, my friend is from Philadelphia, and her friend is from Litiz.

There was a quarrel about the pay due to Seguin[14] and the operatic corps, in consequence of which we were delayed too long to return in the Mail Boat. Ned and I lodged at Burr's,[15] and Caddy at Wilson's.

There is a candor, a sincerity, a familiarity in this girl Caddy, that I cannot sufficiently admire. What will be the result of our acquaintance?

19 February, Sunday.
After crossing the river this morning I went into my sanctum and there staid all day, reënjoying the music and company of last evening and reading Isaiah.

20 February, Monday.
There was a debate to night before the Institute on the capital pun-

---

13. Wilson, daughter of David Wilson of Montgomery County, Pennsylvania, eventually married Cole. See entry of 20 July 1843.

14. Arthur Seguin (1809–52), an English singer, had formed a touring company called "The Seguin Troupe."

15. Joseph Burr's hotel was near the Philadelphia landing of the Market Street Ferry.

ishment subject. I was in the chair and decided in favor of abolishing such punishment.

21 February, Tuesday.

I renewed my studies to-day, but have been playing truant so much of late that the law is hard work.

23 February, Thursday.

Tom Thumb, the dwarf, called at the office to-day to give his compliments to our folks. He had bidden adieu before I got over—so soon is he, and I so late.

This evening the gentlemen of the choir, Baxter, Cowperthwait, Mulford, Gerhart, and myself, agreeably to our promise started off with our instruments for Haddonfield. We supposed we were going to a mere private practicing, but when the waggon arrived at the church we found the audience room lighted up, and filled with about four hundred people. There had been an address and Concert announced, for some charitable object, and we who were to officiate in the latter, had never even seen some of the pieces which we were to play. We were about to apologize for our inexperience when young Clement, who also had a fiddle, said "Never mind, I have only been playing three months." He assured us that the Haddonfield folks would know no difference between good music and bad; and so we tuned up, and went ahead. They had, in their own corps, one treble and one bass violin, and flutes almost innumerable, which together with our aid, were sufficiently noisy. As to the music I say nothing. We played about six pieces, and then had an address on Benevolence from the pastor; then six pieces more and a benediction. The house voted the choir, their thanks "for their admirable performance!"

In coming home Gerhart and I amused the rest by some airs rather more lively than Old Hundred. We gave the Camden people a flying serenade.

26 February, Sunday.

Mr. Parmenter of Rhode Island[16] called at the office to see me last week, about having a Rhode Island meeting in Camden. We fixed on Thursday night next. The object is to start the ball of reform in New Jersey, and also to take up a collection to aid the indigent Suffrage men in our sister state. I drafted a bill and gave it to Hineline, headed "To The Republicans of Camden."

27 February, Monday.

This evening I attended the grand ball of the Fencibles, at the

16. A. W. Parmenter, a leader of Dorr's party, was touring the northeastern states in an attempt to enlist support for Dorr. See entry of 11 May 1842.

Musical Fund hall. The company numbered about four hundred, and was very brilliant. There were many very pretty girls there, and some very good dancers. Being one of Page's intimates I fared very well; being invited down to the banquetting room and served plentifully with all that was good. The cream of the company only were honored with an invitation to sup.

I never dance; but I found inducements nevertheless to remain until the end—which was about five o'clock in the morning. Hazzard and his twenty musicians alone would have detained me. I went to bed at Burr's for an hour or two after the fete; but crossed over home to breakfast.

The affair cost me directly and indirectly, about ten dollars. The price of my ticket was three dollars.

28 February, Tuesday.

I did not go to bed again to-day, nor did I feel much sleepy until tea this evening. Such rows however make me feel badly—they **are** better left alone. The time spent in a private circle would have been more agreeable and more profitable.

2 March, Thursday.

Colonel Page and Mr. Parmenter addressed the Rhode Island meeting to-night in the City Hall. The turn out was quite respectable, though not very strong, on account of the short and imperfect notice given of it, and of the great religious rivalry going on between the two churches in our place. The above named gentlemen and Mr. Davis, and my uncle and myself took supper at Elwell's together. The meeting did not begin until eight o'clock. Mr. Fetters was nominated by my uncle to the Chair; Messrs. Cowperthwait and Cole for Vice Presidents, and Messrs. Mulford and Hineline for secretaries. After two excellent speeches, my resolutions were read by Mulford and unanimously adopted. They take the boldest ground in favor of a reform of the Constitution of New Jersey yet taken—advocating the expediency of spontaneous action by the people, and pledging, the adherence of Camden even to a revolution to effect it.[17] They were ordered to be published in the *Eagle*. A collection was taken up, amounting to nearly ten dollars.

I accompanied the speakers over the river.

3 March, Friday.

Parmenter and his troupe hold a meeting to-night at Trenton. This fellow has been a great rascal I believe, but is a tolerable patriot now.

17. This was bold ground indeed, for it evoked memories of Thomas W. Dorr's abortive "rebellion" in Rhode Island in 1841–42.

The Colonel got a letter the other day from the Post master at Providence, telling him that Parmenter had been once indicted for forgery, but had escaped by a flaw. He referred to the volume and page in which the case is reported, in the Massachusetts series of reports.[18]

I was at Cole's this evening.

4 March, Saturday.

This evening I took Caddy over to hear Maffit,[19] the famous Methodist, in a lecture in the Museum, on "English tourists in America." He was very severe on Dickens. By the by my old friend saw Caddy and myself start. That's bad! The audience was quite large, and seemed to be highly delighted. There were a good many young ministers present, and they in particular relished some of their brother's inuendoes which I thought rather immodest, such as this: he was speaking of Boz's having said that the women of Boston have pretty faces—but that there he must stop. "What!" exclaimed Maffit, "have our women nothing else but faces?" He suddenly halted, and then issued a general laugh in which as I have hinted, the gentlemen with white cravats figured more audibly.

The lecture was over by ten o'clock, but we did not get over until two o'clock to morrow morning—the mail line having been delayed on the way.

6 March, Monday.

This morning I went at my law *novis viribus*. I am reading Blackstone over again, and have now a pretty good knowledge of the first volume, at least.

The Institute met this evening and discussed the question "Has the Roman Catholic church done more good than harm?" I was on the affirmative, which side got beaten.

There was a singular phenomenon in the heavens to night—a luminous belt in the South west, extending from the horizon nearly up to the zenith.[20] It was stationary from seven o'clock till nine. The moon was shining very brightly during this period, and the streak, which some suggest is the tail of a comet, almost equalled it in lustre. It vanished about nine o'clock, by imperceptible degrees. This thing, be

18. *Commonwealth* v. *Parmenter*, 22 Mass. Reports 279 (October Term, 1827). The verdict of guilty was set aside because the prosecution had failed to show that David Parmenter, who had forged a promissory note, had done so in the alleged county.

19. John Newland Maffitt (1795–1850), whose preaching had captivated Southern audiences in the late 1830s, had recently served as Chaplain to the United States House of Representatives.

20. The bright comet Faye had been discovered earlier in the year by French astronomer Hervé Faye.

it what it may, will alarm weak minded people very much. The faith of this class has been so prepared by that madman, Miller, that it would be no wonder if some of them were to take this phenomenon of which we are speaking as one of the symptoms of the world's end, and fold up their hands accordingly.

8 March, Wednesday.

The South-western sign has been observed in all parts of the Country. The New York papers of yesterday mention it. The opinion seems to be gaining ground that it is a Comet, whose nucleus is yet below the horizon. If so it is the most magnificent specimen I have ever read of. It was not visible to-night; the weather being cloudy.

11 March, Saturday.

The *Eagle* appears to-day without any of my help. The editors must come to terms, or I will be spared a good deal of trouble. My conditions are "no delay no alterations," and with these they must and shall comply.

I was at the office an hour, to-day, and then adjourned home; not feeling very well.

The comet was seen again to-night. It is evidently mounting in the heavens.

12 March, Sunday.

I took some medicine to-day, and in the evening went to Church, where I saw one of my old friends, which I do not know—or care! "The last link is broken that bound me to them!"[21]

13 March, Monday.

This is town-meeting day in Camden, and the contest is pretty warm. All the democratic tickets (and their name is legion) have at the bottom the words, "Alteration of City Charter."[22] The measure will be voted by a large majority.

I was at Cole's this evening. Will Madam Rumor change her topic?

14 March, Tuesday.

Returning from the office this afternoon I met Josephine Sheppard, and saw her home—in a few minutes afterwards I met Phoebe, and ditto. At Third and Market Streets on my way down from Sheppard's the second time I met Caddy, and saw her home. Both the Sheppards

---

21. Mickle alters the phrase "The last link is broken that bound me to thee," from a poem, "Song," by the obscure poet Fanny Steers.

22. There was much agitation for changes in Camden's city charter in 1843. A legislative act of 9 March 1844, effected some of the desired modifications, including election of the mayor by town meeting, rather than by the city council, and more powers for the council.

asked why I had been absent so long—and Jo suggested that it had been eight weeks since we had seen each other. I said "Yes, but my examination was approaching, and I found it necessary to study very hard!"

I was at work a little to-day on my "Letters in favor of a reform in the Constitution of New Jersey."

17 March, Friday.

Peter A. Browne, Esq.[23] Page's old preceptor, and chief counsel in the case of young Mercer which shortly comes on, was at the office to-day preparing his argument. He is going to rely on the plea of insanity, which he so successfully made in the outrageous case of Wood, the confectioner, who in 1838, shot his daughter for daring to marry one Peake against his will, at his house in Chesnut Street, opposite Independence Hall. Mr. Browne told the Colonel to-day that this is the last case he shall ever plead without he (the said Page meaning) got into a scrape and required his services.

19 March, Sunday.

This evening about sunset I encountered Ned Cole, who was bound over to the city to see Susan Wilson, his intended. He invited me to go and call on Caddy, who was at home, and would be glad to see company. I accordingly went and passed a very pleasant hour. Prayers were over this time before I got there, and Mr. Cole senior was enjoying his cigar in *otio cum dignitate*. We had a long and to me edifying, conversation on geography, astronomy, religion politics, law, and the Mercer case.

The comet shone with unusual brilliance to night. It is said that the nucleus has loomed so as to have been seen. The stars can be detected, glimmering through the trail, or rather the pilot, of this unheralded visiter.

21 March, Tuesday.

Mulford and I went to a Concert in the City hall to-night, given by the Masters Hughes, Welsh boys and excellent musicians.[24] One little fellow, eight years old, plays the violin very well. He goes beautifully through the most difficult movements, and ascends as high as the fifth and sixth positions with ease.

---

23. A noted Philadelphia attorney, Browne was also an amateur scientist and agriculturalist.

24. The Hughes family, sometimes billed as "Master Hughes and his Infant Brothers," was a group of talented children whose playing often created a sensation in the early 1840s. The two children who had to stand on tables to play their harps appear to have been the hit of the act.

One Bryan sang a song about old maids, which so shocked Catharine and Eleanor Browning, that they rose and left the hall.[25] Ridiculous!

The weather is excessively cold. Quere, does the Comet drink up our share of caloric?

22 *March, Wednesday.*

I went to the Concert with Mulford again to-night. The Cumbrians played the same pieces. Their sister, three years old, who last night sang two or three little airs and made harp accompaniments, was too unwell to appear this evening.

25 *March, Saturday.*

The Hughes gave another Concert to-night. I met Mulford and Dudley there, and the latter showed me an anonymous letter which he had received through the post in the morning, concerning the last number of the Hotch Potch. It abuses myself, Dudley and Mulford, seriatim, for what I hardly know. More anon.

26 *March, Sunday.*

In the house all day. The weather is quite unpleasant. In the evening I crossed over the river to see the New York engine which came on in the mail line to join the procession to-morrow. There was a great bon-fire on Windmill Island made by the Philadelphia firemen in honor of their visiters. They lit it up about eleven o'clock, as the boat was leaving the Camden dock, and the New Yorker's band commenced playing a march in acknowledgment of the compliment. This night's doings will excessively horrify all good Sabbath keepers, and the first blast of the trumpet, as it rang across the water doubtless woke some of the Millerites to a knowledge that sin's end had not yet come, whatever may become of the world.

27 *March, Monday.*

There was a great procession of firemen in Philadelphia to-day. It is said there were twenty five hundred on parade. The pageant was quite pretty, but I soon got tired of looking at it. The streets were very muddy, and about two o'clock as Hague had predicted it began to rain and snow. The weather was so bad at night that we had no meeting at the City Hall.

28 *March, Tuesday.*

Mercer's trial begins to-day. The jury is packed, and will acquit him. I spent the evening with Mulford at Cake's.

25. These were the daughters of Abraham Browning (1769–1836).

29 March, Wednesday.

I am at present reading the II Blackstone, and really imagine that I am making some progress towards an understanding of its intricate doctrines. When I read it before I might as well have been reading Greek or German.

Our Amateurs met to night in the Library Room for rehearsal. We began to play some lively peice, when we learned that there was Church Service going on below, under the Rev. Mr. Burroughs, clerk or clericus of St. Paul's. We of course hung up our fiddles, although we had the right of preoccupancy to the School-house and surrounding premises.

30 March, Thursday.

Mr. Kelley took tea with me this evening, and Mr. Mulford likewise. After smoking a cigar or two to settle our supper and brighten our wit, we went to Sheppard's, and staid till ten o'clock. Ben Browning was there, and Mulford and I concluded from his sheepish look that he knew something about the letter which I mentioned last Saturday. The girls are just as smooth as ever—but I suspect they too had a hand in it.

Kelley and Mulford had a long talk of transcendentalism. They do not think so differently after all.

31 March, Friday.

This evening I spent at Cole's. By the by they say that Ben Sisty,[26] a widower of Philadelphia, and father of two or three children, a stumpy, ugly, Baptist pocket-book maker, is courting Caddy. She will never have him.

Since we are now in "Father Miller's year,"[27] we will have some queer exhibitions of superstition. The comet, coming as it did, all unheralded and sudden, has terrified a good many weak minded persons almost out of their wits. It is said too that strange sights have been seen in the midnight skies, such as fiery crosses and bloody swords. The Sun, I have heard it said by some of the Millerites, has been darkened, and the moon obscured without the intervention of clouds. It is strange that such stories should be believed for a moment by any sensible man; but sensible men really do assure us that they believe, nay have seen, these things. Such is the power of faith! . . .

1 April, Saturday.

Our office is torn inside out, and will not be rearranged completely

26. City directories list Sisty as living and manufacturing pocketbooks on Chestnut Street. He had formerly carried on his trade in Mount Holly.

27. William Miller had predicted that the world would end sometime between March 1843 and March 1844.

for a month. My love of order used to be very great before I began to study music, and it is still so strong in me that I cannot learn anything in the midst of confusion. I will take a holy-day therefore, during the lustration of our sanctum.

2 April, Sunday.
I spent all of to-day in my study. In the evening I went over to Philadelphia and heard Mr. Berg preach a sermon. My Aunt Hogeland goes to his church, but I did not see her to-night. Perhaps she shares my mother's dislike for evening meetings.

5 April, Wednesday.
It has been contemplated for some time to establish a Musical Society among the young men of Camden, to amuse themselves and others during the Summer evenings that are now at hand. The following gentlemen met to night for that purpose in the City Hall:

Cowperthwait and Mickle,	first violins
Gerhart,	second violin
Mulford and Ogden,	second flutes
Atkinson,	first flute
Baxter,	violincello
Mumford, Staigel and Devinney,	vocalists.

Having taken the steps necessary for organization, we adjourned to play, and opened with my little march.

6 April, Thursday.
News came up from Woodbury to-night that Mercer, the murderer, has been acquitted by the leather-headed jackasses who were packed to try him. Jerseymen can say nothing hereafter about Pennsylvania justice. . . .

9 April, Sunday.
This evening I went to Dr. Barne's[28] church on Washington Square, Philadelphia, and heard the best sermon I ever listened to. It was an argument in favor of the divinity of Christ, and was as nearly conclusive perhaps as the nature of the Subject admits.

12 April, Wednesday.
The comet I believe has disappeared from our skies.
The Amateurs met this evening to perfect their organization, and

28. Albert Barnes was pastor of Philadelphia's First Presbyterian Church from 1830 to 1867.

practice a few of Dyer's[29] anthems. We have an accession of two or three new members.

13 April, Thursday.

Mulford and I went to Sheppard's to-night to have some music. Miss Isabella Josephina Segunda asked me to go to Cole's with her next week, and of course I consented.[30] My unreserved manner perhaps warranted this liberty, but—but—

I have not been at the office since Tuesday.

14 April, Friday.

Doctor Mulford wants to see ground broken against the verdict in the Mercer case. He considers it an outrage on law and justice as it is. He told me to night that Gray's columns were open to a series of articles on the subject. Shall I begin it?

15 April, Saturday.

This evening I was at Cole's. About eleven o'clock Mulford, Cowperthwait and I went out a-serenading. We played beneath the lattice of several of the ladies, and of the Methodist clergyman, and wound up by playing Old Hundred for Doctor Mulford.

16 April, Sunday.

Owing to the mild weather of last week and the consequent melting of the snow among the north-Delaware mountains, the river is excessively swollen, and, what is worse, the banks below Kaighn's Point have given away. The "Stream of the Lennape"[31] might puff itself up to the size of the Amazon for what I care, but I do not like to have to pay for its vanity and pride.

18 April, Tuesday.

I accompanied Miss Sheppard to Cole's this evening. We had a queer time of it, but just such an one as I expected, and hoped. "The last link is" now truly "broken," and I am free! . . .

19 April, Wednesday.

The Amateurs met to-night and elected Cowperthwait leader and Casner conductor. We had some very good music. Next Wednesday we admit our friends.

29. Probably English poet Sir Edward Dyer (d. 1607), whose work had been set to music by such composers as William Byrd.
30. Mickle suspects that Josephine is the "Isabella Segunda" who signed the letter he describes in the entry of 25 March 1843.
31. The Lenni Lenape or Delaware Indians inhabited the banks of the Delaware when Europeans first arrived there.

20 April, Thursday.

Devinney and I went to the Philharmonic Concert to-night, at the Musical Fund Hall, Locust Street.[32] Music good—price ditto.

Caddy Cole was to have gone to the exhibition of pictures at the Artist's fund this evening; but Ned's sweet-heart—Susan—and Cole's nurse's child being both sick, we deferred our visit till next week.

21 April, Friday.

This evening I took Isabel's letter to Hugg's, where I contrived to get hold of Mary's Album. In looking over it I saw one nameless piece in the same hand as the superscription of Miss Segunda's communication. Having compared them closely and perfectly satisfied myself, I asked the name of the album writer. It was—**Phoebe Sheppard!** Matters will turn out just as I expected.

22 April, Saturday.

The Amateurs met to-night to rehearse for Wednesday.

During the past week, in which I have not been at the office, I have composed and arranged two concertos, one in three four and the other in common time, for our club. All my science is drawn from Mason's little Manual, and I suspect that said all is about the same size as the book itself!

23 April, Sunday.

This is the day upon which Father Miller first pitched for the grand conflagration, but as the time approached he altered it, and now says that the world will certainly be burned between March 1843 and March 1844! The weather to-day was somewhat unusual; being something like the Irishman's hog, streaks of contraries—now a little sunshine, and now a little thunder and lightning.

This evening I was at Cole's and showed Cad the mysterious letter. She does not know the hand-writing, though she thinks she has seen it before. We compared it with both of the Turners' autographs, and it is entirely different.

Frederic Borrodaile died this morning, and Jacob Ridgway is not expected to live.[33]

26 April, Wednesday.

The Quintette Society met to-night, and as each member had the privilege of inviting his friends, there were a good many people out. Our harmony was very bad. Cowperthwait and I played first violin.

32. The Philharmonic Society, founded in the 1830s, often performed at Musical Fund Hall.
33. Frederic N. Borrodaile, a citizen of Camden, died at age twenty-five.

I have studied very industriously since Monday morning, and really feel much better in health and spirits than when I am idle. There is a joy in being busy, which the lazy can never appreciate. My mother, by the by, would laugh at that remark; for she has trouble enough to get me out of bed to a nine o'clock breakfast.

29 April, Saturday.

At rehearsal to-night Cowperthwait made a motion that the club play sacred music exclusively, which was carried by the Church members, a majority of whom he happened to find were present. We had a warm discussion, the result whereof was that I withdrew from active participation in the Quintette—the original object of which was, as I understood it, to play all kinds of pieces without restriction.

30 April, Sunday.

Jacob Ridgway died about noon today. . . .

Mulford and I, and a common friend from Cape Island, Cape May, went to the Episcopal Church to-night, to witness the confirmation of several candidates. The Bishop—"Lord George" as they called him in England, "Bishop of New Jersey" gave us a rank Puseyite sermon on the laying on of hands.[34] What nonsense!

1 May, Monday.

The Institute met to-night, had a Hotch-potch read, and then adjourned over the summer. Every thing passed off in good feeling and in fine style, and the house was even better than it used to be before the letter of Isabel Segunda. I made a short speech, and concluded with a motion of thanks to "those ladies and gentlemen whose good sense had enabled them to attend our meetings up to the close of the winter session, without offence or any hard thoughts." The motion was carried unanimously.

Holy-days being over, my cousins returned to school this morning.[35] Sally has promised to write to me.

2 May, Tuesday.

. . . This evening I went to De Begnis' Concert. Signor Nagel, the pupil of Paganini, and the first violinist in the world, played some of his favorite pieces in his best manner.[36] He is tall and thin, but not so hideous as Paganini is said to have been. His motions in playing put

34. Bishop Doane may have repeated some of the ideas of English clergyman and scholar Edward B. Pusey (1800–82), an advocate of High Church principles.
35. The Haines girls had been visiting Camden.
36. John Nagel was an obscure violinist with little claim to the preeminent position Mickle accords him. Like some other violinists of the day, he may have merely *claimed* to be a pupil of the renowned Niccolo Paganini.

me in mind of a snake—so flexible are his fingers and arms, and so sqirmy, if I may use the word, in their movements. He plays the harmonics to perfection; and one might readily mistake his performance in this style, by shutting his eyes, for the music of a distant flute. His imitations of the great maestro's staccatos are also very fine. Upon the whole I was entranced with the gifted Swede, and could have listened to him for a day.

I saw Harry Edwards and his sister at the concert.

3 May, Wednesday.

Jacob Ridgway was buried to-day at Laurel Hill. Ex-President Adams attended his funeral. Of Mr. Ridgway posterity can have but little to say that is flattering. He was cold grasping and selfish, and left his immense fortune, with some trifling exceptions to his immediate relatives. . . .

I spent the evening at Cole's. This is the only place in Camden, at present, where I visit with pleasure.

Mercer, the assasin, since his acquittal, has spent much of his time at Woodbury. It is rumored to-day that he has got into a scrape there with some of the girls. The legitimate result of the ridiculous yet sad burlesque which was enacted at the trial of this cowardly whelp has already appeared; for news arrived in town this morning of a most horrid murder in Warren County in this state. Four persons were slain night before last, at one farm; the object of the fiend being supposed to have been plunder, in which he did not succeed.[37] New Jersey never knew so many outrages before, not even in the days of the Tories and Cowboys.[38]

I finished Stephens on Pleading to-day, was examined thereon, and began Tidd's *Practice.*

4 May, Thursday.

Within a week or two back I have learned a good deal of law. My third year as student began yesterday.

This evening I was practising on the fiddle.

6 May, Saturday.

I fell into Cole's again to-night! Confound it—am I going to fall into love again?

7 May, Sunday.

This evening I undertook to listen to a lecture on the Second Com-

37. The murder of John Castner, his wife and child, and John Parke occurred in Changewater, New Jersey, on 2 May.
38. "Cowboys" were pro-British marauders who terrorized and stole from patriots and neutrals during the Revolution.

ing from Mr. Rhees in the City-hall. I was taken with a chill and was obliged to go home before he concluded. He thinks that the Jews are to be restored before that great event. I guess they will be restored and scattered again ere it occur.

My uncle got assurances yesterday from President Tyler that Gray should be removed from the Collectorship of Camden, to make room for Mr. Garrett. The latter gentleman lost some money a year or two ago as surety to a government officer.

11 May, Thursday.

A difficulty has arisen in the Common Pleas of Philadelphia, as to the right of the Court to discharge the Grand Jury. It is a nice point which I imagine must be decided by custom and equity, there being no law in the premises.

This evening I was practising an hour or so on the violin, after which I began Rollin's *History*. This is a long job, but a pleasant one, in prospect. An acquaintance with historical writers is necessary for the complete lawyer, and some-how-or-other I have of late conceived the desire of making myself such a lawyer, if possible.

12 May, Friday.

I have within a few days past made a good deal of progress in Young's *Night Thoughts*. I carry a small edition in my pocket, and read it crossing the river, or while I am waiting for the boat. I cross now four times a day, and the time thus stolen from my arduous studies I will devote to the poets.

13 May, Saturday.

Mulford and I went to Welsh's Circus to-night.[39] Page's family occupied a private box. We crossed the river about midnight in a small boat, having passed a very agreeable evening. I went up from the parquette and sat awhile with Mistresses Breuil and Chambourg, Page's married sisters;[40] but Mulford was too intent on the performances to think of pretty women.

17 May, Wednesday.

This afternoon about four o'clock I called for Caddy and saw her across the river; after which I read law until eight when Ned and I went up Market Street and got the girls, and hastened to the Artist's Fund, where we loitered until nearly ten. The paintings are on the whole very good, but Dickinson, the man who took my likeness, had

39. The theatre more usually known as Welch's National Theatre, or the Olympic Theatre, occupied the corner of Ninth and Chestnut Streets.

40. One of Mrs. Page's sisters was married to C. F. Breuil, a former silk merchant who lived on South Fourth Street.

some that were wretched. He enjoys the reputation I believe of exhibiting the worst pictures that are yearly shown by the society. I met several acquaintances in person, and some in "counterfeit presentment—among the latter was Jo Yeager[41] who really looked from the wall when I entered as if she wanted to say "how do you do?" There is a satirical piece in the exhibition called the *Battle of the Schools* by Winner,[42] which has caused a good deal of newspaper talk. It is an excellent painting, but I did not see its point, not having any knowledge of the painters who are hit off, though one fellow whose head, in the grand melee is about entering a squash that has been broken by his overthrow, resembles the aforesaid Dickinson somewhat.

Ned took Susan his intended and one of his cousins from Princeton, and I took Caddy. They all staid in Market Street, but I went home in the mail-boat.

18 May, Thursday.

I met Miss Cole in Camden this evening, and she says she enjoyed her visit last evening very much. I also met Josephine Sheppard a little while before, but did not speak, not that I was guilty of any rudeness towards so nice a girl, but that I did not see her until we had passed.

20 May, Saturday.

This afternoon I strolled up to the Philadelphia Library and spent an hour or two in ransacking the books relating to the early history of New Jersey. I intend yet to write a work on the Constitution and laws of my native state. . . .

21 May, Sunday.

I went to Saint Joseph's this afternoon, and saw that farce called the elevation of the host, I believe. During this sickening fanfarronade I was the only one in the north gallery who did not go through with the prostration and crossing, and I gloried in my singularity. My anger may rise, but my knees shall never bend at such unmeaning antics. I half regretted during the gymnastics that I had never defended the Catholics.

24 May, Wednesday.

Mulford and I went to a tent-Circus in Camden to-night. The riding was poor—music worse.

25 May, Thursday.

The books which I am now reading are the following: Troubat and

41. Johanna Yeager (d. 1855), wife of Lewis Yeager, a Camden tailor.
42. William E. Winner (*c.* 1815–83) was a prominent Philadelphia portrait painter.

Haly's *Pennsylvania practice*—Blackstone, Tidd, and Sugden's *Letters*. Heretofore I have read the subjoined—

Blackstone's *Commentaries*	4	volumes
Montesquieu's *Spirit of the Laws*	2	
Coke upon Lyttelton	3	
Kent's *Commentaries*	4	
Pennsylvania Blackstone	3	
Furguson on Civil Society	1	
Beccaria on Crimes	1	
Sugden's *Letters*	1	
Jones on Bailment	1	
Duponceau's *View*	1	
Stephens on Pleading	1	
The letters of Junius	2	

27 May, Saturday.

For some time back there have been a good many burglaries committed in Camden; to prevent which a Patrol was organized by the young men of the place, myself among the number included. To-night was my first appearance on duty, and my companion was Mulford. We sallied forth about eleven o'clock, and serenaded the ladies until midnight, and then separated to guard the town. We staid out until four o'clock—during which time we saw three men; one, Sam King who was holding Stivers carpenter shop up about two o'clock. I arrested him and offered to take him home but he said he was waiting for a girl, and was not too drunk to know what he was about. The second was a stranger making out into the woods. And the third was crazy Joel Read. One or both of us watched all three, and saw they were not bent on mischief.

There was a Concert to-night in the Academy—bad music—good audience.

28 May, Sunday.

As I was crossing the river to-day Ned Cole called me aside, and told me that Cowperthwaite came to him this morning and after asking if I went to Sheppard's yet, suddenly turned the subject and asked him if he had heard the reports flying around concerning me and one Miss Barr? This Miss Barr by the by is said to be the mistress of Mr. Jeffers. Ned told him he had not, and left him, as his atrocious villainy deserved, in contempt. There is no such report in existence but from Sam's own mouth, and he knows well enough that I never spoke to the strumpet with whom he endeavoured to connect me.

Cole behaved like a man—he assured that he believed nothing that Cowperthwait told—that he would not believe him upon oath; and that he saw through his design in this affair "which was to stop the few interviews I had with his sister Cad." In the course of the conversation I had ground to infer that the rumor about Benjamin Sisty's courting or attempting to court Cad, was also a lie of Sam's fabrication; and the end of our confab was an invitation to call at Cole's in the evening, which I took up with. So entirely has failed the machination of a contemptible, malicious puppy, who always bites from behind and without barking. The cause of his black-hearted conduct is I presume, my refusal to meet and play with the Quintette Club.

29 May, Monday.
Kelley and I got our likeness taken to-day by the Daguerreotype process. I intend mine as a present to mother.
Since Saturday I have felt something like the piles coming on me; the result I suppose of my assiduous study, for some weeks back, without any exercise.

30 May, Tuesday.
I am approaching the end of Tidd and progressing gradually into Troubat and Haly. In a few weeks I will have added several volumes to the list on the [*previous*] . . . page.

1 June, Thursday.
Summer comes in with very cool weather.* Fires are really indispensable to comfort. The crops in New Jersey, the farmers tell me, are very backward.
I spent the evening at Cole's.

2 June, Friday.
There was ice, a little way back of Camden, as thick as window glass at eight o'clock this morning. So that Byron's exclamation,
　　　　　——No, as soon
　　Seek roses in December, ice in June——
is no longer a banter.[43] The frost was very heavy.

3 June, Saturday.
The adjutant-general of New Jersey has ordered a militia parade for next Tuesday. The Gloucester division is to meet at Chew's Land-

---

* It has been said that the winters of this climate are getting warmer and the summers cooler. I will observe whether this be true or not. [*Mickle's note.*]
　43. Mickle quotes from George Gordon Lord Byron's *English Bards and Scotch Reviewers.*

ing; and to night a meeting was held by "the able bodied men" of Camden, at which there was an evident desire to turn the whole affair into ridicule.

4 June, Sunday.

Mulford and I to-day went to St. Joseph's and heard some excellent singing. In returning we got on the same boat with Ned Cole and Caddy, and Sam Cowperthwaite. The last named looked as if he had been stealing a sheep, or robbing a hen-roost.

6 June, Tuesday.

Mulford, a young man from Cape May named Miller,[44] and myself, a trio of Ms, gave all the girls in the town a serenade to-night. We had several little adventures, too unimportant however to be detailed. I played in all twenty two different airs; to wit:

Slow air from *Zampa*	*St. Paddy's day*
Days of Absence	Quick air from *Zampa*
Swiss Boy	On yonder Rock, *Fra Diavolo*
Original March	*Jim along Josey*
Soldier's Joy	March from *Norma*
Di tanti palpiti, march	*Am I not fondly*
Rose Tree	*Harvest Home*
Portsmouth hornpipe	

Yankee Doodle
Waltz from *Der Freyshutz*
Washington's old march
If I speak to thee
The Cracovienne
Auld Lang Syne
Fisher's Hornpipe

8 June, Thursday.

This evening in strolling up Third Street I met Josephine and walked with her to the Post Office, and thence up to the house. Seeing Phoebe at the window I went in, and paid a short visit. They were all as bland as usual, except Mary, who has been in Camden a month without my having called. I thought she seemed to be a little vexed. When I came away Jo went with me to call on a friend in Market Street, at whose door I left her. She is indeed a lovely girl; and one with far

44. Lafayette Miller was the son of Jonas Miller, proprietor of Cape May's Congress Hall; see entry of 18 July 1843.

more warmth of heart than I have before believed. Heavens! if I have wronged her, what atonement can I make that will be sufficient?

9 June, Friday.

President Tyler arrived in Philadelphia this afternoon, on his way to Boston to be present at the celebration of the completion of the Bunker-Hill Monument. He landed from the Steamboat *Ohio*[45] at the Navy Yard, about half past two o'clock, and after staying a short time at that place was escorted through the city by a splendid line of military under the Command of General Cadwallader. I saw the procession pass the exchange on Third Street, and thought I never witnessed a colder reception. Some of the clerks in the Post-Office undertook to get up a cheer, but it completely failed. Tyler seems indeed to be, as he has called himself, "a President without a party."

The Whig councils of Philadelphia refused to wait upon Honest John.

10 June, Saturday.

The President passed through Camden this afternoon, and was received by our citizens in a handsome manner.

He crossed at the Market Street Ferry about four o'clock, accompanied by Governor Porter of Pennsylvania, Secretaries Porter, Upshur and Spencer, Captain Stockton and several other distinguished men, a band of music, and a numerous train of friends and citizens.[46] When the boat was going through the Canal on Windmill Island, being about to leave the jurisdiction of Pennsylvania, Governor Porter made a short speech, to tell the President that he "now transferred him over to the Jersey Blues[47] who would take good care of him," To which the addressee responded briefly but neatly. My uncle and the other committeemen of Camden then took charge of their illustrious guest.

When the Steamer arrived at Cake's wharf the immense throng sent up a hearty cheer, not so enthusiastic however as it might have been. In a few moments my uncle having the arm of the President, piloted him according to the programme into the garden at the foot of Federal Street; just inside the gate of which were twenty six young ladies, in two equal lines under the direction of Mulford and myself, who had

45. The paddle-steamer *Ohio*, built in 1832, usually made runs to Baltimore or Cape May.

46. The president's party included David R. Porter (1788–1867), governor of Pennsylvania from 1839 to 1845; James M. Porter (1793–1862), secretary of war; Abel P. Upshur (1791–1844) secretary of the navy; John C. Spencer (1788–1855), secretary of the treasury; and Capt. Robert Field Stockton (1795–1866), a senior American naval officer.

47. The "Jersey Blues" was a nickname of a state militia unit during the Revolution.

been got together by Richard Fetters, Esq. to present Tyler with a splendid boquet of flowers from his garden. My uncle not observing the girls, nor expecting the presentation to take place at that stage of the ceremonies, was about passing on between the lines without halting. I caught his arm and pointed him to Mulford who stood opposite with the boquet in his hand. The ladies all now rose, and we gentlemen removed our chapeaus. My uncle, also uncovered, introduced Mulford to Tyler, and Mulford immediately introduced Miss Caroline Fetters the "presenter on behalf of twenty five other ladies of Camden, of a trifling token of regard and esteem." The President receiving the boquet, and looking at the two rows of ladies, made a very pretty little reply—hoping that the twenty six States of the Union might always be as fair as the ladies who on this occasion represent them, or as the flowers which they presented. They then moved on to the octagonal pavillion in the middle of the garden. Here cousin Emma Mulford threw from the second story window a wreath of flowers which alighted precisely upon the President's head. He removed it for an instant, looked at it, and replacing it, bowed very gracefully and passed on.

Beyond the pavillion the procession stopped again, and my uncle who had been selected to deliver the welcome to the shores of Jersey, made a brief address. The President replied, and the surrounding throng gave six tremendous cheers. They now proceeded to the reading room at Elwell's, where Captain Stockton arranged it for the twenty six ladies to shake hands with the object of their courtesy. They, and we gentlemen who were with them passed in detail before him, and all shook hands with him but myself. My uncle beckoned me for an introduction, but I felt no curiosity at all for the honor, and so declined it.

Our battalion of youth and beauty hastened up Bridge Avenue, and stopped in a line upon the pavement fronting our house. In a few minutes a special train of cars moved slowly up, containing the President and suite bound for the residence of Capt. Stockton. We greeted him with our handkerchiefs, and he went out of sight bowing very obsequiously, amid shouts and music, and followed by many an inquisitive eye.

I had a good chance of looking at the President without a party, and I think I never saw a more prominent nose than he can boast! He is tall and spare, and his face is very thin. He is said to resemble my uncle Mulford somewhat; but the resemblance is rather general, that of spareness, than specially confined to any one feature. He is very ready in making speeches, as was proved by the presentation of the flowers, which was entirely unexpected, but received very appropriately, and handsomely, as all say who heard him make his reply.

The new steam-frigate *Union* arrived in the Delaware this morning; and while the President was crossing the river, she was firing a slow salute in his honor. This conspired with other things to make the reception a solemn affair. It has indeed been a great day in Camden; the first day in sooth, in which a man truly great from his station— The President—has deigned to visit us.

11 June, Sunday.

My uncle went on to Princeton last night with the President, and returned about four o'clock this morning. His Excellency was received formally but heartily in all the intermediate towns; Bishop Doane bidding him welcome in Burlington, another minister in Bordentown, I know not who in Trenton, and Professor Dodd in Princeton. His journey through New Jersey promises to be a kind of triumphal procession. He stays to-night, to-morrow, and to morrow night with Stockton; to whom, bidding him good-by, I now leave him.

12 June, Monday.

This evening I spent at Cole's. Caddy and I are to go to the launch to-morrow—weather permitting and the old gentleman willing. But what will Hannah Sheppard say? Last year when the *Raritan* was to have been launched, but was not, I invited her to go, and she actually got ready. Alas! alas! . . .

This afternoon at two o'clock I appeared for the first time behind the bar, as counsel. . . .

The office was quite full of auditors before the case was ended; and in conclusion I have only to add that my aid was altogether gratuitous. My client is a carpenter in the employ of the Ferry Company, and a poor man.

13 June, Tuesday.

This afternoon at half past two Cad and I saw the launch of the frigate *Raritan*, whose keel has been laid for more than twenty years. We were on board of the *State Rights*, and had a pretty fair view. There were a great many boats opposite and near the navy-yard black with human beings; and I think the affair was quite as brilliant as the launch of the *Pennsylvania*. No accident of any consequence occurred, though I saw one that was ridiculous enough in itself. As the frigate was swinging up and tightening her lines one by one, a thick hawser came up immediately beneath a little scow with two men in it. She was raised several feet out of water, and fell again on her bottom, not hurting though doubtless it terrified the fellows aboard, who began to row lustily to get out of such a dangerous neighborhood.

I had a very agreeable jaunt with my fair companion.

16 June, Friday.

This evening I waited on a Mr. Bennaker, a German violinist boarding at Feuring's,[48] to get him to lead a Quartette—He consented, and so we will get at it.

Item. The Quintette, from which Mulford, Mumford, Ogden and myself withdrew some time ago, is in a state of decay.

17 June, Saturday.

This afternoon I strolled out to Ward's woods, to join a Pic-nic party there assembled for a little rustication. There were about two hundred, counting old and young and among the number were the Sheppards and many other fine girls. I took a stroll extra—with Jo, my old friend, and some of her acquaintances, and we had just got back and finished a good but humble supper when it began to rain. Some of the ladies made for a neighboring house—some got under a shed we hastily erected for their accommodation, and some stood it out bravely without any shelter. Mr. Gray turned a barrel over his head for a screen, and cut a very odd appearance as, thus equipped, he was shying through the trees. The rain did not last long—but it dispersed the company a little before they meant to go. I returned along with Carman's girls and Hugg's about half past seven o'clock.

48. William Feuring was a Camden piano manufacturer at Sixth and Market Streets. City directories do not list Bennaker.

The Monument Celebration at Bunker's Hill takes place to-day. All the magnates of the land will be there to hear Webster's oration.

19 June, Monday.

This morning on my way to the office I stopped more for mischief than any thing else, to ask Gray if he would publish some papers on the early governments of New Jersey. He said he could not answer positively until he saw the papers themselves; but when I assured him that they should contain nothing of a partizan character he told me he would publish them with pleasure. We had a good deal of chat—parted good friends—and agreed that the said essays be immediately begun.

I finished Tidd's *Practice* to-day—I finished reading it, I mean; for I have not yet begun to understand it!

This evening I went with Mulford to Cole's. Cad and I arranged a little visit or two together.

20 June, Tuesday.

This evening I was playing with Charley Bontemps. This man is "every thing by turns and nothing long." When I first knew him it was as a musician; then he took to French and sold out or gave away all his musical apparatus; and lately he has procured another flute, and does nothing now but practise on the same.

21 June, Wednesday.

I was practising a little while with Charley to-night.

Item. Mr. Cuyler mentioned to-day that the first gun which saluted the *Raritan* after her launch was fired by a Miss Mary Edwards of Chester. She is a niece of Capt. Engle's[49] and I know her well. She is a beautiful girl; but I do not admire this unbecoming effort at eccentricity.

Item—Again. My old schoolmaster, Samuel Aaron was severely cowhided at Norristown,[50] on last Monday, for something he said in a Temperance lecture offensive to a rum-seller in Lower Merion. This flogging is now the order of the day. A few Sunday mornings ago Mark Ware, the Sheriff of Gloucester County, went down to Black-woodtown and called a man out of Presbyterian meeting and cudgelled him most unmercifully at the door. The flogee's name is Bateman, and his provocation is said to have been that during the trial of Mercer, and in the very cell whence Mercer had been removed to the bar of

49. Probably Commander Frederick Engle, a naval officer since 1814 and a resident of Philadelphia.

50. Aaron was now operating a school in Norristown, Pennsylvania.

the court, he attempted to kiss Mrs. Ware. The Sheriff's family live in the jail.

22 June, Thursday.

Mr. Legare Attorney General of the United States[51] died on Tuesday at Boston; and the President has returned post-haste to Washington. A sudden and gloomy termination to the festivities of the Seventeenth!

It is thought by some that Green of Princeton, N. J. will be appointed Successor to the accomplished Southron. He would make quite as good an officer as my Philadelphia neighbor, Gilpin, whom Van Buren promoted.[52]

Brisbane, the somewhat famous New York "reformer"[53] called on Kelley to-day. He has a sinister, knavish eye; and I would trust him even as far as I could see him.

He is one of those who want to get up a society on the community principle—where each member puts in, and takes out according to rule. Kelley asked him what he would give to the common stock—what he would deposit in order to entitle himself to draw out a subsistence. "O" said he "I shall put in my skill in agriculture architecture and so forth." Yes, thought I, and that is just the curse of society as it now is: every one wants to "put in his skill" and too few are willing to put in their labor. We have too many heads and not enough hands, too much designing and too little doing. If more men would put their hands into the business of life we would soon have better times, and better morals. Each might then produce as much as he could consume, and there would be no occasion for "putting" his hand "in" anothers pocket.

24 June, Saturday.

The *Eagle* appears to day with an editorial complimenting Mr. Aaron, and denouncing the perpetrators of the recent assault upon him. I'll mark a copy with my name and send it out to my domine, to let him know that we are good friends, notwithstanding just cause to the contrary. This is the only article of mine except Capt. Roth's reply to Capt. Engle published in *Eagle* No. 1 that has appeared for a long while. My time has not allowed, nor my temper prompted, much scribbling of late.

We held a meeting to-night in the Library Room, to organize our

---

51. Hugh Swinton Legaré (1797–1843), of South Carolina, was President Tyler's attorney general and interim secretary of state at the time of his death.

52. John Nelson (1791–1860) of Maryland, not Princeton's James S. Green (1792–1862), became Tyler's new attorney general. Gilpin had held the post under Van Buren.

53. Albert Brisbane (1809–90) was most famous for his advocacy of Fourierist communitarianism.

new Musical Society. Bennaker was present, and I find he plays very well.

25 June, Sunday.

Mulford and I spent this afternoon with Kelley in Southwark. He has a well selected library, containing all the Transcendental philosophy of the day; and our time was pretty much occupied with a discussion of this mixed mass of truth and absurdity. He found an opportunity however to read us some poetry—he knows he does it well. One piece, written by Motherwell, was pronounced in a manner that really made me feel inclined to weep—It was addressed to his mistress a few days before the poet died, and is unsurpassed by any thing I ever heard for pathos and sweetness.[54]

This evening I was at Cole's, and Cad and I arranged a visit to Sheppard's for next Thursday evening.

26 June, Monday.

Having got Ned Cole's consent, I wrote a letter to Sam Cowperthwaite to-day, informing him of the cause of my coolness towards him. I now rest satisfied—before I could not.

This evening I gave one Bill Lafferty a lesson on the violin. It may be a delightful task "to teach the young idea how to shoot"—but I declare it must shoot with some other engine than a fiddle-bow. The shots from this gun in the hands of a beginner rack the ear to pieces.

27 June, Tuesday.

I met Sam once or twice to-day and he manifests a decided disposition to skulk. The poor devil looks so sheepish I really pity him. . . .

28 June, Wednesday.

A reply from Sam arrived to-day; but I immediately returned it with this endorsement in pencil: "If the within relates to the affairs of the Washington Library I will open it with pleasure. Our communication on other subjects is at an end." He denies, by the by to Casner that he ever said any thing calculated to injure my reputation.

Colonel Page having presented me with a ticket, I went this evening to the American, to Tommy Downing's Benefit. Tommy was for many years the steeple-man of the city—the alarm-ringer at the State-house, and was quite popular with the firemen. Precious few of these fellows however appeared at the Theatre to-night; there was indeed a most "beggarly account of empty benches.". . .

29 June, Thursday.

This evening Cad and I went up to Sheppards. We had a fine visit;

54. The poem was by Scottish poet William Motherwell (1797–1835).

good singing; and lots of pretty girls. The Rubicon by this visit is passed—to me it was painful in the extreme, and I saw that my feelings were shared by others. I wish I could get at the bottom of the Segunda affair; for I should then be spared the necessity of wounding a heart that once—But enough—for there is no guessing into whose hands this book may yet fall. If I have erred in the affair to which I allude, God knows I have suffered torment enough to atone for it.

30 June, Friday.

The influenza is very prevalent through all the Atlantic cities. It broke out, during the late ceremonies, at Boston; and from that circumstance has been called "the Tyler grippe." The locusts have also made their appearance in New Jersey and some of the neighboring states. An ignorant fellow showed me one to-day at Cake's ferry, and pointed out very particularly that it had the letter W upon its body. I looked and saw the letter very distinctly; but, said I, "what is this the sign of—I am not skilled in such matters." "O," he replied, "we are to have war to be sure."

An article of mine will appear in the *Eagle* to-morrow in defence of Tyler. The remarks by the by about the Aaron affair, have been copied with approbatory comments into the *Public Ledger* and some other papers. As the election approaches I must resume my labors editorial—Curts, stubborn Curts, asks it, and the enthusiastic Hineline insists upon it.

2 July, Sunday.

This morning I took Cad to St. Joseph's church to hear the music. It was very fine, but the weather was too hot to enjoy it. McAllister's thermometer at two o'clock this afternoon indicated 104° in the shade, on the South Side of Chesnut Street! Towards evening there was a heavy blow, and some rain.

4 July, Tuesday.

It is three years to-day since I began to keep this diary; and I hope it will be many more years before I feel disposed to relinquish the labor. Of late I have been quite brief in the recording of my acts and thoughts, for I have been very busy; but some of these days I will give loose again to my tattling propensity, and spin out two volumes a year as heretofore.

The day has been pretty generally celebrated every where but in Camden. My friend Mulford delivers an oration at Cold Springs in Cape May County, and Kelley I believe in Baltimore.

This evening I was at Cole's practising the overture to the *Caliph of Bagdad* with Caroline.

8 July, Saturday.

Uncle and I went to Poplar Hill to harvest to-day. The crop promises very fair and so does that at Walnut grove.

This evening we undertook to organize a Musical Society, but it was a failure. Mr. Bennaker was present, but he plays too well for us; and we must look up another leader.

9 July, Sunday.

Mulford and I waited on the Sheppard's to church to-night. I mentioned to Jo the receipt of Isabel's letter, and I think from her manner, that our former suspicions were right. I care not whether they prove to be or not.

10 July, Monday.

The *Madisonian*[55] copies my article from the *Eagle* in defence of Tyler, and gives it a very prominent place. The *Emporium* and others will now follow.

I was at the office as usual to-day; but studied unusually hard in view of my approaching holy-days.

12 July, Wednesday.

This evening I took Cad up to Sam's Concert. The poor miserable devil was there, but with all his impudence he could not look us in the face, I can imagine how he felt. The music was quite good.

15 July, Saturday.

I leave the office to day for my midsummer holy-day. By taking the Second Blackstone along and reading it of my leisure moments I can at least keep from going behind hand in the law.

16 July, Sunday.

The *Emporium* of Friday has sure enough copied my Tyler article. In the last number of the *Eagle* I had an appeal to the democratic papers of New Jersey about the Constitution. The movement appears of late to have fallen asleep. What effect will my impudence have, I wonder?

To-day I was busied in copying music. To-night I waited on the Sheppards to church.

17 July, Monday.

Ned Cole is to be married on Thursday evening, and I am his groomsman! The time is unfortunate for me, for I have promised my aunt Mulford to go to Cape May with her to-morrow. O for the power of ubiquity during vacation!

55. The *Madisonian* was a Tyler newspaper published in Washington, D. C.

This evening I was playing with Caroline. She is my companion on next Thursday evening.

18 July, Tuesday. Cape May.

This morning my aunt Rachel, cousin Emma and I started for the Capes in the Steam-boat *Trenton,* which the Rail Road Company are running in opposition to Whilldin's boat.[56] We left Walnut Street wharf at nine o'clock and reached the landing at the Cape about five, after a very pleasant passage down. General Wall was on board, and is yet quite feeble from a recent stroke of paralysis. [*John L.*] McKnight and family from Bordentown were also with us.

The houses at the Island are very full; we got in however at Congress hall—the aristocratic establishment—and are doing pretty well. I have already met several acquaintances, and made as many more. Ben Knight is at Ludlam's the Rulon's at McMackins, and young Pitfield at a private house.[57] Lafayette Miller, the son of mine host of Congress Hall, went out on serenades several times early in the summer with Mulford and me. His pretty sister Pauline I have also met at Cake's ferry. She is now at home, but their two hundred and fifty eaters keep her busy.

Frank Johnson gave a Concert to-night in our dining room. The music was good and the audience quite brilliant. Afterwards we had some fireworks, and about midnight a serenade from Frank's band.

19 July, Wednesday. Cape May.

People hardly know what to do with themselves at Cape May, after all its fame as a place of amusement. The bathing is very good, but even the most enthusiastic bather would want to come out occasionally and get dry. To fill up the intervals they have a billiard room or two and several ten pin alleys. You may also pick up shells if you can find any, eat, and look at the women. I tried all these to-day, but without complete success. I was glad when night arrived with a change of employment.

This change we had at Congress Hall, in what is technically called "a hop," that is a sociable dance, in the main saloon. It lasted until midnight, longer than which not even Frank Johnson's admirable music could keep them together. The prettiest girl and the best dancer in the room was Miss McKnight of Bordentown.

56. Wilmon Whilldin's (1773–1852) vessel, the *Sun,* made three trips to the Cape each week during the summer months.

57. Knight and Pitfield cannot be identified, but the Rulons may be one of the several families of that name from Gloucester Township. Knight was at Richard Smith Ludlam's Mansion House, the Rulons at Joseph and Benjamin McMakin's Atlantic Hotel.

Visitors are still pouring down; and to night I and four others slept in the reading room. I have never seen the Island so full.

20 July, Thursday.
This morning I returned in the *Ohio*. The McKnight family were on board, and I had the honor and pleasure of taking care of the belle of last evening. I have known the old gentleman McKnight some time—he is a director in the ferry Company; but his niece is a new and more valuable acquaintance.

We arrived about five o'clock; and the McKnights proceeded immediately to Bordentown and I immediately to get ready for the wedding. Cad and myself, after making our arrangements, met at Ned's house early in the evening. The company, about a dozen, assembled in an old fashioned way, and off I started after the Rev. Mr. Sisty.[58] By nine o'clock Miss Susan I. Wilson was Mrs. Edward Cole; a change which I hope our congratulations will never mock. Every thing passed off very well. Cad and I were alike inexperienced in such affairs, but be difficulties what they may, her ingenuity will overcome them. We did the honors without a single blunder! The new Mrs. Cole is a quakeress, sensible lively prudent and pretty; a good wife for Ned and a worthy sister for Cad. A long life and happy one to the young couple! . . .

22 July, Saturday.
Uncle goes down to the Capes to-day to take care of my aunt and cousin whom I left there day before yesterday. They expect to stay about a week.

23 July, Sunday.
This evening I stopped at Cole's. Mr. Sisty Junior[59] was there, and seems to be no more than a family acquaintance. He is quite sociable, and I guess a very clever fellow.

24 July, Monday.
At home copying music all day. I spent the evening at Hugg's; and about eleven o'clock sat down to read awhile.

There was a Democratic meeting in Woodbury to-day where Hineline and Hamilton fought through a series of reform resolutions which I drew up late last night. There was some opposition, but they finally passed by a handsome majority. I was almost asleep when I wrote them, but they are pretty strong.

25 July, Tuesday.
This morning I started in my boat with a trunk full of clothes and

58. John Sisty resided on North Seventh Street in Philadelphia.
59. This is the Benjamin Sisty mentioned in the entry of 31 March 1843.

music to pass the week at Poplar Hill. I can say with Byron—"Thou, the hall of my fathers art gone to decay,"[60] but I still find a joy in leaving the world behind, and retracing, even with a saddened brow, the footsteps of my childhood.

In the evening I walked up to Camden, to be present at the organization of a Constitution Club. This meeting was very well attended— and Mr. Rhees, a moderate Whig, presided. Mulford made a speech, Hamilton[61] another, and myself too. We were all cheered when we took our seats—a fact I mention, not from vanity but as a matter of curiosity; it being the first applause I ever received from the hands and heels of my fellows.

I was made Chairman of a Committee to draft resolutions and invite Mr. Thompson[62] of Princeton to address us. These things must be attended to.

26 July, Wednesday.

My uncle and aunt came up from the Capes last night, and I returned to the farm this morning. In the afternoon I took my fiddle and practised a while. I pass my time between music and hay making.

27 July, Thursday.

This morning I walked up to Walnut Grove. Moore treated his landlord, to wit, myself, with marked distinction, to wit poundcake and lemonade. I suspect I should not have got any of these luxuries but for their being on the look out for some more young tenants. On my way back to the lower, or in my affections the higher, place I stopped at the Cabin to see old Daddy Tuttle. He made me promise to bring my fiddle along during my visit and play Bonaparte's March for him. This eccentric fellow was a stage dancer in his youth, but afterwards learned the trade of Ship-building. He and his family moved into the upper fish-cabin during the prevalence of the cholera in Philadelphia, and have lived there ever since rent free.[63] Although they own several houses in Kensington they follow cat-fishing very industriously.

The crops at both farms look well.

28 July, Friday.

This afternoon I took my violin up to the cabin to play for my

60. Mickle quotes Byron's "On Leaving Newstead Abbey."
61. Morris R. Hamilton moved to Camden shortly after being admitted to the New Jersey bar, in November 1842. He returned to Trenton in 1849 where he served as a newspaper editor and state librarian.
62. John R. Thomson (1800–62), a prominent stockholder in the Camden and Amboy Railroad, later became United States senator from New Jersey from 1853 to 1862.
63. Tuttle had presumably left Philadelphia during the cholera epidemic of 1832.

cousins who were rusticating there. They and their mother supped with me at Poplar Hill.

In the evening Githens geared up his horses and took two of his eight men and myself to a Camp-Meeting at Gloucester. It was a dull affair, and so we returned about eleven o'clock.

29 July, Saturday.

I sailed up home, with all my duds, this morning. In the afternoon in crossing the river I intentionally insulted the Rev. Jno. Hall, who assumed the liberty of mingling, unasked, in a conversation in which I was engaged; and in the evening I called on Cad. A pretty good day's work!

Item extraordinary! They say Baxter was too drunk on last Wednesday night to play at the Society; and that in consequence they are going to turn him out of Church.

31 July, Monday.

Cad and I spent the evening with Mr. and Mrs. Edward Cole in Philadelphia. Being too late for the mail boat I crossed with Robinson Crusoe.[64] This young couple seem to understand each other perfectly, and to be entirely congenial, and every thing at present promises to them a happy union. May they be so blessed!

1 August, Tuesday.

Kelley goes to Baltimore this morning to be married, and Page goes along to be his groomsman. I accordingly have to bundle over the river to be office tender. I console myself however with the reflection that I might have gone to wedding too—having had a very pressing invitation to do so. But o! How long the day seemed after my late relaxation from study and thought even of study!

In the evening I attended an adjourned meeting of the Reform Club (now The Reform Association, at my motion).[65] They adopted some resolutions of my drafting, and called on me for a Speech. I declined the honor, however, for I am well aware that my name is too young to be identified with such an important movement as this. It will do the cause harm and myself no good, for me to play too open a part. I can nevertheless pull the strings behind the curtain, and enjoy the proud reflection that I help mould the public mind, though I remain to that public an utter stranger. Mr. Hamilton made a speech and a good one. He says his father told him never to go to a Demo-

64. Apparently Mickle's nickname for the small boat owner who brought him across the Delaware.

65. This is the group advocating reform of the state constitution which Mickle mentions on 25 July 1843.

cratic meeting unless he was ready to make an address; and he seems to be an obedient son.

2 August, Wednesday.

Mr. and Mrs. Kelley and Mr. and Mrs. Drakeley arrived this afternoon from Baltimore. I met them at the cars, and supped with them and my gay and gallant preceptor at Feinour's. To morrow we start for Boston. I have only time, amidst the labor of packing up, to say that the two brides are old acquaintances, were married the same day, and are both young and pretty.

3 August, Thursday.   Pacific Hotel, New York.[66]

This morning the Kelleys, the Drakeleys and myself started from Philadelphia and came to Gotham by way of Trenton and Brunswick. We had a very delightful ride; and I like the newly-married mistresses exceedingly. My companions proceeded immediately on to New Haven leaving me behind at my own earnest solicitation. In the evening, having left the money I had and my watch behind, I went to Niblo's and saw an excellent pantomime in which the Ravels performed.[67] Afterwards I took a walk about Broadway and quite late ventured a peep into Leonard Street.

I have fifty dollars with me; and none of it I suppose is expected home!

4 August, Friday.   New York.

This morning I called at the lodgings of my old friend Gideon V. Stivers in Brooklyn. He was not at home, so I left my card, for the Pacific. Having inspected Brooklyn well I passed the rest of the day in doing the same to New York. In the evening Gid came to see me, and we sauntered down to the Battery, to talk over old times. Poor Gid! He says if he only had my chances, how he would study; and I think if I only had his goading spurs I would study too. We parted quite late, and I went home by way of Leonard St.

5 August, Saturday.   "Tontine." New Haven.[68]

Having overslept my time this morning I did not start for Connecticut until four o'clock in the afternoon. My passage up the Sound in the *Champion,* brave a boat as she is, was rather tedious. I knew nobody, and the weather was bad; wind North east—rain—chopping sea. We arrived in this place about nine, and I took lodgings at the Tontine, where I found Kelley's card and address. After tea I hired

66. One of New York's leading hotels, the Pacific stood at 162 Greenwich Street.
67. The famous Ravel family performed a melodramatic pantomime called *Mazulme, the Night Owl* at Niblo's Garden, Broadway and Prince Streets.
68. The Tontine, overlooking New Haven Green from the corner of Church and Court Streets, was reputed to be the finest hotel in the city.

one of the waiters for a pilot and called on him and lady. They are at one Foster's—seemingly a clever fellow, but having a very queer wife. This lady is the only relative Mrs. Kelley has in America.

I have seen nothing curious since I reached here, three hours ago, except the house in which Benedict Arnold once kept store; and this I rather looked at than saw, for it was quite dark when it was pointed out to me.

There is a lovely quietness about this town that I like, and I wished the moment I saw the square and the colleges in the back-ground that I were a Yale boy. Were I out of love and in college, thought I, I should be happy. Such is human fickleness! When I might have entered Princeton I would not; and now—

But a truce to this! I am sleepy, and will crawl for the first time into a Connecticut bed.

6 August, Sunday. New Haven.

This is a lovely town indeed; so regular, so clean, so tasty, so quiet, so decorated with long rows of noble elms, and having around it such beautiful scenery. The public square upon which my hotel faces, with its four churches and State-house is very charming. The avenue through the middle of this area is lined with elms, which meet overhead and form as far as the eye can reach either way a magnificent gothic arch. Beyond the churches, dimly appearing through the trees are the College buildings—a long, frowning pile.

I went to one of the churches in the Square this morning, and heard a Puseyite sermon; or rather a Catholic sermon, from the transcendant virtue which was claimed for the partaking in the eucharist. In the evening I went to another Episcopalean church and heard Dr. Hawkes. He is quite an eloquent man.

During my leisure to day I have been reading *Change for American Notes* by an American lady.[69] It is a sharply written thing, but has enough verisimilitude. She has miscounted, however, and given Boz more than was coming to him. Who can the author be? Not Miss Sedgwick; for if that is the case she praises her own novels. The book mentions by the by, in an incidental way, that there is no poor person in this city of New Haven; and such the inhabitants say is the case.

7 August, Monday. New Haven.

This morning Mr. Foster, Kelley, and I took a carriage and rode out to West Rock, to see the Regicide's Cave[70]—which happens to be no

69. In fact, *Change for the American Notes*, published in New York in 1843, was by Henry Wood, an English journalist.

70. Two officers of Cromwell's army, fleeing from agents of the king, hid for about a month in 1661, in a cave on West Rock, northeast of New Haven.

cave at all, but a nook formed by some huge rocks lying pell-mell on top of the ground on the peak of the mountain. We clambered up these stones, and had a fine view of the city, and Surrounding valley; and the Sound. Afterwards we continued our ride all through New Haven, and had a very delightful time—cost ten shillings.

On our return I called to see my historical friend Howe. He has just returned from a tramp in Virginia, sick. I saw his partner, Mr. Blake,[71] and like him very much.

Mr. Atwill, formerly of the Philadelphia *Evening Journal* and now of the *Courier* in this city,[72] boards at the Tontine. He and I were invited to a party given to-night to the Kelleys by a Mr. Blake,[73] and attended it together. It was a splendid affair, and embraced most of the aristocracy of the town. Among the many beautiful ladies was the daughter of Hillhouse the poet.[74] Last night, by the by, Mr Foster pointed out to me in church the author of *Tecumseh*[75]—a young and unassuming looking man. This is a famous place for literati.

The *Courier* this morning "soaps" Kelley. It speaks of him "as an able and eloquent member of the Philadelphia bar." The same paper announces my arrival by the name of Israel Mickle; a little better than the New York *Express* in which I saw myself metamorphosed into "Isaac Wickles, Canada!"

8 August, Tuesday.   New Haven.

Mr. Foster took us over the College cabinet this forenoon. In passing thro' the Chapel we heard the young gentlemen rehearsing for Commencement, which takes place next week. The fiddles and flutes put me in mind of home. We afterwards went up the state house under the guidance of General Somebody—a good Loco-foco, and Secretary of Connecticut.[76]

After dinner I called upon Howe, who gave me an introduction to Professor Silliman, the gentleman and scholar, at his own residence. We afterwards took a walk through the [*Grove Street*] Cemetery, and saw the tomb of the inventor of the cotton-gin. I returned with him to his office—I mean Mr. Howe's and not the cotton-gin man's—and received two presents from Mr. Barber; his *History of New England* and his *Memoirs of New Haven*. They also loaned me a cut of Van Buren's birth-place, to be printed in the *Eagle*. Howe gave me in con-

---

71. Mickle makes a slip of the pen; Howe's partner was John W. Barber.
72. Winthrop Atwill was editor of the *Morning Courier*.
73. Probably Eli or his brother Philos Blake, local manufacturers.
74. James A. Hillhouse (1789–1841).
75. Mickle probably met former British officer John Richardson (1797–1863), who had written *Tecumseh; or The Warrior of the West* in 1828.
76. Noah A. Phelps was the secretary for the state of Connecticut.

clusion his history of Camden, to be re-written for their forthcoming work on New Jersey.

The Foster's gave a party to night, and of course I was there.

There was a great storm in Philadelphia on Saturday last.

9 August, Wednesday. "Massasoit," Springfield.[77]

We are in old Massachusetts! This state is the mother and nurse of liberty; and should liberty ever pine and die, she will be the last to leave its pillow.

We took passage at four o'clock this morning, by rail road to Hartford. Thence we ascended the Connecticut to this place, in a little steam-boat built very light, to suit the shoalness of the water. Our passage up was very pleasant; its termination was delightful. We approached Springfield just at sunset. The town was shrouded in darkness, but the light still faintly fell upon the peaks of the surrounding hills. It seemed as we glided up the quiet stream, and came into the shade of the valley in which we were to stop, as if we were leaving one world for another.

After an excellent supper at the Massasoit House, we took a walk over the place, without seeing much of it; and returned to our lodgings. Here a curious incident took occurrence: A gentleman who came up the river with us was relating the proceedings of a meeting he attended some time ago in Philadelphia, and describing the part one of the speakers took; which speaker to his great astonishment he learned was Mr. Kelley himself!

We are to start for Boston early in the morning.

10 August, Thursday. "Tremont House," Boston.[78]

We got under weigh betimes this morning, and came to this famous city by the great western Rail Road, through Worcester and a great many less but still very flourishing towns. An air of neatness pervades them all, and the people wherever I have been in New England seem intelligent, honest and happy. They retain much of their primitive simplicity, and appeared to have escaped in a great measure the lax morality of the Southern and middle states.

About eleven o'clock Kelley pointed out from the car window the peak of the monument on Bunker Hill! What were my emotions when I beheld, rising in majesty over the distant city, the column that commemorated the first battle of the revolution! I felt as I never felt before. I seemed for awhile to breathe the air, to live the drama of the glorious

77. Marvin Chapin's Massasoit House stood opposite Springfield's railroad depot.

78. The Tremont House, one of the best and most modern hotels of the era, was on Tremont Street near School.

past; and almost regretted when I roused from my reverie, that the delusion could not have lasted forever.

We soon reached the town, and took a cab. Having left Kelley and his lady at his sister's, Mrs. Curry's,[79] I proceeded to the Tremont House, passing in my way the Common, with which Peter Parley's amusing books had long ago made me acquainted. A hundred historical associations rushed to my mind as we drove by this classic, this sacred spot; and I imagined that a patriot could nowhere sleep the long, sweet sleep of death, so well as there!

I made an acquaintance on the passage from Worcester—a Mr. Turner of New Bedford;[80] a young man about of my age, and travelling like me, to see the world. We got lodgings, after a deal of trouble, at the Tremont—the best house in Boston. In the evening we attended the Museum together, and heard Dr. Valentine,[81] an amusing imitator of characters.

When I arrived at the hotel I met a Mr. Ackley from Camden, and midshipman McCauley who has lately been around the world in the *Boston*.[82] She lies at Charlestown, and her officers have not yet got leave of absence. McCauley is an old acquaintance. I also saw "Lord George Bishop Doane of New Jersey" (as the English papers call him) just going away. There are one or two Governors here also— among them, I am certain at least, of Mr. Hubbard of New Hampshire.[83] The house is very full.

Towards the close of the day it begain raining, and this is a real London evening. The fag end of Saturday's storm has I presume, just "dropped in" upon us. Mr. Ackley, by the by, assured me that the said storm did no injury in or about Camden; though beyond the Schuylkill it was singularly destructive both to life and property.

11 August, Friday. Boston.

Kelley took us around to-day, notwithstanding the drizzling weather, and showed us old Faneuil Hall, the "cradle of liberty,"—the Stone Chapel, famous in many a legend and the Brattle Street Church, in

---

79. Probably the wife of William Curry, jeweler of Court Avenue. Curry's home was on Mason Street, not far from Boston Common.

80. Probably a son of Elbridge G. Turner, an official of the New Bedford and Taunton Railroad.

81. Dr. William Valentine, a comic lecturer, had been a highly popular performer since the mid-1830s. On this night, he appeared in the theatre of Moses Kimball's Boston Museum on Tremont Street.

82. James Ackley was a currier whose shop stood on Market Street above Second in Camden. Edward Y. McCauley had become a midshipman in 1841 and was to rise to the rank of captain by 1872. The *Boston*, an 18-gun sloop-of-war launched in 1825, had been stationed in the East Indies from 1841 to 1843.

83. Henry Hubbard (1784–1857), a Democrat, was governor of New Hampshire from 1841 to 1843.

the front of which still sticks a cannon ball fired there during the battle of Bunker's hill; and many other places of local interest.[84] In Faneuil Hall we were shown the armories of the different volunteer companies of Boston, which are furnished and kept in the best manner. In one of them hung a portrait of my preceptor [*William Kelley*] in his civil dress, looking as natural as life.

I spent the evening with the Currys. The celebrated Brownson was there with us. He is indeed a wonderful man. For inventing a theory which shall reconcile itself with the most repugnant systems and opinions he cannot be equalled. His philosophy, if you will give him time to explain it, is just in accordance with the views of Apostle Paul and Thomas Paine—a kind of an omnibus, in which both orthodox and infidel can unite, and that without any sacrifice of their own previous convictions. Mr. Brownson seems to have forged every link in the chain of his theory in the furnace of deep and ardent reflection. He anticipates every objection and has an answer ready; talks slowly and logically; uses words with great precision; and forces others to believe even when they doubt if he believes himself. Like the preceptor of Pericles who used to demonstrate that there was no such thing as motion, our Chelsea Philosopher, will cheat even a Yankee out of the evidence of his senses. As an instance, he extorted from Kelley to-night the confession that the virtue of the Eucharist was in the mere fact of taking it, in other words, that bread and wine are not bread and wine, but more! Brownson says indeed that he rejoices in the Puseyite movement; and the papers say for him, that he is a greater believer in transubstantiation than even the most ultra of the Oxonians.[85] I hope he may yet be Pope! He would honor the office. As for his democracy, upon which he lays so much stress, I doubt it exceedingly; nor was his remark this evening, that he would support Webster for the Presidency if nominated, calculated to remove the impression I have of his insincerity.

12 August, Saturday.   Boston.

To-day we took a hack and went over to Charlestown. My friend McCauley was on hand, and took us all over the magnificent Navy Yard at this place. The steamer *Mississippi*, our cicerone's quondam

84. Faneuil Hall is still a Boston landmark, revered for patriot meetings held there before and during the American Revolution. Stone Chapel, built at the corner of School and Tremont Streets in 1750, adjoined the cemetery where some "legendary" Bostonians are buried. Brattle Square Church, demolished in 1874, had indeed been struck by an American cannonball during the American siege of Boston, though after the Battle of Bunker Hill.

85. The Tractarian or Puseyite movement, favoring more ritual and other Roman Catholic features in Anglicanism, had begun at Oriel College, Oxford.

domicile, the *Boston,* and several other national vessels were in port. We inspected them, every part of which, together with the dry-dock, the rope walk, and the shiphouses were so explained that even the ladies understood their uses.

From here we proceeded to the Monument, whose gray blocks had been frowning on us, as we wandered over the Navy Yard, as if to reprove us for not visiting it first. We had not time to ascend, either by the steam car, inside, or by the steps; but we saw several go up. The altitude of the monument is 120 feet, and the view from the top must be fine. It has two massive walls; the inner forming a cylinder, and the outer an obelisk; and is built as if to defy time's ravages. It bears no inscription yet; and when they do incribe it I hope they will not allude to the disgraceful fact that a public dancer made the last contribution towards erecting it.[86]

From the Monument we drove to Chelsea, to see Mr. Brownson. He lives in a snug little cottage, on top of a hill from which a fine view extends of Boston, the rivers, and the neighboring towns. Nahant—the place where a few years ago so many fools resorted to see the Sea Serpent—is also visible in the distance. It is indeed a magnificent spot— I mean this Chelsea hill; and it is no wonder its tenant has great ideas. If his own theory be true, a glance from one of his study-windows would inspire any man.

We found Brownson at work, as usual. He came out, when we drew up, and welcomed us very heartily to what he called "the philosopher's den." The philosopher, however—especially since he expected ladies at that hour—looked rather shabby. His fine curly hair was in the greatest confusion—Mrs. Kelley whispered to me that it had not seen a comb for a month; his coat was ancient and a little ragged; and his feet, though it was now one o'clock, still retained their morning slippers. From his *tout ensemble* in his den I should think he was about as lazy as Goldsmith,[87] who used to fling his shoe at the candle when he wished to extinguish it. He ushered us into his library where he was copying A College Address for publication, and introduced us to his lady—a sickly, unintellectual, but not unhappy looking woman. They tell some strange stories about Boston concerning the treatment she receives from her husband; Mrs. Curry however denies them. Thus they say that Mrs. Brownson once went to a party with a pair of her lord's gloves on—a pair of white kid gloves, and too big for her by a mile. This Mrs. Curry most emphatically rebuts by averring that Mr. Brown-

86. Fanny Ellsler had contributed over five hundred dollars for the completion of the monument.
87. English writer Oliver Goldsmith (1730?–74).

son never had any white gloves. *"Non est nobis tantas lites componere."* It may be so and then again it may not.

The library was of course **in** character—that is, beautifully **out of** order. It was however a splendid collection of books—such as they were. A few will serve to give the general character of his collection: Voltaire, Volney, Carlyle, Hume, Paine, Channing, and Emerson. There were several of his own works. On the mantle was the Latin Grammar, "the first and last book" to a Latin student; and all around lay the classics and works in French in the greatest confusion. The only picture in the room was a portrait of M. Cousin,[88] who is, I believe a great favorite with Browny, as our guest is called by his clique in Boston.

Having spent an hour in very sublimated confab—for Kelley be it remembered is a good Transcendentalist and Mrs. Curry, like Juvenal's wife, *"novit, quid toto fiat in orbe,"*—I got an autograph, and we came away.

13 August, Sunday. Boston.

This morning I took an early walk over the Common. In the afternoon I went to the "old Stone Chapel" in Tremont Street. And the evening I passed with the Currys. Nothing worthy of note occurred at either place.

14 August, Monday. Boston.

This morning we ascended the State House and had a beautiful view of the city. We were annoyed by a company of negroes who were up at the same time with us "lookers on in Venice." Negroes are inconceivably insolent in this land of hot-headed abolitionism, where some of the whites consider them at least equal "if not a little more so." In coming down we asked the man who keeps the book in which visitors to the cupola register their names if the negroes above had entered theirs. "Of course they did" said he to Mrs. Curry "and who has got a better right?" If I had heard this fellow I should have offended him.

In the afternoon all our party but myself visited Mount Auburn and Fresh Pond;[89] taking tea on their return with Murdock the actor. I preferred strolling about town. I dropped in, in my rambles, at Burnham's, Cornhill, and bought an opera, the *Metamorphosis*,[90] some other music, and a present for one of the young Currys, who read for me the other day very well.

---

88. Victor Cousin (1792–1867) was a French philosopher and minister of education under King Louis Philippe.

89. Mount Auburn was a cemetery in Cambridge overlooking the Charles River. Fresh Pond, a popular spot for outings, was nearby.

90. C. Burnham, bookseller, of 58 Cornhill, sold Mickle a copy of William Jackson's comic opera of 1783.

In the evening I went to the National Theatre.[91]

15 August, Tuesday. Steamboat Rhode Island: Long Island Sound, bound down.

This morning we visited several Reading Rooms and Libraries; and in the afternoon the Currys and Kelleys went to Nahant and Lynn. Having become tired of Boston I bade them "Au revoir" and started for New York at four o'clock by way of Providence and Stonington.

A little way from Boston our cars ran over and mashed to pieces a Jersey man who had fallen off. His mangled carcass could hardly be taken up to be brought on. The curiosity among the passengers to see him was very great; but among all the questions they asked I could not but observe none inquired "Is he a poor man? Has he left a wife and children to lament their sudden loss and curse the world's cold charity?" He had children indeed; for a fine boy was along with him. He says his father fell among the wheels and jumped off at the risk of his own life to assist him. The poor fellow's sorrow was indescribable.

In crossing the river at Providence I left my coat behind; and not having time to return I requested one of the ferrymen to forward it to Howard's Hotel in New York. He declined any pay. His name is Tram Frost; but if he sends my bang up along I shall conclude that the stream of honesty is not yet quite frozen up.

It is impossible to sleep in this moving palace. Her roaring fires keep before me the fate of the *Lexington* and banish Slumber.[92] I took the precaution when I came on board to find out a bouyant box among the merchandize to which I could fly at the alarm of fire, and trust for an escape. We arrived safely at New York however about six o'clock in the morning, and I made for Howard's.[93]

16 August, Wednesday. New York. Howard's Hotel, Broadway.

While waiting for breakfast this morning I saw Ned Humphreys go into a store on the opposite side of the street. I was glad to have discovered an acquaintance and went over to him. He is clerk to his brother at the establishment I saw him enter. We made our arrangements about passing the day—and night—and separated *pro tempore*.

The morning I passed in various ways—the afternoon as follows. Humphreys invited me to a pic-nic at the Elysian Fields, Hoboken,[94]

91. The National, on Portland Street near Traverse, was a highly popular theatre from 1836 to 1852.

92. The steamship *Lexington* had burned in Long Island Sound on 13 January 1840, with the loss of over one hundred lives.

93. The Howard Hotel, on the corner of Broadway and Maiden Lane, was one of New York's newest and finest hotels.

94. The Elysian Fields were a large expanse of fields and woods on the west banks of the Hudson, just opposite New York City.

which I accepted. In addition to the ladies and plenty to eat, there was a balloon ascension and music. What with these and the Sybyl's cave, and the spot where Aaron Burr shot Hamilton, and the place where the murdered body of the beautiful Mary Rogers was discovered I had enough to do and look at and think about.[95] The time passed very agreeably—the more so as I was on the soil of my native state, after an absence of nearly a fortnight!

In the evening Ned called for me and we went to several public places, among the rest to Pinteux's and la Duchesse de Berri's in Duane St.[96] The music at the former was good.

Having to start very early in the morning I did not sleep or undertake to sleep much to-night. *Ce n'est pas chez la Duchesse et ses belles charmantes qu'on peut regarder le passage des heures.*

17 August, Thursday.

Kelley and wife came through the Sound last night; I joined them on the Philadelphia boat, and came on with them home. I found all our folks well—and went to sleep on my own sweet bed! So ends a jaunt which has cost me two weeks time and a little over fifty dollars; but which was very agreeable and instructive, and to which I can long refer with pleasure and profit.

18 August, Friday.

It took me all to-day to recruit from my fatigue and loss of rest. In the evening I got out and went over to call on Kelley.

19 August, Saturday.

This evening I was playing with Cad. How glad I was to see her! . . .

24 August, Thursday.

To-day I was busy writing an Address on the Constitution. A committee of twenty five were appointed to do this, at a Democratic meeting held some time ago in Woodbury, and they have delegated me.

25 August, Friday.

John R. Thompson Esq. of Princeton lectured to-night in the City Hall on a reform of the Constitution. He had a very good house, and his production was quite excellent, although his arguments were, of

95. The Sybyl's Cave, a man-made cavern, was a principle tourist attraction in Hoboken. The body of New York tobacco shop clerk Mary Rogers was found floating near its entrance in July 1841, providing the inspiration for Edgar Allan Poe's *The Mystery of Marie Roget* of 1842.

96. John Pinteux was proprietor of an eating place, the "Cafe de Mille Colonnes," at 307 Broadway, with a rear entrance on Duane Street. New York City directories provide no reference to "la duchesse de Berri's." In the light of Mickle's next paragraph, it may have been a brothel.

course, the same we have heard of long ago. Captain Stockton was present as an auditor, but was called up, and avowed himself a reformer. He is a gallant fellow, but a very laborious speaker. Col. Alexander and Mr. Perrine of East Jersey[97] were also present, and the former made a short speech. So did Mr. Jeffers. The cause is progressing bravely! To night we had all the Amphictyons of democracy, present, and their gray hairs become the great measure of reform much better than my young friend Hamilton's curly and well-oiled soap-locks, or my own smooth face.

26 August, Saturday.

This evening I attended a Reform meeting in South Camden, and was called up. I spoke about forty minutes. Hamilton read the Charter, and Mulford closed the exercises by a very neat address.

27 August, Sunday.

The Sheppards except Mary are all at home. I dropped in a little while this evening. They borrow the *Eagle,* I find from some of their Democratic neighbors, for they quiz me about my "disorganization." By the by, the Address I was writing was so much like Mr. Thompson's lecture in some parts that I destroyed it.

29 August, Tuesday.

To-day I wrote a pamphlet of eight or nine pages on the Constitution, and helped Mr. Kelley move to his new house in Sansom Street! If that is not a good seven hours' work I'll give up and call myself lazy. In truth I never wrote so fast nor with so little trouble before. I had put off the Address until the election was at hand, and had no choice but to go ahead; it was a matter of necessity; but I flatter myself that it is done better than job-work in some cases.

31 August, Thursday.

To-day I went on the Company's Bay Excursion with Mrs. Morgan and Miss Champion. We started at seven o'clock in the morning; took boat to Bordentown, cars to Amboy, boat again up the bay by way of the Narrows, by New York fifteen miles up the Hudson to see the Palisades; then returned to Amboy by the west passage round Staten Island, and came home as we went; arriving in Philadelphia about eleven, in time for me to cross in the mail-boat. The weather was fine and we had an agreeable trip, with good music and good eating. To-day a month ago I entered New York with Kelley.

97. William C. Alexander (1806–76), an attorney since 1828, would later serve in both houses of the New Jersey legislature and run for governor in 1857. Lewis Perrine (1815–89) was a Trenton lawyer and railroad executive.

So ends a summer in which I have been flying all over the country; and hereafter for study!

1 September, Friday.

This evening Caddy and I were at Ned's. We had a very agreeable visit, which I was obliged to break off to cross in the mail-boat.

A man named Hunt, residing on Doctor Mulford's place, is now laboring under the hydrophobia. He was bitten about five months ago at Trenton, and has been well up to four or five days ago when the Doctor was called upon to visit him. The disease did not manifest itself, although the Symptoms were very unusual, until some water was given him to wash down some powders he had been taking; at which his features were so horribly distorted that the Doctor was frightened and ran from the room. He was for the first time in the presence of a rabid man! From that moment, Hunt has been subject to violent spasms, and to night he was to be removed to the Hospital in Philadelphia.[98]

2 September, Saturday.

This evening I took a music lesson of Mr. Osbourne. We are to play together twice a week for ten dollars a quarter. We use Pleyel's duettes.[99] I crossed in the mail boat—for the third successive night in the present week. The Brownings and some other very pious folks thought I must be very dissipated last winter for being in Philadelphia so often at night; I wonder what they would say now?

3 September, Sunday.

At home—rains like the devil—that is to say it rains every where, for about these times the devil does seem to reign every where. Cousin Delia[100] spent the day with us; the man with the Hydrophobia died yesterday morning at the Hospital, and the printers moreover have got two pages of my address set up.

5 September, Tuesday.

At my office-studies to-day. Began Chitty's *Pleadings*.

In the evening I was at a Reform meeting in the City Hall and was made Secretary.

Late at night Charley Bontemps and I went out and serenaded Sheppards, Turner's and Delacours! He is a married man, and was yesterday presented by his lady with a second heir, representative and responsibility.

98. Benjamin Hunt died at Philadelphia Hospital on September 2.
99. Ignaz Joseph Pleyel (1757–1831) was a disciple and imitator of Haydn.
100. Mickle's visitor was Adelia Hogeland.

7 September, Thursday.

Capt. Stockton's steamer, the *Princeton*[101] was launched from the Navy Yard to day amidst a pelting north-east rain.

This evening I was at Cole's. Cad goes away on Saturday of this week.

8 September, Friday.

Cad and I were at Ned's this evening, and staid all night.

9 September, Saturday.

I had a thorough examination this afternoon on Bills of Exchange. In the evening there was another Reform meeting in the City hall. It was but thinly attended, and I had to do most of the talking. The only regular speech that was delivered however was by a South Camden mechanic named Nicholls. He made out very well.

How lonesome it will be for a while now that Cad is gone! Time however is a great physician, and I guess I shall survive her absence.

10 September, Sunday.

At home to day studying Mason's little book on music. I begin to understand something of the construction and sequence of chords.

In the evening I called on the Sheppard's and took two of them to Baptist Church. My intercourse at this family's house is apparently as familiar as ever, but there is wanting the warmth I once entertained.

11 September, Monday.

My pamphlet is published this morning![102] It contains eight pages; and the typographical part is done very neatly. The composition, I begin to fear is too labored to please the people.

12 September, Tuesday.

The Philadelphia *Ledger* of this morning contains a Synopsis of my Appeal.

To-day I was at my office reading Chitty's *Pleadings,* and in the evening we had a rehearsal at our house.

14 September, Thursday.

This evening according to promise I took my violin over the river and accompanied Mrs. Kelley for an hour or so. She sings very well and plays the guitar quite tolerably.

101. Stockton, commanding officer of the ship, was a student of naval architecture and had also assisted in its construction.

102. Mickle's pamphlet, ostensibly written by "The Democratic Citizens of Gloucester County, New Jersey," bore the title *An Appeal to the People of West Jersey in Favor of a Convention to Frame a State Constitution.* It advocated more separation of the three branches of government and extension of the suffrage and the right to sit as a juror, among other reforms.

16 September, Saturday.

This afternoon there was a grand regatta on the Delaware between six Indians from Lake Superior and six Kensington fishermen. The former rowed a tin canoe and the latter a brig's gig, and the Indians beat about one length. I say the canoe was rowed—but in truth she was paddled, and her coxswain, a squaw, paddled as hard as any. The distance run was from the Rail Road Hotel to a flag boat off Kaighn's Point, and back again. There were thousands of people over to see the affair, and the river was studded over with little boats and big ones, moving about among each other in a very animated style. Col. Page, and some other friends and myself were on top of Elwell's house, and had an excellent view.

In the evening I inducted Mulford into the mysteries of Theatrical life. The play was—I forget its name; but this I remember we were at the American. I crossed in the mail-boat, but Mulford staid all night.

17 September, Sunday.

This morning in crossing the river I encountered Miss Mulford one of my quondam playmates, and a nice girl. She had been all night at her and my uncle's—the Doctor's, and was returning to her boarding School in Chesnut Street above Thirteenth. Of course I accompanied her to the door.

In the evening Bontemps and I went to Baptist Church.

18 September, Monday.

Ned Cole and his wee wife and I went up this morning to see Cad. She is staying at an aunt's on the Moorestown road and near the said town. We remained until after dark and had a most delightful visit. Cad sent two lovely peaches to my mother. She is enjoying herself finely among her good old fashioned kinspeople, and has the brightest glow of health in her cheek. She is free now from the tyranny of her stepmother, and is happy, as she deserves always to be.

19 September, Tuesday.

There was a Buffalo Hunt in the field north of Cooper Street and east of Love lane this afternoon, which was witnessed by thousands upon thousands of people from the city. Some western speculator, whose name I did not learn is the head man in this piece of humbug. He first makes a bargain with the ferries to divide the spoils, and then attracts the public eye by his huge advertisement heralding "a grand gratuitous exhibition in Camden." The good citizens take the bait, and are diddled out of ten cents apiece without knowing it.

The field used to-day contained maybe eight or nine acres, and around its circumference at the distance of ten feet from the old fence a temporary paling was erected to make a track something like a race course. "I wonder who pays all this" exclaimed some gawky Philadelphian as he looked at the bran new boards that were employed in this "gratuitous" Show, or rather in the arrangements for it. "Why you do, you damned fool" said Bontemps who was walking with me "you pay ten cents towards it." But the fellow could neither feel the insult nor see the truth of the remark; so Charley got off with a whole nose.

At the time appointed the herd of buffaloes were let out of the pen and began to run around the enclosure. A man painted and dressed like an Indian, mounted on a horse and armed with a lasso started after them. By dint of diverse thumps and blows from the spectators the poor calves were forced into a pretty lively trot, and gave the man some trouble to catch them. At last, some of them, enraged beyond endurance at the accumulated provocation which they received from the double line through which they passed, broke out into Love Lane and made towards Camden. The lane being full of people, of course a ludicrous scene ensued. Men and women, horses and carriages, hand carts and pie-men, news paper-boys, prostitutes, sweeps and dogs made for the adjoining corn-fields, over and through the fence and over one another, as if the old boy himself had been at large. Such screaming and tugging and sweating and cursing I never saw. Very fortunately however no one was hurt. The calves squandered through the town, the woods, and fields and each one was followed, by a crowd, yelling and whooping like a pack of Savages. The farmers, in the neighborhood received a good deal of damage from the carrying off of their truck, and I suppose the ferries, being partners as to the profits of the day, will be obliged to pay for it.

In this kind of folly all the afternoon was passed. Camden was overrun with people, and a large proportion of the mass seemed to vie with each other in making fools of themselves. It was in short such a time, that every good citizen wished the plagued buffaloes and their speculating keeper a thousand miles beyond the Rocky Mountains.

Mr. Osbourne gave a concert to-night in the Court House. The music was only tolerable, and the house slim, but highly respectable.

20 September, Wednesday.

I missed a music-lesson to-day and will be unable to practise much with Osbourne until after election.

The *Mail* of to-day calls Mulford, Hamilton and myself a "triangle of young patriots," and accuses us with being the main agitators of the Reform movement in West Jersey, and moreover advises us to "tarry in Jericho till our beards be grown." The article is quite keen, but is no more than we might have expected. I was glad it appeared; for it gave me an opportunity of coming at an explanation which I have long desired. I accordingly wrote Gray a letter and left it at his door in the evening.

Middy McCauley, Mulford and I went up to the Hadyn's rehearsal to-night.[103] Sam looked somewhat sheepish—poor devil!

21 September, Thursday.

To day, having finished Chitty on Pleadings, I took up his work on Bills. It is a dry subject, but *"n'importe."*

The Whigs make their County ticket at Woodbury to-day. They are going to try to run Sheriff Ware out for caning Bateman; and in sober truth I do not care if they succeed. There is too much of this lawless disposition abroad, and I want to see it curbed.

22 September, Friday.

Tom Gray gave me a letter from his father to-day. It is quite fair, considering some parts of my note of Wednesday. He wants an interview—*pour quoi,* I wonder. *Nous verrons.*

Colonel Page has received a letter from Rives of the *Globe,* expressing great doubt of the result of the next Presidential election. That generally true prophet says that Van Buren will be the nominee of the Convention, in which case, Calhoun and Tyler will unite forces and oppose him.[104] If they can divert one-eighth of the Democratic votes Clay will be elected. So fears the *Globe* man; but God forfend!

24 September, Sunday.

Ned and I went to see Cad again to-day. She is now near my uncle Hugg's among friends who think a great deal of her. We had a very pleasant visit—and did not return until quite late.

26 September, Tuesday.

This evening I called on Gray at his residence, for he told me this morning it was out of the question to have any pleasant talk at his office, where people were continually coming in. He saluted me quite cordially, and took me into a private room, and locked the door after us. He then opened the matter between us, and said there had been but two articles in the *Eagle* which hurt his feelings. He repeated their tenor, and fortunately, I was able to assure him that I had nothing to do with either of them. We talked over the violent character of our organ, and the dangers of my connection with it. He spoke highly of my ability and of my future prospects; but complained that there was

103. Camden's Haydn Music Club was an amateur group of musicians, perhaps the successor to the "Amateurs' Club" mentioned earlier in the diary.
104. The Democrats eventually abandoned Van Buren to prevent the opposition of Southern leaders.

a tendency to virulence in every thing that I wrote. He was aware of the authorship of the "Farmer's Letters" and of the pamphlet on the Constitution, but thought the note on page 3 was not true.[105] He said that Governor Pennington was incapable of uttering such a sentiment. I told him my authority—the *Emporium* at Trenton; and assured him that I believed it to be true. The Whigs in Camden he also said wanted to write to the governor and get him to disclaim it, but he dissuaded them from it, as the mischief was already done. He entered quite deeply into a defence of his conduct on the bench in the Mercer case, and I thought showed his soreness at a paragraph in my pamphlet, about the Judges "squeezing themselves upon the bench at exciting trials to disgrace the State in the eyes of her neighbors." He disclaimed any intent to hurt our feelings or detract from our character in his late article about the "triangle of young patriots," but gave as a reason for writing it, that he wanted to let us know that he understood our movements. It is needless to follow the conversation through. I staid till nearly midnight, and after all proper acknowledgements on both sides I promised that after the eighteenth day of next month I would have nothing to do with the *Eagle* anonymously. My sacred word is passed that I will either become the controlling editor, or cut entirely loose from the concern. Mr. Gray did not ask me to make this engagement, but I did it upon a clear conviction that my present relations with the *Eagle* are dangerous to my character and interests both now and in time to come. That I write many of the articles for the editorial columns of this paper is notorious all over Camden. This will make me many enemies where I am known, while it gives me no credit where I am not.

27 September, Wednesday.

A rustic friend called on me to-day at the office and I took some pains to impress upon him the advantage of keeping out of the law's meshes entirely. In the height of my remarks upon the subject Col. Page came in and wanted two witnesses to a power of attorney he was about executing. I signed and then asked John to do so, "No indeed," he replied "I am not going to get myself into a scrape." I had a great deal of trouble to undo the clown's prejudice and prevail on him to attach his name. He is a simple fellow, but he brought me the good news that Cad is well and happy.

29 September, Friday.

This evening I spent at Ned Cole's in Market Street. I had just

---

105. There are no extant copies of Mickle's pamphlet and newspaper reviews of his arguments do not mention the note about Governor Pennington.

returned by the mail-boat and got to bed when I heard the alarm of fire. I found on arriving at the spot, that it was the Vauxhall-Garden. It and an adjoining building were entirely destroyed. Mr. Gray's house was in great danger, but was saved by covering the roof with blankets and keeping them saturated. The Garden is no loss to Camden, it has been for many years a low rum-hole and gambling shop.

30 September, Saturday.

We undertook to have a rehearsal to-night at our house, but it was "no go." Gerhart, our second fiddler, lives opposite the scene of last nights fire and I suppose he is drunk on the liquor that was carried into his house for safety.

1 October, Sunday.

At home reading Euclid. It seems to me that I am duller of apprehension or weaker in memory than I used to be. I really cannot retain even the simple theorems of the first book of the *Elements* now without a great deal of labor. My mind seems to have lost its capacity for the exact sciences. It has been wandering in the labyrinth of the law until it has lost its fixedness and its ability to be fixed.

2 October, Monday.

Mr. Elmer the Demo Candidate for Congress in the first district addresses a meeting in the City Hall to-night. Mulford and I concluded we had better go to see the French Opera troupe now playing in Philadelphia and did so. They performed the *Crown Diamonds* by Auber,[106] but as they sang and talked in French I don't know what the plot was. Music however, is a universal language; that we could understand, and it was very fine. Mad. Calvé is the prima donna.[107] She is quite pretty. The acting of the Company is much more chaste than that of our own players; there is none of that hauling and mauling, that excess of kissing, that overt blackguardism which you are sure to see in ordinary plays, with our native "talent." From the character of the French I did not look for an example in them, of delicacy and propriety....

3 October, Tuesday.

There was to have been a meeting in Fetterville to-night, but a party of Methodists got possession of the School house first, and were singing and praying away lustily. Of course we adjourned, though some of

106. Daniel François Auber's (1782–1871) *The Crown Diamonds* appeared at the Chestnut Street Theatre.
107. Julie Calvé was a highly popular singer in the 1840s, often performing with a French opera company from New Orleans.

the reformers would have ejected the tenants of the room and gone ahead, if they could have had their own way.

As the election approaches we will have a good deal of work to do. Mr. Gray's "triangle of young patriots" must make a considerable jingling, especially upon the Constitution question. A new Constitution we must have.

5 October, Thursday.

There was a meeting of "the friends of Sheriff Ware without distinction of party" at Jennett's house at Mount Ephriam to-night.[108] I rode out with Hineline or rather he rode with me, for of course I had to pay for the horse and waggon. It was a very good meeting. I was appointed on the Resolution committee, and prepared a set which were adopted by acclamation; they then called on me for a speech, which I declined on account of my youth. My uncle and about a dozen others spoke. Their addresses were short but not very sweet.

At home about midnight.

6 October, Friday.

This evening I addressed a Democratic meeting at Wilson's in South Camden.[109]

At home at eleven o'clock.

7 October, Saturday.

We had a splendid caucass to-night at Long-a-coming. "The triangle," and Curts and Miller[110] went up from Camden. Hamilton spoke first, then myself (and I never before made a speech with which I was satisfied afterwards) then Mulford, and finally Miller. The last speech was very humorous and kept the house in a roar. The meeting I think will do some good in old Waterford.

At home at three o'clock.

9 October, Monday.

There was another Ware meeting at the Buck-tavern to-night.[111] Hamilton and Miller spoke. I declined. They say that Mark will get four or five hundred majority, but this is thought by others to be an over-estimate. The election of to-morrow and next day is going to be very warm in old Gloucester.

At home a little before midnight.

108. James Jinnett was proprietor of the old tavern at Mount Ephraim from 1827 to 1860.

109. James H. Wilson was proprietor of the Washington Hotel in South Camden.

110. Miller was probably Lafayette Miller of Cape May.

111. One of old Gloucester County's most famous inns, Buck Tavern was located on the road from Gloucester City to Woodbury in present day Westville.

10 October, Tuesday.

There was a strong poll in Camden to-day. In the evening Mulford and I went over to get the returns from Philadelphia, but found out about midnight that we would not be able to learn any thing until morning; and so came home in a small boat.

11 October, Wednesday.

The election concludes to day. They finished counting off in our township a little after one o'clock, and Mr. Garrett and I started for Woodbury with the returns. Just as we were leaving Cake's hotel we met Mr. Gray and Mr. Cooper coming home from the out townships. We asked them the result, and Gray replied "Faith Garrett I shouldn't wonder if you have elected your whole ticket! We have got but thirty one majority in Waterford, Union and Newton." The majority in Camden for Ware was a hundred and seventy eight, and on the rest of the ticket a hundred and fifty. With this good news we started, and drove through, pretty smartly. We reached Woodbury a little after two in the morning. Smallwood, or "Ephriam Smooth" was standing before his house when we passed, and followed us down to Pearce's hotel.[112] Sheriff Ware, Joel G. Clark, Ben Roberts, young Caldwell and Bob Smallwood, Bill Fisher, Clerk Bradshaw, and a good many others there waiting for Camden and Washington; all the other townships having arrived.[113] Without these two Ware was two or three hundred ahead, and the rest of the ticket uncertain. The heavy majority from Camden decided the result at least as to Wood and Stratton on the Assembly ticket and Browning on the Council.[114] The Loco-focos then gave way to rejoicing and gladness, and such a noisy set I never saw. The Sheriff invited us into the jail, where we took supper, after which they gave three cheers for Camden. Gray, Browning, Cooper, Dudley, Morgan, Hineline and Cassady had come down immediately after us, but the four first being Whigs pretty soon went home sick. At four

112. John C. Smallwood (1797–1878), one of Gloucester County's most powerful politicians, would soon begin four terms as president of the New Jersey Senate. Ephraim Smooth was a character in John O'Keeffe's popular play, *Wild Oats*, which had been performed at several Philadelphia theatres in recent months. Thomas A. Pearce was the current owner of Woodbury's Washington Hotel.

113. Clark was a Gloucester County judge in the 1830s and 1840s; Roberts was probably Benjamin Morgan Roberts who died at Haddonfield in 1853; Caldwell was probably a son of James W. Caldwell of Deptford Township, who ran, unsuccessfully, for sheriff in this election; Robert M. Smallwood (1827–56) was the young son of John C. Smallwood; William C. Fisher (1824–49), son of Woodbury attorney Michael C. Fisher, was a law student; Henry Bradshaw had been Gloucester County clerk since 1837.

114. Thomas B. Wood, Gloucester City storekeeper, and Nathan T. Stratton of Woolwich Township won seats in the state assembly. Joshua P. Browning (1800–85), of Gloucester, was elected to the legislative council or state senate.

o'clock "the old General" not having come in, an express was sent for the returns to the Burnt House.[115] About five we had the whole county in, and sure enough Ware's majority is over five hundred. Browning is elected, and so [is] Wood and Stratton. Mr. Elmer on the Congress ticket leads Wales a few votes.[116] This is a glorious victory; one however that nobody expected.

12 October, Thursday.

We got back from Woodbury about half past six o'clock, and I immediately forwarded the Gloucester returns to the Trenton papers. At nine o'clock, without a wink of sleep, I started for Moorestown with mother on a visit to Hugg's. They are about moving into their new house. We had a very pleasant time, though I occasionally felt a little drowsy.

I arrived in Camden about eight o'clock. Enough has been heard to satisfy me that New Jersey is redeemed.

For a wonder I was in abed to-night by eleven o'clock.

13 October, Friday.

Every thing is ours! All the Congressmen, but the one from the Essex district, where an Independent is elected—and both branches of the Legislature. The Constitution movement has been the cause of this great revolution. To the Whigs the result is overwhelming. Poor Mr. Gray actually wept, when he heard the returns from East Jersey. The new counties which Pennington and Company cut out to secure the Whigs in the ascendancy have gone against them![117] They are blown clear out of water.

14 October, Saturday.

The Whigs have very long faces. Hineline is almost crazy with joy. It is wise perhaps for us to rejoice now, for I hardly imagine the Whigs will give us a chance next year.

I endeavoured to-day to make up for my recent losses of sleep.

16 October, Monday.

I resumed my studies at the office this morning. For the last three weeks I have done nothing much but electioneer. The Whigs having been most essentially trounced I can go on with Chitty cum laeto corde.

---

115. Mickle means that the voting returns from Washington Township had not yet arrived. The identity of the "Burnt House" is uncertain, but it may have been a name for the Green Tree Tavern at the intersection of Egg Harbor and Green-tree Roads.

116. Elmer's opponent was Edmond L. B. Wales of Cape May.

117. Atlantic, Passaic, Mercer, and Hudson Counties had all been formed during William Pennington's tenure as governor, 1837–43.

17 October, Tuesday.

At the office.

This evening I was at an old visiting place in Camden. When I departed the youngest lady accompanied me to the door, and proposed a walk. I told her to get her bonnet, and she did so and took my arm. We went away up Love Lane. In returning the following conversation took place; one, it may be, of a good deal of significance.

"O, do tell me where Caroline Cole is!"

"Indeed, Miss, I do not know. She is in the country somewhere near Colestown."

"I haven't seen her for an age."

"Your acquaintance I trust is not to be interrupted—Cad would feel heavily the loss of a friend."

"Does she feel it more keenly than I?"

"Well, no—yes—I rather think she would. You have near and dear connections, lovely sisters and a doating mother. Cad has not. In their love and friendship, you have a treasure for which Cad must sigh in vain."

There was no reply made. When we reached the door I took the beautiful hand of my companion in mine. Perhaps I pressed it, for I felt that my conduct has unnecessarily wounded a heart as pure as noble as ever breathed, and but for **that letter**, and my cursed pride, I could have asked her forgiveness. . . .[118]

18 October, Wednesday.

This morning Edward Cole, his lady and one of her sisters and myself went upon a visit to Miss Caroline Cole, who is staying at a relative's upon the road leading from Ellisburg to Moorestown, and within a short distance of Cole's Church. We found Cad in excellent health—with cheeks as red as a milkmaid's and spirits buoyant as air. She is far happier in the country than at home; for here she has no step-mother to tyrannize over her.

After dinner we took a stroll up to the Church.[119] This is one of the oldest buildings in this part of the country, and by far the oldest Episcopalian church in Gloucester county. It is built of wood, and the boards are covered with moss. There is an air of antiquity about it, with which the sycamores and poplars around it, now seer with the frosts of autumn, well correspond. The tottering house and the blighted trees, alas! are not the only monuments of Time's changing power. All

118. Mickle again refers to the pseudonymous letter first mentioned in the entry for 25 March 1843.

119. St. Mary's Protestant Episcopal Church, better known simply as the Colestown Church, was built in the 1760s and destroyed by fire in 1899.

around, beneath, within, above, us, tells that we too must pass to decay. Where is Morgan Starn, the romping boy who used to dandle me on his knees, and tell me he would work for me, when I became a man? I become a man this day; but he sleeps beneath a little mound west of the church—a sleep free from toil and void of trouble. And where are his brothers Benjamin and Abner? They lie by his side, and all of them that is left is the name.

In one corner of the yard repose George and Franklin Browning. Frank was my most intimate friend. We had lived for many years of our boyhood side by side, and we loved each other with the affection of brothers. While I was at Burlington School he took the scarlet fever and died; and his family say that during his rational moments up to the moment of his death he continued to ask why I did not come to see him. O Frank! if I could have embraced thee once, the tears I now shed would not have been so bitter. I can hear thee now chiding my cold neglect—but thou dost me injustice. Such was the suddenness of thy departure that the news of thy sickness and thy death came together. But why this apology? Thou knowest all things now, I hope. Thou knowest I loved thee then and that I love thee still.

The last time I saw Frank he told me candidly that he loved the girl who now hanging on my arm, was looking with me at his grave; and Frank's warm heart loved not weakly or doubtfully; its affection was strong wild and enthusiastic. We gazed at the narrow abode of our common playmate until our eyes began to fill with tears, and then turning away I hinted at the confessions he had made to me. I saw the allusion was painful to my lovely companion, and turned the conversation.

The visit to the grave-yard left a gloom upon my spirits throughout the afternoon. Yet I enjoyed myself very much, and was very loth at sunset to say good-bye to Cad, and start for home.

Since I am now entering upon manhood, and shall have more calls upon my time, it will be necessary for me to confine the memoranda of my diary to important things and events only. Amidst the press of business, and the turmoil of actual life of which heretofore I have only been a loop-hole spectator, I will be unable to find hours to devote to bagatelles. I have got into the way of saying something every evening, and I suppose it will come handy to continue the habit. I cannot quite comply with the golden rule "When there is nothing to be said say nothing," but I can come pretty near it by saying very little under those circumstances.

21 October, Saturday.
I spent the evening at Ned Cole's very agreeably too. Susan has an

excellent disposition, and is better looking than her husband, though there is much in his countenance that I like.

23 October, Monday.

At the office, reading the book by Thomas F. Gordon on Decedents. This is the man who wrote the *History and Gazetteer of New Jersey.* If his law is not more correct than his history, I would not give much for it. He was a member of the Philadelphia bar—a very large man, Colonel Page says, whom the lawyers used to call Goosy Tom, from his stupid look.[120]

24 October, Tuesday.

This evening the Board of Trustees of the Washington Library Company met for the last time. There were present Messrs. Cowperthwait, Ogden, Folwell, Baxter and myself. We had got through with some business, when the question came up whether we should return to the shareholders of the old Camden Library Company, the books we had got from them. Cowperthwait and Ogden went against returning them, and Folwell for it—Baxter being neutral and I in the Chair. Notwithstanding my position, however, I went with Folwell for returning the books, believing it to be no more than an act of common honesty since we were about to exist no longer as a public company. In the course of the debate, Mr. Cowperthwait said, "The gentleman is willing enough to return the books, for he gave none to the society when it started." And so I own I did not; but I found the Company a room and fire-wood for three years as a recompense.

The remark however whether true or false was not to be borne from such a fellow as Sam. I sprang from my chair, and went around the table to him, and said in an angry tone "I have never robbed the Society, sir, as you have!"—accusing him of having cut the plates out of the *Casket,* which several members believe he did. The coward tho' put this in his pocket, and said he could not be insulted. After exhausting my invective in attempting to provoke him to strike me, I filliped him under the nose. He jumped up and asked me if I meant to strike him? I replied of course I did. He then stepped back to pull off his coat, and I approached him but waited while he was thus engaged. Suddenly before he had got his coat unbuttoned and while I was yet off my guard he struck me upon the right side of the nose and made it bleed. While I was yet stunned I closed with him and threw him, but he turned me, and then the others separated us.

By this time I was entirely recovered from his first blow, and we

120. Gordon (1787–1860), a Philadelphia lawyer, wrote some fifteen books on law or history, but Page has confused him with another attorney of the same name. See entry of 12 February 1845.

went at it again. I struck him once and knocked him through the window, again, and he reeled against the book-case. After this last blow he wanted to explain, and said two or three times "Mickle, there must be some mistake!"—not heeding which I continued to thump him about the head and face. He was unable to stand his ground, but backed twice around the room, saying sometimes "I dont want to hurt you," sometimes "Take care I'll kill you," and sometimes calling upon the by-standers not to let me follow him. At last he got into the entry, and they shut the door; and here the fight stopped.

We resumed our seats at the table and took up the business where it had been so unceremoniously broken off. Sam's left eye by this time began to get black, and I remarked to him that he had a liar's badge upon his face. As soon as we finished the business he began to make off in a great hurry. "Stop!" said I, "you are going out of the room with the epithets liar and coward unrevenged." But he only hurried the faster, muttering something I did not hear.

The rest of us put up the stove-pipe which had been knocked down in the fray, and arranged the chairs in order. We then shut up, and I went down to the ferry and helped Bob to gear up his horses to go home. The last words I heard him say as he whizzed out of sight were "I guess Sam will not go to the office to morrow!" After this I went around to our house and washed my face and hands and tucked in my collar; and then dropped in at Delacour's. So little had I suffered that no body suspected I had been in a fight. Indeed the first blow I received was the only one I felt. When I was on my look-out he could not strike me about the face at all.

After having trounced this miserable puppy I enjoyed a sweet night's rest.

25 October, Wednesday.

My face is not marked in the least degree. I was at Delacour's this morning, and even Jim could not smell the rat. Baxter witnessed also that I am unscathed.

I was at the office to-day, and in the city this evening. My nose feels a little sore, and by some kind of irresistible propensity I keep pulling and rubbing it.

26 October, Thursday.

I have succeeded at last in pulling my nose out of shape. It is a little swelled.

27 October, Friday.

The bruise upon my nose is more apparent, so much so that instead of going out I remained at home reading Virgil. It also prevented me from attending a party at Sheppard's this evening.

29 October, Sunday.

My face is entirely well—since I have stopped meddling with it, with my fingers. Charley Bontemps spent the evening with me, and says Sam's eye is "black as hell" which I imagine must be pretty considerably black. He says also that Sam has reported that he could have whipped me, and that he got his black-eye, by a blow from behind!

30 October, Monday.

Mr. Gray gave me a book in M.S. on France and her Government by M. DeLammenais, (translated by M. Surault)[121] this evening to revise. He is still willing to call upon "the triangle" for favors.

31 October, Tuesday.

I crossed in the boat with Sam to-night. His eye is black enough, and he has a whipped look. I pitied the poor devil even while I peered very inquisitively into his discolored peeper.

2 November, Thursday.

This evening I spent at Ned Cole's. At Walnut Street Ferry on my return, I saw the famous Marshal Bertrand[122] the most faithful of Napoleon's friends. He had come on in the mail-line from Bordentown, and was attended with two or three French gentlemen. He appears quite infirm, and stoops somewhat in his gait.

3 November, Friday.

My cousins return to school to-day. They stay at West-Chester for a year yet.

I finished the revision of Lammenais' book this morning; and

In the evening I accompanied Miss Josephine Sheppard in a call on Miss Mary Gray.

4 November, Saturday.

The Haydn Society had a Concert on Wednesday night last; and Sam's mother told my aunt Mulford that I had said I meant to black his eyes so he could not assist therein. He did officiate however on that occasion, although his eye is yet quite black.

5 November, Sunday.

I read two hundred lines of the *Aeneid* to-day. Virgil's Latin is not so hard as I supposed.

121. Mickle refers to French religious writer Félicité Robert de Lamennais (1782–1854) and to François M. J. Surault, who lived on Second Street, Camden.
122. Henri Gratien, Comte Bertrand (1773–1844), French general and biographer of Napoleon, was currently touring the United States.

6 November, Monday.

This evening I went to the National Theatre. They played the *Swiss Cottage* which I had seen twice before.

9 November, Thursday.

To-day I rode up to Cooper's Creek to look at some timber mother is about to sell. After which I went to Ellis's Tavern and got dinner, and then proceeded on to see Cad, at Fellowship.[123] She is well. She had heard of my recent battle, and *damnabile dictu,* that I knocked Sam down, but that in the end he mastered me! Of course I set this right. I found the story had come through Haddonfield.

In the evening I called at Ned Cole's with a violin. He and his wife insisted on my taking the same to her mother's in Race Street—a prim old Quaker lady's; which I did. We had a Quaker dance, and a good deal of amusement, which we kept up so late that the mail boat left me.

10 November, Friday.

Colonel Richard M. Johnson arrived in Camden to day from a tour over New Jersey. I was introduced to him, and spent a half an hour or so in his private room at Elwell's. He is a fine looking old fellow, and wears an old velvet red vest, which he says is the same he had on when he killed Tecumseh.[124] He limps a little; but it used to be a saying in Washington when he was Vice President "The Colonel has got his lame leg on this morning." He addressed the citizens of this place this afternoon, but I did not hear him. His private conversation satisfied me that he can fight quite as well as he can talk. His object in all this travelling and speech making is of course to get the nomination for the Presidency. I was invited to make the welcoming speech to-day but declined. Mr. Jeffers was selected as the orator.

11 November, Saturday.

I sold my mother's wood to day for thirty six dollars an acre to Jacob Troth. Heulings Haines and Joseph Stoy wanted it for thirty, and I told them that if Troth did not deal they could have it.[125] His coming down and closing the bargain supercedes the negociation with them.

123. The Waterford Hotel at Ellisburg, six miles southeast of Camden, was operated by members of the Ellis family for many years. Fellowship is a small town two miles southwest of Moorestown.

124. Johnson claimed to have killed Shawnee chief Tecumseh (1768?–1813) at the Battle of the Thames in the War of 1812.

125. Troth (d. 1857), a sawmill owner, was a prominent citizen of Delaware Township who was to serve as a New Jersey assemblyman in 1848. Stoy (d. 1881) held land north of the Marlton Turnpike, just east of today's Stoy's Landing Road.

13 November, Monday.

I challenged Cowperthwait to another combat to-day, through Charles Bontemps. He showed the white feather completely. My reason is his continuing to deny that he was whipped. I wish to demonstrate it to his own satisfaction.

15 November, Wednesday.

This morning, I rode up to Cooper's Creek to assist Charles Beck Esq.,[126] to survey the timber which I lately sold for my mother. It was an unpleasant work, and required me to crawl through briars and stand in mud and water from nine o'clock in the forenoon until nearly sunset.

16 November, Thursday.

Captain Sloan, Recorder of Camden, Isaac Winner, Methodist Pastor,[127] Mr. Delacour the druggist, and myself, went together this morning to the quarterly meeting of the Gloucester County Temperance Society at Haddonfield. It was a very slim meeting and a very dry one. But for the comical grimaces of President Sloan in putting motions before the house it would have been intolerable. The old gentleman would get part the way through, then forget the next word, and commence a most ludicrous bobbing of the head and twisting of the features, which he would continue until the delinquent word occurred to him. My object in attending this meeting was not so much, I confess, to forward Temperance, as to administer an antidote to the lie which Cowperthwait has circulated among his relatives in this town.

This evening Mulford and I were at Sheppards. By the by said Mulford is now an Esquire—he was admitted to the bar yesterday.

17 November, Friday.

This evening I accompanied two of the Sheppards to a little soirée at William Coffin's, Front Street, Camden.[128] We had the aristocracy forsooth; to wit the Brownings—and Mrs. Jeffers! . . . There was, however, quite an agreeable company, and I did not regret going. Miss Josephine sang *A life on the ocean wave,* and Catherine Browning *the old arm chair.* The latter lady is so fat that she entirely submerges the piano-stool.

126. Beck, formerly a resident of Camden County, was currently a Burlington County attorney.

127. Winner had recently become pastor of Camden's Third Street Methodist Church and would remain in that post until 1844.

128. William Coffin, Jr. (1801–72) had a glass factory on Front Street, above Plum. He was later active in the glassworks at Winslow, a cobalt and nickel refinery in Camden, and in the Camden and Atlantic Railroad.

18 November, Saturday.

Troth paid earnest to day on his timber-purchase. I have lately sold twenty acres of my own timber, also; Joseph Githens and William Guy are the purchasers at Githens' own offer, three dollars a cord on the stump.

19 November, Sunday.

This evening I was in the city; *at quomodo actus sum non audeo, vel volo, scribere.*[129]

20 November, Monday.

At office; *Nec possum, ob res gestas proximâ nocte, multum discere. Non tamen mente tanto quam corpore invalidus sum—Infandum!*

22 November, Wednesday.

O for another fight, or something to break this awful monotony! It is nothing but, "at the office," "at the office."

25 November, Saturday.

Doctor Harris, the President of the Ferry Company, died to-day.

This evening I was in Philadelphia at a Book auction. I bought Ewing's *Philosophy*, Breckinridge's *Tour* and Paley's *Theology*. They sold an articulated skeleton for about six dollars!

27 November, Monday.

Cad got back to-day from her three months visit. I spent the evening at her father's, with herself, her brother and wife, and her cousin.

28 November, Tuesday.

There was a little gathering at Ned Cole's to-night, in commemoration of Cad's return. We had another Quaker dance, I, a Quaker also, doing the fiddling. I slept at Burr's.

I subscribed to-day for the Philharmonic Concerts, which begin tomorrow evening. The holders of tickets have the privilege of being present at their rehearsals.

29 November, Wednesday.

This evening Ned Cole and Susan, and Cad and I, went to the opening Concert of the Philharmonic. The music was grand. Monsieur Bley[130] performed a grand violin solo, but he is inferior to Nagel. The country by the by, is full of great violin players just at present. Besides

129. Mickle's reluctance to tell his whereabouts, and his weary comments of the following day, are indications that he may have visited a brothel.
130. Jules Bley was an obscure violinist who billed himself as "first Violin Solo at the Gymnase Musicale, Paris."

the two I have named there are Monsieur Artot, Ole Bull, young Wallace and many more.[131] Ole Bull has the greatest reputation.

I lodged at Burr's again to-night.

1 December, Friday.

It snowed so hard this morning that I concluded not to go to the office. . . . I reviewed several of the rules of Algebra. My taste for the mathematics was never so keen as at present. I really enjoy the labor of solving an equation, or evolving a remote root.

6 December, Wednesday.

This evening I took Miss Josephine to the Baptist Church, to hear a debate on the right of selling rum. The fellow who contended that it was right used two others up, who argued the contrary. I believe however all the parties are members of the Temperance Society. Captain Taylor[132] is now the President of the Camden Association, which has very considerably flagged under his direction. They invited me to preside over the discussion to-night, but no, thank'e.

7 December, Thursday.

It has been snowing hard all day. In the morning I concluded I would remain at home and read Virgil; but having read until noon, I left Aeneas, and Dido . . . and went over to the office. Here I finished Espinasse on Evidence. Since the 25th of last May, I have read the following books: Buller's *Nisi Prius*, Tidd's *Practice*, 2 volumes, Chitty on Bills, Chitty's *Pleadings*, Gordon on Decedents, Gilbert on Rents, Espinasse on Evidence, II and III Blackstone's *Commentaries*, Several Cases; and Much miscellaneous law matter.

8 December, Friday.

This evening King and Hamilton and I undertook to go a-sleighing; but we only got as far as Ward's lane, where seeing nothing but mud ahead, we turned around and came home.

15 December, Friday.

This evening I called with Cad and Cousin Em, on Miss Ann Mulford at the Misses Gill's School out Chesnut Street.[133] She entertained us very politely except she forgot to ask the girls to take off their

---

131. Alexandre-Joseph Montagney Artôt (1815–45), a Belgian, and William Vincent Wallace (1812–65), an Irishman, had recently completed tours of the United States. Ole Bornemann Bull (1810–80), a Norwegian, was truly one of the great violinists of his day. He made five tours of the United States in the early 1840s.

132. Joseph Taylor, a Camden boat-builder, was also active in local nativist groups.

133. The school was probably at the home of Sarah Gill, 504 Chestnut Street.

bonnets and cloaks. I had a good laugh at their expense, for knowing something about boarding-school manners I had left my over-coat behind me at Ned Cole's.

18 December, Monday.
Writing a New Year's Address for old Levi Beckett,[134] the carrier of the *Eagle,* and reading law.

Col. Shamburg has got into a war with the editor of the *Forum*[135] about Captain Stockton and the *Princeton.*

19 December, Tuesday.
I stay now at the office from nine till two, then come home and read Virgil till dark.

22 December, Friday.
To-day I concluded an arrangement with Hineline and Curts, by which I shall become editor of the *Eagle.* They will intimate as much in to morrow's paper.

23 December, Saturday.
At the office.
Some people are on the qui vive as to who is the young man that is going to associate himself with the *Eagle* men. They announce the fact in this morning's paper with a great flourish of trumpets, I suppose. At all events, it is known out of doors, that a change will be made.

25 December, Monday.
I arranged a little party for this evening, in order to make certain matters straight—to wit: Mulford invited Cad to go to an exhibition in Philadelphia, and she consented. I soon dropped in to see her, and invited myself to join her and Mulford with the Sheppards. With Hannah and Jo, therefore, I met them at the Artist's Fund Hall, where there was a good display of pictures by West, and other eminent artists—among them the famous one of *Death on a pale horse,* at which I could gaze for a month.[136]

We all returned in the mail-boat, after passing a very pleasant evening—and to me an important evening too.

134. Camden city directories list Beckett as a laborer, living on Reese Street, above Spruce.
135. James S. Wallace was editor of the *Forum,* a short-lived Whig daily, with offices on Chestnut Street.
136. Benjamin West (1738–1820) had first exhibited this renowned work in 1817.

26 December, Tuesday.

It is hard to study during this festive season, but I did study to-day and that very industriously.

30 December, Saturday.

The *Eagle* this morning announces the arrangement of Friday week—I expected it last Saturday.

This evening, Miss Ann Mulford, I beg pardon Miss Anna Mulford, and I called at Sheppard's.

31 December, Sunday.

The last evening in the year I spent in a moon-light walk with Josephine. I left her at McCalla's,[137] and went in the meanwhile to see Mr. Gray and apprize him of my initiation into the fraternity. We had a long talk on politics, and my new relations; and I never stopped for my sweet companion until nearly ten o'clock.

137. The home of Aulay McCalla, cashier of the Camden Bank, was on Cooper Street, above Front.

Cape May Island

1844

1 January, Monday.   New-Year's day.

The new year opens with cold but pleasant weather; it is evident, however, that we are going to have quite a mild winter, as we have had for some years back. There is a manifest change operating in our climate, which as I have elsewhere hinted, is attributed by some to the clearing off of the western country, whereby the snow is sooner melted, and to the increase of hearth-fires consequent in civilization. Still we are many degrees behind the corresponding latitude of Europe even in mountainous countries, and we may reasonably expect the mollification to go on until we have the same climate they have. . . .

2 January, Tuesday.

The political prospects at the beginning of this year are dark for the Democratic party. A strange infatuation has seized our leaders, and they seem determined to nominate Mr. Van Buren again; and if that is the case the opposition who are united upon Mr. Clay, will elect him. Col. Page read me a letter some time ago from Mr. Blair of the *Globe*,[1] the leading Van Buren organ in the republic, wherein that

1. Mickle's entry of 22 September 1843 reported that the letter was not from Francis P. Blair (1791–1876), but from his co-editor, John Cook Rives.

acute politician expresses his fears that Calhoun and Tyler will unite to defeat Martin's election; which he opines they will do, if they can draw off one eighth of the democratic votes. It was an impolitic move in the democratic press to refuse to welcome Tyler into the party when he sought it, and as things now look, we shall reap the fruits in Harry Clay's election.

3 January, Wednesday.

I to-day began my new duties as editor. . . . Mr. Gray, by the by, in his paper of this morning alludes to the arrangement of which I informed him a few evenings ago, soaps me with the adjectives "capable and ardent," and concludes by appending an extract which proves that some young men become attached to their party without a why or wherefore! We will, however, get along very smoothly.

4 January, Thursday.

Having recently showed Isabel Segunda's letter to the Sheppards, they gave me to understand they knew nothing about it. Their opinion is that Angeline Turner wrote it, and I guess that is the true one. Now therefore I can be as intimate as ever at the Parsonage—but how can I ever apologize sufficiently for my conduct to Josephine? . . .

5 January, Friday.

This evening I took two of the Sheppards—it was either to night or last night and I'll be hanged if I can now remember which!—to a lecture in the City-hall, on magnetism. This, however, I do remember, that Professor Rodgers[2] was the lecturer, and that some of the experiments were quite convincing. A Miss Carter, one of the audience was magnetized collaterally, as it were, and went through several demonstrations in neurology; but Miss Carter aforesaid is a Methodist, and Methodists are generally very credulous and easily influenced through the imagination. . . . It will not do to reject this new wonder—not very new either is it, for Hannah More mentions it, and so did Lafayette in a letter to Washington, and my friend Crump of the *Inquirer*[3] contends that it was even known to the Greeks and Romans, and used it in their oracles—it will not do, I say, to reject it, for that is not fashionable among those who wish to be esteemed intelligent; but on the other hand it is hard to believe.

2. Probably Henry D. Rogers (1808–66) of Philadelphia, a professor of geology at the University of Pennsylvania, or his brother James B. Rogers (1802–52), professor of chemistry at the Medical Institute of Philadelphia.
3. More (1745–1833) was an English author, largely of religious material. William Crump, listed as an editor in the Camden city directory for 1850, was probably an employee of the Philadelphia *Inquirer*.

7 January, Sunday.

To-day I was setting type to help the printers get out their paper. It is surely a "work of charity" however to enlighten the public.

9 January, Tuesday.

At the office, reading the *Pennsylvania Blackstone*.

This evening I took Cad to the second concert of the Philharmonic Society.

10 January, Wednesday.

This morning Mulford and I took a sleigh-ride up to Jacob Troth's, to resurvey the tract of timber which my mother lately sold. Mr. Nicholson and we ran it off again.

Gray's paper this morning gives me a pleasing notice, but lashes Hineline and Curts without mercy.

11 January, Thursday.

This morning I took up as the lumbermen say, that is took an account of, the wood I recently sold to Guy and Githens. I had a bad cold when I went upon the ground but standing for two hours in the snow seems to have mended it.

13 January, Saturday.

The *State Gazette* this morning notices me favorably. My promise of moderation seems to have conciliated the Whigs.

There was a private exhibition before twenty of us this afternoon in magnetism, for which we paid ten dollars. The experiments on the Rev. Mr. Sisty, were very unsatisfactory, but "sure the pleasure is as great of being Cheated as to cheat."[4]

14 January, Sunday.

To-day I was busied in preparing some sketches of the history of Gloucester county. In the evening I accompanied the Sheppards to church. Mr. Taylor[5] preached an excellent sermon. He said among other things "There are dark days ahead of the church! I believe that there are young men in this congregation who will yet see blood shed to save her!" This exclamation, earnest and sincere, brought the sleeping deacons to their consciousness, and thrilled the whole house. And Mr. Taylor is right in fearing that there are signs in our country which predict a dreadful contest. A hundred causes are now conspiring to

---

4. Mickle quotes Samuel Butler's *Hudibras*, Canto 3, line 1.
5. Thomas R. Taylor, pastor of Camden's First Baptist Church from 1842 to 1854.

make infidels, and I expect, should I live an ordinary life, to see a re-enactment of the French revolution.

15 January, Monday.

I spent this afternoon at the Philadelphia library, in ransacking the old books relating to the history of West Jersey.[6]

Mother got a paper from Iowa to-day, announcing the marriage of my uncle, my mischievous uncle, Charley C. Morgan. He has married a Smith—a daughter of the ubiquitous John Smith.

17 January, Wednesday.

Mr. Gray's paper continues to treat me with marked courtesy. All but the Democratic papers of Trenton have extended to me the right hand of editorial fellowship. Upon them I imagine young Hamilton for some reason or other has brought an unfavorable influence to bear.

18 January, Thursday.

This evening I had a most delightful visit with Josephine to Miss Gill's school. Miss Anna did not forget this time to treat her visitors politely. We stopped for a few moments at a Concert in the Museum, but found the music ordinary enough. We returned in the mail-boat, after a *tete-a-tete* which reminded me of old scenes.

20 January, Saturday.

The *Eagle* is not out regularly to-day, notwithstanding I helped set type myself for two or three hours.

I saw a member of our Legislature to-night, and from what I could learn they are doing but little save divorcing ill-contented benedicts. There will be a great number of changes wrought at the present session in township lines, and probably a new county will be made. There is an effort on foot to divide our county of Gloucester at Timber creek, and to erect a new county of the northern portion, called Delaware. This movement was begun by my uncle and a few others in 1838, since which time till now it has slept. The fate of the project is very doubtful.[7]

21 January, Sunday.

To-day I was engaged at home in writing my Sketches of Gloucester. I would digest them, and present something like a history to the public, but young Snowden of Mullica's Hill, an old school-mate, has a

6. Mickle refers to the Library Company of Philadelphia, then located on Fifth Street near Chestnut. He had now begun the research which would eventually result in his *Reminiscences of Old Gloucester* (1845).

7. Most proponents of the new county believed that it would be more likely to vote Democratic than Whig. The plan was being revived in 1844 because Democratic control of the state legislature now made its passage possible.

pre-emption right to the subject.[8] At all events I can furnish him with material; and that I'll do.

22 January, Monday.
This evening I was at Ned Cole's with my fiddle. We had a regular cotillion party, and I enjoyed myself much. One Quaker fiddling, and six dancing! What a spectacle for the overseers that would be!

23 January, Tuesday.
The *Sheet-Anchor* at last notices the new arrangement in the *Eagle* office, and that quite handsomely—so I did Hamilton or Mills, or both perhaps, injustice, in charging upon them a conspiracy.[9]

24 January, Wednesday.
I received a letter from Mr. Elmer to-day. Things look black in Washington for the Democratic party, but they may resume their brightness before next fall.

26 January, Friday.
Last night brought the first really cold weather of this winter. The thermometer stood this morning at—but I forget that somebody has stolen ours, and that our neighbors never had any. . . .

27 January, Saturday.
The remains of Commodore Porter, lately brought home from the Levant, were to day taken by a showy procession from The Navy Yard to St. Stephen's Church Yard. "The paths of glory lead but to the grave."[10]
The estate of poor Ogden was sold at Elwell's to-day under the Sheriff's hammer.[11] The old-man was there, tremulous with grief and wan with poverty—unpitied poverty. He seemed, as he saw house after house, farm after farm, go off at half its worth, as if he could have willingly jumped into the Delaware to rise no more. And there stood two of his lazy, worthless, sons, apparently unmoved at the wreck

8. William H. Snowden (1825–1909), who had attended Aaron's High School in Burlington with Mickle, collected materials on local history, but never published anything on the subject.
9. Franklin S. Mills was a prominent Trenton newspaperman and politician from 1839 to his death in 1885. He published the *Sheet Anchor of Democracy* between April 1843 and July 1845. For the "conspiracy," see entry of 17 January 1844.
10. David Porter (1780–1843), a prominent naval officer in the War of 1812, had died in Constantinople while serving as United States minister to Turkey. St. Stephen's Church was on Tenth Street near Market. Mickle quotes Thomas Gray's "Elegy in a Country Churchyard."
11. Robert W. Ogden's estate was sold to satisfy debts owed the state bank in Camden. He had served as cashier of the bank from 1827 to 1843.

which they had wrought and unsympathizing with the emotions of their gray-haired father.

29 January, Monday.

This evening I called upon Miss Josephine, now boarding in Arch street Philadelphia, and took her to the Museum and to the ingenious representation of Paris, now open in Chesnut Street, and which cost the maker sixteen year's labor. We had, or I had, at best, a delightful, a very delightful time, of which more anon.

30 January, Tuesday.

The river is very full of ice—so much so as to make the crossing very tedious and unpleasant; in consequence whereof I to-day commenced boarding with aunt Eliza in Cherry Street. I am writing now, at ten o'clock, at the office, with feelings that teach me that it is not to boys only and to weak school-girls, that "there is no place like home."

31 January, Wednesday.

I went home—that is to my Jersey home—this afternoon, to read the proof of the first side of the *Eagle*.

In the evening I went up to Sheppard's, but stopped on my way to see the body of Captain Ezra Rudderow who had just been mashed to death among the machinery of the steam-boat *Farmer*.[12] He was lying on the floor at Hollingshead's[13]—his brains dashed out, and his forehead touching his breast—a horrid sight! He was a school mate of mine at the Greenville school-house on Cooper's creek.

The politics of our country bear at present a singular aspect. Clay, who is by no means the choice of the Whig party in general is to be forced into nomination by the leaders—and Mr. Van Buren, notoriously unpopular with the mass of the Democratic party is to be made his competitor, whether or no. Buchanan has declined—Calhoun is to stand neutral or go over to the opposition—Tyler's case is hopeless—Stewart is forgotten—and Colonel Dick[14] is willing to take the nomination for the Vice Presidency, or any other smaller favor. Between Clay and Van Buren it seems the next match must come off—and the question will be, not who can run the fastest, but who cannot run the slowest. I fear exceedingly that Clay is to be elected, and this fear is the secret of the *Eagles* opposition to Mr. Van Buren. If the people will not look at principles, hold before them something that they may regard. It is better to amuse them even with a little humbug than to

12. Rudderow was killed when the *Farmer*'s engineer inadvertently set some machinery in motion while the captain was inspecting it.
13. Joshua Hollingshead's tavern was at the Market Street Ferry landing.
14. Colonel Dick was Richard M. Johnson.

suffer the Whigs to get the ascendancy. If expediency does not require a sacrifice of our principles, for heaven's sake, let us follow it, and save ourselves from another defeat.

1 February, Thursday.

At the office reading in Troubat and Haly's everlasting book of practice. Examination day is now only three months off, and I must pull up stoutly if I want to redeem the pledge that I made to Page when I called on him first about coming into his office. I really feel quite apprehensive about my qualifications now; but my very fear may save me.

This evening I called on Josephine, but went home in the mail-boat.

2 February, Friday.

This is proof-night again, and of course I had to be in Jersey. The *Eagle* printers are so stupid or so careless, that but for continual watching they would have the paper full of errors. No. I of my Sketches of the County will appear to-morrow. If they take well, and Mr. Snowden of Mullica Hill does not object, I will publish them in book form.

3 February, Saturday.

At home, reading law and geometry by turns. Boarding in town seems to be rather tough work. A very slight excuse indeed suffices to take me back to my little study, my old arm chair, and my mother's smiles.

5 February, Monday.

There was a slight earthquake a few days ago at Trenton and New Brunswick. It rattled the windows a little and scared the inhabitants a good deal and then ended. The same thing has been observed at Trenton before.

7 February, Wednesday.

Mr. Gray's paper is very attentive to the *Eagle* to-day. Last week he did not allude to "us"—that is the editorial Isaac Mickle; and so in Saturday's *Eagle*, "we" as aforesaid did not allude to him. As he gives he shall receive, but I will not be behindhand in returning courtesy....

Snowden of Mullica Hill called on me to-day about his History of the County of Gloucester. He has seen most of the authors who throw any light upon the subject, and seems to have read them well. He may produce a book that will be worth reading. He says he has no objection to my publishing the "Reminiscences" in a substantial form.

10 February, Saturday.

There was a meeting at Woodbury to-day, to appoint delegates to the Democratic Convention in Trenton, on the 22nd instant. The object of that convention is to appoint delegates to Baltimore—seven to represent New Jersey.[15] This is considered a Van Buren move, and will not give entire satisfaction. Some of the counties and districts have already named their representatives at Baltimore, and it is doubtful whether those delegates will consider themselves superceded. I drew up the Resolutions passed to-day. They protest against any departure from old party usages, and instruct our delegates to go first for Col. Johnson's friends, and secondly for those of Gen. Cass.[16]

14 February, Wednesday.
The *Mail* to-day is mum!
This evening I went at Col. Page's solicitation to hear one Major Tochman[17] an exiled Pole, deliver a lecture on the revolutions of his native land. It was a pretty good thing though two or three times he forgot what word he wanted to employ, and got into a terrible muss. Jo was to have gone with me—I called for her at her boarding house, but she was sick.

18 February, Sunday.
. . . This evening I accompanied Mr. and Mrs. Kelley to a debate or rather a lecture on Capital punishment. Some of the Philadelphians are crazy upon this subject at present, and seem determined to have the criminal law still further relaxed and mollified, although even now it is far too weak to restrain the wicked.

21 February, Wednesday.
In the 5 o'clock train this afternoon I went to Trenton with several other Democrats old and young.
At nine o'clock a grand Caucass met in the Council Chamber, to prepare for the Convention of to morrow. My uncle offered a resolution recommending said Convention not to appoint more than two Senatorial delegates to Baltimore. After a pretty hot debate it was laid on the table, and the Caucass adjourned, after some unimportant business. It is evident all is not going smooth to morrow.

22 February, Thursday.   Trenton.
I got to bed very late last night and slept but little. After the grand Caucass there was a sub-caucass in Mr. Green's room, composed of the anti-Van Buren men. I was sent for and went in. There were

15. The Democratic National Convention would be held at Baltimore in late May.
16. Lewis Cass (1782–1866), a Michigan politician and an advocate of national expansion, would receive the Democratic nomination in 1848.
17. Gaspar or Kaspar Tochman was one of the most active and famous Polish exiles in America. On this occasion, he spoke in the lecture hall of the Chinese Museum.

present Mr. James S. Green, James C. Zabriskie, Joseph A. Yard of the *Emporium,* Joseph Justice the Post-Master of Trenton, my uncle and one or two others.[18] Their course in Convention was agreed on, and to-day it was acted out. The Van Buren men are very intolerant—

Just after the Convention, which was very full, had organized, I departed—being committed to go to the Ball at Woodbury, to which end it was necessary I should take the noon train.

A little after eight o'clock—with darkness inpenetrable and wretched roads to cheer me, I started alone to our goodly shire town. I arrived in about two hours, and found the room full and the cotillions going on merrily. I never dance, but in promenading and looking at others I passed the night very agreeably. About half past two o'clock, Sheriff Ware and John W. Watson[19] came into the saloon—the latter pretty indefinitely drunk. They had just returned from Trenton, and gave me an account of the outrageous proceedings of the Van Buren men. Thereat I was so confounded that I really introduced Watson, in his booziness, to the belle of the room, Miss Doughton of the village of Westville.[20] My head was so full of Convention and log-rolling and wire-pulling and protesting and quarelling, that I really forgot that it was hardly according to Gunter to ask the handsomest girl to dance with the most intoxicated man, in the room. However I got Miss Doughten's attendant, Benjamin H. Browning, to explain and apologize to her, and perhaps the matter will all be right.

The fiddling and the dancing kept on until broad day-light. I started home about Six, but got the wrong horse. I went down with a Rosinante, but the hostler gave me a Bucephalus.[21] Thinking he needed the whip as much going as he did coming, by way of getting my hand in I gave him a cut just as I turned out of the tavern yard. Away he went with a tremendous bound—indistinct shouts were heard after me—on kept the unmanageable steed, down the hill, over the creek and up the hill again, as if the devil was after him. Observing that the harness had come off, by great exertion I curbed him in, and at last got him to stop entirely. Then, being overtaken by a wagon, I was told that I had made a mistake, and sure enough I had got Ned Andrew's firey gray instead of Charley Garrett's unfirey ditto. I returned,

18. Zabriskie (1804–83) was a banker and lawyer of New Brunswick; Yard, the editor of the Trenton *Emporium*; and Justice, a newspaperman and long-time postmaster of Trenton.

19. John M. Watson (1796–1878), a prominent Woodbury Democrat, had recently been appointed a common pleas judge.

20. Probably a daughter of Isaac Doughten, an important merchant in the village of Westville.

21. Rosinante was Don Quixote's tame mount, a quondam plowhorse. Bucephalus was Alexander the Great's spirited battle-charger.

exchanged teams, and came home; and thus ended my first ball in Jersey.

The Constitution Bill became a law to-day!

23 February, Friday.

I slept a few moments this morning while mother was getting breakfast, but after that kept awake the whole day.

In the evening the Concert and Lectures came off in the lower story of the Baptist Church. The house was jammed full. First came a piece or two of horrid music; then Mulford delivered an address of forty minutes . . . ; then came more excruciating music; then Isaac Mickle, Esq. read a lecture of fifty minutes on The duties of young Men, or any thing else he might have called it; then more music and the house dissolved. The people were drawn together I imagine more by Tom's incomprehensible announcement than by any respect for either him or me, or any love for joining ten cents apiece to a charitable object.

24 February, Saturday.

But did I not sleep last night? Ask the old clock, which told twelve to-day, before I saw day light. For once, the *Eagle* was in the dining-room before I was. It kicks a little this week against the proceedings of the Van Buren men—Wall in particular; and but for the new county, whose fate my course I am told will influence at Trenton, it should have kicked much more unequivocally. We raise to-day the flags of Col. Johnson "subject to the decision of the people fairly expressed."

26 February, Monday.

This morning Mulford and I undertook to go [*to*] Woodbury but our horse ran away and came near breaking our necks. We returned and got another, and succeeded in getting through, however, about noon. My business was to copy some old records in the clerk's office, concerning the early history of our county. In the course of my investigations I found that one Archibald Mickle figured quite conspicuously in juries grand and petit, as early as 1691.[22]

27 February, Tuesday.

Nothing is thought of or heard of now but the new county proposed to be called Delaware. Camden goes for it strongly and Woodbury and Haddonfield against it.[23] If carried, Timber Creek is to be the line between it and old Gloucester. My uncle has taken board at Trenton

22. Archibald (d. 1706) was the first Mickle to settle in the Camden area.
23. Camden was eager for the creation of the new county, partly because the city stood an excellent chance of becoming the county seat. Woodbury, the Gloucester County seat, would suffer by the change, of course, and Haddonfield residents were probably concerned about any added power or prestige for the upstart city on the Delaware.

as a member of the third house.[24] A new law, by the by, has been passed at his instigation, in place of the old Act of 1713, concerning the meadows between my fast land in Newton and that of the Kaighn family.[25]

29 February, Thursday.

This is the scape-day of leap year! I passed it in reading till evening, and afterwards by listening to some pretty good music at the Museum in Philadelphia.

News reached town to-day of the explosion of Captain Stockton's big gun, called the "Peace Maker," and the consequent death of Secretaries Upshur and Gilmer and four other magnates of the nation.[26] A terrible accident!

1 March, Friday.

The excitement in relation to the new County, now proposed to be called Camden, continues to increase. The bill has passed the lower house, notwithstanding the opposition of many influential men.

2 March, Saturday.

The *Eagle*, for fear of driving some of the Van Burenites into opposition to the making of Camden County is quiet to-day about the late Convention. I shall open my batteries as soon as that matter is out of the way, for I had rather, in the language of the last resolution passed upon the Candidates for the Presidency at the said Convention, "die by the right than live by the expedient."

The manner of log-rolling against which I complain is briefly this: The County of Gloucester, and a majority of the first Congressional district, do not want to see Mr. Van Buren nominated again. A vast majority of the delegates from the five lower counties, declined *protestando* to the Constitution of the Convention, to appoint any delegate; believing that the whole contrivance of the 22nd ultimo was intended to promote Van Buren's nomination. The protest was read in Convention, and all supposed the matter would there rest.

But Joseph Kille of Salem[27] afterwards rose, and taking the pro-

24. That is, as a lobbyist.

25. The new law, of 16 February 1844, authorized owners of the Little Newton Creek meadows to create a board of managers who would "put and keep in repair, the Tide-bank and Water Works" which protected the meadows from the tide in the Delaware. The law repealed an act of 13 February 1713, which had authorized a similar body.

26. Secretary of State Abel P. Upshur (1791–1844) and Secretary of the Navy Thomas W. Gilmer (1802–44) were killed when a gun exploded on board the battleship *Princeton*, commanded by New Jersey's Robert F. Stockton.

27. Kille (1790–1865), born near Bridgeport in Gloucester County, moved to Salem before 1822. He had recently served one term in Congress (1839–41).

testants by surprize, asserted that they had concluded to change their minds. He thereupon nominated one Ward of Cumberland as delegate, and the Convention ratified the appointment.[28]

Now the manner of Kille's appointment was as follows: At Salem Court (so says Newell[29] of the Bridgeton *Chronicle* and Clerk of Assembly) three or four persons pretending to be the democracy of the next county but one, Cape May, concluded they would nominate a man as delegate to Trenton. Leaving Cape May, as if she had no Democrat who could afford to go to the seat of government, they pitched upon Richard P. Thompson of Salem; and made him the representative of the Cape County. He being busy and not able to go, transferred his delegated and suspiciously delegated authority to Joseph Kille, a stuttering, head-strong, thick sculled companion, also a Salem man; and in his proxy he Thompson, who had no instructions himself instructed Kille to go for Van Buren men as delegates to Baltimore. And being thus the shadow of a ghost, Kille claimed his seat at Trenton, and the Convention admitted him, and he appointed Ward, a Van Buren man, as aforesaid. This much is necessary to explain the course of the *Eagle*. I am placed thereby in a ticklish position, and may do myself lasting injury as a politician—but whether or no, I am going to stand by the First District, whose dignity has been infringed, and whose voice has been basely perverted.

3 March, Sunday.

Curts dined with me to-day, and we were engaged for some hours in important deliberations concerning our forthcoming history of Old Gloucester. We at last concluded to publish it in octavo, an edition of five hundred, with three or four engravings, myself to indemnify any loss that may be sustained.

4 March, Monday.

Uncle came home from Trenton Saturday, but he returned this morning to watch the new county affair. How popular he will be hereafter in Haddonfield and Woodbury!

5 March, Tuesday.

At the office so far this week very assiduously. I generally spend most of the afternoon in the Philadelphia Library, ransacking for authority to be used in my history.

7 March, Thursday.

County stock is down! It is said some of the democrats in Council

28. The new delegate was James Ward, a Cumberland County judge.
29. James M. Newell (d. 1851) was a prominent citizen of Bridgeton and editor of the Bridgeton *Chronicle*.

are dodging. Clap your hands, O Haddonfield and Woodbury! Enjoy your triumph while you may!

8 March, Friday.

There was a full and hot Caucass to night for the township officers of Camden. I mixed not therein, not even by voting.

9 March, Saturday.

The news from Trenton to-day is rather unfavorable to the prospects of our new county. The bill has passed the lower house handsomely, but in Council—owing to the opposition of Mr. Browning and the Vice President, Patterson, its fate is very doubtful. An amendment has been tacked on requiring an election by the people on the Subject; and a motion to reconsider the said amendment failed yesterday by 9 to 8— Nelson[30] of Salem, a friend of the bill in the form its friends ask, being out of his seat. The whole matter is now postponed until Monday.

10 March, Sunday.

The friends of the new county are very busy—the wicked rascals!— in getting names to petitions for their scheme. They have had wonderful success, and probably will get enough signers to turn the now wavering scale. So mote it be—though as an antiquarian I dislike to see old Gloucester thus dismembered. . . .

11 March, Monday.

The first meeting of the holders of meadow on Little Newton Creek under the new law was held to day at Kaighnton. Charles Kaighn, John M. Kaighn, Elias Kaighn, William D. Kaighn, John Cooper and myself were present. I was made Clerk for the ensuing year—John Cooper and John W. Mickle managers—John M. Kaighn Collector—and Richard Fetters and Joseph Saunders appraisers.[31] What other business we did will more fully and at large appear by reference to my minutes.

A strong delegation from Woodbury and other places opposed to the new county went up to Trenton this morning, and an equally strong body of friends. Both sides are sanquine of success, and the rivalry in zeal is really amusing. There is a good deal of hard feeling between the opposite parties.

30. Joseph C. Nelson was a land surveyor from Pittsgrove.
31. The Little Newton Creek Meadow Company was organized to reclaim the low land near the Delaware River, long the property of the Mickle and Kaighn families. Among its organizers were Elias Kaighn (1799–1864), mayor of Camden from 1838 to 1840, and Charles Kaighn (1806–68), who would become mayor in 1845. Charles, John and William R. Kaighn were children of the late Joseph Kaighn (d. 1841); John Cooper of Woodbury had married their sister Mary. Joseph Saunders, a frequent office-holder in Deptford Township, had served in the New Jersey Senate from 1842 to 1843.

To-day at the town-meeting in Camden township I polled my first vote. My friend Mulford was moderator. I went the solid Caucass ticket agreed on, on Friday night last. . . .

12 March, Tuesday.

Certain news reached Camden to-day that the County bill has become a law, without the amendment. On receipt of the intelligence Messrs. Cowperthwait, the Mayor, Garret and Cole of the Council[32] and myself held a little caucass and concluded we had better organize the party of Camden County immediately for the election of a delegate to frame the new Constitution. The Whigs of old Gloucester have nominated Abraham Browning, but it is said three of the townships were not represented in the nominating convention, and that a majority of those present from the district now composing the new county were in favor of Doctor Isaac Mulford.

13 March, Wednesday.

We had another caucass this morning in Cole's shop and ratified the determination of yesterday, and agreed to call a convention at Camden on Saturday next. I immediately started for the country to get signers to the call. I visited Delaware, Newton and Union townships and procured a very respectable list of names—among the best that of old John Clement, the most violent Democratic opponent of the new county scheme. Very fortunately the *Mail* was delayed, so we could get our call published in it. When I gave it to Gray he turned to Dudley and said "with these fellows it's 'whistle and I'll come to you my lad.' It would take the Whigs a week to get these names!"

Mr. Jeffers arrived in Camden to-night with a certified copy of the county law. He came down on purpose to get that done which I have just said we did do. They talk of Jeffers, of Esquire Clement and my uncle for the delegate. Jeffers said in my presence to night. "There is but one man that we must think of—that is Captain Mickle; he must go." But I do not believe he can get the nomination.

15 March, Friday.

The Whigs of Camden County have called a Convention at Cake's Ferry for to-morrow, simultaneous with ours, to appoint a candidate for the Constitution honor. They had nominated Charles C. Stratton and Abraham Browning in old Gloucester before the division; and they cannot well get out of confirming Abraham's appointment. The other candidates are Joseph Porter and Doctor Mulford. The Doctor

32. John K. Cowperthwait was the current mayor of Camden. Isaac Cole and Charles S. Garrett were members of the common council.

thinks and with reason that there was some wire-pulling used at Woodbury, to give Browning the nomination.

The prospects of my uncle getting the appointment on our side,
begin to brighten. Mr. Garrett went up into Delaware [*Township*]
to day, and drummed out some who will prevent John Clement from
being chosen.

16 March, Saturday.

The Commissioners appointed in the law making the new county
met today at Woodbury. John W. Mickle, John K. Cowperthwait, Isaac
Hinchman and Joseph C. Collings were duly qualified; but Joseph
Saunders declined, and William R. Cooper after being sent for and
brought to Woodbury did the same—saying he wanted to know first
what the people thought of the law.[33] Mulford and I were also in our
old shire-town—I to get materials for my history. At the Convention
this afternoon neither my uncle nor I was present; but he got the
nomination unanimously, though young John Clement and the Brownings from Union were present.

17 March, Sunday.

Having got the Compromise tickets printed, with the names of
John W. Mickle and Abraham Browning thereon, I started this
morning to distribute them; being attended by Joseph Stetser[34] as
driver, and Mulford and Bontemps as companions. This being an
election without parties I thought it best to take Charley along—his
whiggery serving in a measure to neutralize the loco-focoism of us the
other three. We visited Union, Gloucester, Waterford and Newton
townships. Every thing looks calm, but I fear a mine. It is not likely
that my uncle, after his violent advocacy of the new county will be
elected without opposition. We got in Haddonfield a little before sunset, and Charley, who is a nephew of Judge Clement, and I called
upon the old man at Browning's request, to leave him some tickets.
He told us that thirty would be enough for Newton township, as there
would be no contest; and he insisted upon our staying to supper. We
did not avail ourselves of his kindness. Indeed I strongly suspect his
sincerity. He told me that young John was not at home—that he went
away after dinner. The thought crossed me that he was at Woodbury
or in Philadelphia getting ballots struck with his father's name.

33. The legislative act creating Camden County designated these six men to
meet on this date in order to divide the property, funds and tax burden of old
Gloucester County. Cooper, Hinchman, and Saunders were to represent the new,
smaller Gloucester County; Mickle, Cowperthwait, and Collings would represent
Camden County.

34. Stetser was a blacksmith of Plum above Front Street.

18 March, Monday.

Soon after the polls opened this morning news reached Camden that tickets were going in, in the country townships with the name of Clement on instead of my uncle's. We immediately sent an express, to rouse up our men and prevent the old hypocrite's treachery from doing much harm. We also went to work and got out a pretty full compromise vote in Camden township, which will probably save the caucass ticket.

I was in Philadelphia this evening. When I returned in the mail boat I found that my uncle led Browning in our township forty three votes. After waiting for the country returns until one o'clock in the morning I went to bed.

19 March, Tuesday.

Of course there can be no study until I learn the result of yesterday's election in our county. The townships come in slowly. In Newton and Delaware Clement has a heavy majority. If there is as much splitting in Waterford, Gloucester and Washington, my uncle is defeated. In Union a ticket was run with the names of Clement and Porter. This is the work of Joshua P. Browning. The modest gentleman could not find it in him to run "father-in-law Clement" and "cousin Abe" both at once; so the latter was discarded. These rebels shall pay for this!

20 March, Wednesday.

I believe John W. Mickle will after all help to make the new Constitution; the lower townships having adhered to the compromise, and Waterford having given Clement only three majority.

21 March, Thursday.

On Tuesday I last sent my compliments to old Clement, congratulating him upon his election, and the means by which he procured it. I was a little too fast. It is certain now that his treachery and hypocricy have failed.

This evening I took Miss Josephine to Gray's.

Yesterday young Howe the historian called on me and gave me a copy of his New Jersey book. He dined with me, and wrote a letter of introduction to Watson the Annalist,[35] which I shall use as soon as I have leisure. I showed Howe the proof of the first form of my *Reminiscences*, and he passed upon it quite a handsome compliment.

22 March, Friday.

Clement and Browning have behaved so badly about the new county

35. Philadelphia financier and publisher John Fanning Watson (1779–1860) had written his *Annals of Philadelphia* in 1830.

that I mean to give them a slight rub in to-morrow's *Eagle*. What shall I do? Ah! Clement shall be denominated a Whig, as he was at Trenton on a late occasion much to his discomfiture; and that will touch both him and his son-in-law.

25 March, Monday.

The Washington Manufacturing Company, incorporated at the last session of the New Jersey Legislature, want to buy the land in Newton belonging to my uncle and myself. Mr. David Brown, the head man of the concern has taken a great fancy to that property, and has insinuated that they would give us eighty thousand dollars for it. The land has been in the name so long and we want money so little that we concluded not to sell. My uncle left the answer to me, and I said **no**.[36]

This evening Ned Drayton and I were on a musical visit to Sheppard's.

26 March, Tuesday.

Colonel Page examined me to-day, and complimented me on my proficiency in the II Bla. *Comm.*[37] The said compliment was as unexpected as—undeserved!

In the evening Ned and I were at Cole's.

The first form of my pamphlet history was printed yesterday. I read proof some six times; yet one **n** is upside down—Christina is made Christiana—and Manaathan is misspelt.

28 March, Thursday.

A great meeting was held at Woodbury to-day to show the unpopularity of the law making Camden County. The Commissioners also met at the same place.[38] Thinking that probably there might be some hard talking and even a little fighting about the vexed question, I went down (as I was invited to by the *Constitution* of last Tuesday) to hear, look on, and if needs be stand by the dignity of the state in general, and of my uncle the Commissioner in particular. The meeting was quite large—several speeches were made, in which the editor of the *Eagle* in common with all Camden received some pretty hard Thrusts. The Court being in session I dropped in there after being considerably abused in the Court House yard. Abraham Browning was making a speech in the case of *Bateman* against *Ware*,[39] and in the

36. It was a testament to the family's wealth that Mickle and his uncle decided not to sell their land to Brown. Brown eventually located his successful new company in Gloucestertown, radically improving the economy and perhaps ensuring the continued existence of that town.

37. The second part of Blackstone's *Commentaries*.

38. See entry of 16 March 1844.

39. The suit for damages resulting from Ware's attack on Bateman (see entry of 21 June 1843) ended with a verdict against Ware. Bateman was awarded one hundred dollars and costs.

course of his argument while I was leaning unobserved over the rail he passed quite a compliment on the manner in which the *Eagle* has been conducted since it came into my hands. A Whig squire of old Gloucester whose name I do not know turned to me and said "Browning speaks of you quite handsomely" or something to that effect. And so this I will offset to the *per contra* of the nullifiers[40] on the outside of the court house. I dined with Judge Elmer at Humphrey's,[41] and spent most of my leisure time in the Clerk's office, copying old records for my book.

In the evening I called at Sheppard's.

30 March, Saturday.

The *Eagle* charges the anti-county men with being nullifiers, and so they are. The number issued to-day contains a brief of the proceedings at Woodbury on last Thursday, and the second communication signed "Vindex,"[42] which by the way is partly mine and partly Mulford's.

1 April, Monday.
At the office all day.

In the evening I took my fiddle—poor, neglected friend! and went with Mulford to Sheppard's. The old lady was away, and so we had a merry time—yea, even—who'd a-thought it?—even dancing.

2 April, Tuesday.
The *Constitution* is full of replies to last Saturday's *Eagle*.[43]

I was examined again to-day by my sanguine preceptor. Would that he could impart a little of his confidence in my acquirements to myself! ...

5 April, Friday.
The democrats have been beaten in Connecticut. About this time four years ago began the disasters of the good old cause. Our prospects now look even worse than they did then; but there is a gleam of day break in the question of the annexation of Texas which may yet floor Harry of the West.[44]

---

40. Mickle calls the protesters "nullifiers" because they want to nullify the act creating Camden County. The term was highly pejorative because it summoned up memories of South Carolina's nullification of a national law in 1832–33.

41. Daniel Elmer (1784–1848), of Cumberland County, was a justice of the New Jersey Supreme Court from 1841 to 1845. He and Mickle dined at Smith's Tavern, sometimes called Paul's Hotel, then run by Richard Humphreys.

42. "Vindex" argued that Camden was the best location for the seat of the new Camden County.

43. The Woodbury *Constitution*, opposed to the creation of Camden County, was responding to Mickle's charges that anti-county men were "nullifiers."

44. Mickle and other Democrats hoped that Henry Clay would express opposition to the United States' annexation of Texas and lose the election as a consequence.

6 April, Saturday.
This evening I was at the Walnut Street Theatre.[45]

7 April, Sunday.
Writing the IX Chapter of my pamphlet. I stole time enough however in the morning to go with Mulford and his brother to see the Easter mummeries at St. Joseph's.

10 April, Wednesday.
The Native Americans have carried the City of New York.[46]

An incident occurred recently which foreshadows the nature of the coming political contest. The Steamboat *New Philadelphia* belonging to the Camden and Amboy Rail Road came out of the repairing dock last Monday with the picture of a coon exulting over a fox painted on each side of the wheel-houses.[47] A great hubbub was made and last night the pictures vanished! They were forced to take them down and say they were stolen.

11 April, Thursday.
Between my pamphlet history, my editorial labors and my legal studies, my diary must be somewhat lean for the balance of this month.

14 April, Sunday.
Busily engaged all day upon my pamphlet. I find by my researches in the Philadelphia Library and elsewhere there is material enough for a very full history of the eastern bank of the Delaware. Of this, if the pamphlet now in hand succeeds, I may avail myself and write a history of West Jersey.

This evening I called for the Sheppards and took them to the Methodist Church.

15 April, Monday.
This morning I was a while at the office but did not read much. I am examined frequently by Col. Page, who tells me I am sufficiently qualified to pass. For my part I doubt that same thing very much, yet my head is so full of various other things that I cannot set about making up for my deficiency. . . .

16 April, Tuesday.
The *Constitution* of to-day is silent about the new county. The fact

45. Mickle saw Richard B. Sheridan's *School for Scandal* and an obscure play called *Sleeping Beauty, or The Enchanted Wood.*
46. Nativism had waxed in America in the late 1830s and the American Republican Party was founded in New York City in June 1843. That party formed a coalition with Whigs in New York City in 1844 and succeeded in electing a nativist mayor.
47. The coon was a symbol of Clay, the fox of Van Buren.

is Mr. Barber[48] was too fast when he wrote that "the people meant not to regard the law as binding until passed upon by a future legislature" and now wants to back out.

17 April, Wednesday.

Mr. Bradley, the agent for Barber and Howe's *Historical Collection of New Jersey* has arrived in Camden, and is selling the work quite rapidly. That rascal Howe has attached to my account of Camden a history of the Heberton murder, which I by no means thank him for.[49]

20 April, Saturday.

To-day I went to Woodbury to make a search for John Richmond,[50] who thinks he has some claim upon an estate at Longacoming. I dined at Humphrey's with Abraham Browning and John B. Harrison.[51] The latter made some jocular remark about the "Buzzard," as the Whigs call the *Eagle*. "What do you mean, sir?" I inquired firmly and sternly; whereupon he apologized like a gentleman.

24 April, Wednesday.

An old domestic of ours, Sarah Collins, came to me in great tribulation to-day, to get me to procure her a divorce from one Thomson whom she has unlawfully married through ignorance. He has a wife living, and Mr. Taylor's church[52] of which both Sarah and her quasi husband are members are making a great fuss about it. I promised to see Mr. Taylor, and to file a petition for a divorce as soon as I am admitted to the bar.

25 April, Thursday.

This afternoon I walked down To Catharine Street to see the clergyman mentioned yesterday. He was not at home, but I had a talk with his wife.

Towards evening yesterday there was a gust or whirlwind that passed over Camden and did considerable injury. It blew down Elias Kaighn's new factory[53] near our house, and unroofed the boat sheds being built

48. Augustus S. Barber (1808–95), a native of Pennsylvania, was the founder (1834) and current editor of the Woodbury *Constitution*.

49. Mickle had cause for anger. The book, *Historical Collections of the State of New Jersey* (New York, 1844), credited him with the authorship of a four-page description of Camden, one-third of which was devoted to a gossipy account of the Heberton murder.

50. Probably the John Richmond who lived on Federal Street in Camden in 1850.

51. Harrison, a native of Gloucester County, was one of the senior lawyers in the county bar.

52. Philadelphia city directories show a Rev. John S. Taylor living at 47 Catherine Street, but do not identify the church with which he was associated.

53. Neither the Camden *Mail* nor the *Eagle* mentions any destruction at Kaighn's factory.

just south of the Rail Road. The hail broke several panes of glass at the Poplar Hill mansion, and I learn that a boy was picked up by the wind near the Newton meeting house, and carried a considerable distance. I never saw so hard a blow, but it did not last four minutes.

In the evening of to-day I finished my account of the Indians of West Jersey.

26 April, Friday.

Great preparations are making for the Whig Mass Meeting at Baltimore. I suppose they will have a large gathering to nominate Clay.

27 April, Saturday.

Whig delegates are flocking to Baltimore. It is evident from their conduct that they mean if possible, to revive the system of electioneering which they employed in 1840; but Clay, alas! is not a General—he has never killed an Indian.[54]

28 April, Sunday.

Mr. Clay has just come out with a letter against the Annexation of Texas.[55] This matter until now has made but little talk; but it is destined to exercise great influence over the next Presidential election, and for him who goes for Texas the country I think will go. It is expected that Mr. Van, who now has a majority of the nominating delegates, will follow with an annexation letter.

29 April, Monday.

Alas! alas! Mr. Van Buren has come out against annexation too! He has a long and able letter in the *Globe* of Saturday night, dated three days after Mr. Clay's, taking decided ground—not, like Mr. Clay, against annexation "in any view of the case," but against immediate annexation.[56]

30 April, Tuesday.

There is a great stew in politics just now on account of Mr. Van Buren's course on the Texas question. He must be—he will be, dropped.

1 May, Wednesday.

The impression begins to be fixed that Mr. Van Buren will be dropped as the Democratic nominee. So many of his friends, particularly in the South, have committed themselves to the annexation, that

54. Mickle jokes about the current vogue for military heroes in politics.

55. Clay's so-called "Raleigh letter" was first published in the *National Intelligencer* of 27 April. It rejected annexation as a likely cause of war between the United States and Mexico.

56. Van Buren's letter, which also expressed a fear of war with Mexico, is generally considered to have been the death blow to his pursuit of the Democratic presidential nomination in 1844.

they cannot unite on him. Col. Page, John M. Reed,[57] Mr. Dallas and other leading Van Buren men, recently got up a meeting in Philadelphia, to pledge their candidate as it were to annexation, and thus deprive Tyler of the sole advantage which he now has upon that question. Col. Page wrote the resolutions, and he has seen no reason I imagine to change his position since. In the democratic ranks men do not doff and don principles to suit their favorites.

2 May, Thursday.

Yesterday finished my three years in Colonel Page's office, and I am now entitled to admission—if qualified in other respects—to the Philadelphia bar. That I have sadly abused my privileges and wasted my time, my own conscience as well as the foregoing pages of this diary, attests. Yet while I own that I might have been much more studious than I have been, I can say in all sincerity I could not have been more pleasantly situated than in the office of my preceptor. Since the absconding of Bill Vanarsdale, there has nothing turned up to interrupt in the least the harmony and good feeling of my relations at No. 101, while the stern integrity, the unwavering democracy and the ever ready wit and ever open generosity of my tutor, have left upon me impressions which a thousand years could not efface or dim. Indeed had I never opened a law book at all, my tutelage would have been invaluable. As "evil communications corrupt good manners" so intercourse with men of the stamp of James Page elevates while it pleases, and strengthens while it refines.

I was registered as a student on the 3d of May 1840. My admission will not probably take place for some time.

3 May, Friday.

The storm against Mr. Van Buren continues to increase. The South in particular seem determined to cast him overboard. Well, well! "Nothing for men," as the fellows said when they threw Jonah into the sea—"let us take care of the good old ship, whatever becomes of them."

4 May, Saturday.

The *Eagle* opens to day upon Mr. Van Buren; but I am determined not to say one word upon which the Whigs can seize, if, after all I should be obliged to sail under Mr. Van Buren's flag. . . .

6 May, Monday.

There was a meeting held in Kensington this afternoon, by the Native Americans, which ended in a row, and murder. The only

57. John Meredith Read, an attorney since 1818, had offices at 85 South Sixth Street.

principle of this new party is antipathy to Irishmen and the Catholics, and they went to day into the midst of a Catholic neighborhood, Second and Master streets, to hold their meeting. Such unprincipled men as Lewis C. Levin were the speakers—they addressed the assembly in the most indiscreet manner, abusing the Irish outrageously. There were some Catholics among the audience, and of course their blood boiled with rage. One of them and a Native got into a debate—from that they proceeded to blows—others participated—the Irish retreated towards their houses west of the Market—clubs and stones were hurled after them—and for a few minutes the Natives seemed to have entire possession of the Market ground and the adjoining streets. But the Irish returned to the attack with musquets, some firing from their doors and others from the windows. The Natives fled, leaving two or three killed and several wounded. An American flag which was used as a rallying point for the meeting, was knocked down and trampled upon in the melee, the Natives say, by the Irish, but I imagine by both parties indiscriminately. I was on the ground about dusk, and saw parties and knots, all of Irish, at the corners and in the streets talking the matter over. A general riot is expected to-night or to morrow.

7 May, Tuesday.

This afternoon Washington Page and I went from the office up to the scene of yesterday's riot. We found things pretty quiet, but about half past four o'clock a meeting of Native Americans which had been convened in the State House Yard were seen coming up Second Street in procession, headed by the flag which was tattered yesterday, and along side of which on a large placard was the inscription: "This is the flag that was trampled upon by the Irish Papists." The procession numbered I should think some three thousand. It took possession of the Market house and planted the banner opposite the house of the Hibernia Hose.[58] The Irishman, many of whom were before in the street in knots reading a conciliatory letter from the Catholic Bishop,[59] had now retired into their houses. The women sitting in the doors were pelted by some boys who came up from the city with the Natives, and this was the signal for a general fight. The Irishmen commenced firing from the windows and allies, and many of the Natives who had brought arms along with them returned the shots. One man among the latter showed great bravery—he stood for some time at the North end of the market firing at the Irish, and lying down to reload. He shot thirty or forty times and at last escaped, himself, unhurt. The Natives having broken open the house of the Hibernia Hose, took the Carriage out and removed it down Second Street where they demolished it. After this the Irish seemed for a while to have the advantage. The main body of the procession had dispersed from the Market House when the firing first commenced and only a few now returned the shots from the houses. These few were at length assailed by the Irish who came out from their ramparts and fought in the open fields. I was standing all this while near the North end of the Market with Samuel Garrett,[60] and we saw several duels fought near us, and heard shots in every direction. At length we thought prudent to retire to Second and Cadwallader streets, where the crowd was immense, and increasing every minute. Here several men were carried by me, some dead and some only wounded. The Natives took past me one Irishman who it was said had killed three of the Natives—they beat him in a most shocking manner, and as I learned from a Catholic with whom I boarded at my Aunt's last winter, and whom I met on the ground, they were hanging him when he came up Second Street, after having dragged him several squares with a rope around his neck. It is rumored that St. Michael's church in Kensington near the first scene of riot is filled with arms and Irishmen, and that St. Augustine's in the city has likewise been turned into a garrison.[61] The indignation against these

58. The Market house was the so-called "Nanny-Goat Market" on Washington Street above Master. The Hibernia Hose Company, not to be confused with the Hibernia Fire Company, had its building on Cadwalader Street near Washington.

59. Francis Patrick Kenrick (1797–1863), bishop of Philadelphia from 1830 to 1851.

60. Samuel W. Garrett was a Camden "coach trimmer" of Second Street, near Market.

61. Saint Michael's Church was at Second and Jefferson Streets, Saint Augustine's on Fourth Street, north of Race.

two places runs very high, and if something be not speedily done to arrest it, they will be burnt. The Sheriff [*Morton McMichael*] came upon the ground last night, and staid a little while, when he became scared and ran away. The military meet in their armories at four this afternoon, and report to the Major General at five. At six o'clock when I left the ground they had not arrived, although the mob was increasing fast, and seemed more bitter than ever. For squares around the scene of riot, Irish families were seen this afternoon moving away. Many it is rumored have gone into the woods above Philadelphia, whence the Catholic men mean to make an onslaught to-night, to recover their ground. At six o'clock the firing was still brisk and wounded and dead Natives continued to be taken past Second and Cadwallader.

Having got my tea at home, and collected five companions I returned to Kensington. Soon after dark the obnoxious houses about the Market had been fired, and the Market itself and a wide reach of frame and brick tenements were now in a blaze. The military had reached the ground and formed a circle in front of the burning district, to keep the mob at bay. The latter sometimes pressed the volunteers close, catching hold of their bayonets and saying "you dare not fire—you know us!" At one time they seemed on the very point of driving back the Fencibles. Col. Page jumped in front of his men and made some appropriate appeals to the crowd. They gave him three cheers and retired. At nine o'clock the military maintained their posts unmolested. The mob stood in silence surveying the awful but magnificent scene before them. All my companions having deserted me but Curts, we two went away west of the military and penetrated the midst of the scene, to see what was going on where we heard an occasional random shot. This was on Cadwallader St. where there were none but the remaining Irishmen. These people were trying to save their effects, for the rear of their houses was already on fire. One poor fellow was trying to drive out a pig whose pen was in imminent danger; but the more the Irishman tried to get him down the alley the more the pig would go up. The game was completely blocked—and the Irishman looked at the hog and the hog at the Irishman with mutual wonderment and despair. At this juncture Curts and I interfered, and by seeming to want the animal to run into the fire got him to run out. The Irishman thanked us, exclaimed "Sad business this!" and went his way.

I staid upon the ground until near eleven, at which time the firing had entirely ceased, and the mob evidently abated in numbers as well as in wrath. Curts and I met our cowardly companions at the Ferry, and crossed with them in a small boat.

8 May, Wednesday.

All this afternoon I was on the scene of the riots. St. Joseph's church[62] was abandonned by the military to the mob and fired about three o'clock. When the cross fell in the Natives gave three cheers. The priest's house adjoining the church was pillaged and burnt also, and his library scattered to the winds. In both of these buildings I thought I heard guns go off among the ashes. The sacred implements were removed from all the Catholic churches this morning to some place of safety, and it is said that thirty theologians of that denomination went down the Delaware this forenoon. In the neighborhood of St. Joseph's all the Irish who yet remained in their houses hung out little American flags which were respected in every instance by the mob.

In the evening Mulford and I hearing that St. Augustine's was to be burn[ed] went there. Fourth Street was crowded with people, whom Mayor Scott[63] and other dignitaries were addressing, but with little effect. A troop of horse was stationed in Fourth Street just below Vine, and might easily have saved the building by charging down and halting before it. This they did not do; but on the contrary went entirely away and did not return until after the torch had been applied. Nine o'clock was tolled by the ancient bell in the steeple, and in a few minutes a stone was hurled through the window on the north side of the front. The boys kept up an occasional fire for some time—then the door was broken in by a battering ram of scantlings—and shortly afterwards I saw the tapestry on fire. Before ten o'clock St. Augustine's old bell was done telling the hour! Mulford and I stood at the Third Street end of New Street, and saw the flames mount up, up—and at last reach the cross. This soon fell in, and thousands of throats yelled applause, just as the Jews must have done when Jesus died upon the same emblem. I left the ground immediately after this, disgusted with the things I had witnessed, and almost ready to question the capacity of the people to govern themselves.

The citizens are beginning to organize themselves into companies to keep the peace. The Governor[64] has come down from Harrisburg to direct the defensive measures which are to be taken.

9 May, Thursday.

The city is now under strict martial law, and soldiers and armed citizens are seen patrolling in every direction.

62. Mickle means St. Michael's Church.
63. John M. Scott was mayor of Philadelphia from 1841 to 1844.
64. David R. Porter was governor of Pennsylvania from 1839 to 1845.

This evening I called with a lady upon my cousin in Chestnut Street.

10 May, Friday.

The city is apparently quiet, though a deep feeling evidently prevails against the Catholics. This is nourished by the *Sun* and the *Native American,* two reckless sheets, over the first of which Mr. Levin presides. The whole number of killed, so far as I can get correct information of the riot, is about twelve; but it is said that some of the Irish corpses were burnt in the houses.[65] The city is still under martial law.

11 May, Saturday.

The Catholic bishop has issued a Circular closing his churches on to-morrow; whereupon Major Gen. Patterson[66] put forth his orders announcing that he has sufficient men under him to "protect all religious denominations" in the exercise of their rights. All the Catholic churches have been under guard since Tuesday night, especially St. John's in Thirteenth St. which the mob seemed determined to assail.

14 May, Tuesday.

To day meets the Convention which is to frame a new constitution for the state of New Jersey. It was intended so to compromise the election as to choose half Whigs and half democrats; but the County of Monmouth refused to accede to this arrangement, and selected one democrat more than she was entitled to have, under the compromise apportionment. The result is the democrats will have a Majority of two in the Convention. I got a letter from my uncle to-night telling me they had made ex-Gov. Williamson[67] President, and Mr. Patterson Secretary.

Great efforts are being made to throw Mr. Van Buren—they will, I think, succeed.

15 May, Wednesday.

The city of Philadelphia is still under martial law—a queer sight for the place of "brotherly love."

16 May, Thursday.

The Colonel gave me an office examination to-day previous to the "grand tug" which the President of the Committee, Mr. Kane,[68] has fixed for next Tuesday, if I can persuade a quorum to attend. I have

---

65. Philadelphia newspapers, in July 1844, summarized the riot casualties as at least thirteen killed and fifty wounded.
66. Robert Patterson (1792–1881) was a Philadelphia manufacturer and politician when not commanding militia units.
67. Isaac H. Williamson had been governor of New Jersey from 1817 to 1829.
68. John K. Kane (1795–1858), a prominent attorney, would soon become a judge of the United States district court in Pennsylvania.

been running about all this afternoon, calling upon the gentlemen of the board with that view.

17 May, Friday.

Peace, if not good feeling, is again restored in Philadelphia, and armed soldiers are no longer seen patrolling the streets. But for Levin and a few others on the side of the Natives, who are worse than Jesuits, the flame of discord would soon go out.

18 May, Saturday.

A new paper called *The Hickory Club*[69] was sometime ago started in the *Eagle* office by Mr. Hineline, designed only for the campaign. They are now engaged in printing three thousand Extras of this sheet, filled with the letters that have lately appeared from distinguished democrats in favor of the annexation of Texas. The design hereof is of course to throw off Mr. Van Buren. The job is paid for by Jno. M. Reed Esq. Joseph A. Pugh[70] and other late Van Buren men in Philadelphia.

19 May, Sunday.

Since Page assures me that I can pass examination without much trouble, I tho't I could afford to-day for my pamphlet; and have accordingly been at work at it pretty industriously.

20 May, Monday.

To-day I studied law hard—indeed I did! The book upon which I was engaged was Anthon's *Abridgement of the Commentaries.*

21 May, Tuesday.

"The agony is over," and I am virtually a member of the Philadelphia bar. My board were: John K. Kane, Prest., Eli K. Price, Benjamin Rush, Jos: A. Budd, Henry McIlvaine, James Paul, Kinderton Smith, Henry M. Watts, Robert Hare, Jr., of whom the first named six were the quorum in attendance.[71] This board examines for the District Court for the City and County, and the sitting to-day is the last they are to have during the six months for which they are appointed. We met at a little after four o'clock in the Law Library on Sixth Street.[72]

69. The *Hickory Club* appears to have published very few issues, perhaps only that of 17 May 1844. Hineline announced its demise in the *American Eagle* of 15 June.

70. Pugh, formerly editor of the Mount Holly *Herald* was now a Philadelphia attorney.

71. This distinguished group of lawyers included prominent Philadelphia attorneys, such as Price and Rush, and relatively obscure men like Watts and Paul, who had themselves recently joined the bar.

72. Founded in 1802, the Library of the Law Association of Philadelphia was the oldest such institution in the United States. It was located in a room of Congress Hall, Sixth and Chestnut Streets.

The President, Messrs. Price and Budd, and the Secretary were punctual; the rest lagged behind for a considerable time, during which the Fencibles marched up Sixth Street in inverted order and with solemn step, escorting to his last home poor Jack Dutton, a Lieutenant of the Company, who caught an inflammation of the lungs, while doing duty the other night at the riots. At length Mr. Rush, the last of the Board necessary to constitute a quorum, appeared. We took our seats, and I found that the familiar manner in which Mr. Kane had been telling professional anecdotes during our waiting, had entirely dispelled the feeling, almost amounting to awe, which I had erst entertained for this ordeal. I was perfectly calm and collected when the President ordered Mr. Rush to proceed. This gentleman commenced with, "What is law?" and then proceeded to question me in the outlines of the science. I believe I answered every interrogation promptly and correctly. Mr. McIlvain then put some queries to me in the doctrine of estates. He soon stopped, and the President asked Mr. Price if he had any questions. That gentleman said no, and Messrs. Budd and Secretary shook their heads to the same effect. Mr. Kane then took me up upon political economy and constitutional law, and concluded by asking me a few questions upon bills of exchange and promissory notes. By very fortunate guess work, I replied instantly and correctly to every one. In less than twelve minutes after the first interrogation by Mr. Rush, the president said, "Mr. Mickle, if you will retire for a moment we will confer together." I did so, took a turn in the vestibule, and was recalled. My certificate was already signed, and as Mr. Kane handed it to me he remarked "Now Mr. Mickle, that we have made a lawyer of you— or rather given you the stamp, for the metal was there before—I hope you will help keep our folks right at Baltimore." I bowed, and thanked him. Mr. Rush then said "Give my compliments to the Colonel, and tell him that you have passed one of the best examinations I ever knew." "Excuse me sir," said I "but were the praise merited, it would not do for me to be its bearer." He smiled and added "Well then I'll tell him myself." I thanked the Board for their politeness, took my papers and gave room to another young gentleman who looked very much scared. And thus end my three years sergeantship in the office of Col. Page.

I have often had occasion to remark that my time has been most wofully abused, and notwithstanding the flattering character of this examination I feel yet that such is lamentably the case. Hard study yet however may atone for the past, and I will now go at it.

22 May, Wednesday.
This morning I took the Attorney's-oath at the bar of the District

Court, and am now fairly initiated into the ancient and honorable fraternity. It is my intention to hang out a shingle for one year with Colonel Page in Walnut Street, and then remove to Camden.

23 May, Thursday.

My admission is announced this morning in the *Ledger, United States Gazette* and *Pennsylvanian,* and the day has been pretty much passed in receiving the congratulations of my friends. One queer fellow wished me "sharp sheers and abundant fleece."

24 May, Friday.

This evening I attended a Tyler meeting in Mercer Court House, Trenton. It was a very spirited affair. Mr. Zabriski spoke and also Mr. Green. The latter gentleman is for dropping Tyler if he be not nominated by the regular Convention, but Zabriski seems to go Tyler whether or no. They will all come in, I imagine, for the regular nominee.

25 May, Saturday.

This afternoon I started in company with many other Jerseymen for Baltimore. We left Dock Street Wharf in the *Ohio* at four o'clock and reached Baltimore about two in the morning. We had a warm time in descending the Delaware, between the Van Buren and anti-Van Buren men. Many New Yorkers being on board, the Van Buren men seemed to have the advantage. A few men from upper Jersey were in favor of the sage of Lindenwold,[73] but our state was decidedly for a new man. The first district, on account of the manner in which Mr. Ward was appointed, was very numerously represented.[74] We were called "First District Protestants," and some of us were pretty animated in our resistance to Van Buren's nomination. The Van Buren men talked of ducking Hineline at New Castle, but of course it was all talk.

Most of our district took lodging at the Eagle Hotel.[75]

26 May, Sunday.   Baltimore.

There is much stronger opposition here to Mr. Van Buren than his friends expected. Were not many of the delegates pledged to go for him he could not any how be nominated [;] as it is, it is very doubtful. Barnum's[76] is full to overflowing, and the anti-Van Buren men are busy enough electioneering against him. The policy agreed upon by them is

73. "Lindenwold" was Martin Van Buren's farm at Kinderhook, New York.
74. See entry of 2 March 1844.
75. Baltimore's Eagle Hotel, owned by William Whitman, was on Pratt Street, east of Light Street.
76. One of the first of America's lavish new hotels, David Barnum's City Hotel was completed in 1826.

to adopt the rule requiring two thirds to nominate.[77] If this rule be carried it is believed, nay known, that some new man will be taken.

There are several Tyler men staying at the Eagle. They have a convention also to-morrow, but it will not amount to much.[78]

27 May, Monday.   Baltimore.

The city is full of democrats, and the most intense interest pervades them all respecting the nomination. The strong array of anti Van-Buren men from New Jersey will awe four out of the seven delegates into opposition to that gentleman; but Mr. George Vroom[79] who is instructed to go for Cass is going for Van Buren. Mr. Ward from the first District is "all right." I was introduced to him this morning at Barnum's, and I thought he was a little cool. No wonder however if he read the *Eagle* just after his appointment.

The two thirds rule was adopted to day—many going for it who are under instructions to go for Van Buren. The Pennsylvania delegation stood twelve for the rule and thirteen against it; Mr. Benjamin Brewster and the President of the Convention, Hendrick B. Wright leading off in this way against Van Buren.[80] This vote is considered by all a test. Van Buren cannot be nominated.

I have not been in Egyptian Hall to-day:[81] not caring much about the preliminaries which the Convention have been busy in discussing.

This evening I went to the Front Street Theatre.[82]

28 May, Tuesday.

I went into the Convention to day, as a member of the press. Mills of the *Sheet Anchor* and Allison[83] of the *Somerset Messenger* were with me. On the first balloting Mr. Van Buren had a decided majority, Mr. Cass being the next highest. At each successive attempt the former lost and the latter gained, and when at the eighth trial—no, the

77. The famous two-thirds rule, which influenced Democratic party nominations from 1832 to 1936, allowed a minority of convention delegates to reject a candidate.

78. Whig dissatisfaction with Tyler's stubborn Democratic philosophy during his term had made the president a man without a party. The Tyler meeting in Baltimore was his attempt to found a third political party which might carry him to another term in the White House. Though he received his party's nomination, his campaign languished and he withdrew from the race on 20 August.

79. Convention records list George A. Vroom as a substitute delegate from the fourth congressional district.

80. Brewster was a Philadelphia attorney; Wright was a member of the Pennsylvania legislature from Luzerne County.

81. The Democrats were meeting at the Egyptian Saloon of the Odd Fellows Hall on Gay Street.

82. Baltimore's Front Street Theatre was a very large house, first built in 1829 and rebuilt, after a fire, in 1838.

83. Thomas Allison, of Somerville, was sole proprietor of the *Somerset Messenger* from 1837 to 1851.

seventh—it was found that Cass was approaching the two-thirds necessary, and that the large states Pennsylvania and New York were splitting in his favor, the Van Buren men carried an adjournment. The scene that preceded the adjournment I shall never forget! It seemed inevitable that the Convention must break up: The Ohio Van Buren delegation behaved very indiscreetly. One of its members after the seventh balloting jumped up and offered a resolution declaring that Mr. Van Buren having received on the first balloting a majority of the votes was duly nominated. Babel itself was orderly compared with the confusion that followed. A dozen were on the floor at once—hisses, plaudits, laughs and sneers betokened the different feelings of different sections of the Union. A momentary calm being obtained a man from Pennsylvania nominated General Andrew Jackson. This was laughed incontinently down. I sat between the Georgia and Kentucky delegations during this intensely interesting crisis. Those fellows, hot-headed as they are, behaved much better than the Ohio men. Once or twice some of them rose and were about to speak; but young Ritchie[84] of the Richmond *Enquirer* besought them to keep cool and they obeyed. One of the Kentucky men indeed took me to task for helping to hiss the Ohio proposition. "Every thing" said he, mistaking me for a Georgia delegate "depends upon our calmness now—let that young fellow talk himself dry, and we will get a Texas man."

In the midst of this storm the motion to adjourn was carried, and we left the house with sad hearts. But it cannot be that Clay will be made our next President—some opening will offer though we see none now to save us. After this day's proceedings however it is clear that the Van Buren men will never allow Cass to get two-thirds. They blame him more than any other for the defeat of their favorite, and will in turn defeat him. There is moreover an objection to Mr. Cass to which I think much importance ought to be attached; viz: the fact that he bases his opposition to a United States Bank and his friendly disposition towards annexation upon the supposition that the people don't want the first and that they do want the second. A constitutional question, anyhow, ought not to be made pendent on the popular impulse of a day.[85] Cassism, however, like Johnsonism and Stewartism, and Tylerism in the main, only means anti-Van Burenism, and the friends of Cass will readily forego their preferences for any new man.

This evening I went again to the Theatre, and afterwards meeting with some jovial friends took a look at "the lions." Baltimore is great

84. Thomas Ritchie (1778–1854) was editor of the Richmond *Enquirer* from 1804 to 1845 and of the *Union*, organ of the Polk administration, from 1845 to 1851.
85. Arguments about the constitutionality of a United States Bank had been current since the 1790s.

for two things at least: her monuments and her pretty women, and the latter are by no means confined exclusively to the paths of virtue. I could not help thinking to-night at the ball at Mrs. Osbourne's, that the morals of the people were likely to be kept vigilantly if they were entrusted to the conductors of the press; for strange to say there were three New Jersey editors with me dancing at this famous place. The ball broke up about half past two o'clock in the morning.

I dined to day with the Drakeleys. Mary has beaten Harriet Kelly![86]

29 May, Wednesday. Baltimore.

This morning the eighth balloting took place and showed a slight gain for Mr. Van Buren—the result of caucassing and boring last night. It was evident however that the game was blocked, and that the Convention must take up a new man. Accordingly at the next trial, James K. Polk of Tennessee was nominated nearly unanimously.[87] The few votes given for others were called "mistakes" and rectified. The enthusiasm which this nomination excited cannot be described. It must be—it will be triumphant.

In the afternoon Silas Wright[88] was nominated nearly unanimously for Vice President. The news was immediately transmitted to Washington by that wonderful invention of Morse's, the electric telegraph, and it was said just as we were leaving the wharf in the steamboat that a declination had been immediately returned.[89] I was in Convention when the states were balloting for this office. The vote of Massachusetts was given by the historian Bancroft[90] in a very neat manner. I also had an opportunity of hearing Senator Walker, Gov. Hubbard, Hon. B. F. Butler and many more great men address the Convention.[91] The "conscript fathers" of the democracy were an extraordinarily fine and intelligent looking body of men; and after a happy issue out of

86. See entry of 1 September 1844.
87. Often called the first dark horse presidential candidate, Polk (1795–1849) had served as Speaker of the national House of Representatives, 1835–39, and as governor of Tennessee, 1839–41.
88. Wright (1795–1847), a political ally of Van Buren, had been a United States senator from New York since 1833.
89. Samuel F. B. Morse (1791–1872) had experimented with his telegraph since 1832 and first put it into operation over a line from Baltimore to Washington on 24 May 1844. So new was the invention that delegates refused to believe that Wright had declined the vice-presidential nomination until confirmation by more conventional means.
90. George Bancroft, best known as an historian, was active in politics throughout much of his life. He would soon serve Polk as secretary of the navy and minister to Britain and Germany.
91. The speakers were Robert J. Walker (1801–69), senator from Mississippi and soon to become Polk's secretary of the treasury, Henry Hubbard (1784–1857), Democratic governor of New Hampshire from 1841 to 1843, and Benjamin F. Butler (1795–1858), former attorney general of the United States and prominent New York attorney.

their dissentions had lit up their faces with satisfaction, they were a pleasant sight to look at.

I entirely forgot to mention that the Tyler Convention met in Carroll Hall on Monday morning and nominated Honest John.⁹² The New Jersey Tyler men wanted to wait a while, to see if the other Democrats would take up Van Buren, but the ultras put the suggestion down, and even talked of putting Zabriskie and Yard out of the window. Just as they were commencing proceedings a portrait of John Tyler fell from its hook over the rostrum and broke to pieces—an omen!—an omen!

This morning I visited the great monument and ascended it to enjoy a bird's eye view of the city.⁹³ I was amply repaid for my trouble.

Most of our Jersey men left this evening. There was so much enthusiasm on board the boat on the Delaware that there was no sleep. The Van Buren men were in particular very noisy; and one of them, either to show his joy or to bedevil us lucky ones who had monopolized all the cots, went up and down the cabin half the night ringing a tremendous dinner-bell and singing *Lucy Neale*.⁹⁴ We reached Philadelphia about five o'clock, and gave three cheers for Polk at landing. Some of the Whigs had come down to quiz us for breaking up in a row, but they soon went away, looking wonderfully chop-fallen. Yet I confess I felt disappointed at the enthusiasm created by our nomination. True it was great—but confound it! it ought to have been an hundred times deeper, louder, and more lasting.

30 May, Thursday.

Sleep! Sleep! Sleep! Blessed indeed, as honest Sancho Panza has exclaimed, be the man who first invented that same.

31 May, Friday.

I have hardly caught up yet, though I slept almost all of yesterday. I did not on an average sleep more than two hours a night during my trip to Baltimore. I guess the *Eagle* will be leaden enough to-morrow.

1 June, Saturday.

The late riots in Philadelphia have given an impetus to the Native American movement in several parts of the country. This humbug had its origin in New York, where Bishop Hughes⁹⁵ very properly remon-

92. Mickle errs here. The Tyler convention was held at Calvert Hall, at the corner of Saratoga and Sharp Streets.

93. Baltimore's Washington Monument, a two hundred foot high tower, was completed in 1829.

94. One of the most popular songs of the mid-1840s, *Miss Lucy Neale* was written by James Sanford.

95. John Joseph Hughes (1797–1864) was bishop of New York from 1842 to 1864.

strated a year or two ago against the reading of the Protestant Bible in the public schools, to Catholic children. The bigots of various sects seized upon this remonstrance, and the success with which it met, as a theme for denunciation; and they raised such a storm, and collected such a party, that at the last municipal election in the city of New York, the Natives elected their entire ticket. Since the riots the Natives have organized themselves in Camden, and on one or two occasions they have been addressed by some ignorant jack-an-apes who had pistols sticking out of their pockets as if they expected mortal fight! If these fellows run a ticket in the new county, the whigs will beat us—the Natives being nearly all Democrats.

2 June, Sunday.
The nominations are very well received by the people, and Clay stock has fallen quite low in consequence.

4 June, Tuesday.
I was at what they call a Ratification Meeting to night in Trenton. It was very enthusiastic, and wound up with a torch-light procession through the streets. The Whigs look sadder than ever.

5 June, Wednesday.
I have not been regularly at the office since my admission.

6 June, Thursday.
The fire spreads—the nomination of Polk and Dallas gives universal satisfaction.[96]

7 June, Friday.
Every morning that I go down to the *Eagle* office to look over our exchanges, gives me stronger evidence of the popularity of Polk's nomination. The Van Buren men everywhere have come in nobly, and we are united and must be triumphant.

10 June, Monday.   West-Chester Pa.
My aunt and cousin Emma having come out here on Saturday, I went after them this afternoon. The Haines' are well. I had a pleasant but sultry ride, but found it cool enough among the hills. I made some acquaintances among the democrats of this place, and was glad to see them in such good spirits.

11 June, Tuesday.
This afternoon we returned.

96. Democrats had chosen Philadelphia lawyer George M. Dallas to be their vice-presidential candidate when they were satisfied that Silas Wright would not accept the nomination.

Mr. Van Buren has written a letter to a large meeting in the Park, declaring his intention to support the nominees.

13 June, Thursday.
Our Polk Dallas and Texas affair to-night, notwithstanding a heavy rain, went off admirably. The court-house was jammed. Mr. Rhees presided—Col. Page made an excellent speech—Miller drew some capital resolutions, and the band performed a number of grand airs. I had a seat, during the meeting, in the window, and Page several times made me blush by using my name. Alack-a-day! When shall I learn to lose my modesty?

18 June, Tuesday.
I took my mother and aunt Eliza up to Hugg's this morning, and brought them back before dusk. Old Joseph gave me a good many new incidents for my pamphlet.

In the evening I went with Mulford to Philadelphia—heard the Hon. Silas Wright and other distinguished men deliver excellent speeches at the democratic reading room—and then looked in for a few minutes at Number Twenty-One.[97]

19 June, Wednesday.
Since I began to receive the income of my farm I have laid out the chief part of it in books. I bought a good many to day.

20 June, Thursday.
Mulford and I—Number Twenty One!

22 June, Saturday.
At our meeting on Thursday week Miller inserted at my suggestion a resolution nominating John R. Thompson Esq. of Princeton as Governor under the new Constitution. This of course was adopted. It made a good deal of stir, my uncle tells me, in the Convention among the "old Hunkers."[98] But this morning several papers came to hand seconding the motion with all heartiness.

23 June, Sunday.
The prospects of the democracy brighten every day. Betting whigs are growing scarce.

25 June, Tuesday.
"The whigs of old Gloucester" as they called themselves, undertook to have a meeting last Thursday at the Point. It was a failure.

97. In the absence of a street name, it is impossible to determine where Mickle visited this night and again on 20 June. Perhaps he merely refers to the Sheppards' pew in Philadelphia's First Baptist Church; see entry of 27 February 1842.
98. Mickle means among conservative Democrats.

27 June, Thursday.

This evening we had a delightful moonlight-walk to Kaighn's Point—no, we had a pic-nic in the woods this afternoon, and the walk last night. Mary Gray was along on both occasions. She and I understand each other very well, if I and her papa do occasionally quarrel with each other through our papers.

28 June, Friday.

This evening I addressed a small democratic meeting at the Spread Eagle Tavern on the Moorestown road. Young Clement from Haddonfield officiated as Secretary. He and his kith want to get back into traces.

29 June, Saturday.

This evening I, along with the rest of the "triangle,"[99] addressed a large meeting of democrats at Long-a-coming. My hand is not yet in at stump-speaking, and I fear I make an awful fist at it. But *n'importe!*

1 July, Monday.

This evening I made a twenty minute speech at Wilson's in South Camden. I begin to understand the art and mystery of stumping.

3 July, Wednesday.

I started for Malaga[100] this morning, along with my old friend Remak, the Pole, who is also an "orator of the day." We had an infernal ride from Woodbury, in a crowded stage, and in the midst of a heavy rain. We were received at Malaga by Judge Rosenbaum,[101] and treated very politely. What to talk about I have not yet made up my mind.

4 July, Thursday.   Amer. Indep. Ann. LXVIII.

The Native American party is to have a grand celebration to day in Philadelphia. I think this will be the culminating point of their enthusiasm. I hope so at least.

I was awakened this morning by the firing of a cannon. I found the weather admirably adapted to our *fete champetré*; clear and cool, with just wind enough to unfurl the flags, and with no dust to mar our dinner "in the arbor." Soon after breakfast people began to flock into the village. A procession was formed at the Judge's school house, and thence we marched to the woods where the exercises were to take place. Remak, myself and a good-natured Methodist itinerant had a

99. The triangle was composed of Mickle and his friends Thomas Mulford and Morris Hamilton. See entry of 20 September 1843.

100. The town of Malaga was built around a glass factory which had attracted German immigrants to the area.

101. John G. Rosenbaum (1794–1860), a German immigrant, was a prominent miller and glass manufacturer in Malaga where he also served as a local judge.

place near the van, where we could be tortured by the horrid music of the band.

When we arrived at the forum and got seated, I estimated the number of people at six hundred, but the Minister said there were a thousand, and so I let it go. The drama opened by prayer. Then we had music. Then the Declaration of Independence was read in English. Then the itinerant gave us a queer kind of an Address. Then my turn came. I spoke—just a half an hour—concerning Native Americanism, the love of money, Count Pulaski—Leonidas and Xerxes and so on. Just such a speech I guess nobody ever heard before, and I doubt if ever any body will want to again. After this we adjourned to dine. Near two hundred sat down to a long table spread in the grateful shade, and partook of an excellent dinner prepared by Mrs. Rosenbaum. After eating was done with, we proceeded again to "the flow of soul." Remak made a beautiful address in English; then read the Declaration of Independence in German and commented upon it, briefly but effectively. This part of the programme Rosenbaum's Dutchmen highly relished. After this some gangling red-headed fellow got up and gave us a Temperance address, but he did not go down at all. Then the itenerant aforesaid told the people they had been edified— a hymn was sung—a benediction pronounced—and the meeting—ladies and all, adjourned into the village in procession and dissolved. The Malaga people are delighted with the manner in which the day has passed, but for my part I am mortified with myself for making such a speech. Remak upon the contrary tells me it was excellent, and says he never made so bad an address as he did to-day. My allusions to the Natives made some Whigs a little wrothy, but if that had been all I would not have cared. It is to my want of connection that I refer with mortification and chagrin.

In the evening Rosenbaum and we "orators" stopped in at one of the glass-blowers houses to hear some singing. We had songs in five languages, and then they got me a violin and I played them a few jigs and reels. I went to bed heartily tired with The Fourth.

5 July, Friday.
This morning Remak and I returned home, bringing with us the thanks and I hope the good feelings of the Malaga people.

6 July, Saturday.
We put the *Eagle* in mourning to-day for the imprisonment of Dorr.[102]

102. Rhode Island Democrat Thomas W. Dorr was tried for his "insurrection" of April-May 1842 and, on 25 June 1844, was sentenced to life imprisonment. He was amnestied and released in 1845.

There were indications of another riot to day in Southwark, and the military in consequence are out.

7 July, Sunday.

As I predicted, there has been another and a serious outbreak in Philadelphia. The cause was the arming of St. Philip de Neris' Church, in Queen St. above Second, Southwark. The arms were discovered on Friday and removed by the Sheriff. A mob of people however began to collect, and yesterday they threatened to burn down the building. Gen. Cadwallader arrived on the ground last night, and one of the rioters caught hold of his horse's reins. The General cut his arm. Others continued to press upon him, and he ordered his artillery to be discharged. Then Chas. Naylor[103] jumped before the piece, and begged the men not to fire. They did not; but Naylor was taken under arrest and put in the Church. The mob got some old cannons, which had been planted along the wharves, and this morning fired into the church and rescued their champion.[104] Afterwards the Hibernia Greens[105] were put in the obnoxious building to defend it. This only incensed the people still more. At last it was arranged that the Greens should have liberty to come out and depart in peace. They did come out, but were pursued and pelted. They disbanded, and each went his own direction. One of them being chased into a strange house, and clear into the attic fired upon his pursuers. This affair, with many additions, flew over the city and of course increased the excitement.

In the afternoon I was on the ground. In Commissioner's Hall[106] they had some of those who had been wounded by the Irishmen, and also some of the Irish who had been much beaten. The Church was in possession of Grover,[107] Levin and other leading Natives, who pretended to desire the protection of the Church itself and the peace in general. I heard Levin make a speech, and ask the people whether they would defend the Church or not. They voted they would not. Levin then sent word up to Head Quarters that he was unable to stay the mob; and the troops therefore were again assembled by the ringing of the State House bell, and prepared to march down.

103. Naylor (1806–72), a Philadelphia lawyer since 1828, had been a congressman from 1837 to 1841.

104. In fact, wet powder prevented the nativists from firing their two cannon, so they used a battering ram to rescue Naylor. Nativists did fire cannon at the church later in the day, however.

105. The Greens were a company of Irish militia.

106. The Southwark Commissioners' Hall, built in 1811, was on Second Street, above Christian.

107. Thomas D. Grover, a Philadelphia wharf-builder, became one of the vice-presidents of the nativist American Party, at its founding in Philadelphia in July 1845.

While I was on the ground this afternoon the Natives had entire control. It was extremely dangerous to make a remark not fully approving of cutting Catholic throats, and burning all Catholic churches. I nearly got into a scrape for daring to express the abhorrence I have for mobocracy.

In the evening Gen. Cadwallader went down to Queen St. with the First Division, in which are Col. Page and the Fencibles. A cannonading immediately began, up and down Queen St. and in Second and Third St. I was sitting at Elwell's ferry when Cadwallader's first shot came booming across the water. The flashes now visible in the twilight, became more and more frequent. A terrible sight for a Sunday eve in this Christian land! At nine o'clock I went over with Billy King.[108] We approached no nearer than Front and Mead St.[109] where there was a party of cut-throats, armed with muskets, and rum, robbing a store which they had broken open. They had also a cannon ready to go into the fight. The shooting about the church was now rapid on both sides, and exaggerated accounts of the number killed were flying over town. Terror and dismay pervaded every body.

At ten o'clock the firing had in a measure ceased, though we still heard musket shots at intervals by no means long. At this hour we left the city, and found Camden almost as much excited as Philadelphia. One fellow at the wharf was going to "smell me out when the day of retribution comes" for saying that the Catholics had as much right to arm their churches as he had to arm his house. I put him down however and made him ashamed of himself.

8 July, Monday.
The Military triumphed last night after a combat of five hours. Col. Page was on duty twenty four hours without sitting. He lost a man or two in the fight—not killed, but wounded. Poor Lawyer Bob Scott they say is killed, or will die.[110]

9 July, Tuesday.
The Governor arrived in town to day, and troops are gathering from all quarters. There was no disturbance yesterday or to day. The military were withdrawn yesterday, by the mismanagement of Patterson, from the church. The authorities of Southwark now pretend to guard it.

10 July, Wednesday.
Troops still continue to come in. The city looks quite martial.

108. Mickle probably refers to his neighbor William T. King.
109. Mead Street ran east from Second Street, beginning at a point north of Catherine Street.
110. Robert K. Scott, a Philadelphia attorney since 1834, survived his wounds.

11 July, Thursday.

Levin and others have been arrested for "inciting to treason." That is right.

I addressed a large meeting to night at Clementon. I rode up on horse back, and feel very sore.

13 July, Saturday.

The Natives at last have heard of my speech at Malaga, and do not like it. Well, well! They know their alternative.

14 July, Sunday.

Five thousand troops are now in Philadelphia.

15 July, Monday.

The Whigs say they have carried Louisiana. That's bad for Polk and Texas.

16 July, Tuesday.

The weather is very hot.

It appears from the returns from Louisiana that the Whigs have gained one Congressman, but I imagine they have not carried the Legislature.

17 July, Wednesday.

I was to have started this morning for the Capes, but deferred it till to morrow. In the evening I called to say farewell pro tem to the Sheppards.

18 July, Thursday.

This morning at eight o'clock I embarked on board the *Morris* for the Cape. I found Pugh, a Philadelphia lawyer, and formerly a Jersey democratic editor also bound down. Captain West, a Mexican merchant and a client of Col. Page's, is my *compagnon du voyage*. He is a glorious fellow.

We arrived at the Island about four o'clock, and found it so crowded that Miller could not do better for us than give us a room to sleep in out in the country about two miles.

19 July, Friday.

Our wagon came for us and took us "in town" early this morning. They tell us that if we will camp out to-night, they will contrive afterwards to get us into the hotel.

My place at table is alongside a Mrs. Heberton, the mother of the roué who was assassinated on board of the *Fitch*.[111] She is a very lady-like, but a very weak-minded woman. Just beyond her sits Char-

111. See entry of 10 February 1843.

lotte her daughter, a lovely girl of seventeen. Opposite to me are George Heberton and Miss Hutchinson.[112] Altogether it is a very pleasant coterie, and—since they have done me the favor to send their valet to serve me—I will tell Miller that I dont care to change quarters.

20 July, Saturday.

West, tired of camping out, went home this morning; but in the afternoon Dr. Lippincott[113] from Woodbury came down.

My cousin John Cooper and his family are here. They say that Louisa is accomplished and pretty. *Nous verrons.* The Doctor gave me an introduction to Cooper this afternoon, and I shall before long find out his step-daughter.[114]

Pugh introduced me to-day to a Miss Wright, the sister of the young man of that name who was accidentally shot in the Kensington riots.[115] I also have added to my list the somewhat famous J. Washington Tyson.[116] He is quite a gentleman.

21 July, Sunday.

I have at last got a nook in the Hotel.

This evening I met my cousins[117] the Rulons, and Miss Stockton at the Mansion House.

22 July, Monday.

My time is passed here a little differently from the common mode. I neither go into bathe, dance nor drink. In the morning, instead of ducking, I walk along the shore—in mid-day, instead of drinking I read D'Aubigné[118]—in the evening, instead of dancing, I generally talk politics with some of my Whig friends. Then I ride occasionally, and flirt a little with Miss Stockton or the Misses Webster. Thus day rolls in and rolls out.

23 July, Tuesday.

Some body gave me an introduction this morning to Judge Camp-

112. George Heberton was probably a brother of the victim and Miss Hutchinson a cousin.

113. This was probably Dr. Franklin Lippincott who died near Woodbury in 1846, in his twenty-ninth year.

114. Mickle had attended a meeting with John Cooper, of Woodbury, on 11 March 1844 but had not been formally introduced at that time. Cooper's mother had been a Mickle.

115. John W. Wright had been shot in the head and killed on May 6.

116. Tyson (1811–60), a Philadelphia attorney, was assistant postmaster-general of the United States.

117. Mickle refers to the Coopers.

118. Théodore Agrippa d' Aubigné (1552–1630) was a French poet and Huguenot soldier.

bell[119] of our Philadelphia Common Pleas. I find him a very pleasant fellow.

24 July, Wednesday.

I have made some fifty acquaintances here since my arrival, and met with a good many old friends. The gayest and prettiest of my lady acquaintances is Ellen Stockton; and with her therefore I now and then enjoy a flirt in the hop-room or on the beach. A lively girl is Ellen!

25 July, Thursday.

To-day I took a long ride on horseback. Carriage-hire, and all other items, bring my expenses here up to about five dollars a day.

I have had several talks with Miss Louisa Heulings.[120] She is a sensible girl—fond of conquests and likely to make them. Among the male acquaintances whom I have added to my list within a few days are Charles C. Stratton of Gloucester, Dr. Spencer of Moorestown, Mr. Hoy the present Post-master of Philadelphia, and Andrew Sinnickson Esq. of Salem.[121] My cousin Cooper and I have got quite intimate. He tells me that my uncle "is neither fish, flesh nor fowl," but that I am quite a decent fellow—"much too good to be a Locofoco." John is a little cracked—just enough to make him agreeable.

26 July, Friday.

It has rained all day long, and given the blues to Dr. Gardiner,[122] Comly, Pugh and all the rest. For my part I have been abed most of the time reading D'Aubigné.

For two or three nights past I have slept in the reading-room where I staid last year. The oven is immediately under this, and of course it is hot as Tophet. Before I was put here I was in the cock-loft. I'll be off to morrow, I will, faith!

27 July, Saturday.

To-day I came up in the *Sun*, with Miss Mary Turner under my charge. I used to dislike Whilldin very much, and a year or two ago I actually insulted John Hall for taking his part. But I heard him the other day declare himself in the midst of a dozen bitter whigs at Miller's, declare himself to be a democrat; and for his independence I

119. James Campbell (1812–93) had served on the court since 1842. He later served as postmaster-general of the United States under President Pierce.

120. Heulings, who died in Camden in 1898, was probably the daughter of Elizabeth Heulings of Smith's Row, Camden.

121. Mickle had met Dr. Jonathan J. Spencer, a prominent physician in Burlington County for many years, James Hoy, Jr., Philadelphia postmaster since June 1844, and Andrew Sinnickson, a young lawyer and businessman of Salem.

122. Gardiner was probably Dr. R. Gardiner of Catherine Street, Philadelphia.

like him and determined to support him. He lost several passengers by his bold avowal of his colors, and I feel it my duty therefore to stand by him. I mean also to write an apology to Hall.

I found my dear mother and all the rest very well.

28 July, Sunday.

After the excitement of Cape May the sameness of home makes me feel stupid. I slept nearly all of to-day.

29 July, Monday.

I spent most of to-day in reading D'Aubigne. In these Native American times it is necessary for me to understand both sides of the Catholic question.

30 July, Tuesday.

Mr. Jeffers[123] and I fixed it at Cape May that we are to go to Saratoga together this summer. We were to have started to day, but Camden Court promises to hold so long that we don't know when we shall be able to start.

31 July, Wednesday.

Allison, my brother of the *Somerset Messenger* is in Philadelphia. He says that Samuel R. Gummere, Whig clerk in Chancery has been endeavoring to stir up the Whigs in East Jersey to oppose the new Constitution.

1 August, Thursday.

The election returns from Louisiana, to which all parties have looked with great interest, have at last come in. The democrats have elected three out of four of the members of Congress, a majority of the Constitution Convention, and nearly half of the Legislature. They have gained considerably in the popular vote. Upon the whole there is little reason to complain.

3 August, Saturday.

The printers are on my heels with my *Reminiscences*. To-day therefore I was busy in getting out of their way. William D. Cooper Esq., Lemuel H. Davis and Joseph Hugg Esq. have promised me some anecdotes for which I have been waiting. The book will sum up I fear to seventy five pages.

4 August, Sunday.

To-day my old chum William Shaw dined with me. He is a great Native American, but an entire disbeliever in the Bible. I proposed to him the idea I have of forming a society of the Sons of Liberty in

123. Mickle refers to William N. Jeffers, Esq., the uncle of his friend Will Jeffers.

Camden, and he consented to become an honorary member. He is a queer fellow.

6 August, Tuesday.
At home reading.

I hear that Mr. Winner the pastor of the Methodist Church in Camden is going to open batteries through the *Mail* upon the Catholics. Let him do it!

7 August, Wednesday.
Sure enough, Winner is out to-day over the signature of Amicus. I wrote a pretty tart reply which will be very apt to sever our friendly connections.

This afternoon Mulford and I took Caroline and Josephine down to Walnut Grove to eat watermelons. We had a very pleasant time, but I guess Jo will think I am an incomprehensible fellow.

8 August, Thursday.
The Camden sessions still detain Jeffers and me from Saratoga. There are several nuisance cases which progress very slowly.

9 August, Friday.
The North Carolina election returns are in, and I hardly know whether to consider them favorable or not. We have gained greatly upon the popular vote, while our opponents have gained in the Legislature. One thing is evident: that the Whigs are making a dead-set for the Federal Senate through the state legislatures.[124]

10 August, Saturday.
This evening, at my suggestion, a few young gentlemen of Camden met in conclave in Mulford's office, to form a Society to resist the progress of the Native American cause. There were present Mr. Garrison, a Whig,[125] studying law under Browning, Mr. Dooley a Fetterville mechanic and two or three of his friends whom I did not know; and Messrs. Mulford, Hamilton and Mickle. I made a short speech setting forth the dangerous tendencies of Nativism, and the necessity of meeting it by counter organization. Mr. Mulford followed in the same strain. The result of these addresses was to confirm Garrison who was a little wavering. We resolved to form an association, and after some debate the name of Sons of Liberty was agreed upon at the intimation of my friend Mulford. This little meeting was conducted

124. Until the adoption of the Seventeenth Amendment in 1913, United States senators were elected by state legislatures, not by popular vote.

125. Charles Grant Garrison, a native of Swedesboro, had practiced medicine there for six years before deciding on a legal career.

with a solemnity amounting to sadness. We knew that we were about to incur the opposition of the intolerant, the ignorant and the bigoted; but we remembered, too, that we were about to make a stand for the very dearest rights of man. Though sad, therefore, we were firm. We dispersed to meet again in two weeks, to fix a plan of organization.

11 August, Sunday. City of New York.

Jeffers and I left home this evening at five for Saratoga. We arrived here at eleven and took lodgings at the Astor.[126] There is an immense deal of travelling this summer, and it is a lucky thing to get a bed in any decent house.

12 August, Monday. Troy, N. Y.

Just after we retired last night there was a brawl in the street by the Park. This kept me awake so long that I was afraid to go to sleep again, lest the North river boat should leave me.[127] Without a wink of sleep therefore I started at five o'clock in the magnificent steamer *Empire*, for this place. This boat is just the sixteenth of a mile long, and is perhaps the best boat afloat.[128]

Becoming very sleepy I took a berth and enjoyed several good naps during the passage. I was awake, however, when we passed West Point and Dunderberg—the latter of which I have wanted to see ever since I read Irving's description of a thundergust upon the Hudson.[129] The monument of Koskiusko it may be imagined made me more than ever a Son of Liberty.[130] It is an eloquent argument against Nativism.

It is needless for me to dwell upon the scenery of this heavenly river. What I saw of it I enjoyed as every one must enjoy it who has a soul. And what I did not see—I hope to look at when I come down.

We took lodgings at the Hotel facing the public square in this city about five o'clk. After tea we took a stroll over the place, in the course of which I looked in at a bookseller's and bought Howe's *Lives of Eminent Mechanics*.

13 August, Tuesday. Saratoga.

We came hither this morning by rail-road. The United States being full we quartered at the old Congress Hall, once the leading house but now number three in the scale of popularity. I met with none

126. The Astor, at Broadway and Vesey Street, was one of the city's leading hotels.
127. That is, the boat going north on the Hudson.
128. The *Empire of Troy*, built in 1843, was a wooden paddle steamer, 307 feet in length and of 1012 tons displacement. It was owned by the Troy and New York Steamboat Company.
129. Mickle may be thinking of the Postscript to Irving's "Rip Van Winkle."
130. The white marble Kosciusko monument, designed by John H. B. Latrobe, had been erected at West Point in 1828.

whom I knew except ex-President Van Buren. He is at the States. We called on him this evening and had a short interview. He looks well, and says that political affairs in New York look ditto.

14 August, Wednesday.

I have made a few acquaintances here, and among the rest one with Charles Secor,[131] a New York democrat, and one of those who were going to throw Hineline overboard on our way to Baltimore for opposing Mr. Van Buren. I find him to be a very clever fellow.

There is but little beauty here, but of course a great deal of folly. The most distinguished flirts at all the houses are as ugly as the devil.

The water here improves with use. When I first drank it, it went down like medicine. Now I can drink five or six tumblers with ease. It has had a considerable effect in opening my bowels.

I called to-day on the two democratic editors here.

15 August, Thursday.

Carman's girls arrived here to-day from the north.[132] Being the only ladies I know of course I do the gallant to them, though the elder one is horridly ugly. I have made several other acquaintances among the gentlemen, among them with Josiah Randall, Esq.[133] of our bar.

16 August, Friday. Utica.

Jeffers and I held a consultation to-day and resolved to go to Niagara. Accordingly we paid all our bills—as a good many do not who visit the Springs—and started at noon, via Schenectady, for this place. We arrived here at ten—got tea—and ought immediately to have gone to bed. This indeed Jeffers did, but I found some politicians in the bar room, with whom I have been engaged until the clock has told me it is midnight. In two hours more I must be again in the cars.

17 August, Saturday. Buffalo.

From two o'clock this morning until ten to-night! What an everlasting journey would it not have been but for two things—my bob-tail coat, with which I made a very comfortable pillow; and a pretty Miss whose occasional glances served very materially to while away the time. We put up at the American,[134] and my pretty companion sat so near me at tea that I had the honor of serving her.

131. Charles A. Secor was a New York City shipchandler with his home on Franklin Street.
132. Probably the daughters of William Carman of Camden.
133. A member of the Philadelphia bar for over thirty years, Randall had offices on Washington Square near Walnut Street.
134. An imposing five-story structure built in the mid-1830s, the American stood on Main Street near Eagle.

18 August, Sunday.   Niagara.

This morning Jeffers and I called upon the quondam Miss Charlotte Jeffers, now Mrs. Westcoat.[135] Her husband, Lieutenant Westcoat, is connected with the garrison here, and his lady lives with him in the barracks very contentedly.

At five o'clock this evening—leaving Jeffers, who cared more for his niece than the Falls, which he has seen before—I took the cars for the "great rush of waters." Near me on the passage sat a gentleman and a lady, either brother and sister or husband and wife. The latter was young, pretty and amorous. Whatever be her relation to her comrade I confess she quite eradicated from my mind the Baltimore beauty who sat opposite to me last night at table! I like these occasional acquaintances with the ladies. In the present case, judging from the grave looks of my Othello, there is just danger enough of cold steel to give the adventure an agreeable spice!

Before I got my lodgings arranged at the Cataract House[136] it was so dark that I could not see the grandeur and majesty of the Falls as I wished. I went over however to the island and proceeded to the point which commands the best view of the American Sheet. The roar of the rapids, as they came on, on, faster and faster still, and at length took their final leap into the now imperceptible abyss below, gave me an idea of eternity—of God—of all that is grand—that no time can efface. It was a terrible sensation that came over me, as I stood there looking at the stupendous scene! I felt that the Eternal was all around me—in all that I saw and all I heard; and for once I realized my own nothingness as I ought, and put a proper estimate upon human littleness. He must be a beast indeed who is not religious when he first sees Niagara!

19 August, Monday.

This morning I arose betimes and went down to look at the wonders of the mighty Niagara. I descended Biddle stairs, and on the ledge below I met my gazelle-eyed beauty of yesterday and her mysterious companion. The latter recognized me, and we soon got into a conversation. They like myself were bound to the Cave of the Winds; but the spray flew so thick that we changed our minds. After standing awhile to contemplate the stupendous scene, the lady began to move up the hill. She slipped and extended her hand to me for assistance. I took it—a beautiful hand it was!—and aided her up the crags, leaving

135. Jeffers' niece had married George C. Wescott, or Westcott, an army officer, in June 1841.
136. One of the two hotels in the town of Niagara Falls, the Cataract was famous for its elegant appointments.

her comrade, like Papegoia in *Printz Hall*,[137] examining minerals and flowers. I had a delightful flirtation with my nameless girl; and came to the conclusion at last that the beau who accompanied her had been made her husband against her will. He joined us at the top of the hill after we had had a teté-a-teté, and I left them forever.

Mr. Jeffers arrived from Buffalo this morning and began to hurry me off. We left the Falls just after dinner intending to return by way of the lake and Oswego. When we got down to Lewiston I discovered that I had left my baggage behind. I told Jeffers to go on. I returned to the Falls, along with another young man from New Haven, who was in the same predicament. My baggage was safe enough at the Cataract House, but whether he found his I do not know.

My start being now put off a day I took several other views of the Falls from different points, but did not go over to the Canada side. I wish to reserve some thing for my next trip.

20 August, Tuesday.   Syracuse, N. Y.

This morning, having made sure of my baggage, I took another peep at the Falls and got into the cars for Buffalo. At this place I fell in with a company of ladies and gentlemen from Virginia, of whom more anon.

Being desirous of overtaking Jeffers at Albany, I did not even stop in Buffalo to breakfast. It was my luck to get into the same cars with the company above alluded to, among whom was a lady who appeared to have no companion—that is she was attended by her brother. With him I got acquainted. Until dinner the said lady appeared very offish. We exchanged a good many sheep's eyes, it is true, but they prove but little at best. From Rochester we rode in the little old-fashioned round-bodied cars. The Virginians occupied one apartment and an old bachelor and myself another—the two communicating by sliding windows. Being very much fatigued, as evening began to close in, I lay down upon the seat adjoining my pretty neighbor, and had well nigh forgotten her, Niagara, the Camden *Eagle* and every thing else, when I felt a soft pressure upon my hand. I opened my eyes and found that by some accident I had clasped the plump white and soft hand of my pretty friend. She had reached through the window to arouse me, and ask me to hold her bonnet. I picked myself up as soon as possible—put her bonnet in a safe place—and went to sleep again.

137. John Papegoya, son-in-law of Governor John Printz (1592–1663) of New Sweden, assumed control of the province in 1653 when Printz returned to Sweden. Printz Hall was the governor's mansion on Tinicum Island in the Delaware. Mickle has probably read the anonymous *Printz Hall: A Record of New Sweden* (Philadelphia, 1839), a novel in which Papegoya is portrayed as a scientist, so interested in collecting "botany and mineral treasures" that he neglects his political and husbandly duties.

About ten o'clock we reached this place—famous in politics—where we took tea. My Norfolk friend and I, got, by some mishap, opposite to each other, and as I caught her eye I observed a slight blush upon her dimpled cheek. She is a merry piece, and loves fun better than most. Her brother is a good-natured fellow, but he cant see all things.

I find, from talking with the politicians here, that the Democrats are in fine spirits. Betting, the test of the spirits with a certain class, runs in favor of Polk.

21 August, Wednesday.   Albany, N. Y.

I left Syracuse this morning along with the Virginia company. They stopped at Schenectady en route to Saratoga. This is I trust the last time I shall allow the ladies to keep me from appreciating the natural beauties of the country I have come so far to see.

This evening I called at the *Argus*[138] office and introduced myself as a democratic editor from New Jersey. Croswell himself was not in, but a few minutes after I left my card Mr. Kramer, assistant editor of the *Argus,* called on me at the Stanwix House.[139] We attended a concert, and were together most of the evening. He kept saying continually "Why you're very young—You're very young." I pleaded guilty to every charge, but in a few minutes he would take another survey of me, and again break forth with the same expression. He's a queer fellow I guess. He says that New York is doubtful,[140] and that the Camden *Eagle* is "a very pleasant paper."

22 August, Thursday.   New York City.

I came down to-day in the *Empire,* and took lodgings at the Astor. This evening I went to Niblo's.

Mr. Jeffers went on to Philadelphia yesterday, so that I shall stay here until Saturday. I'm under positive obligations to behave well. I can stay here without carousing and without deserving any credit for so doing. By the by, for the first time since I signed the Temperance pledge I the other day took a glass of wine without the plea of medicine. Jeffers at Saratoga ordered some Madeira, but he found himself the only toper at table. I took a glass merely to help him out of his unpleasant singularity. The fact is the Temperance cause has been merged of late in Native Americanism, and the latter is a humbug which I do not care to be thought to sanction in any way.

138. The Albany *Argus,* one of the leading conservative Democratic papers in the state, was edited by Edwin Croswell (1797–1871), with the assistance of John Kramer.

139. Stanwix Hall, at the corner of Broadway and Maiden Lane, was a popular haven for railroad passengers.

140. Kramer thought New York "doubtful" in that it might not deliver its electoral votes to Polk.

23 August, Friday.

To-day I visited the different democratic newspaper offices in the city. At Tom Englishe's[141] I fell in with a Norfolk Tyler man who roomed with me last night. He is a glorious fellow.

This evening I went to the Bowery.[142] A greater set of blackguards I never before saw together. The first tier of boxes was about equal to a Philadelphia pit.

24 August, Saturday.   Camden, N. J.

I came home in the first line this morning to be present at a democratic Mass Meeting this afternoon in the Camden woods. The affair cost me five dollars, but that I do not regret if it be the means of doing any good. The turn-out was pretty strong, and the spirit quite as warm as I expected. My uncle presided. Mr. Potts, Mr. Elmer and Col. McCahen[143] made speeches. Mulford drew the resolutions. The Fencibles band made the music. And Tom Florence[144] and his company of hard-riders did the singing.

In the evening I called at Sheppard's.

25 August, Sunday.

For the chief part of to-day I did nothing but sleep. The little I read was in Dumas' *Democracy in France.*

26 August, Monday.

The new party of Native Americans held a mass-meeting in the Camden woods this afternoon. It was quite large, but some of the speeches were so indiscreet that several of our Camden converts have back-slidden—among them Jo Githens, who now damns the Natives as heartily as a week ago he did the foreigners.

The Philadelphia *Spirit of the Times* a few days back noticed our society, The Sons of Liberty, in a very favorable manner. The article has been copied in several of the Eastern papers, and has made quite a stir among the liberals.

27 August, Tuesday.

This evening I was at Sheppard's. Miss Josephine has now finished her education and set out for a young woman. With me "the light of the other days is faded." The foolish notions that disturbed me when a boy have left me, never, I hope, to return.

141. Thomas Dunn English (1819–1902), poet and journalist, was editor of the New York *Aurora* in 1844.
142. The Bowery, a popular theatre, opened at the corner of the Bowery and Elizabeth Street in 1826.
143. John J. McCahen was a Philadelphia newspaper editor and an accountant.
144. Philadelphia Democrat Thomas B. Florence (1812–75) would run for Congress in 1846 and would serve in the house from 1851 to 1861.

28 August, Wednesday.

Between the Natives and ex-councilor Browning I think it is very probable that the Whigs will carry the new county of Camden in the coming election. Mr. Browning has the face to ask us, after his conduct last winter, to take him up again; and he throws out ominous hints of an independent ticket, should we refuse.[145] There is also some difficulty concerning the Sheriffalty. Too many want to suck the same teat at once.

29 August, Thursday.

To-day I was engaged principally in getting matter ready for the next *Eagle*. This playing the editor is becoming a very great bore.

30 August, Friday.

Since Bossee sold out to Curts it has been as much, and a little more than the bargain to get the paper out in due time.[146] To-day they were considerably behind-hand; so I turned to and helped them. I am a pretty good type-sticker, and can I guess earn my bread at that if I cannot at pleading law.

31 August, Saturday.

This evening The Sons of Liberty met in Mulford's office and adopted without alteration a Constitution of my drafting. It is short, terse and comprehensive.

1 September, Sunday.

This evening I stopped at Kelley's. Harriet's hopes are soon to be realized; but Mrs. Mary Drakeley has beaten her several months.[147]

2 September, Monday.

This evening our Stumping Club were at the Green Tree in Washington.[148] I talked about half an hour, *ad captandum*. My companions tell me it was the best speech I have yet made. The night being very dark, we lost our road in coming home, and got to Woodbury. We were foolish enough to wake Humphreys up to get something to drink; so now, I suppose the old county men will have the laugh on us completely!

---

145. For Joshua P. Browning's earlier behavior, see entry of 19 March 1844.

146. Henry Bosse had purchased Hineline's share of the *Eagle* in May 1844, but was forced by ill health to abandon the newspaper business only three months later.

147. That is, she had gotten pregnant first.

148. The Green Tree Tavern, at the intersection of Egg Harbor and Greentree Roads, was one of the most famous inns and stage stops in Washington Township. Thomas Crees was the current owner.

3 September, Tuesday.

I bought some miscellaneous books to-day, being desirous now while I have some money to widen the foundations of my library.

This evening I went to Trenton, to attend the first State Convention under the new Constitution, which is to take place to morrow. Thomson's chances for nomination are very good. He was first publicly nominated at my suggestion in the Court House in Camden on the 13th of June. The old hunkers, Wall, Vroom, Ryall[149] and Co. kick a little, but it will be in vain.

4 September, Wednesday.

The Convention this afternoon nominated John R. Thomson almost unanimously. Hard work however is before him and us. That rail-road is—all must forsee—a heavy drag.[150]

5 September, Thursday.

To day there was a tremendous Mass-meeting at the Capital. Every part of the State was fully represented, and the proceedings were very enthusiastic. I will have to write a full account of the affair for the *Eagle*—which, if you are curious, see. I came home in the mail line to night.

6 September, Friday.

I am half resolved to drop the editor—I am sick of Curts' intolerable stupidity.

7 September, Saturday.

The *Eagle* appears to-day with a short card from me announcing my withdrawal from the concern. Mr. Jeffers however and several of our democratic friends object so strongly that I will be obliged to reconsider my resolution.

8 September, Sunday.

The Whigs have put us upon the defensive with reference to Thomson. They urge the monopoly with which he is supposed to be beneficially connected with irrisistable force. The contest begins to be doubtful. Of this however I am well assured, that no man deserved nomination and election better than "the father of our new Constitution."

9 September, Monday.

This evening I made a so-so speech at Mount Ephriam. Joshua P.

149. David Bailey Ryall (1798–1864), an attorney from Freehold, had recently served as a congressman (1839–41).

150. Thomson was a major stockholder in and director of the Camden and Amboy Railroad, the most disliked corporation in New Jersey.

Browning was present. He is going to make a desperate push to get upon our ticket. If he succeeds, our game in this county is up.

10 September, Tuesday.
I took a peep in upon my friend the Colonel to-day. He is sanguine of the election of Polk. The Natives however in Philadelphia will join the Whigs in a body.

This evening I paid a social debt.

The Whigs have nominated Charles C. Stratton for Governor.[151] My uncle has beaten him two to one in old Gloucester; but he has that negative reputation which I fear. He is one of those harmless creatures about whom nothing can be said pro or con.

11 September, Wednesday.
To-day, for a wonder, I was at the office, and read a little law.

12 September, Thursday.
The democrats have carried Maine—glorious news! The Whigs will now make a dead set upon New York and Pennsylvania.

There was an excellent meeting to night at Clementon. I talked about an hour.

14 September, Saturday.
This evening I made a speech at Haddonfield.

151. Stratton won the November election and served as governor from 1845 to 1848.

View in Morrestown

1845

1 January, Wednesday.

This morning I went to Woodbury to collect from the county records some facts which are necessary for my "Reminiscences." I had a long conversation with the ancient Michael Fisher, Esq.[1] who gave me much information. He told me, for instance, that the Horseheads, mentioned in the *Memoirs of the Gloucester Fox Hunting Club*,[2] is a place about three miles south east of Woodbury, where seven roads come together. The people from all these roads bring to the junction all their horses which have died, and the waggoners in passing hang up their sculls on the trees. My old friend says he has seen hundreds of these horse-sculls suspended here abouts. He mentioned also an instance of female courage which ought not to be forgotten: Some Hessians going, after the battle of Red Bank to a house near Blackwoodtown, where the matron only was at home, she met them at the door with a noggin full of hot water, and forbade them to enter. They pushed their bayonets at her, but she maintained her post bravely, until at last an officer

1. The influential Michael C. Fisher was currently director of the Gloucester County Board of Freeholders.
2. Mickle refers to William Milnor's *Memoirs of the Gloucester Fox Hunting Club, near Philadelphia* (Philadelphia, 1830).

came up, and addressed her very politely. Him she let in, but the others she would not. Of the town of Upton, which is occasionally mentioned in the earliest records of the county, Mr. Fisher knows nothing definite. He seems to think, however, that it was situated where the old King's Road crossed Little Gloucester River.[3] There was, a few years ago a tavern in ruins at this place; but now there is nothing but a hand bridge, to mark the spot. The site is upon or near the property of Joshua P. Browning, Esq. This Mr. Fisher is by marriage a distant relative of mine. He is of one of the oldest families in the county—has been for a long time a distinguished man—remembers well things which occurred sixty years ago, and delights in conveying his knowledge to others. O that such men would only write all they remember! What light would they throw upon the history of the past!

When dining at Humphrey's—the old Matlack Tavern, in which the County Courts used to sit, while the present Woodbury Court House was in course of erection—I sat alongside of Mr. John B. Harrison, a briefless lawyer, an "*anceps syllabarum*" as Tully[4] would have called him. He had read, it seems, my sketch of Haddonfield, published in a late number of the *Phoenix*,[5] and began pretty soon to take exceptions to its accuracy. He had heard some body say that an old man had told his grandmother's cousin that it was not Ben Haines, but some body else, who accompanied old Sage on his reconnoitering trip from Haddonfield to Gloucester.[6] I convinced him of his utter ignorance of matters of local history by asking him whether some of his ancestors' buildings were not burnt by the British at Gloucester. He had never heard of any such thing! Afterwards he asked if I had weighed the title of my book well. I told him I had. He then entered into a long argument to prove that the title *Reminiscences* was a misnomer, inasmuch as I am entirely too young to remember as far back as the erection of Fort Nassau in 1623![7] I only smiled and asked him if he had not read Butler's *Reminiscences* written not many years ago, which reach back to the deluge?[8] He replied very gravely, "Yes that

3. Fisher was incorrect. Upton, settled in the late seventeenth century, had been on the south branch of Big Timber Creek, near present Blackwood. The King's Road was the Salem Road, the first authorized in West Jersey.

4. "Tully" is Marcus Tullius Cicero.

5. Curts had changed the name of the *Eagle* to the *Phoenix*, starting with the issue of 23 November 1844. Mickle was no longer associated with the newspaper.

6. Miles Sage's trip is discussed in the entry of 7 March 1841.

7. A more accurate date for the construction of Fort Nassau, the first white settlement in old Gloucester County, is 1626. The fort was located within the bounds of modern Gloucester City.

8. Mickle seems to be referring to Frederick Butler's *Sketches of Universal History*, the last edition of which was published in 1832, but the word "reminiscences" does not appear on the title page of that book.

is true, but——." And the rest of his answer slipped down his throat with a piece of lemon pudding. The ignorance of some men is astonishing.

My stay at Woodbury having been prolonged till sunset I was obliged to run my horse all the way home, in order to redeem my promise to Emily Harley, to wit, to call upon her this evening, if I was alive. I just succeeded in getting on board the last boat to Philadelphia. Mulford, Master Tom Ridgway, and Misses Cole and Ridgway were also on board bound to the same place. We had a merry time, although the grave, Mesmeric and deistical Doctor Coates[9] was present a great part of the time.

2 January, Thursday.

This morning I was obliged to hurry across the river to be present at the close of the case of *West* vs. *Stokes* before Judge King, in Equity. Col. Page and Mr. Dallas, the Vice President elect are for the plaintiff, and Morris and Tyson for the defendant.[10] The argument was opened last week by Col Page, who took the best part of two days. The defense took another day; and Mr. Dallas began his argument on Tuesday. I have been engaged as note-taker and precedent hunter on the side of the complainant. While Tyson was speaking his Honor stopped him, and remarked: "I now begin to see this case; it divides itself into two branches." He then stated the two phases, and concluded with the singular bull: "The first view of the transaction is very simple, but the latter is equally simple, only a little more complicated." The Vice President looked across the table and observed to me, "That's queer, isn't it?" The Judge however is excusable for being just now a little bemuddled. He has been nominated by President Tyler, as successor to Judge Baldwin in the Supreme Court of the United States, and his nomination is yet unconfirmed by the Senate.[11] Of course his mind is not in a State to examine a dry point of equity with a great deal of care and deliberation. During the course of this trial several amusing bar-anecdotes have transpired. For instance, Dallas in a kind of episode this morning asked Tyson if he remembered the warrants which old Mayor Wharton[12] used to issue for the apprehension of "base ill-looking fellows." "No," said his Honor "for the apprehension of persons 'suspected of being base ill looking fellows.'" Such pleasantries afford a proper relief from the tedium of a trial in chancery. Dallas made a powerful argument for West, and I think we shall get a decree.

9. Reynell Coates (1802–86), a Philadelphia physician, later moved to Camden. In 1852, he secured the vice-presidential nomination of the Native American ticket.

10. Edward King was president judge of the court of common pleas. Phineas Pemberton Morris was a young attorney with offices on Prune Street.

11. Justice Henry Baldwin (1780–1844) having died, Tyler nominated several successors, none acceptable to the United States Senate.

12. Robert Wharton had been mayor of Philadelphia from 1820 to 1824.

3 January, Friday.

My *Reminiscences,* the publication of which has been much delayed by the hurry in the *Eagle* office consequent upon the election, seem now in a fair way to be brought out. Curts has employed an extra hand who works continually upon them, and keeps me pretty busy in finding copy. We have already got out more than fifty pages, and will probably have the whole complete by the middle of February. There will be about eighty pages, instead of thirty two as we first supposed.

4 January, Saturday.

This evening my French lesson with M. Surault detained me so long that I could not attend the Reading Circle at Chapman's; so I took my violin to Cole's and practised awhile with Miss Caroline. That Reading Circle, by the by, is a very pleasant affair. Miss White,[13] the young lady who gives us lessons, is quite an expert locutionist, and recites very well. She gave instructions to the Rev. John Maffit of the Methodist ministry, whose style is just like her own, and to many other distinguished men. She is young, not pretty, but intelligent and, if I read eyes aright, amorous. It was she who delivered the address at the whig meeting, at Kaighn's Point, on delivering a flag to my friend Dudley. Poor Tom forgot his reply, and had to produce it from his pocket. Lo, it had been written in pencil and was rubbed out! He made a perfect farce of the affair, to the infinite amusement of the democrats present, and to the utter disgust of my aunt Hugg, who vows she will never attend another meeting of the kind!

5 January, Sunday.

Some time ago my friend Chapman bought at an auction in Philadelphia a lot of four or five old books for five cents. On examining his purchase, he found a perfect copy of Gabriel Thomas' *History of Pennsylvania and West New Jersey,*[14] which he presented to me. I gave him in return the *Memoirs of Lord Eldon,* which cost three dollars and a half. The news of the sale of this book having got abroad among the connoiseurs and booksellers Chapman was several times offered ten dollars or more for it. He told inquirers that he had given it away to me. Yesterday, being in Ward's book-store in Fourth Street, Ward related to me the premises—concluding by saying that a young lawyer named Mickle now had the work, and that Mr. Paulson of the Philadelphia bar, and several others wanted it very much and would

13. Miss White, of Camden, whose first name is not given in newspaper accounts, had spoken at a Whig meeting of 20 June 1844, on behalf of the "ladies of Camden." She was the daughter of Lemuel G. White of Market Street, Camden, who was also a "teacher of elocution."

14. Thomas's (1661–1714) *An Historical and Geographical Account of the Province of Pennsylvania and West New Jersey* was first published in 1698.

give almost any price for it.[15] I replied "I am that young lawyer, but expect to retain old Gabriel as long as I live, and then give it to the Historical Society of New Jersey, if there should be one in existence."[16] He offered me fifty dollars for my treasure, which I promptly and positively declined. I told Chapman of this, and he was delighted. "I will spread it" said he "wherever I go."

6 January, Monday.

This morning my dancing-master, Whale,[17] put into my hands for collection a bill against Prince Murat of Bordentown. Of all pay Princes are the worst![18]

7 January, Tuesday.

I spent last evening with two very respectable, lively girls in Lombard Street in Philadelphia. I was struck with the approximation which our manners are making to the ante-Revolutionary manners of the French people. Our ladies now speak upon subjects which a few years ago they would hardly have dared to think about. Thus last night we struck accidentally upon the Heberton affair, and finding the girls communicative, I played off just as far as my modesty would allow. They entered into all the minutiae of that revolting farcico-tragedy with a freedom which I confess astonished me. They agree with me fully that Heberton was quite as much sinned against as sinning. One of them by the by has promised to procure me an introduction to Charlotte Heberton, whom I met at Cape May last summer. She is certainly a charming girl.

This evening, for the first time, I attended the Cotillion Party given by my dancing-master in the Assembly Buildings. It was a shabby affair. I saw some of the Harvey boys there, and several counter-hoppers from Second Street. I soon got wearied, and retired.

8 January, Wednesday.

I had some invitations extended to me to dine to-day with different companies of Democrats who were thus celebrating the defeat of Packenham and Clay.[19] I did not attend. Col. William Polk—the

15. Townsend Ward was the owner of the book shop. He later published Mickle's *Reminiscences of Old Gloucester*. Charles A. Paulson, Jr., had joined the Philadelphia bar in July 1844.

16. The New Jersey Historical Society was founded in 1845 and Mickle was an early member. He apparently never donated a copy of the Thomas book to the organization, however.

17. Henry Whale's dancing school was held at the Assembly Buildings at Tenth and Chestnut Streets.

18. That is, of all who owe money, princes are the worst. Achille Murat, son of Napoleon's marshall, immigrated to the United States in 1823 and gained the reputation as an untrustworthy debtor.

19. Henry Clay had just lost the presidency to James K. Polk.

brother of the President elect—was at the dinner in the Chinese Museum, and seems, it is said, to be in charge of Hoy and others of the Young Democracy—that is the anti Van Buren portion of the Democratic Party. By the by, the only two papers that have complimented me upon my withdrawal from the editorial chair of the *Phoenix* are the *Hunterdon Democrat,* and the Philadelphia *Spirit of the Times,* both organs of the Young Democracy. My warm opposition to the renomination of Van Buren has caused me to lose caste with the old Hunkers.

This evening Mr. Coad delivered a lecture in explanation of his improvement of the Galvanic Battery, in Bontemps Hall, Camden.[20] The audience was very small, and the only absolutely young lady present was Miss Mary Gray. Notwithstanding the hostile relations between her father and myself, we had quite a cosy talk. She looks as well as ever. After the lecture, Mulford and I called at Cole's, where we found Tom Ridgway. He is a fine looking fellow, and his exterior may be more powerful with Cad than the internal merits of Mulford. Cad however is a sensible girl, and *nous verrons!*

9 January, Thursday.

I made my debut to-day as a pleader before Judge Stroud[21] in the District Court. The case was *Barnet Rice* vs. *the County of Philadelphia,* under the Act of 1841, for the compensation of losses occasioned by mobs. The plaintiff, a harmless Irishman, occupied the house at the South East corner of Second and Master streets, Kensington, as a grocery store. In the Native riots in May last this house was fired and destroyed, and thereupon this action was brought nominally for one thousand dollars, the loss being according to Rice's own estimate some five hundred and twenty dollars. The jury without going out of the box gave us the whole amount and costs. I opened in a short speech to the jury, and Col. Page concluded. Henry M. Phillips[22] and Peter A. Browne Jr. defended the county. The former committed one blunder, which to me would have been very mortifying. He rose and said to the Court: "I wish, may it please your honor, to raise one point which has never yet been construed— Can personal property come within the statute?" The Judge interupted him, "Does not the statute expressly provide for compensation for the loss of personal property?" "I think

20. Patrick Coad, of Philadelphia, had invented a "Graduated Galvanic Apparatus" to help people with hearing impairments and other ills. The lecture may have been held in a room in Charles Bontemps' gunsmith shop near Second and Plum Streets.

21. George M. Stroud was an associate judge of the Philadelphia District Court from 1835 to 1868.

22. Phillips, a Philadelphia attorney since 1832, had offices on South Sixth Street.

not" replied Phillips; and taking up our volume of the Pamphlet Laws for 1841 he began to read, p. 416: "In all cases where any dwelling house or other building or property real or personal——." At the word "personal" he dropped the book, and said he would withdraw the point. Since Phillips has been assistant Solicitor for the County for some time back, and has defended many riot actions of a similar nature, such a blunder was inexcusable. Neither he nor Mr. Browne had read the law! This incident may serve to teach me the lesson that impudence is as necessary as knowledge in acquiring a reputation.

David Paul Brown sat by me during my speech, and after Court rose I walked with him towards his residence. He promised to give me some facts in the history of Gloucester county, of which he is a native. His father was an inebriate, and in a drunken frolic fell overboard at Market Street Wharf and was drowned. It will hardly do to note this down among other reminiscences of the men of Gloucester.

Mr. Coad's audience was about the same as last evening. His battery was brought to bear this morning upon the ears of Mrs. Henry Curts, who has been deaf, or nearly deaf, for a long time; and as she says and believes, with a very beneficial result. From the lecture Mulford and I adjourned into his office below, where we were joined by Bontemps and Martin, and afterwards by Denny,[23] who had quite a cotillion-party—I being fiddler.

10 January, Friday.

The foolish haste of us republican, democratic Americans to adopt the dress and ape the manners of the foreigners who visit us, is sometimes ridiculed by our press; but is too deeply fixed to be eradicated. When Ole Bull, the great Norwegian violinist, played in Philadelphia, he brought with him an outlandish cap. . . . Immediately the hatters on Chestnut St. began to make caps after the same fashion; they were called "Ole Bulls," and in a few days every fop in town had mounted one upon his head. The rage of "ole bulls," was at its height about Christmas; but by this time the loafers had taken a great dislike to them, and began to cry them down. On that day, the Streets were full of promenaders, and in the morning a great many "ole bulls" were visible. About noon companies of young men of rowdyish character, having mounted mock "oles" with great tassels of various colored paper, began to parade up and down together; and whenever they met a gentleman so unlucky as to have one of the obnoxious caps upon his head, they would cry out "Ole Bull, Ole Bull!" and raise such a disturbance that the man would be glad to get into the nearest hatter's,

23. John Denny is listed as a sailor in the Camden city directory for 1850.

to purchase some other kind of head dress. The consequence was that "ole bulls" disappeared from the street as quickly as they had come. Towards evening a very few had the courage to wear them upon the promenade; and some of these I heard were pursued by the loafers and mobbed. A similar emeute occurred in Philadelphia last summer a year, about the French blouse. That comfortable article of dress was driven entirely from use; and "Ole Bull caps" will, I guess, also disappear.

11 January, Saturday.

The case of *Rice* vs. *the County* having been reported in the *Ledger* with the names of the counsel, several of my friends have tendered me their congratulations. Whether their friendship is seated deeper than upon their lips, I know not. I am becoming misanthropic. I have seen too much treachery and hypocricy not to feel an incontinent desire to laugh, whenever any one would persuade me that he, or she—aye, she— "there's the rub!"—is my friend. If I could find a comfortable cave, big enough to hold me and a few books, and situated where I could dig up plenty of roots and see no human being—No—no, I would'n't either! I have a mother, a dear old mother, for whom alone I would live though life were purgatory! While she breathes, I have one true friend who would love me for myself! . . .

12 January, Sunday.

To-day I wrote the XVIII Chapter of my *Reminiscences*. Being obliged to write as much every Sunday as the printers can get through with in the following week, I have to compose very rapidly. I fear very much the last part of my pamphlet will be very crude. . . . If I had had less time then and more now, I should, perhaps have made a better whole.

13 January, Monday.

This evening I attended the Annual Ball of Col. Page's corps, the State Fencibles. Owing to the superior tact of my esteemed father in the law, and the great care he takes to make his company as select as possible, the Fencible balls are the most recherché of any given in Philadelphia. The newspapers have been busy for a month back in sounding the note of preparation; and the high expectations which they excited concerning this year's fete were realized and more than realized. The Musical Fund Hall contained no less than a thousand people; and the company was composed of the best families and the most beautiful girls in the city. I had the honor to wait upon Mrs. Chamburg, or Schaumburg, as she spells it, Miss Page and the beautiful little Miss Schaumburg. The Hon. John R. Thomson of our state, who was present, agreed with me that Mrs. Schaumburg was by far the most splended woman pres the room.[24] I was invited down to supper about midnight, and disarranged my digestive organs I fear by mixing champagne and other liquors. I turned in at Burr's about five o'clock.

14 January, Tuesday.

This evening I visited the Musical Fund Hall again to hear Ole Bull. Mulford and Caroline were also there. The great Norwegian played his *Niagara,* a piece which has made some sensation in the city of New York. It contains some magnificent music; but I think he might have just as well called it *Mount Vesuvius* or the *Roaring Maelstrom.* The most significant part of the whole affair, was a passage upon the kettle drum—a crescendo—which resembled the noise one hears in approaching the cataract with woods intervening. Niagara, I rather imagine, was not made to be represented, even upon the omnipotent violin. Its sublimity was intended to be felt—and with this man ought to be satisfied. Our maestro, however, was much more successful in *The Norwegian Pines.* I could hear the wind sigh fitfully through the desert of trees; and almost felt the house shake as some monarch of the forest, yielding to a stronger blast, fell crushing and splintering among its fellows. Ole Bull is a tall and spare man, something like what I take Paganinni to have been from the likenesses I have seen.[25] His shoulders are broad, and his waist slender. He wears a long frock-coat, like most of the north-Europeans. His face is expressive of a fervid imagination, which he undoubtedly has. In playing double and triple trills, his fingers can hardly be seen, they move with such rapidity. I observed that he would correct the pitch of his strings and resume the piece, without any observable break. When he was in the crisis of his concertos he seemed to be a madman; yet his gestures had none of the horrid ungracefulness which made Paganinni so ridiculous. But his playing is by far less graceful than Nagel's.

15 January, Wednesday.

Col. Page introduced me to day to Dr. Ferris of Rhode Island.[26] The form observed by my preceptor on presenting me to the Dorrites is generally as follows: "This is Mr. Mickle, who is almost the originator of the new Constitution of New Jersey." The compliment always makes

24. The word "pres" is apparently Mickle's abbreviation for "present in."
25. Niccolo Paganini (1782–1840), by far the most famous violin virtuoso of his time, never toured America.
26. There was no Dr. Ferris among the prominent supporters of Governor Dorr. Perhaps the man referred to is Peter W. Ferris, whom Providence city directories list as a teacher in 1844 and a dentist in 1850.

me feel awkward. By the by such partiality is not confined to the Colonel: for the other day I received a copy of Hineline's paper—published at New Albany, Indiana,[27] wherein I am called "the Dorr of New Jersey." The Lord forbid that my humble efforts in behalf of Constitutional reform in New Jersey should cause me to have my head shaved and my diet reduced to bread and water. Dr. Ferris brings with him a book called *Might and Right*, containing, he says, the true history of the Dorr movement.[28] I bought a copy, and will see.

16 January, Thursday.

My French teacher, M. Surault, put into my hands a few days ago a little vaudeville which he has translated for the Walnut Street Theatre. It is called *Yelva, or the Russian Orphan*,[29] and is a very neat little piece. It is intended to be produced when Taglioni,[30] the famous danseuse comes out to make a fortune from us simple, humbug Americans. The translation is by no means the best that can be made; but as people will go to see Taglioni's legs rather than to hear the dialogue, it does not matter much. I made some alterations at Surault's request.

To-night I wrote the chief part of the XIX Chapter of my pamphlet.

17 January, Friday.

This afternoon I was engaged, when I ought to have been at my office, in arranging my library. I have spent a good deal of money of late in books, and have made a good many acquaintances among literary men. Among the rest Mr. Chapman has become very attentive to me. He is about to set up a book-store with his library, and has already sold many of his books. I have paid him near fifty dollars for law and general literature; having bought of him, inter alia, *The Secret Memoirs*, in French, in thirty nine volumes.[31]

18 January, Saturday.

The winter has so far been remarkably mild, and the opinion is every where expressed among scientific men, that instances of mildness are of late years more frequent and more signal than they used to be. We are yet in a climate some degrees colder than that of the corresponding latitude in Europe; but there can be no doubt that the

27. Hineline lived in Indiana for a brief period before returning to Camden in 1845.

28. *Might and Right* was a defense of Dorr, written pseudonymously by Frances Harriet Green (1805–78) and published in Providence in 1844.

29. Surault did not secure a performance of his version of *Yelva* in the years following this entry. Other translations of Augustin Eugene Scribe's play had been used in Philadelphia performances in the 1830s.

30. Marie Taglioni (1804–84), one of Europe's leading ballerinas.

31. Mickle's purchase was Louis Petit de Bachaumont's *Mémoires secrets pour servir a l'histoire de la république, de lettres en France*, published in 1777–89.

effect of felling the forests and subduing the wilderness yet remaining to the west and north west, will be to give us the same uniformly mild winters.

19 January, Sunday.

To-day I finished the XIX chapter of my book. The booby Curts gets along so slowly with it that I have determined to give it to Ned Chandler to finish. I am impatient to get it out.

20 January, Monday.

Owing to the death of Judge King's wife, the Common Pleas have adjourned for a week. We have two or three cases returnable to this term which of course go off. Among them is one riot-case, wherein I think we shall easily beat the county. . . .

21 January, Tuesday.

The fate of the Texas project before the Congress is yet somewhat doubtful.[32] Bob Tyler, the son of the President, who is practising law in Philadelphia, said to day very confidently that the bill would pass the house handsomely and have a majority of one in the Senate.[33] He ought to know; but whether he does or not—*nous verrons*.

22 January, Wednesday.

John K. Kane, my principal examiner, is for certain to be made Attorney General of Pennsylvania. My friend Kelley will, in this event be made Prosecutor for Philadelphia county.[34]

Kelley, by the by, gave me a case the other day to look into, which may be of some consequence. A United States sailor, named Joshua Howell, died some years ago in Boston at the house of a man named Casey; having before made a will bequeathing to Casey some thirteen hundred dollars in cash, and making also a general devise of all his real estate. It is said that Howell had a right to a moiety of a large estate in Gloucester county, now in possession of Robert K. Matlack. I fear there is some mistake about the matter; but at all events I will examine it to the bottom. The celebrated Hallett[35] is the counsel retained by

32. President Tyler had failed to gain congressional approval for the annexation of Texas in the spring and summer of 1844 and was now trying to secure a joint resolution to that effect.

33. Tyler, an attorney with offices on Seventh Street, was not far off. The senate vote for annexation, on 27 February, was 27 to 25, the house vote, on the following day, 132 to 76. Texas was formally admitted to the Union on 29 December 1845.

34. Kelley became deputy prosecuting attorney for the city and county of Philadelphia later in the year.

35. Benjamin F. Hallett (1797–1862), editor, prominent Democrat and one of Massachusetts' leading attorneys.

Casey in Boston. He was in Philadelphia some time ago, and Page introduced me to him as "the Originator of the New Constitution of New Jersey." What would Thomson say, if he knew that I sometimes blushed in feathers belonging to him?

23 *January, Thursday*.

This evening young McCollum,[36] one of the Colonel's protegés, took a benefit at the Olympic Circus. He is a beautiful rider and most graceful vaulter. I accepted an invitation from my preceptor, and took a seat with him and Mrs. Schaumburg in a private box.

Last evening I was at Whale's cotillion party, and danced—actually danced—two or three of the setts! Miss Emily Harley was there, and promised to take me through. I observed in the room a son of Ross the Cherokee Chief, with whom I had a slight acquaintance some years ago,[37] during a sojourn of a few days at Lawrenceville. There is not much of the Indian in him; his mother having been, I believe, a full-blood white woman.

24 *January, Friday*.

The Whigs, headed by Governor Stratton and John C. Smallwood of Gloucester, the President of the Senate, are going to make a desperate effort to set Camden County back.[38] This will raise a family quarrel among them, for since it went last fall for the Whigs, many of their own number are for retaining it. They will have stormy caucasses this winter at Trenton. In the meanwhile it is clearly the policy of the democrats to stand off and laugh. A meeting to oppose the reunion is to be held on next Thursday evening at the Race Coarse Tavern—a Whig House.[39]

25 *January, Saturday*.

Dropping around to my favorite bookseller's—Townsend Ward's—this afternoon, I met Chapman, and found that he is about putting his splendid library in the market. He does not care, however to own this in so many words. He calls it "exchanging books, as all literary men are fond of doing." Soon after my return to Camden he sent me a list of several works with prices annexed—so that I conclude he will not object to "exchanging" for money.

I stopped at Alderman Mitchell's this morning to learn what judg-

36. Thomas McCollum, then touring with the Rufus Welch circus troupe, was to astound New York critics with his riding and jumping skills the following week.
37. See entry of 7 November 1838.
38. Stratton and Smallwood hoped to win repeal of the law creating Camden County. They were not able to do so.
39. At the Camden and Philadelphia Race Course.

ment be rendered on Thursday against Thibault, in our case.[40] Lo! he informed me that he had decided against us! I reported this to Page, who without being at all surprized remarked: "It generally happens that Aldermen go for the plaintiff." We are going to appeal, and I think the Common Pleas will certainly reverse this inequitable decision.

26 January, Sunday.

This evening I called upon Jeffers at his office, and requested him to enter me as a student in New Jersey. There is nothing like making, "assurance doubly sure."

28 January, Tuesday.

I gave Wannan some days ago several volumes of old pamphlets to bind for me. I desire to catch up to Col. Page, who has a pamphlet-library of some sixty volumes. Many of those which I now have on hand are rare—having been collected by my father and grand father.

29 January, Wednesday.[41]

This evening I was to have attended a meeting of the "Camden Haydn Society," of which I have been elected instrumental leader. A child in the family of the vocal conductor having died, our rehearsal was postponed. . . .

My friend Mulford went to Salem post haste on Saturday last, to hear as he believed the last words of his father, who has had a very severe paralytic stroke. We got news to-day that the old gentlemen is not withstanding likely to recover; of which on Tom's account I am very glad! He is too good a fellow, this, ever to have any trouble in this world or the next.

[SD] J'arrive ce soir chez la belle Caroline, et y porté mon violon pour l'accompagner dans des chansons de l'opera *The Bohemian Girl*.[42] Lá je recontrai ma vieille amie, la jolie Josephine. Il y a eu peu d'amité entre nous depuis quelques mois—ce que je ne dirai point á present. Quand je me fis introduire dans le salon, elle rougit—soit par modestie ou par mauvaise honte—et elle repondit á mon salut avec formalité.

Apres que Caroline et moi nous eûmes accompli plusieurs piéces,

40. Joshua Mitchell, a Philadelphia alderman, lived on North Sixth Street. The case of *Thibault* v. *Welsh* had been argued on 20 January, with Mickle representing Welsh. Thibault was suing Welsh for money he claimed was owed him for construction materials.

41. From this date until February 27, Mickle kept two diaries, though there are not entries for every day in both. Hereafter the first entry for each day will be from the regular diary; shifts from one diary to another will be indicated by the abbreviations (*RD*) for regular diary and (*SD*) for secret diary.

42. Michael William Balfe's opera had seen its first United States performance in New York City in 1844.

nous nous arrêtâmes; et comme le bruit des deux instrumens expiroit j'appris de Josephine, qui parlait á Mme. Ridgway, celle remarque: "Nous n'existons que pour voir de plus en plus la deception des hommes!"

Mes yeux rencontrerent ceux de Caroline—nous souriâmes l'une et l'autre, mais nous noustairîmes.

A dix heures il faut que j'accompagne ma vielle amie á sa demeure. Nous marchons comme des soldats aux obsèques de leur general—ni l'une ni l'autre de nous ne parle—elle me renvoie sans m'offrir sa main—nous nous separons avec déplaisir et peine.

Je suis bien aise de cette affaire; elle m'a rendu homme libre. Desormais je resterai libre!

30 *January, Thursday.*

. . . [SD] The nomination of Judge Edward King to fill the vacancy upon the Supreme Court bench occasioned by the death of Associate Baldwin, is still unconfirmed.[43] This is said to be owing to certain intrigues in which James Buchanan is implicated. It seems that Governor Porter, on his term expiring, was suspected of managing to get himself into the Senate in place of Mr. Sturgeon.[44] Buchanan can make Sturgeon vote pretty much as he pleases, but with Porter for a colleague he thought probably that he would have a good deal of trouble. He therefore interfered to keep off the confirmation of King, with the intent no doubt to have it rejected if Porter should have come into the Senate, and then get the nomination for himself from President Polk. But Sturgeon having been reelected, it is likely that Buchanan's opposition to King will cease, and that sound lawyer will be confirmed.

By the by, Peter D. Vroom is making efforts to keep off the appointment aforesaid until the new administration comes into power, hoping that he may then get in. He has had his recommendations at every county court in New Jersey, and the other day, according to the Trenton correspondent of the Newark *Daily Advertiser,* he procured the names of nearly all the members of our legislature to a paper urging him as a suitable person for that responsible trust.

When Wall and others of Vroom's friends first began this movement, my faithful advisor, Lewis Perrine Esq. of Trenton immediately advised me of it. I told Page, and he mentioned it to King. Perrine and all the Young Democracy—that is those who opposed the renomination

43. President Tyler had named Pennsylvanian King to the Supreme Court in mid-1844. The Senate blocked his appointment until February 1845, when Tyler withdrew King's name.
44. Daniel Sturgeon (1789–1878), a Democrat, was one of Pennsylvania's senators from 1839 to 1851.

of Martin Van Buren—are unwilling to see Vroom, or any of the Wall clique, honored by the new administration. All this set of old "Hunkers" behaved badly at our state election. General Wall opposed the nomination of John R. Thomson as Governor to the last moment; his son, James W. Wall[45] told me himself that he had won fifty dollars by Thomson's defeat. Peter D. Vroom refused to address democratic meetings until after the October election. Stacy G. Potts openly proclaimed that he would not vote the regular Governor's ticket. And Ryall in Monmouth, and all of the rest of the "Hunkers," did us infinite harm by proclaiming among the weak bretheren that "the Monopoly would crush any man who had to carry it." In fact they have never behaved well since their favorite, Van Buren, was laid on the shelf at Baltimore.

The new administration it is thought will favor the Young Democracy—at all events it will not allow the Hunkers to monopolize its smiles. As for our New Jersey clique, Thomson has told me repeatedly that both Polk and Dallas understand them. If so, Wall, Vroom and their confrerie will not be so powerful at the Capitol as they were under Jackson and Van Buren.

31 January, Friday.

[RD] This evening having been at a cotillion practising at Whale's Saloon, I met on the mail-boat my friends Souville and Surault. We had a good deal of conversation in French, which I find myself becoming able to carry on without much difficulty.

1 February, Saturday.

Col. Page to-day made me a present of a beautiful bound copy of Longacre's *National Portraits,* and wrote in each volume a very flattering inscription. Verily, verily, it is better to be born lucky than rich or wise.

[SD] I wrote a letter to Governor Stratton some days ago, asking him to tell me where, in our county, he was born, and to communicate whatever other facts in his history he might feel disposed to let the public know through the medium of my "reminiscences." Yesterday Dudley waited upon me with a message from his Excellency, that he, the said Governor would be in Camden next week, and would with pleasure give me the information I seek.

Well, well! I find that all men have a weak point, if you can only approach it in the proper way. The idea of figuring in a pamphlet which is to last perhaps for a quarter of a century was enough to make Stratton send a very prompt and very civil answer to one whom I

45. Wall (1820-72), only son of Burlington's Garret D. Wall, was practicing law in Trenton and later would serve briefly as United States senator.

know he does not like; and even Fennimore Cooper, in consideration of the additional immortality which I promised him, took time from his libel-suits to write me half a novel![46]

2 February, Sunday.

[RD] This evening Mulford and I called upon Charley Humphreys and his wife, late Miss Fetters. The marriage took place last week, and was perhaps hastened by causes other than—the convenience of Charley.

[SD] Madam Rumor is busy in circulating accounts of new love-intrigues in which Bob Matlack of Woodbury has been engaged. He has made it a point ever since he was quite a young man to be kicked out of the old Smith Tavern[47] by every fresh landlord that hostel has had. Dick Humphreys has been spared this duty for a year; but recently Bob insulted Miss Caroline Fetters, the sister of Dick's wife, and the betrothed (now the wife) of his brother Charley. Thereupon— so says report—Dick gave him a severe lecture, and threatened to apply his foot to that peculiar part of the body which a gentleman considers the most sensitive of all the rest. The consequence was, Bob left Woodbury, and had staid in Philadelphia for some time.

It is said that this scoundrel has deceived Miss Eliza Thorn of Mount Ephriam—a pretty, but weak girl, who was surrounded with honest bumpkin beaux, who have all left her in consequence of the cordial welcome which she extended to Bob. The story in question may have had its origin among some of these disappointed fellows.

3 February, Monday.

[RD] We have several trials marked for next week, and per consequence I must read pretty industriously for some days to come. Moreover as I shall apply in May for admission in New Jersey, I must begin to read New Jersey law.

[SD] Governor Stratton has nominated Oliver S. Halstead of Essex for the Chancellorship—Thomas P. Carpenter of Woodbury as Judge of the Supreme Court, vice Elmer, resigned—and Abraham Browning of Camden, as Attorney-general. These names have been before the Senate for some time and are not yet confirmed.[48] The Whigs at Trenton, and indeed all over the state, are in much trouble. They like not the appointments which the Governor would have the Senate make, and

46. Mickle had written James Fennimore Cooper in December 1844, asking about his birthplace. Cooper, in a letter of December 6, responded that he had been born in Burlington, and had returned there for tutoring after his family had moved to New York State. Cooper had recently been involved in libel suits with Whig newspapers which he thought had defamed him.
47. Smith's Tavern, sometimes called Paul's Hotel, was in Woodbury.
48. The Senate soon confirmed all three men.

many in West Jersey desire that Halstead may be rejected. As for Tom Carpenter, he is a very clever fellow but the idea of his going upon the Supreme Court bench is ridiculous. He has been prosecuting the pleas in Gloucester county for two or three years back, and I am told, in one case actually drew five indictments before he got one that would hold water. Halstead, it is said, in some of the papers is not always sane; and as for Browning he well deserves the character which the lobby-members of the Constitutional Convention gave him—to wit "the gravest fool in New Jersey." I have heard several intelligent Whigs express their utmost contempt for these three fellows. Mr. Chapman in particular is very much put out by the stupid selections which Stratton has made. I dropped in at his office the other day, and found him conversing with Mr. Kinsey of Burlington, a son of the former Chief Justice.[49] He like Chapman is a good Whig; but they both concluded that the state would certainly "go for the Loco-focos" next year. And so she will, for what Stratton has not done to blow his party out of the water, the miserable set of Jackasses in the legislature will do.

4 February, Tuesday.
[RD] The first serious snow of the season fell to-day. It is supposed to have been very heavy to the eastward as the mail-line due at ten o'clock is not in now, (at midnight).

5 February, Wednesday.
This evening I took my cousin Adelia to Whale's party, where I met Emily Harley. I turned in very late at Burr's, much fatigued with standing and dancing. The New York mail lines of yesterday have not yet arrived.

6 February, Thursday.
The river is so full of ice that I cannot get over to Philadelphia in time for my dancing-lesson. All communication between us and the New Yorkers is cut off by the snow.

7 February, Friday.
I have been engaged for an afternoon or two past in making a MS. copy of Beauchamp Plantagenets *New Albion*, from the one, or rather the piece of one, in the Philadelphia Library. This copy which is I believe the only one now known to be extant,[50] has been so much

49. Charles Kinsey (1783–1850), son of James Kinsey (1731–1803), chief justice of New Jersey from 1789 to 1803.
50. While the original edition of Plantagenet's *A Description of the Province of New Albion* (published in 1648) was quite rare, a new edition had been published by Peter Force in Washington, D. C., in 1837.

mutilated by the carelessness of the binder, that I have to supply letters, syllables or words on almost every page. The sense however generally directs me so that I cannot err.

8 February, Saturday.

The cuts have been at last dug out of the rail-road between Brunswick and Jersey City, so that the cars can pass. At Bergen-hill it is said the snow lay in heaps like mountains.

9 February, Sunday.

My pamphlet having come to a dead stop by Ned Chandler's breaking a blood-vessel, I was able to-day nearly to make a finish of copying Plantagenet. It will be when done a valuable addition to my library, although perhaps none but myself can read it readily.

10 February, Monday.

I was introduced again to-day to Eli K. Moore of New York, who had to spend three days in getting here. He was on the rail-road from Tuesday evening until Saturday noon. By the by a marriage was arranged on last Thursday at the Quaker meeting in Arch Street—the Company assembled to see the ceremony—the dinner was all prepared—the wife *futura* dressed in her best, etc. etc. But lo the groom came not! He was stuck fast on the New York rail road, unable to get one way or the other. The guests therefore demolished the dinner, and separated after long waiting, to try it over again in more favorable weather. But *revenons nous á* Moore. I wonder if he knew that I was the editor of the Camden *Phoenix*, when that article appeared touching his interview with Mr. Van Buren, after the sending in of the Subtreasury Scheme to Congress?[51] The notice of that event was copied into almost all the democratic papers of New York and New England, with credit to the *Phoenix*.

11 February, Tuesday.

I copied several pages to-day of *New Albion*. What will Mr. Pennington say, to my taking this trouble, after all his pains to prove Beauchamp Plantagenet nothing but an arrant liar?[52] I think however that Mr. Pennington, in his paper in the *Memoirs of the Pennsylvania Historical Society*, has not made his case. How could Plantagenet have

51. See entry of 10 February 1843.
52. John Pennington's "An Examination of Beauchamp Plantagenet's Description of the Province of New Albion" appeared in the *Memoirs of the Historical Society of Pennsylvania*, Vol IV, Part I (1840). In it, Pennington argued that Plantagenet's book was "not an authentic document," but rather a fraud written to make money for its author and Sir Edmund Plowden. According to Pennington, Plowden (d. 1659), a Catholic adventurer from Hampshire, had never visited the banks of the Delaware, but learned a little about the area from Dutch sailors.

hit the names Eriwoneck, (like Vanderdoncks[53] Ermomex) and Ram-
cock, (like our present Rancocas) unless he, or the one from whose
narration he wrote, was upon the Delaware.

12 February, Wednesday.

I have had some correspondence of late with Mr. Gordon the Historian of New Jersey. He manifests quite a friendly disposition. . . .
Alas! alas! I was told that the author of the *Gazeteer* was Thomas
"Goose-head" Gordon as he was called, of Philadelphia, who has been
dead for some years.[54]

13 February, Thursday.

. . . [SD] Confound it, what evils come from forgetting that good old
rule. "Think twice before you speak once!" Sometime before the Presidential election, when everything looked gloomy for the cause of
democracy, I playfully remarked to my old friend, Ariadne, that I
would take her to Washington to see Polk inaugurated.[55] Since matters
have turned out as they have, no alternative is left me but to go or to
forfeit my word. The first I would not do for a hundred dollars, but
the other I would not do at all; so go I must. I have invited cousin
Emma, and to night I called upon Ariadne in company with Caroline,
to invite her also. My invitation was so formal, and the circumstances
under which it was given were so peculiar, that I trust my disposition
in the affair is no secret to the invitee. *Nous verrons, nous verrons!*

14 February, Friday.

[RD] I felt so indisposed to make a speech to-day, that I did not go
over to the office at all. There is much in being "in the vein.". . .

I consented to-night to deliver an Address before the Jefferson
Society[56] on the evening of the Twenty-Second.

15 February, Saturday.

. . . [SD] . . . Dropping in at Ward's book-store to day I met Hall,
the publisher of the *Port Folio*, and Young Sergeant, a grandson I
believe of the former Governor of the South-western Territory.[57] They

53. Adriaen van der Donck (d. 1655) was a Dutch navigator who published a
History of New Netherland in 1655.

54. The author of the *Gazetteer of the State of New Jersey* (Trenton, 1834)
was Thomas Francis Gordon (1787–1860), a native of Philadelphia.

55. Ariadne was Mickle's nickname for Josephine Sheppard.

56. Camden's Jefferson Debating Society was apparently a recent addition to
the town's cultural organizations.

57. Harrison Hall (1785–1866) had been the last publisher of the respected
literary magazine *The Port Folio,* which had ceased publication in Philadelphia in
1827. Winthrop Sargent (1825–70), currently a student at the University of
Pennsylvania, was to become a lawyer and author of historical works. His grandfather of the same name (1753–1820), had been first governor of the Mississippi
Territory, 1798–1801.

are both very ardent Whigs, and one of them pretty soon assailed the *Democratic Review*,[58] throwing out also some slings against the Democratic Party. This touched me, and led me to reply. A warm debate ensued upon the principles of the two parties, in which I took a broad, radical position which soon silenced my antagonists' guns. I never met the man yet, who, with the doctrine of the brotherhood of our race as his fundamental postulatum, could not out-talk a room-full of opposers....

Young Sergeant is a gentlemanly fellow, with a fortune I believe to make him independent. We have on two or three occasions met at the rendevous kept by my friend Ward, and measured swords. He has a good mind and a thorough education; but advocating as he does a restoration of property-qualifications, an assimilation of our government with that of England, and an adoption of the doctrines of the Natives in all their proscriptiveness, he is soon led to absurdities of which he is himself ashamed. The other day he carried his nonsense so far that I told him "if he uttered such sentiments abroad, I wondered he had not been stoned to death." I felt a strong desire to add, that such sentiments deserved such a reception; but remembering Jefferson's maxim that Error is harmless where the Mind is free, I only smiled at the ridiculous positions of the young aristocrat.

I am to deliver an Address before a literary society in Camden on the evening of the Twenty-Second. To-night Garrison called upon me, and in a round-about way attempted to persuade me to make my lecture a phillipic against the Natives. A snake! a snake! I saw through this fellow at once, though I contrived to let him believe he was playing upon me.

16 February, Sunday.

[RD] To-night, about eight o'clock, I finished the text of my pamphlet, *Old Gloucester*. O! how rejoiced I felt! How well I understand the feelings which Gibbon describes himself as having, at Lausanne, after he had got through with his *Decline and Fall*. This may be comparing very small things to very great ones; but I imagine there is no difference in the nature of Gibbons' emotions on that occasion and mine now. Hereafter I will have my evenings at my command to read French, to write to my fair cousins or visit my pretty and amiable friends in Plumb and Cooper Streets. I burnt the notes from which I have been so long writing, with an *"Evoe!"*

17 February, Monday.

There is a great rush of people from Camden and Gloucester counties

58. The *United States Magazine and Democratic Review*, currently being edited by New York radical reformer John L. O'Sullivan, was the most prominent Democratic magazine in the county.

to-day, on account of the attempt being made by Smallwood and his friends to merge the two divisions together. Gov. Vroom and Gov. Pennington are to argue the matter for Camden county before a committee of the house of Assembly to-morrow night, and Bill Halsted for Gloucester. It is my opinion that Smallwood will carry his point; for there is a pack of fools at Trenton this winter who will do any thing.

[SD] This afternoon when I returned from the office I found Governor Stratton waiting for me at Elwell's, to answer my recent letter to him. He gave me some anecdotes of his mother, who was a Creighton, and lived in Haddonfield during the Revolution. She was the daughter of Hugh Creighton,[59] the keeper of the inn which Old Shivers now keeps. She is yet alive, and lives with the Governor at Swedesboro! She saw Miles Sage after he had been so unmercifully bayonetted by the British, as I have related in my *Reminicenses,* as Curts spells the word. In my conversation with his Excellency, by the by, I was rather more candid than polite. We were speaking of the singular coincidence of his residing at 'Coon creek, when the coon was the party emblem of the Whigs. Says I, "We boys who canvassed Camden county used to tell the people that we were going to move your quarters from Coon Creek to Salt River;[60] but unfortunately we turned out false prophets; or rather," I added, "fortunately, as you will think." He laughed at my queer blunder, and awkward correction—but, strange to say, did not blush.

Miss Sheppard Ariadne, is, I hear making active preparations for her trip to Washington. Em is also getting new dresses and laces ad in finitum. I saw Cad to-night, and she seems to be struck with my gloominess. Have I not reason, under the circumstances, to be sad? Were my will and not mine honor concerned, Cad should accompany my cousin and myself to Washington instead of Ariadne. . . .

I must try, after my return from Washington, to avoid female society altogether. I will shut myself up, and turn hermit, until Mulford marries Cad, and Time, Time, that great doctor! eradicates from my heart the stubborn partialities of childhood. Mulford is my friend; a noble, sterling friend. He is, I know devoted to this girl, and he is far more worthy of her than I am. He is not like me, fickle as the winds; he has not, like me, plunged to the eyes in the frivolities and dissipations of youth. He will make her a good husband, and as I desire her

59. Creighton was the proprietor of the Creighton House, now called the Indian King, in Haddonfield from 1777 to 1790. Samuel E. Shivers was the current landlord.

60. Stratton lived in Swedesboro near Raccoon Creek. Rowing or sending someone up Salt River was a nineteenth century slang term for defeating him politically.

happiness and my own I would like to see him marry her. For his sake and hers; for the sake of friendship and honor; I will pluck from my bosom the first and most vivid picture engraved there in my boyhood, and make that bosom again a blank.[61]

18 February, Tuesday.

[*RD*] Plitt[62] writes me from Washington that it will [*be*] very difficult to find quarters for the girls. What shall we do—adjourn our trip? No——I want it over too badly for that.

19 February, Wednesday.

After dancing at Whale's party until about midnight this evening, Jack Browning and I started for the "Adelphi" where Souville had a promiscuous gathering of some forty couple.[63] It had broken up, on account of some difficulty as to the pay, before we got there. This Souville is a great rascal. He has swindled me out of about ten dollars—devil take him!

20 February, Thursday.

This evening I attended a most delicious ball at Humphrey's in Woodbury. The room was about comfortably filled—the ladies were full of life—the wine was excellent—the supper superb. I began to dance at the second sett, and did not, I believe, miss a cotillion afterwards. About five o'clock the ladies retired; but we hauled the music out of their beds and set them to playing again for a stag-dance which lasted until six. There was a wild set of boys there.

21 February, Friday.

This carousing is playing the deuce with me—it must be stopped. Of course after being up two nights, I could not go over to the office to day. The wine and the hard exercise of last evening made my head feel rather dull this morning. The pleasure however of dancing with Eveline[64]—especially since now she is the object of so much talk among the prudes—more than counterbalanced the stupidity I now feel. She has acquired an embonpoint of late which makes her doubly interesting. Her husband introduced me—his good nature not caring for the little flirtations which Rumor attributes to his prettier and—better half.

22 February, Saturday.

This evening, in accordance with my engagement, I delivered an

61. Caddie Cole and Mulford were married in Camden in November 1847.
62. George Plitt was a friend to whom Mickle had written for help in finding a room.
63. Souville's party was at Adelphia Hall, near Walnut and Fifth Streets, Philadelphia.
64. Evaline Fetters Humphreys was the wife of Richard Humphreys.

Oration before the Jefferson Debating Society, in Bontemps Hall. The affair was not published in the papers, but circulars were printed and sent around to the best families, announcing the celebration, and inviting an attendance. The result was, that the boys had a crowded and very select house—one of the best indeed that I have ever seen in Camden. I was surprized at the great number of pretty girls who turned out. Where they came from I cannot tell—many of them I had never seen before.

Mr. Garrison, the President of the evening, made a short speech in introducing me, and unfortunately dived right into the middle of the topic which I proposed taking up. Per consequence I had to throw away my skeleton, and make an address altogether extempore. A more radical set of doctrines I guess the good people of Camden never listened to. I saw one or two of our ministers squirm a good deal, and Mr. Fetters, the "Native" candidate for Mayor, seemed to sit very uneasily. The gist of my address was that we have not realized the idea of the Revolution—the equality of man; that we are too much in the habit of allowing others to think for us; that whether we differ from or agree with the world we ought to speak forth our thoughts, "speak forth and leave the rest to God." I felt perfectly at ease, and talked, I think, with more fluency than ever before. The address, I have no doubt will make some fuss among the church-people.

After I had concluded, my cousin and namesake read a part of Washington's valedictory, but I had so far overrun my time that he had to omit some of the most important parts. The members and the audience seemed to be very much pleased; and for a wonder I can say that I was satisfied with myself. The decorations of the room were devised by Garrison, and were very tasty. The speaking was from a temple made of festooned flags, and over our heads was the name of "Washington" in evergreens.

I felt so stupid in the early part of the evening that I sent word to Caroline, and some of the members of our family not to come; that I was going to make a most signal failure. She was so disobedient as to come; but the rest did not. Feeling the want of some stimulus, I drank an ale-sangaree and a glass of brandy before going to the Hall, but I think I derived no aid from this source, and mean not to try it again.

23 *February, Sunday.*

I attempted to write the Preface to my pamphlet to-day; but found I had not sufficiently recovered from the dissipations and labors of last week.

There was a severe thunder storm this afternoon, accompanied with heavy rain. The spring seems to have made an early and permanent opening. The farmers in the neighborhood of Camden have been ploughing for a week.

24 February, Monday.

A great many people are winding their way to Washington. The town must already be full.

25 February, Tuesday.

The *Phoenix* concern will I guess be blown out of water. Mr. Bosee has put Curts' bond into my hands for collection, and instructed me to go ahead.[65]

26 February, Wednesday.

The girls are ready, I believe, to start for Washington. Our trip I understand gives much uneasiness to some of the old maids in Camden.

27 February, Thursday.

Blessed be heaven! My pamphlet is out.[66] Wannan sent me up fifty copies to-night ready for delivery. I immediately dispatched most of them to my friends of the press, and those who have helped me to collect material.

28 February, Friday.

[SD] This afternoon at four o'clock Miss Sheppard, cousin Em and myself departed on our trip. The good people in Camden have, I am told, a great concern for our welfare; and some of the friends of Josephine have even had the impudence to wonder publicly that her mother "would trust her to such a libertine as young Mickle!"

We met at the depot with Captain Schaumburgh, under whose care I put Miss Sheppard. We reached Baltimore without accident about eleven o'clock at night, and put up at the Exchange Hotel.[67] The Captain made himself very agreeable, and the girls like him exceedingly. He has been pretty much over the world and is, in the ordinary acceptation of the word a perfect gentleman.

1 March, Saturday.

We went to the city of Washington by the first line this morning— The Captain still keeping our company. The place was already filled, and many more arrived in our train; so that I apprehended much difficulty in finding quarters. We took a hack, and drove to Brown's.[68]

65. The *Phoenix* continued publication, though sometimes irregularly, until at least 1858.

66. Mickle's book was titled *Reminiscences of Old Gloucester: or Incidents in the History of the Counties of Gloucester, Atlantic and Camden.*

67. The Exchange, one of the country's leading hotels, occupied a wing of the Merchant's Exchange on Gay Street.

68. Brown's Hotel, or the Indian Queen, on Pennsylvania Avenue had been the city's most popular hotel for several decades.

The landlord came out, told us he was overflowing, but recommended us to a Mrs. Smith's, near his hotel. We went there, but I found the house to lack cleanliness, and so passed on to another boarding-house upon the Avenue. The landlady came, or rather was coming to the carriage, when I discovered that she had red hair. "Drive on, drive on!" said I without waiting for a parley—for red hair I detest. We next went to Mrs. Mount's[69] on the hill in front of the Capitol, where we found very clean and pleasant quarters, a civil hostess, and respectable and distinguished company. They gave me a front room facing the Public Place, and adjoining a similar room occupied by my girls. This was just the arrangement I wanted, and so here we concluded to stop.

As soon as our baggage was delivered, I hastened over to the Capitol to see the two houses, and take a turn in the Rotunda. Very fortunately I met Wiley of Virginia, an old friend and correspondent of the *Eagle,* who knew all the distinguished men and pointed them out to me from the ladies' gallery.[70] The most remarkable man in the lower house was John Quincy Adams.[71] Amid the incessant din and turmoil that surrounded him he sat like some old rock amid the billows of the ocean. His head was resting on his hand, and his back partially turned towards the Speaker's chair during the time we were in the gallery—about a half an hour. The physiognomy of the House struck me very favorably—there was much more personal beauty among the members than we ordinarily see among the same number of men.

I can not describe the feeling that came over me as I entered the other house—the hall where the illustrious fathers of our land have so many of them figured. As I leaned over the rail of the gallery I not only saw Benton, Choate, Woodbury, McDuffie and the other leaders who were tangibly present; but Calhoun, Wright, Webster and the great Clay were also before me, and the lank form of Randolph, the red face of Pinckney, the grave countenance of Burges—a long panorama of reanimated magnates glided past my fancy's eye, and carried me back to simpler and better times![72] O! if there be such

69. Mount's Boarding House was located on First Street between East Capitol and A Streets.

70. Mickle does not mention Wiley elsewhere in his diary or correspondence.

71. Ex-president Adams had been a member of the House since 1831.

72. Mickle refers to Senators Thomas Hart Benton (1782–1858) of Missouri, Rufus Choate (1799–1859) of Massachusetts, Levi Woodbury (1789–1851) of New Hampshire, George McDuffie (1790–1851) of South Carolina, John C. Calhoun (1782–1850) of South Carolina, Silas Wright (1795–1847) of New York, Daniel Webster (1782–1852) of Massachusetts, Henry Clay (1777–1852) of Kentucky, John Randolph (1773–1833) of Virginia, and Charles Pinckney (1757–1824) of South Carolina. Mickle's final reference is probably to Tristam Burges (1770–1853), not a senator, but a famous member of the House from 1825 to 1835.

thing as Patriotism I felt it as I indulged in this reverie! I felt—I know not why—but I know I felt the whole force of that line in Horace—"*Dulce et decorum est pro patria mori.*"[73]

After spending some time in the Senate I took a walk down the Avenue, to see who of my acquaintances had arrived. I found plenty of good company at Coleman's[74] and Brown's, and with them I spent the day until dinner-time—to wit, five o'clock. At the table I made an acquaintance with a young democrat from Baltimore named Hiss—a wild, good, clever devil, just of the mould I like. In the evening we took a stroll together, and I found that he "knows the ropes," as the phrase goes, of this city as well as Baltimore.

2 March, Sunday.

The weather being very fine this morning, and Mr. Wiley calling in to see us, we concluded to take a hack and go over to Georgetown. The ride consumed all the afternoon. After dinner, I went down to Coleman's and called upon the Vice President[75] and John R. Thomson of our state. They were both very affable. Mr. Dallas is, indeed, by far the most democratic man I have yet met with in Washington. He deserves to be, and has my wishes for being, the next President. I also called upon several others of my acquaintances, and found a good deal of log-rolling going on. It is understood that Mr. Buchanan is to go into the state department, and that Bancroft of Massachusetts is to be made Secretary of the Navy. The latter appointment is much objected to even by some of the New England democrats.

I waited upon Mr. Allen of Ohio[76] with my letter from Page towards evening. He received me as civilly as he knew how; but he is [*in*] manners a brute. I have become much better acquainted with Jarnagin[77] without any introduction than I ever could with Allen. By the by, in a conversation which I had with Jarnagin to-night he said to me: "We consider it a little ridiculous out in Tennessee that Jim Polk should have been made President—but so it is." He also told me to my surprize that Dayton[78] of our state is regarded as one of the ablest speakers in the Senate.

About seven o'clock we have what they call "tea"—to wit, a cup of tea and a cracker in our hands, which is just sufficient to remind me

73. Mickle quotes Horace's *Odes*, 3.2.13.

74. Samuel S. Coleman was the proprietor of the National Hotel on Pennsylvania Avenue.

75. Mickle means the vice-president-elect, George M. Dallas.

76. William Allen (1803–79) was a Democratic senator from Ohio, 1837–49.

77. Spencer Jarnagin (1792–1853) was a Whig senator from Tennessee, 1843–47.

78. William Lewis Dayton (1807–64) was a Whig senator from New Jersey, 1842–51.

of the necessity of patronizing some refectory. To-night after I had dispatched my oysters and ale, I took another bout with young Mount, the landlady's son and Hiss. We called upon the famous Mary Hall, whose monument over Green, her paramour, excites the jokes of every visitor to the Congressional Cemetery.[79] We walked up and down town till pretty late, and I turned in with quite as much wine in my belly as consisted well with my digestion.

3 March, Monday.

This afternoon I went to the President's house to witness Tyler's withdrawl. He and his pretty wife and all his family were assembled in the "blue room" to receive the hands of the citizens. Gen. Van Ness,[80] an old inhabitant of the District read an address while we were there, bidding the President Adieu and thanking him on behalf of the people of Washington for his kindness, hospitality and courtesy. Tyler made a very neat reply, and such replies by the way he is just the man to make. He alluded to his having had to contend with the opposition of both parties—protested that he had only followed his conscience, and appealed to future history to do him justice. He spoke in glowing language of the just consummated overture to Texas, and challenged investigation into the whole course and tenor of his administration. When he had done I observed several sturdy old fellows weeping like children, and I confess I felt like it too. In this tribute to the setting sun I thought there was not—could not be any unworthy motive.

This evening I was at a ball on Jersey Avenue, and danced with the celebrated Eliza Kyle—who is, without exception, the most beautiful girl in Washington. I told her I had come from Philadelphia on purpose to enjoy the honor of her hand in a quadrille. We had a little badinage but it amounted to nothing. A fellow named Moore, who is an applicant for some office—a Jerseyman and a neighbor of mine, was along with me. Will he tell tales? I guess not, for I took care to drink him drunk as a loon before we went to the hop.

About three o'clock in the morning, the ball winding up and my boarding house being closed, I went on board the steamboat *Express* with a friend, and turned into a berth until about six. I got back to Mount's before my girls were out of bed.

4 March, Tuesday.

The weather to-day has been very uninviting, and tended greatly to

79. Mary Ann Hall lived at the corner of Maryland Avenue and Four-and-one-half Street, S.W., in a house some Washingtonians thought "shameless." In short, Mickle again seems to be visiting a brothel. Green's identity is obscure.

80. John Van Ness (1770–1847), an officer in the District of Columbia militia, was a prominent banker and former mayor of Washington.

mar the festivities and parade of the Inauguration. Before nine o'clock I sent the girls off to the Senate chamber, with the young and pretty Miss Mount; and by the politeness of Mr. Jarnagin of Tennessee they got a good seat, and had a very fair view of the Inauguration of Dallas. About noon, with the other ladies who were admitted to the Chamber, they proceeded to the portico, and saw the President inducted. Having business in another part of the city, I crossed the public grounds in front of the Capitol during the ceremonies and saw his Excellency for a few moments while he was engaged in reading his Inaugural address. It was raining at the time, and a man held an umbrella over him. All the officers of the government, the foreign ministers and invited guests who occupied the platform which had been raised over the steps, had also umbrellas over them. The area in front had the appearance of a sea of Silk and cotton.

The escort which conducted the President from Coleman's to the Capitol was rather a poor affair. The famous Empire Club from New York[81] formed a prominent part of it, much to the mortification of many good democrats; for it is notorious that a greater set of blackguards never existed. They are commanded by a fellow called Captain Rynders,[82] an out and out bully and blackleg.

In the evening I took the girls to the ball at Carusi's—the ten dollar, aristocratic affair.[83] It was so full and so hot that my head began to ache in a very few minutes. It was brilliant enough—but not such a place as I would voluntarily seek pleasure in. The supper set in the lower room was the most splended affair I ever saw in the line of suppers. It consisted of everything and "*quibusdam aliis.*" John Cooper and lady, Harry Edwards, Postmaster Hoy, Governor Thomson (that ought to have been) Strickland, the architect,[84] and scores of others whom I knew were present. Cousin Em seemed to be delighted with the pageant, but the excitement was too much for her; and so, to forestall the sick head-ache which she knew she would bring on by staying, we took our carriage a little after one, and returned home.

An incident occurred at the door to-night which may be worth mentioning. I had some difficulty about my ticket—it having been put into a side-pocket, where I did not think of looking. The door-keeper told

81. The Empire Club, on Park Row, was the Tammany political center of New York City's Sixth Ward and the headquarters for the notorious Five Points gangsters.

82. Isaiah Rynders, gang leader and Tammany boss of New York City's Sixth Ward, had founded the Empire Club in 1843.

83. One of the two inaugural balls held on this night was at Gaetani Carusi's popular Assembly Rooms at Eleventh and C Streets.

84. William Strickland (1787–1854), of Philadelphia, was a leading exponent of the Greek revival style.

me I had better buy another ticket, and have the matter made right before the Managers to-morrow. Just at this juncture Mr. Dallas came in sight, and saw me. Advancing, and extending his hand very cordially, he asked, "Why, Mr. Mickle, how are you? When did you arrive?" I answered him, and had a little conversation about the weather, the fullness of the ball, etc. when his daughter appeared at the dressing-room door, and took him off. The door-keeper immediately came up to me, and said "Pass in, Mr. Mickle; never mind your ticket— never mind." "I thank you," I replied, "Mr. Mickle will take another ticket if you will show him where the managers are sitting." He did so and I got my second ticket. Soon after we entered the room, however, I found my first one, and immediately returned it to the committee who paid me back the ten dollars I had given them.

During the time I staid at the ball I was merely a looker on. I had left my light boots in the carriage that had brought us from Mount's, and could not therefore undertake to dance. As amusement therefore, my friend Harry Edwards and I took several strolls into the Champagne room, where we punished several glasses of that pleasant beverage. Harry towards one o'clock had become pretty well heated; so much so that when he went to waltz with a young lady from Chester, I feared sometimes he would capsize. For myself, having ladies with me kept me strictly within bounds.

5 March, Wednesday.

I called upon Mr. Thomson and several other friends at Coleman's and Brown's this morning; and went with some of them to see the President. He appeared very sociable, but has not got the hang of the White House yet.

In the afternoon I got a carriage and took the girls to the White House to see Mrs. Polk. She is a pleasant and dignified woman, but not pretty by any means, the newspapers to the contrary not withstanding. The President was in Cabinet Council, and him therefore we did not see.

The author of *Might and Right* met me to-day at Coleman's, and introduced me to Several of his Rhode Island friends as "The Dorr of New Jersey."[85] Delightful compliment this! to be compared to a State-prison convict.

This evening I was with Moore, that everlasting pest. Every night since he has been in Washington, he has got gloriously fuddled. I left him and his party about one o'clock and wended my way up Capitol

85. Mickle obviously does not know that the author of *Might and Right* was Frances Harriet Green. The man discussed here may be the Dr. Ferris mentioned in the entry of 15 January 1845.

Hill towards home. I had just drunk enough wine to loose my thoughts from the anchorage of fact, and set them afloat upon the sea of fancy. Being very much fatigued with my day's work, I sat down near the north gate of the Capitol grounds and began to wonder if I should ever be entitled to sit in the building before me as the representative of my fellows. It was a queer idea, that, and one for which I cannot account. I saw how ridiculous the vagary was, and banished it from my mind. As soon as I was a little rested I proceeded to my quarters and got to bed.

People are leaving town very fast. My friend Garrett and his sister went to-day. Hiss, also, departs to-night. We are to go to-morrow.

6 March, Thursday.

The girls having seen the Inauguration, the wife of the President, the Patent office, the heights of Georgetown, the grand ball, and whatever else is curious or worth seeing, are like good girls, ready to start at my suggestion. Accordingly this afternoon at four o'clock we took the cars for Baltimore, where we arrived in time for tea. We staid at Whitman's, opposite the depôt where I put up at Convention. Hon. David Narr and Jos. C. Potts of New Jersey are here also.[86] We have had so far very good luck in the way of travelling acquaintances; for there has not been any moment since we left home that I have not been with gentlemen whom I know well, and whom I can introduce to my cousin without scruple.

In the evening Mr. Henry Garrett called upon us—I having found him at Barnum's where we expected to have stopped. He is a very pleasant fellow, and has taken I think a kind of liking to Josephine. His sister and my cousin became quite intimate, and have promised to correspond. Garrett and I are under a similar engagement.

7 March, Friday.

A pleasant party was there of us for Philadelphia this morning—to wit: John Cooper and lady, Judge Campbell of the Common Pleas, Jos. C. Potts of Trenton, Hon. David Narr, Mr. Hoy and lady, and Henry M. Phillips Esq. These and ourselves took up the private apartment of one of the ladys' cars, and had lots of chat! It was indeed the most pleasant portion of our journey to me, and I guess to the girls too. We were sorry when we arrived in Philadelphia, and had to separate.

I reached home about dark—used up—used up!

86. Naar (1800–80), of Elizabeth, was an Essex County judge, and later editor of the Trenton *True American*; Potts, brother of Stacy G. Potts, was a lawyer in Trenton, later in Jersey City.

8 March, Saturday.

I am told that during my absence with the girls the old women in Camden have been making themselves very busy indeed. We are entirely too young, they say, to take such a journey. They feared, too, that we would meet with no one whom we knew, and would consequently be at a great loss how to pass our time. They missed it most gloriously; for had we been able to stay a month longer we could have found an agreeable employment for every moment. For my part, the dissipation to which I was unavoidably forced, was the only thing that interfered with my pleasure. To stay up all night—and that after a day of active exercise—is itself enough to sicken one; to say nothing of about a bottle of wine, which one found himself forced to put under his jacket in the course of the evening. The trip cost the girls thirty-two dollars and a half, apiece; and me near a hundred dollars. Such extravagance as this may do once in four years, but not oftener.

9 March, Sunday.

I think this late trip to Washington affords me the very opportunity for which I have long been looking, to break off my intercourse at the Parsonage. Several times of late I have heard that it was currently reported that I was engaged to be married to my old young friend; and some of the busy bodies about town even seem anxious to hasten the day. I have left the sunny hours of childhood now, and cannot carry on these little flirtations with impunity. I must retreat or go ahead! I must look coldly upon that laughing eye which once it seemed harmless to respond to. I must consider that soft white little hand the property of some unknown one, not to be invaded by me. Marry her I cannot and will not. Love her, I do not, and never could, as one should love the being with whom he intends to consort for life. That I have somehow loved her 'twere vain to conceal; but it was a flame which could not last. Her appearance and manners conspired to kindle a superficial attachment which I know she would be the first to condemn and repress; for with all her warmth of feelings, her principles are firmly rooted and unshakeable. I am no sensualist—and therefore I have done forever with this dangerous girl! From this time forth I will visit her house as seldom as good-breeding will allow; and will draw myself within my shell, when I do go there, as closely as a terrified turtle. During our trip I was strictly non-committal. I was cold, unimpassioned as a statue. I knew I hurt her generous heart on two or three occasions, and was very [*sorry*] that I had to do so; but heaven—which sees all things—knows that my very iciness, perhaps, was the best thing for both her and my own future happiness, that could have happened.

10 March, Monday.

The new administration is now fairly afloat, and there is a good deal of speculation as to whether the Tyler men will be removed from office or not. So far, there have been no important changes, except in the Cabinet. To me this matter is somewhat interesting; for if the Tyler men walk the plank, Hoy will leave the Philadelphia post-office, and probably Col. Page will be made his successor.[87] If these two circumstances do turn out so, I am to take charge of the Colonel's business, as partner, taking half the profits. Thus I should find myself immediately in the receipt of an income of about one thousand or fifteen hundred dollars a year, without the usual prelude of starving for half a decade before being able to get under weigh.

11 March, Tuesday.

When I was at the Inauguration I thought I observed signs of a smart blow-up in the ranks of the democracy. Calhoun and his friends were said not to have been at all pleased with the complexion of the Cabinet; and the other wing of the army, the Van Buren men, or "old Hunkers"[88] as they have come to be called, show manifest symptoms of displeasure because the President has not dismissed the Tyler men holding important posts in the great cities. They think a week is long enough for the new administration to have made a beginning at least, to clean out the stables.

12 March, Wednesday.

The whig press and party are at present quiescent. They have given over their attempts to create a "panic," and concluded, it would seem, to lie back and enjoy the squabble which is about commencing among us. The President's Inaugural Address has not been as severely attacked by the organs upon the other side as I expected; but they are quite tart upon us for allowing the Empire Club of New York to officiate in the installation of Polk. They complain a good deal, too, that Mr. Dallas should be seen conversing with Captain Rynders of that Club, and walking arm-in-arm with Tom Dunn English, of the *Aristidean*.[89] I confess that, democratic as I am, I would have been loth to be seen in Washington in company with either of those scamps.

87. Page, who had served as Philadelphia postmaster from 1833 to 1841, did not succeed James Hoy in that capacity. Instead, Polk appointed him collector of customs for the port of Philadelphia.

88. Van Buren would no longer seem allied with the conservative Hunker wing of the Democratic Party after the election of 1848, in which the New Yorker split with his party and ran for president on the Free Soil ticket.

89. English edited the short-lived *Aristidean* in New York City from March through December 1845.

13 March, Thursday.

The Tyler men begin to think they are pretty safe, as no considerable removals have yet been made. Polk is too thorough a tactician to be in haste to do so unpleasant a duty as to dismiss those who voted for him.

On last Monday evening I was at Mr. Chapman's, at the meeting of Miss White's Reading Class. Mr. Chapman was well as usual, and more lively than I have seen him for some time. On Tuesday afternoon about five o'clock, I stopped at Bloodgood's Oyster Room for a moment, and taking up an afternoon paper, the first article that met my eye, was an announcement that my friend had fallen dead, about nine o'clock that morning, while attending to his ordinary duties in his office. I learned when I got across the river, that in the course of some directions which he was giving to a client, he stopped, put his hand to his breast, exclaimed "O, my God!" and rolled from his chair a corpse! His wife, a singular, nervous lady, will not yet believe that he is dead; but has had him placed upon a couch, and perseveres in applying hot bricks to his feet, and bathing him with various embrocations to restore him from what she takes to be merely a trance. My respected friend was in the prime of life, unexceptionable in his character and habits, and beloved by all who knew him.

14 March, Friday.

The town-meeting last Monday in Camden was conducted with great animation. The democrats, whigs and "natives" each had a ticket, and the "natives," by our negligence elected all their men, except the Mayor, by a majority averaging about a dozen. Howell being the Whig candidate for the Mayoralty, and Fetters the "Native," our men concluded to make no nomination so as to elect Howell and thus repay Fetters for his dividing us, and causing us to be beaten last fall. We had a caucus last Saturday night at Elwell's, at which I was forced to make a speech. In the course of my remarks I bore pretty hard upon the Natives, and per consequence have had several of them down upon me. The Whigs are done coquetting with this miserable set of fools, and I think before another year rolls around the whole party will want an epitaph.

15 March, Saturday.

Poor Chapman was buried this morning; the services taking place in St. Paul's, Camden. The attendance was large and respectable. In the evening Mulford and I called upon his widow, and sat for an hour.

16 March, Sunday.

My pamphlet, which was published on the eve of my departure for the Capital, has been noticed much more extensively and much more favorably than I ever expected. All, or nearly all the Philadelphia papers have done me the honor to praise my brochure quite emphatically, and even my late brethren of the New Jersey press, with whom I used to have so many quarrels have done the same. An editor at twenty—an author at twenty two is a fair beginning for a vagabond at thirty. I will stop writing!

17 March, Monday.

Saint Paddy's day, as usual, brings all kinds of weather. Nevertheless this afternoon I attended a very pleasant Polka party at Whale's room. He gets some of the girls together and then as a mark of special favor sends for a few of us gentlemen to come and dance with them. I have had the honor to be thus selected on several occasions of late, and have got so now that I can go thro' the steps and figures quite readily.

18 March, Tuesday.

I read a little law to-day, but it was very little. I really think that one more year of idleness in Philadelphia would not only bankrupt me in the pocket, but in morals too. For months back I have been in a dream—have hardly seemed to touch the earth and its realities. The opera, the soiree, music, women and wine, billiards, jaunting, picnicing and what not have been my bill of fare. Having kept no regular accounts of my income and outgo, I cannot tell what this frolicking has cost me; but I am sure it does not fall much short of two thousand dollars, for the past twelve months!

19 March, Wednesday.

This evening I took Emily Harley to the last of Whale's soirees. We remained until the concluding waltz, and had a very pleasant time. She is a lively girl, but blessed with uncommonly good sense: and having seen a great deal of the world, she is just one of those creatures with whom a man of the world delights to meet.

20 March, Thursday.

The last number of Curt's paper, in speaking of "Nativism," alluded to something that "our esteemed friend Isaac Mickle Esq." said in his speech the other night at the Caucus. The Native paper, the *Advertiser*,[90] promises "our esteemed friend" aforesaid a going over at its earliest convenience. The devil take the newspapers—I thought I had at last got out of their clutches; but alas! not yet is that happiness mine!

21 March, Friday.

My pamphlet still continues to make a noise. Ward, I suspect, is at

90. The Newark *Daily Advertiser* was founded in 1832.

the bottom of this. *N'importe*—I am sure at least of one thing—I do not, like Tom Dunn English, write my own puffs.

22 March, Saturday.

Some few removals have been made by Polk; but I consider Page's appointment now so remote a contingency, that I shall base no calculations upon it all. Upon the contrary I shall read the New Jersey practice, and apply for admission there in May.

23 March, Sunday.

Most of my time to-day was passed in reading Moliere's admirable play: *le Bourgeois gentile-homme*, over which I laughed more than will answer me for a week. I consider that to read this alone, in the original, would amply repay one the labor of learning the French language.

24 March, Monday.

I attended a case this morning before Alderman Campbell in Moyamensing, but the other party not being ready, we continued it over for a week. It is a trifling matter, and his Honor has already signified to me that he should give us judgement.

25 March, Tuesday.

The bill to abolish Camden county, after having been defeated in the House, has been revamped in the Senate, and is now under consideration. The first proposition was to repeal the law of last winter immediately and unconditionally. The present bill contemplates the submission of the question—Camden county as it is, or Gloucester County as it was, to the people, at a special election. The first bill was defeated in the lower house by two; but what luck the Woodbury men will have now, it is hard to divine.[91] A weaker legislature never before met in Trenton, than the present is.

26 March, Wednesday.

Mirabile Dictu! I got through with several cases of Harrison's *Reports,* to-day, and understood them. I am improving—I certainly am!

27 March, Thursday.

I got a note today from a needy relative politely intimating that if [*it*] was altogether convenient I might pay some seventy dollars to her landlord. Very pleasant, in sooth, very pleasant! but do it I shall have to.

28 March, Friday.

I saw his Excellency Gov. Stratton, the other day, and had a long confab with him about my book. I mentioned to him that we thought of getting out another and better edition, and that I would like to embody in it a cut of his birth-place. Governor as he is, he seemed not to dislike this idea, and proffered me his services in that or any other particular in the premises.

29 March, Saturday.

The *Congress* frigate[92] has arrived at Norfolk, so my chum Will Jeffers will be at home shortly.

30 March, Sunday.

It is really too bad. I have not been at the Parsonage but once since our return from Washington. What will the world say now? That the match is broken off, I suppose, that I fell in love with some of the District girls, am going to "deceive" my old friend again, and thirdly and lastly, deserve to be hung. Very well, very well! But I forget—it is not very well, and never will be very well until the old lady pays me those thirty two dollars which her daughter cost me. I will be off to the Parsonage soon, if not sooner!

91. A number of plans to destroy or weaken the new county were proposed in the two years after its creation. Camden County's friends in Trenton were able to defeat all of them.

92. U.S.S. *Congress,* launched in 1841, had recently been stationed off the east coast of South America.

INDEX

Personal Names

Aaron, Samuel, xiv, xxiii, 70, 73, 105, 237, 276, 280–81, 310, 379, 380, 382
Ackley, Thomas, 289, 392
Adams, John Quincy, 52, 92, 369, 498
Alexander, Fulton, 307, 341
Alexander, William C., 398
Allen, Enoch, 83
Allen, William, 499
Allison, Thomas, 450, 463
Andrews, Edward (Ned), 428
Andrews, John R., 127, 270, 277
Apple, Charles, 292
Appleton, James, 305, 307, 318, 351
Artôt, Alexandre-Joseph Montagney, 416–17
Ashbrook, Joseph, 176–77
Atkinson, Josiah R., 156, 233–46 *passim,* 289, 290, 314, 316, 318, 319, 325–44 *passim,* 365
Atwill, Winthrop, 390

Badger, George E., 145
Baldwin, Henry, 476, 487
Ballantine, James, 12, 19, 127, 133, 263, 290, 291–93, 299, 302
Ballantine, John, 78, 225, 231
Bancroft, George, 344, 452, 499
Barber, Augustus S., 439
Barber, John W., 278, 390, 439
Barnes, Albert, 365
Barnum, David, 449
Barnum, P. T., 355
Barrett, John W., 4, 33
Barton, Anna, 235, 236

Barton, Charles C., 235
Barton, Mary, 72
Bates, William, 164
Baxter, John H.: attends meetings, 100, 104, 114–15, 343, 411; accompanies Mickle, 111, 215, 226, 296; musical activities, 182, 233, 282, 323, 327, 329, 334, 336, 349–50, 358, 365; mentioned, 297, 306, 315, 339, 387, 412
Beck, Charles, 415
Beckett, Levi, 418
Bender, Peter, 225
Bender, Thomas, 267
Bennaker, Mr. (violinist), 378, 380–81, 383
Bennett, James Gordon, 214, 264, 354
Benton, Thomas Hart, 137, 179, 182, 222, 498
Berg, Joseph, 143, 276, 277, 365
Biddle, Nicholas, 113, 147–48
Bishop. *See* Ivins
Blair, Francis P., 420
Blanco, Don Pedro, 246
Bley, Jules, 416
Bolton, William Compton, 246
Bonaparte, Joseph, 27
Bontemps, Charles: plays music with Mickle, 223, 228, 229, 287, 379, 399, 480; accompanies Mickle, 320–21, 401, 434; mentioned, 402, 413, 415, 479
Borrodaile, Frederic, 367
Bossee, Henry, 337, 471, 497
Boyer, Jean Pierre, 196
Bradshaw, Henry, 407

511

Bready, James Hall, 255, 261
Brewster, Benjamin, 450
Brisbane, Albert, 380
Brown, Charles S., 77
Brown, David Paul, 100, 101, 105, 152, 162, 238–39, 240, 241, 480
Brown, David Sands, 436
Brown, George, 246
Browne, Peter A., 362
Browne, Peter A., Jr., 479–80
Browning Family, 134, 257, 261, 415, 434
Browning, Abraham, 28, 290–91, 363, 407, 433–39 *passim*, 489–90
Browning, Benjamin Franklin, 108, 410
Browning, Franklin H., 428
Browning, Benjamin W., 242, 245, 260–61, 277, 280, 284, 364
Browning, Catherine, 363, 415
Browning, Eleanor, 363
Browning, George, 410
Browning, John, 273, 495
Browning, Joshua P., 407, 408, 432, 435, 471, 472–73, 475
Brownson, Orestes, 161–62, 163, 168, 185, 193, 257–61, 393, 394–95
Bryant, William Cullen, 76, 240
Buchanan, James, 182, 239, 268, 337, 425, 487, 499
Buckstone, John Baldwin, 306
Budd, Joseph A., 447–48
Budd, Paul C., 109
Budd, Priscilla B., 109, 123, 124, 130, 190, 195, 199, 218, 241
Buffington, Henry, 280, 287, 324
Bulkley, Chauncey, 107, 232
Bull, Ole, 416–17, 480–81, 482
Bullock, Isaac, 6, 88
Burges, Tristam, 498
Burleigh, Charles C., 279, 280
Burr, John, 290–91
Burr, Joseph, 291, 357
Burr, Nicholas, 198
Burrough, William, 23
Burroughs, Henry, 149, 174, 293, 294, 325, 340, 364
Burroughs, Marmaduke, 237, 243, 273
Butler, Benjamin F., 452

Cadwalader, George, 283, 285, 289–90, 293, 329, 350, 375, 458–59
Caldwell, James, 407
Calhoun, John C., 137, 403, 420–21, 425, 498, 505
Calvé, Julie, 405
Campbell, Alexander, 241
Campbell, James, 462, 503, 508

Carlyle, Thomas, 353, 395
Carman, James, 290–91
Carman, William, 24, 291, 466
Carpenter, Thomas P., 489–90
Carusi, Gaetani, 501
Carvalho, Solomon Nunes, 134–35
Cass, Lewis, 427, 450–51
Cassady, James M., 350, 407
Chambers, John, 172, 276, 340
Chambourg. *See* Schaumburg
Champion, John, 200
Champion, Mary, 200
Champion, Samuel C., 11
Chandler, Edward, 280, 484, 491
Chandler, George, 103
Chandler, Joseph R., 154, 175, 275–76
Channing, William Ellery, 174, 395
Chapin, Marvin, 391
Chapman, Thomas, 165–66, 477–78, 483, 485, 490, 506
Choate, Rufus, 498
Cilley, Jonathan, 36–37, 39–40
Clark, Joel G., 407
Clark, Mrs. (acquaintance of Mickle), 218, 245, 265, 286, 299, 313
Claxton, John W., 300
Clay, Henry: and 1844 election, 125, 137, 210, 216, 335, 403, 420–21, 425, 437, 440, 451, 454, 478; as possible dueler, 130–31; bank bill of, 214; mentioned, 438, 498
Clement, John K., 78, 130, 433, 434, 435–36
Clement, John K., Jr.: expelled from Washington Library, 78, 326; as speaker, 88, 122, 169; relationship with Mickle, 103, 136, 139–40, 200, 211, 233, 244; attends meetings with Mickle, 104, 342; newspaper activity of, 109, 353; and Sheppard family, 232, 242, 244, 245, 260–61, 267, 275, 301; others' opinion of, 265–66, 308; plans to move west, 275; as musician, 358; and campaign of 1844, 456; mentioned, 191, 198, 263, 323, 434
Clement, Meriam, 172, 257, 260–61, 321
Coad, Patrick, 479, 480
Coates, Reynell, 476
Coffin, William, 415
Cole, Caroline (Caddy): returns to Camden, 177, 291, 416; Mickle visits, 203, 293, 295, 299–303, 350–87 *passim*, 400–410 *passim*, 414, 418, 436, 479, 486–87; visit to Cranberry, N.J., 344, 345, 349; Mickle's fondness for, 352, 494–95; Mickle accompanies, 356–99 *passim*, 416, 417, 422, 464; plays music with Mickle, 382, 384,

397, 477; and Thomas Mulford, 482, 495; mentioned, 294, 476, 492, 496

Cole, Edward (Ned): visits Mickle, 12, 139; speech by, 33; accompanies Mickle, 120, 241, 355, 357, 370, 401, 403, 409–10, 416; elected trustee of Washington Library, 127; Mickle visits, 344, 387, 399–416 *passim*, 424; marriage of, 383, 385; mentioned, 177, 300, 345, 349, 350, 362, 367, 372–73, 374, 381, 418

Cole, Isaac, 177, 255, 293, 359, 362, 416, 433

Cole, Jesse, 225

Coleman, Samuel S., 499

Collings, Joseph C., 434

Collins, Sarah, 439

Colt, John C., 340

Conner, Ned, 269

Conwell, Henry, 279

Cooper, James Fenimore, 54–55, 489

Cooper, John, 432, 461, 462, 501, 503

Cooper, Joseph B., 41, 74–75, 120, 212, 220, 236, 325

Cooper, Joseph W., 164–65

Cooper, William D., 334, 463

Cooper, William R., 236, 237, 434

Cousin, Victor, 395

Cowperthwaite, John K., 234, 332, 338, 351, 359, 433, 434

Cowperthwaite, Samuel S. E.: visits Mickle, 4, 5, 58, 59, 134, 140, 146, 151, 154, 221, 286; as speaker, 33, 114–15, 122, 181; relations with women, 61, 218; organizational activity, 78, 98, 100, 127, 190, 277, 264; accompanies Mickle, 127–29, 132, 138–39, 151, 159, 187, 193, 200, 226, 229, 233, 273, 277, 288, 290, 293, 315, 340, 341, 344, 358; Mickle visits, 134, 147, 182, 209–10, 215, 326; musical activity of, 172–86 *passim*, 211, 220–41 *passim*, 264, 273, 276, 282, 289, 294, 303, 307, 322–36 *passim*, 349–50, 365, 366, 367, 368; disputes with Mickle, 294, 372–73, 381, 411–13, 414, 415; mentioned, 102–3, 133, 152, 212, 258, 260, 266, 284, 300, 306, 351, 374, 383, 403

Cox, Benjamin, 310

Cox, John, 308–10

Cox, Oliver, xiv, 5–11 *passim*, 16–23 *passim*, 33, 107–9, 228–29, 311

Creighton, Hugh, 494

Crittenden, John J., 227

Crockett, Davy, 30, 37

Croswell, Edwin, 469

Croxall, Morris, 6, 88, 130, 194

Crump, William, 421

Currey, Lewis V., 240

Curry, William, 392–93, 394–95, 396

Curts, Henry: as publisher of *Eagle*, 336–37, 382, 418, 471, 472, 475, 497; as publisher of *Reminiscences*, 431, 477, 484; mentioned, 348, 406, 422, 444, 494, 507

Cushman, Robert W., 284, 318–19

Dallas, George M., 232, 288, 441, 454, 455, 476, 488, 499, 501, 502, 505

Daugherty, Edward, 18, 262, 305, 316–17, 322

Davis, Lemuel H.: visits Mickle, 98, 230; organizational activity, 104, 115, 169, 197, 332, 337, 340, 342; 353; in accident, 187; accompanies Mickle, 193, 291–93; similarity to Mickle, 262, 265; mentioned, 211, 238, 258, 260, 264, 338–39, 463

Dayton, William Lewis, 499

de Begnis, Giuseppi, 288, 368

Decatur, Steven, 31, 287

Delacour, James, 412, 415

Delacour, Joseph Charles, 151, 213, 265, 296–97, 316–17

Delacour, Sarah, 262, 399

Denny, John, 480

Denny, Joseph W., 31

Devinney, William, 229, 365, 367

Dickens, Charles, 47, 270, 360, 389

Dickenson, Daniel, 88, 89, 90, 92, 94, 370–71

Doane, George Washington, 262, 275, 368, 377, 392

Dod, Albert Baldwin, 377

Dodson, Richard W., 134

Donop, Carl Emil Kurt von, 15, 127, 164–65

Dorr, Thomas W., 284, 285, 297, 358, 359, 457, 482–83

Dougherty. *See* Daugherty

Drayton, Edward (Ned): accompanies Mickle, 6, 21, 43, 285–86, 291–93, 298, 305, 436; plays chess with Mickle, 16, 19; on school holiday, 230; visits at Sheppards, 232, 277, 298, 315, 316, 331, 436; visits at Stivers, 279, 303; begins study of law, 286; musical activity, 295–96, 334, 335; at debates, 332, 335; mentioned, 42, 301, 326, 328, 333

Drew, Samuel, 80, 88, 91, 310

Drew, Thomas, Jr., 259, 260

Driesbach, Mr. (lion-tamer), 305–6

Ducachet, Henry, 42

Dudley, Thomas H.: visits Mickle, 211; in debates, 270, 332, 337, 342, 353; accompanies Mickle, 304–5, 363; helps Mickle in legal research, 345; mentioned, 198, 326, 407, 433, 477, 488
Duer, James, 218
Dunn, Nathan, 240, 309
DuSolle, John, 264
Dutton, John, 448
Dyott, Thomas W., 15, 163–64, 225

Eastlack Family, 128, 172, 210
Edmonds, Nathaniel, 25, 123
Edwards, Henry, 176, 180–81, 190, 197, 199–200, 239, 278, 285–86, 369, 501, 502
Edwards, Mary, 180–81, 369, 379
Elfreth, Samuel D., 296
Ellis Family, 414
Ellsler, Fanny, 104, 109–10, 329, 394,
Elmer, Daniel, 437
Elmer, Lucius Q. C., 238, 248, 405, 408, 424, 470, 489
Elwell, James, 88, 274
Emerson, Ralph Waldo, 353, 395
Engle, Frederick, 379, 380
English, Henry, 23
English, Israel, 25, 287
English, Thomas Dunn, 470, 505, 508
Espy, James Pollard, 56, 64
Eustace, F. A., 233, 271
Ewing, Thomas, 227

Faye, Hervé, 360
Ferdinand Philippe (son of King of France), 320
Ferris, Peter W., 482–83, 502
Fetters, Caroline, 376, 489
Fetters, Richard, 26, 143, 151, 157, 273, 279, 359, 376, 432, 496, 506
Feuring, William, 378
Finch, Mrs. (friend of Mickle family), 190, 195, 199, 274
Fisher, Michael C., 407, 474–75
Fisher, William, 407
Fisler, Lorenzo F., 195, 267, 307, 350
Fitzwilliam, Fanny, 306
Florence, Thomas B., 470
Forrest, Edwin, 43, 246
Fortiner, Elwood, 104, 114, 115–16, 169
Fortiner, Samuel, 104, 169
Foster, Samuel S., 9, 50, 155, 236
Fowler, Orson Squire, 71, 213
Fox, Henry Stephen, 131, 144, 226
Frelinghuysen, Theodore, 36
Fritz, Peter, 289–90
Fullerton, Alexander, 300

Gall, Franz Joseph, 213
Garrett, Charles S., 50, 255, 287, 370, 407, 428, 433, 434
Garrett, Henry, 503
Garrett, Samuel W., 443
Garrison, Charles Grant, 464–65, 493, 496
Garwood, Hamilton C., 114
George, James, 290–91, 298, 319, 331
Gerhart, Mr. (acquaintance of Mickle), 334, 358, 365, 405
Gill, Sarah, 417, 423
Gillett, Abraham D., 349–50
Gilliams, Jacob, 272, 273
Gilmer, Thomas W., 430
Gilpin, Henry D., 266, 282, 380
Girard, Stephen, 348
Githens, Joseph, 128, 387, 416, 422, 470
Goodrich, Samuel Griswold (pseud, Peter Parley), 8, 106, 392
Goodwin, John D., 289
Gordon, Thomas F., 24, 202, 411, 417, 492
Gotera (African chief), 246
Graves, William J., 36–37, 39–40
Gray, Mary, 151, 336, 413, 456, 479
Gray, Philip James: association with Mickle as writer, xvi, 35, 39, 40, 46, 49, 50, 109, 199, 240, 243, 261, 266, 267, 271, 379, 413; in fights, 38, 239; as Collector of Customs, 130, 194, 370; as Justice of the Peace, 146, 345; Mickle visits, 151, 403, 419, 435; supports Library Company, 155–56; subject of articles by Mickle, 330–38 *passim*; house threatened by fire, 405; and election results of 1843, 407, 408; opinion of Mickle, 421, 422; mentioned, 26, 28, 172, 212, 229, 243, 269, 278, 353, 366, 378, 406, 423, 426, 433, 479
Gray, Thomas M., 130, 340, 403
Green, James S., 278, 380, 427–28, 449
Greene, Christopher, 15, 65, 164–65
Greene, Nathanael, 127
Grover, Thomas D., 458
Gummere, Samuel R., 337, 463
Guy, William, 416, 422

Hackett, Isaac, 77
Hague, Thomas, 193, 363
Haines Family, 57, 213, 235, 332, 413, 454
Haines, Benjamin, 475
Haines, Heulings, 304, 414
Haines, Mary, 5, 8, 87, 97, 183, 200–209 *passim*, 213, 276, 303, 305, 331, 332

Haines, Rebecca, 5, 201–9, 368
Haines, Samuel, 5
Haines, Sarah M. (Sally), 5, 201–9, 368
Hall, Harrison, 492–93
Hall, John, 132, 387, 462, 463
Hall, Mary Ann, 500
Hallett, Benjamin F., 484–85
Halsted, Oliver S., 36, 489–90
Halsted, William, 494
Hamill, Samuel, 43
Hamilton, Morris R., 385, 386, 387, 398, 402, 406, 417, 423, 424, 456, 464–65
Harbord, Richard, 324
Hare, Robert, Jr., 447
Harley, Emily, 476, 485, 490, 507
Harris, Samuel, 160, 186, 257, 261, 308, 416
Harrison, John B., 439, 475–76
Harrison, Josiah, 26, 345
Harrison, William Henry: election of 1840, xv, 60, 74, 75, 77, 93, 96, 214, 217; inauguration, 125–26, 130; death, 143–57 *passim*, 166, 217; mentioned, 99, 218, 219, 231, 237
Harvey, George, 179
Haslett, John, 190
Hazard, John L., 104, 169
Hazelhurst, Isaac, 133, 136
Hazzard, Mr. (bandleader), 283, 359
Heberton, Charlotte, 460–61, 478
Heberton, George, 461
Heberton, Hutchinson, 355–56, 439, 478
Henderson, John, 269, 289
Heulings, Elizabeth, 462
Heulings, Louisa, 461, 462
Heyl, Elizabeth, 123, 291
Heyl, William, 290–91
Hicks, Elias, 260
Hillhouse, James A., 390
Hinchman, John, 70–71, 145–46, 182
Hineline, Charles D.: as newspaper publisher, xvi, 280, 324–38 *passim*, 382, 418, 447; at Rhode Island meeting, 359; and Democratic politics, 385, 406, 408; in Indiana, 483; mentioned, 348, 358, 407, 422, 449, 466, 471
Hogeland, Adelia, 143, 168, 195, 213, 399, 490
Hogeland, Eliza, 143, 164, 276, 287, 323, 365, 425, 455
Hogeland, Mary, 143, 195, 317–18, 324
Holahan, Jacob, 215
Holcomb, Chauncy P., 104
Holland, Mr. (schoolmaster), 273–74
Hollingshead, Joshua, 425
Hollingshed, Charles, 305, 307, 320, 326, 328, 330, 337, 342, 345
Holmes, William, 309, 310–11, 314

Houston, Sam, 37
Howe, Henry, xxii, 278–79, 316, 318, 390, 435, 439, 465
Howell, Joshua, 484
Howell, Richard W., 234, 286, 507
Hoy, James, Jr., 462, 479, 501, 503, 505
Hubbard, Henry, 392, 452
Hugg Family, 164–65, 288, 289, 299, 302, 319, 320, 335, 336, 378, 385, 408, 455
Hugg, Anna, 172, 239, 270, 315, 331, 336, 344
Hugg, Charles, 333
Hugg, Hannah, 20, 164, 477
Hugg, John, 288
Hugg, Joseph (grandfather), 164–65, 287–88, 455, 463
Hugg, Joseph (grandson), 21, 164, 287
Hugg, Mary, 21, 367
Hugg, Richard, 21, 200, 403
Hugg, William, 172, 239, 261, 263, 267–68
Hughes Family (musicians) 362–63
Hughes, John Joseph, 453–54
Humphreys, Charles, 93–94, 488
Humphreys, Edward, 396–97
Humphreys, Evaline Fetters, 495
Humphreys, John C., 290–91
Humphreys, Richard, 437, 471, 489, 495
Hunt, Benjamin, 399
Hunt, Thomas P., 131–32
Hupfeld, Charles, 288
Hupfeld, Charles Frederick, 288
Hupfeld, John, 288

Ide, George, 152, 154, 174, 307
Irwin, Samuel, 170, 325, 326
Ivins, Bishop, 147, 182, 215, 329

Jack, Charles James, 142
Jackson, Andrew: as president, xv, 12, 16, 147; as general, 19, 37, 254, 349; Mickle writes to, 295; mentioned, 137, 226, 245, 266, 282, 451, 488
Jarnagin, Spencer, 499, 501
Jeffers, Charlotte, 467
Jeffers, William N. (nephew), 54–68 *passim*, 74–95 *passim*, 142–43, 145, 147, 234–35, 463, 509
Jeffers, William N. (uncle): as lawyer, 36, 198, 299; Mickle visits, 95; political activity, 112, 398, 414, 433; trip to New York State with Mickle, 463–69; mentioned, 234, 239, 338, 372, 472, 486
Jinnett, James, 406
Johnson, Frank, 186, 194, 195–96, 252, 384
Johnson, Ovid J., 328

Johnson, Richard M., 77, 137, 334, 337, 354, 414, 425, 427, 429, 451
Justice, Joseph, 428

Kaighn Family, 26, 430, 432
Kaighn, Elias, 432, 439
Kaighn, John, 183, 260
Kaighn, Joseph, 123, 432
Kane, John, 83, 87
Kane, John K., 446, 447–48, 484
Kelley, Harriet, 388–97 *passim*, 400, 427, 452, 471
Kelley, William D.: as politician and reformer, 77, 161, 162, 163, 211, 227–28, 230, 279, 339–40; speaks in Camden, 123, 178–79, 190–99 *passim*, 241, 242–43, 286; as lawyer, 154, 159, 160, 176, 189, 354; general description and character of, 168, 211–12, 227–28; as friend of Brownson, 258, 260, 394–95; accompanies Mickle, 279, 364, 427; visits Mickle, 322; visits Emerson, 353; Mickle visits, 381, 397, 471; marriage and honeymoon, 387–97 *passim*; mentioned, 174, 185, 193, 214, 217, 220, 233, 257, 271, 276, 289, 323, 335, 373, 380, 382, 398, 484
Kenrick, Francis Patrick, 443, 446
Kille, Joseph, 430–31
King, Edward (Ned): Mickle meets, 229; Mickle visits, 230; visits at Sheppards, 232, 234, 277, 286, 298, 305, 306, 307, 315, 321; musical activity, 233, 279, 288, 290–91, 306–7, 319–27 *passim*; relations with women, 286, 308; accompanies Mickle, 292–93, 298, 304, 417; trip to Bridgeton, 316, 318; leaves Camden, 329–30; letters from, 343; mentioned, 252, 281, 289, 303
King, Edward, 476, 484, 487
King, Samuel, 372
King, Samuel Ward, 285
King, William R., 130–31
King, William T., 459
Kingdon, Jabez, 310
Kinsey, Charles, 490
Kinsey, James, 490
Kneeland, Abner, 245
Knight, Benjamin, 384
Knisell, John, 137–38
Kramer, John, 469
Kyle, Eliza, 500

Ladd, Ann, 201–9
Ladd, Samuel Hamilton, 201–9, 213
Lafferty, William, 381
Landis, John, 179
Lane, James, 23
Lanning, Charles P., 309

Lanning, Samuel, 229, 322
Lardner, Dionysius, 269
Latrobe, John H. B., 465
Lawrence, James, 31, 287–88
Lee, Robert M., 289–90
Legaré, Hugh Swinton, 380
Lehr, Jacob W., 75
Lenhart, John L., 297, 323, 332
Lescure, Mr. (acquaintance of Mickle), 228–29
Levin, Lewis C.: temperance activities of, 261–62, 263, 276, 280–81, 317, 350, 351; nativist activity, 442, 446, 447, 458, 460; mentioned, 271
Lippincott, Franklin, 461
List, Christopher, 322
Little, Archibald, 61
Lord, James A., 4
Lougee, Noah, 307, 341
Louis Philippe (King of France), 230, 395
Ludlam, Richard Smith, 384
Lummis, Samuel, 315, 325

McCahen, John J., 470
McCalla, Aulay, 419
McCalla, William S., 152, 245, 246, 270, 279, 280
McCauley, Edward Y., 392, 393–94, 403
McChesney, Charles G., 256
McCollum, Thomas, 485
MacCulloch, Francis L., 239, 241
McDuffie, George, 498
McIlvaine, Henry, 447–48
Mackenzie, Alexander Slidell, 343
MacKenzie, William Lyon, 37
McKnight, John L. 384, 385
McKnight, William, 100
McLeod, Alexander, 144, 210, 222, 231
McMakin, Benjamin, 384
McMakin, Joseph, 384
McMichael, Morton, 119–20, 261, 272, 444
Macomb, Alexander, 188
Madison, Dolly, 183–84
Madison, James, 183–84
Maffit, John, 360, 477
Manly, Henry, 293, 294
Martin, James K., 163–78 *passim*, 228, 254, 272, 324, 480
Mathew, Theobold, 132
Matlack, Elizabeth, 290–91
Matlack, James, 3, 180
Matlack, James, Mrs., 180
Matlack, Mary, 3, 29
Matlack, R., Mrs., 181
Matlack, Robert, 489
Matlack, Robert K., 185, 216, 220, 484
Mercer, Hugh, 101–2

Mercer, Singleton, 355–56, 357, 362, 363, 365, 366, 369, 379, 404
Mickle Family, xiii, 7, 9, 36, 178, 183, 320
Mickle, Andrew F. E., 3, 36, 180, 216
Mickle, Archibald, xiii, 429
Mickle, Benjamin, 90
Mickle, Benjamin W., 3, 29, 74, 90, 183
Mickle, Isaac (father of diarist), xiv, 71–72, 117, 486
Mickle, Isaac (grandfather of diarist), 29, 486
Mickle, Isaac W., 74, 102, 496
Mickle, John W.: and Mickle's career choice, xiv–xv, 126, 141–42, 155; and business affairs, xv, 5, 7, 9, 17, 19, 22, 29, 35, 36, 66, 69, 84, 134, 137, 350; and politics, xv, 48, 76–77, 88, 237, 370, 406, 427, 428, 433–35, 446, 470; and formation of Camden County, xvi, 423, 429–30, 431, 434, 436; letters of, xix, 28, 29, 446; *faux pas* of, 30; visit with Van Buren, 135; friendship with Page, 142, 155; and Mickle property, 183, 216, 220, 436; travel, 187, 190, 191, 218–20, 304–5; and visit of President Tyler, 375–77; mentioned, 9, 40, 83, 85, 94, 167, 186, 194, 211, 218, 229, 234, 291, 321, 359, 383, 430, 432, 455, 473
Mickle, Rebecca Morgan: influence on Mickle, xiv–xv, 92, 118, 126, 154; sells farm to Mickle, xvii; marriage, 45; visits to friends and relatives, 97, 151, 164, 287, 305, 408, 455; education, 180; illness, 221, 293–94; Mickle's love for, 481; mentioned, 66, 71, 186, 190–91, 208, 209, 242, 268, 304, 321, 306, 368, 373, 414, 426, 429, 462
Mickle, Sara Wilkins, 183
Middleton, Robert, 233
Miller, Jonas, 460, 461
Miller, Lafayette, 374, 384, 406, 455
Miller, Pauline, 384
Miller, William, 247, 319, 339, 361, 364, 367
Mills, Franklin S., 424, 450
Mitchell, Elizabeth, xix
Mitchell, George P., 187
Mitchell, Joshua, 485–86
Moffett, Craig, 351
Monroe, James, 92
Montgomery, John C., 157, 166, 231
Moore, Eli K., 354–55, 491
Morgan, Charles Joseph, 423
Morgan, Edward, 333
Morgan, John, 297
Moriarty, Patrick Eugene, 117, 149, 223, 234, 277

Morris, Edward Jay, 105
Morris, Phineas Pemberton, 476
Morse, Samuel F. B., 452
Muhlenberg, Henry, 38
Mulford, Anna, 5, 106, 417–18, 419, 423, 446
Mulford, Emma, 5, 132, 178, 209, 210, 376, 384–85, 417–18, 454, 492–503 *passim*
Mulford, Isaac S.: borrows books from Mickle, 5, 9; Mickle visits, 7, 21, 32, 88, 112, 127, 135–36; speeches of, 17, 28, 148, 155, 156, 182, 242, 256, 264, 266, 267, 278, 316, 318; as physician, 80, 123, 148, 221; opinion of horse-racing, 171–72; political views, 176; visits "Poplar Hill," 305; resemblance to President Tyler, 376; visits Cape May, 385, 386; candidate for constitutional convention, 433; mentioned, 245, 299, 327, 356, 366, 399, 433
Mulford, Mary, 124
Mulford, Miss (niece of Isaac Mulford), 401
Mulford, Rachel Mickle, 5, 319–20, 331, 332, 383–85, 386, 413, 454
Mulford, Thomas W.: Mickle meets, 299; in debate, 330, 332, 338–39, 340, 342, 353; newspaper work, 330, 338, 353; visits Sheppards, 333, 343, 364, 366, 415; musical activity, 334, 339, 358, 365, 366, 374, 378, 437, 480; accompanies Mickle, 336, 362–63, 368–81 *passim*, 401, 403, 405, 407, 422, 429, 434, 438, 445, 455, 464, 489, 506; helps in legal research, 345; in Salem, N.J., 350, 486; at Rhode Island meeting, 359; and visit of President Tyler, 375–76; and Constitution of 1844, 386, 398, 402; speeches of, 406, 429; admitted to bar, 415; and Caddy Cole, 418, 479, 482, 494–95; and presidential campaign of 1844, 456, 470; helps establish anti-nativist organization, 464–65, 471; mentioned, 326, 337, 352, 382, 383, 384, 433, 476
Mulford, William B., 104
Murat, Achille, 478
Murdoch, James Edward, 185, 395

Nagel, John, 368–69, 416–17, 482
Narr, David, 503
Naylor, Charles, 458
Neall, Thomas, 23
Nelson, John, 380
Nelson, Joseph C., 432
Newell, James M., 431
Newton, Mr. (Mormon speaker), 170, 173

Nicholls, Mr. (speaker at meeting), 400
Nicholson, Mr. (surveyor), 422
Nolen, Spencer, 42

O'Connell, Daniel, 19
Ogden, Francis, 158, 182, 225
Ogden, Robert W., 424–25
Ogden, Robert W., Jr.: accompanies
  Mickle, 69, 79, 161, 229, 233, 240,
  245, 268–69, 290, 291–93; organiza-
  tional activity, 100, 127, 411–12; plays
  cards with Mickle, 133; musical activ-
  ity, 235, 241, 255, 294, 318, 334, 365,
  378; visits Mickle, 263, 286; men-
  tioned, 254, 291, 333, 339
Ogden, William H., 334
d'Orléans, François Ferdinand, Prince de
  Joinville, 230
Osbourne, J. G., 172, 182–83, 188, 216–
  17, 220, 221, 252, 357, 399, 402
Osbourne, Mr. (minister), 295, 336, 337,
  339
Osbourne, Mrs. (Baltimore hostess), 452
Ostler, George, 104
O'Sullivan, John L., 493

Packenham, Edward, 254, 478
Paganini, Niccolo, 368, 482
Page, George Washington, 167–68, 176,
  185, 322, 442
Page, James: as Mickle's law tutor, xv,
  141–42, 154, 158, 227, 228, 238, 436,
  437, 438, 441, 446, 449; as politician,
  72, 77, 159, 162, 163, 211, 359, 441,
  455; as political officer-holder, 157,
  182, 187, 277, 505, 508; description
  of, 167, 284; as militia leader, 190,
  263, 283, 289, 320, 322, 323–24, 329,
  444, 459, 481; as lawyer, 246, 307,
  476, 479; mentioned, 154, 185, 204,
  214, 231, 232, 233, 260, 264, 266,
  283–95 *passim*, 325, 344, 347–48, 354,
  362, 370, 381, 401, 403, 404, 411, 420,
  426, 427, 447, 448, 456, 460, 482–88
  passim
Parkinson, J. W., 247
Parkinson, R. B., 247
Parley, Peter. *See* Goodrich, Samuel Griswold
Parmenter, A. W., 358, 359–60
Parmenter, David, 360
Parrish, Joseph, 312
Partridge, Alden, 328
Patterson, James, 351, 432, 446
Patterson, Henry S., 140–41, 162, 176,
  193, 258, 260, 265–66, 267
Patterson, Robert, 446
Paul, George M., 201–9, 222

Paul, James, 447
Paul, Mary Ann, 201–9, 213
Paul, William S., 25
Paulding, James K., 84, 145, 266
Paulson, Charles A., Jr., 477–78
Peak, Edward, 186, 362
Peale, Charles Willson, 12
Pearce, Thomas A., 407
Pennington, John, 491–92
Pennington, William, 48, 236–37, 338,
  340, 351, 404, 408, 494
Perrine, Lewis, 398, 487–88
Perry, Matthew C., 159
Peterson, John W., 157, 334
Phelps, Noah A., 390
Phillips, Henry M., 479–80, 503
Pine, Mrs. (choirsinger), 315, 321, 323
Pinteux, John, 397
Pitman, Charles, 280
Plankinton, Joseph, 277
Plantagenet, Beauchamp, 490–92
Plitt, George, 495
Plowden, Edmund, 491
Poe, Edgar Allen, 185, 397
Polk, James K., xvi, 451–60 *passim*, 469,
  473, 478–79, 487–508 *passim*
Polk, William, 478–79
Porter, David, 424
Porter, David R., 38, 162, 204, 234, 375,
  445, 459, 487
Porter, Edward, 98
Porter, James M., 375
Porter, Joseph, 433, 435
Potts, John, 116
Potts, Joseph C., 503
Potts, Stacy G., 232, 263, 338, 351, 470,
  488
Price, Eli K., 447–48
Pugh, Joseph A., 447, 460, 461, 462
Pusey, Edward B., 368

Quimby, Phineas P., 240

Rainer Family (musicians), 283, 288
Randall, Josiah, 466
Randolph, John, 498
Ravel Family (actors), 388
Read, Joel, 372
Read, John Meredith, 441, 446
Read, Thomas Buchanan, xvii
Reed, John, 315, 324
Remak, Gustave, 272, 276, 322, 456–57
Renshaw, James, 93
Rhees, John, 176, 261, 369–70, 386, 455
Richmond, John, 439
Ridgway, Jacob, 56, 69, 72, 84–85, 190,
  201, 367, 368, 369
Ridgway, Thomas, 476, 479

Ritchie, Thomas, 451
Ritner, Joseph, 38
Rives, John Cook, 337, 403, 420
Roberts, Benjamin, 407
Rogers, Henry D., 421
Rogers, James B., 421
Rogers, Josiah, 114, 327, 342
Rogers, Mary, 397
Rogers, Samuel (Camden), 114
Rogers, Samuel (Burlington), 242
Rogers, William, 104
Rosenbaum, John G., 456–57
Ross, John, 43
Ross, John, Jr., 43, 485
Rossell, Joseph, 209
Rossell, William, 209
Roth, William, 265, 380
Rowand, Mrs. (Caddy Cole's grandmother), 300–302
Rudderow, Ezra, 425
Rue, John, 38
Rulon Family, 384, 461
Rush, Benjamin (d. 1813), 52, 130, 136
Rush, Benjamin, 447–48
Rush, Samuel, 130, 136
Ryall, David Bailey, 472, 488
Ryerson, Thomas C., 3
Rynders, Isaiah, 501, 505
Sage, Miles (grandfather), 127–28, 165, 278, 475, 494
Sage, Miles (grandson), 100, 104, 127–28
Sammis, Dr. (lecturer), 152, 243–47 *passim*, 255, 265, 267
Samuels, Henry, 104, 111–12, 114–15, 181, 315, 319, 321
Sargent, Winthrop (grandfather), 492
Sargent, Winthrop (grandson), 492–93
Sartain, John, 283
Saunders, Joseph, 432, 434
Sawn, Josiah, 12, 304
Schaumburg, Capt. (Page's brother-in-law), 418, 481–82, 497
Schaumburg, Mrs. (Page's sister), 370, 381–82, 485
Scott, John M., 445
Scott, Joseph Warren, 193, 237
Scott, Robert, 459
Scott, Winfield, 189
Scull Family, 333
Scull, Joab, 12, 114, 255
Scull, Joab, Mrs. 114, 172, 242
Scull, Samuel, 163
Seargent. *See* Sergeant
Secor, Charles A., 466
Sedgwick, Catharine Maria, 389
Seguin, Arthur, 357
Sergeant, John, 222, 224
Shamburg. *See* Schaumburg

Sharp, Joseph, 317
Shaw, John K., 310
Shaw, William, 34, 55, 306, 463–64
Sheppard Family, 143, 150, 152, 190, 200, 232–80 *passim*, 290–400 *passim*, 413–38 *passim*, 455, 460, 470
Sheppard, Hannah (mother), 199, 238, 241, 253, 296, 308, 316, 319, 329, 437, 509
Sheppard, Hannah (daughter): accompanies Mickle, 253, 267, 272, 275, 286, 318, 320, 356, 361; Mickle visits at Dr. Smalley's, 311, 312; trip to Bridgeton, 316, 318; mentioned, 133, 252, 256, 302, 321, 331, 377, 418
Sheppard, Joseph, 45
Sheppard, Josephine: Will Jeffers visits, 143; meets Mickle, 172–73, 243, 349; Mickle visits, 232, 241, 268–69, 311–14, 315, 344, 346, 426, 427; discussions with Mickle, 235, 253, 298, 325; accompanies Mickle, 246, 255–56, 266, 270–95 *passim*, 317–18, 320, 332–43 *passim*, 361, 366, 374–75, 378, 409, 413, 417, 419, 423, 425, 435, 464; visits Caddy Cole, 299–303; romance with Mickle, 281–82, 305, 313–14, 315, 316, 321, 327–28, 332, 340, 409, 486–87, 504; trip to Washington with Mickle, 492, 494, 497–503; mentioned, 41, 133, 143, 252, 356, 360, 371, 382, 383, 415, 418, 421, 470, 509
Sheppard, Mary, 133, 232, 244, 247, 252, 265, 273, 280–81, 293–99 *passim*, 316, 335, 340, 374
Sheppard, Phoebe; Mickle visits, 268–69, 277, 279, 284, 307–08; Mickle accompanies, 295, 308–14, 315, 320, 341; mentioned, 133, 152, 174, 237, 244, 252, 261, 268, 287, 293, 294, 299, 321, 328, 333, 367, 374
Sherman, James T., 232, 254, 256
Shivers, Isaac, 127
Shivers, Samuel E., 494
Silliman, Benjamin, 390
Simmons, R. R., 181, 278, 315
Simpson, Joseph, 292
Sinnickson, Andrew, 462
Sisty, Benjamin, 364, 373, 385
Sisty, John, 385, 422
Slamm, Levi D., 354
Slicer, Henry, 340
Sloan, James W., 183, 267–68, 317, 415
Smalley, John, 311, 312, 337
Smalley, Joseph B., 302, 310–11
Smalley, Joseph B., Jr., 237, 241, 308, 310–12, 314, 337
Smalley, Joseph B., Mrs. 237, 311, 312

Smallwood, John C., 407, 485, 494
Smallwood, Robert, 407
Smith, Jesse, 31
Smith, Joseph, 170, 173, 176
Smith, Kinderton, 447
Smith, William W., 256, 273, 330
Snowden, William, 43
Snowden, William H., 423–24, 426
Southard, Samuel L., 92, 146, 234
Souville, Mr. (acquaintance of Mickle), 488, 495
Spain, George, 114
Sparry, Charles, 124
Spencer, John C., 343, 375
Spencer, Jonathan J., 462
Spencer, Philip, 343
Stanley, Edward, 227
Stetser, Joseph, 434
Stevens, Robert Livingston, 84–85
Stewart, Charles, 136–37, 167, 170, 179, 182, 189, 210–16 *passim*, 222, 268, 425, 451
Stivers Family, 279, 286, 303, 319
Stivers, Elizabeth, 306, 319
Stivers, Gideon V., 78, 161, 372
Stivers, Gideon V., Jr.: organizational activity, 78, 120, 127; accompanies Mickle, 98, 104, 155, 159, 176; at debates, 114–15, 169, 181; as singer, 147; visits Mickle, 161, 232; Mickle visits, 388; mentioned, 178, 199, 306
Stockton, Ellen, 461, 462
Stockton, Robert Field, 375–76, 398, 400, 418, 430
Stockton, Thomas H., 335
Stone, Charles, 118
Stoy, Joseph, 414
Stratton, Charles C., 433, 462, 473, 485, 488–89, 490, 494, 509
Stratton, Charles S. (Tom Thumb), 355, 358
Stratton, Nathan T., 407, 408
Strickland, William, 501
Stroud, George M., 479
Stryker, Peter C., 309
Sturgeon, Daniel, 487
Sullivan, John Turner Sargent, 116, 121, 232, 240
Surault, François M. J., 413, 477, 483, 488
Swartwout, Samuel, 60, 74
Swift, John, 166, 172, 229

Taglioni, Marie, 483
Taylor, Edward Thompson, 5
Taylor, John S., 439
Taylor, Joseph, 417
Taylor, Mary A., 58, 59, 61, 62, 63, 68

Taylor, Thomas R., 422–23
Thomas, Gabriel, 477–78
Thomas, Henry, 345
Thompson, Charles Wes, 255, 273
Thompson, John R., 386, 397–98, 455, 472, 481, 485, 488, 499, 501, 502
Thompson, Richard P., 77, 232, 256, 257, 269, 325, 431
Thorn, Eliza, 489
Tindall. *See* Tyndall
Tochman, Gaspar (or Kaspar), 427
Todd, Charles Steward, 231
Todd, Dolly. *See* Madison, Dolly
Todd, John, Jr., 183
Tom Thumb. *See* Stratton, Charles S.
Toms, Benjamin, 327
Toole, Ebenezer, 26
Toy, Isaiah, 20, 25
Treadwell, Stephen, 271–72
Troth, Jacob, 414, 416, 422
Turner, Angeline, 241, 243, 254, 288, 305, 306, 322, 338, 367, 399, 421
Turner, Elbridge G., 392
Turner, Mary, 147, 243, 305, 322, 367, 399, 462
Tyler, John: as president, xv, 145, 146, 150, 157–58, 166, 175–76, 214, 218, 222, 224–25, 254; difficulty with Whig party, xvi, 145, 210, 215–16, 217, 225, 226, 227; in Camden and Philadelphia, xxiv, 375–77; vetoes, 213–25 *passim*, 316; as candidate for president in 1844, 216, 254, 403, 420–21, 425, 449, 450, 453; presidential messages of, 225–26, 245, 342; and Dorr "rebellion," 285; mentioned, 237, 271, 370, 380, 382, 383, 441, 450, 451, 476, 487, 505, 506
Tyler, Robert, 484
Tyndale, Clara, xvii, xix, xxiv
Tyndale, Robinson, xvii
Tyndale, Sarah Thorn, xvii, xix
Tyndall, Napoleon Bonaparte, 45, 69, 135, 150, 155, 170–78 *passim*
Tyng, Stephen H., 17
Tyson, J. Washington, 461, 476
Tyson, Job R., 113

Upshur, Abel P., 375, 430

Valentine, William, 392
Vanarsdale, William, 322, 441
Van Aurburgher. *See* Vanbrugen
Van Bergen. *See* Vanbrugen
Vanbrugen, Daniel, 44
Van Buren, Martin: election of 1840, xv, 96, 97, 125–26, 212; possible candidacy in 1844, xvi, 125, 136–37, 267,

268, 355, 403, 420–31 passim, 440–54
passim; John Mickle meets, 135; Mickle
meets, 266, 466; on bank war, 354–55;
on annexation of Texas, 440; men-
tioned, 53, 60, 62, 77, 99, 214, 216,
294, 380, 390, 438, 479, 488, 491, 505
Vanburger. *See* Vanbrugen
Vandenburg, Mr. (song-writer), 217
van der Donck, Adriaen, 492
Vandever, Lydia, 278, 335
Vandever, William, 331
Van Dyke, James C., 355–56
Van Ness, John, 500
Vansciver, Isaac, 257
Victoria (Queen of England), 37, 144,
186
Vroom, George A., 450, 472
Vroom, Peter D., 72, 77, 487–88, 495

Wainwright, James, 269, 272–73
Wales, Edmond L. B., 408
Walker, Robert J., 452
Walker, Thomas, 26
Wall, Garrett, 43, 72, 77, 384, 429, 472,
487–88
Wall, James W., 488
Wallace, James S., 418
Wallace, Mr. (lecturer), 255, 266
Wallace, William Vincent, 416–17
Wannan, William, 134, 486, 497
Ward Family, 178
Ward, James, 430–31, 449, 450
Ward, John, 177, 200, 322
Ward, Mr. (music director), 290, 335
Ward, Townsend, 477–78, 485, 492, 493,
507–8
Ward, William, 177, 200, 229, 244
Ware, Mark, 379–80, 403, 406, 407, 408,
428, 436
Washington, George: birthday celebra-
tions, 22, 32–33, 266, 496; mentioned,
15, 16, 20, 27, 54, 104, 119, 169, 421
Watson, John Fanning, 435
Watson, John M., 428
Watson, Mrs. (singer), 288
Watts, Henry M., 447
Waugh, Beverly, 283
Weatherby, Joseph, 25, 123, 127–35
passim, 189–202 *passim*
Webb, James Watson, 39–40, 216, 225
Webster, Daniel, 111, 130, 131, 144, 197,
199, 216, 226, 245, 379, 393, 498
Weight, John J., 223, 243, 254, 263, 264,
286–93 *passim*, 303, 316, 321, 323
Welch, Rufus, 485
Wescott, George C., 467
West, Benjamin, 309, 418
West, Charles, 176
West, John, 20
West, Mr. (merchant), 460, 461
Westcoat. *See* Wescott
Westcott. *See* Wescott
Whale, Henry, 478, 485, 490, 495, 507
Wharton, Robert, 476
Whilldin, Wilmon, 384, 462–63
Whitall, Ann Cooper, 59, 165
Whitall, James, 15, 59
White, Lemuel G., 477
White, Miss (speaker and teacher), 477,
506
Whitesides, Henry F. M., 21
Whitman, William, 449
Wiley, Mr. (Kelley's law student), 354
Wiley, Mr. (acquaintance of Mickle),
498, 499
Wilkes, Charles, 294
Wilkins Family, 177–78, 264
Wilkins, Abby, 305
Wilkins, Benjamin, 42, 264, 278
Wilkins, Edward L., 66
Wilkins, Isaac, 305
Wilkins, Job Whitall, 58–59, 79, 81, 186
Wilkins, Rufus, 235, 278, 285–86
Wilkins, William, 58, 59
Wilkins, William Wood, 183–84
Williams, Hampton, 264
Williamson, Isaac H., 36, 446
Wilson, Benjamin, 273
Wilson, David, 357
Wilson, James H., 267, 406
Wilson, Susan, 357, 362, 367, 371, 385,
410–11, 416
Winner, Isaac, 415, 464
Winner, William E., 371
Wise, Henry Alexander, 39, 227
Wise, John, 42–43
Wolf, George, 38
Wollstonecraft, Mary, 258
Wood Family, 177–78, 278
Wood, Henry, 389
Wood, James, 186, 362
Wood, James, Mrs. 186
Wood, Thomas B., 407, 408
Woodbury, Levi, 498
Woolman, Burr, 242
Woolman, Franklin, 242
Wright, Frances (Fanny), 258
Wright, Hendrick B., 450
Wright, John W., 461
Wright, Silas, 452, 454, 455, 498

Yard, Joseph A., 428, 453
Yeager, Johanna, 371

Zabriskie, James C., 428, 449, 453

Subjects and Proper Names Other Than Personal Names

Abolition, 181, 395. *See also* Slavery
Abstinence, 262, 292, 461, 469
Accidents: reported, 50, 145–46, 187, 396, 425, 425 n.12, 430, 430 n.26
Actors: encountered, 185, 269, 306 n.85
Addresses, political: made, 456, 460
Africans, 246. *See also* Blacks; Negroes
Agriculture, 164, 169–70, 373, 383, 386
Alcohol: sale of, 129, 131, 379, 417; use of, xvii, xix, 471, 482, 495, 496, 500, 503, 504. *See also* Drunkenness; Temperance
Alexander, 7
Alliance, U.S.S., 220, 220 n.158
"Alms House, Old," 313, 313 n.96
Amateurs Association: formation of, 264; meetings of, 267, 271. *See also* Amateurs Music Association
Amateurs Music Association: formation of, 334, 334 n.123, 365–66; meetings of, 336, 341, 349, 352, 364, 366, 367
American (hotel): visited, 466, 466 n.134
American Eagle. See Eagle
American Republican party, 438 n.46
American Theatre: attended, 40, 40 n.67, 47, 381, 401. *See also* Walnut Street Theatre
Antinativism. *See* Sons of Liberty
Architecture, 7, 51, 111, 312
Arch Street Theatre, 286
Aroostook "War," 110, 110n.77
Arrests, 179, 261–62, 263, 304, 345
Artists' Fund Hall, 159, 159 n.71, 418
Astor Hotel, 465, 465 n.126

Baggans, Burr v., 198
Ballooning, 42–43, 43n.74, 397
Balls, 263, 284, 358–59, 428, 452, 481–82, 495, 500–501. *See also* Dancing
Baltimore (Maryland): visited, 449–53
Bank of the United States (second): constitutionality and, 451, 451 n.85; derided, 147, 148; as political issue, 15, 16 n.6
Banks, 274–75; failure of, 268; positions on, 26, 26 n.39, 147–48, 157, 197, 211, 213, 214, 215–16, 218, 222, 224, 245, 254, 354; run on, 112–13. *See also* Fiscal Bank bill; names of banks
Baptist Church: attendance at, 17, 45, 86–87, 149–50, 159, 178, 180, 223, 233, 239, 241, 245, 253, 256, 270, 273, 293, 310, 315, 321, 324, 338, 400, 401. *See also* First Baptist Church
Bar: examination for, 447–48. *See also* Law
Bateman v. *Ware*, 436, 436 n.39

Bathing, seashore, 461
Battery (New York City), 388
Battery House, 94, 94 n.57
Beatings, 379–80; in nativist riots, 433
Bethlehem (Pennsylvania), 201–4
Betting: on elections, 97
Bible: discussed, 72, 89, 116–17; read, 74, 80; in schools, 163
Bigotry, 200
Billiards, 123, 127, 247, 252, 281, 320–21, 384
Blacks, 311. *See also* Africans, Negroes
Blackstone, 159, 161, 174, 179
Blue laws, 229–30. *See also* Sabbath
"Blue lights," 39, 39 n.65
Boats, 7, 8, 187. *See also* Excursions, boat; Rowing; Sailing; Steamboats; names of boats
Books, xiv; collecting of, xiv, 166, 477–78, 486, 490, 491 (*see also* Books: purchased); cost of, 7, 8, 90, 92, 118, 166; lent, 4, 5, 9, 12, 114, 195; purchased, 7, 8, 17, 20, 22, 55, 90, 92, 118, 122, 166, 416, 455, 472, 483, 483 n.31. *See also* Library (personal); Reading: titles comprising; specific titles
Boston (Massachusetts), 391–96
Bowery, The (theatre): visited, 470, 470 n.142
Brandywine Chalybeate Springs, 67–68
Brattle Square Church. *See* Brattle Street Church
Brattle Street Church: visited, 392–93, 393 n.84
Bridgeton (New Jersey), 47, 62
Brooklyn (New York), 388
Brothels, 396 n.96, 500 n.79. *See also* Prostitution
Brown's Hotel, 497, 497 n.68, 499
Buffalo hunt, 401–2
Bunker Hill, 379, 391
Burglaries, 66, 291, 372
Burials, 90, 101–2, 122, 190, 369, 506. *See also* Funerals
Burlington (New Jersey), 111; educated in, xiv, 105; visited, 187, 242, 245
Barnet Rice v. *the County of Philadelphia*, 479–80
Burr's (hotel), 357, 357 n.15, 359
Burr v. *Baggans*, 198
Business affairs, 430, family's, 69, 84–85, 137–38, 183, 216, 218, 220, 304, 383, 414, 415 (*see also* Camden and Amboy Railroad; Camden and Philadelphia Steamboat Ferry Company; Canal: through Windmill Island); own, 416, 455

Cadwallader Street: nativist riots and, 444

Cafe de Mille Colonnes, 397, 397 n.96

Camden (New Jersey): described, xx, 24–27; elections and, 89–90, 129, 361, 506; history of, 24, 391, 439, 439 n.49; illustration of, 250

Camden and Amboy Railroad, 5, 17; and campaigning, 438, 472; characterized, 472; discussed, xv, 5 n.11, 26

Camden and Philadelphia Steamboat Ferry Company, 69, 72

Camden and Woodbury Railroad, 22 n.22, 26

Camden Bank, 157

Camden Classical School, 5 n.8. *See also* Oliver Cox's school

Camden County (New Jersey): abolition of, 508–9, 509 n.91; creation of, xvi, 423, 429, 429 n.23, 430, 431–32, 433–36, 434 n.32, 437 n.40, 438–39; and elections, 471, 485

Camden Garden, 199

Camden Haydn Society, 486. *See also* Haydn Music Club

Camden Literary Association, 156

Camden Temperance Society, 19, 262. *See also* Union Temperance Society

Camden Township: elections and, 234, 334, 407. *See also* Camden: elections and

Campaigning, political, 73, 89, 211–12, 231. *See also* under names of political parties

Canada, 37; United States and, 110, 131, 131 n.133, 144, 144 n.53

Canal: through Windmill Island, 19, 22 n.22, 29, 29 n.41, 44, 250

Canton (China): England and, 182, 184

Cape May (New Jersey), 384–85, 420, 462

Capewell Glass Works, 260, 260 n.12

Capital punishment, 265, 279, 279 n.43, 357–58, 427

Caroline, 131, 131 n.33, 144, 144 n.53

Cataract House, 467, 467 n.136

Catholics, 360; criticized, 149, 371; intolerance toward, 124, 124 n.20, 152, 232, 276, 464 (*see also* Riots: nativist)

Census, 94, 110

Chess, 16, 19, 67, 74, 134, 139, 140, 145, 146, 151, 154, 161, 176, 210, 221, 263

Chester (Pennsylvania), 180–81

Chestnut Street (Philadelphia), 14

Chestnut Street Theatre, 109, 269, 405. *See also* "Old Drury"

Childhood, xiv

Children, xviii, xix

China, 110

Chinese Museum, 280

Christmas: celebration of, 16, 106, 247, 344

Churches: in Camden, 25

Cincinnati Society, New Jersey, 193

Circus, 260, 332, 344, 371

Clairvoyance, 269, 270, 272–73

Class, social: distinctions made in, 111, 115, 134, 160; in republic, 189

Classics, 105, 117, 120. *See also* Greek, Latin

Climate, 420, 483–84

Clothing, 83. *See also* Fashion: in dress

Coins: collections of, 84, 87, 120, 212, 266, 325

Coleman's. *See* National Hotel

Columbia Garden (Camden), 25. *See also* Columbia Pleasure Garden

Columbia Pleasure Garden (Camden), 123 n.19

Comet: sighted, 360–61, 362

Communitarianism, 380, 380 n.53

Concerts: attended, 121–22, 217–18, 288, 349–50, 357, 358, 362–63, 367, 368, 383, 402, 423, 429, 482

Congress Hall (Cape May), 374 n.44, 384, 465

Constitution, New Jersey: revision of, xvi, 346, 346 n.139, 352, 353, 358, 359, 362, 371, 383, 387 n.65, 397–98, 400, 400 n.102, 402–3, 406, 408, 429, 446, 463, 482–83, 485 (*see also* Constitution Club; Reform Association)

Constitution Club (later Reform Club, Reform Association), 386. *See also* Reform Association

Conventions, political: national, 267, 440; state, 35, 38, 324–25. *See also* under names of political parties

Copenhagen (game), 298, 298n. 75

County of Philadelphia, Barnet Rice v., 479–80

Court cases: discussed, 3–4, 36, 136, 198, 210, 246, 326, 345, 362, 363, 365, 366, 436, 436 n.39, 476, 479–80, 484–86. *See also* Murderers: trial of; names of specific court cases

Courting: instances of, 49, 57, 58–60, 81–82, 107–8, 133, 134, 138–39, 150–51, 152, 172–73, 180–81, 190, 199, 231, 232, 239, 241, 243, 244, 246, 257, 264, 268–69, 271, 272, 275, 284, 286, 288, 295, 299, 302, 307, 315, 319, 320, 326–27, 335, 337, 338, 341, 343, 350, 352, 356, 357, 360, 361–62, 366, 370–71, 377, 378, 382, 401, 425, 456, 461, 464, 466, 467–69, 500, 504. *See also*

Courting: instances of *(continued)*
    Ladies: interaction with; Romances
Crime, 164, 179, 277. *See also* specific
    offenses
"Custom House Boat," 6; identified, 4
    n.5; sailing in, 4, 13

Daguerreotype, 373
Dancers, professional, 109–10
Dancing: discussed, 67, 359, 384, 416,
    452, 461; participated in, xvii, 485,
    490, 495, 500, 507; studied, 478, 488;
    viewed, 50, 53, 59, 187, 304, 329.
    See also Balls
Death(s): discussed, 90, 123, 143, 144,
    145–46, 148, 188, 322, 367, 368, 380,
    410, 416, 425, 425 n.12, 430, 430 n.26,
    448, 506. *See also* Burials; Duelling:
    instances of; Funerals; Killings, Mur-
    ders; Suicides
Debates: heard, 27, 29, 110–11, 114–15,
    279, 328, 332, 335, 351–52, 417; par-
    ticipated in, 12, 27, 112, 114–15, 118,
    163, 169, 179, 181, 184, 220, 223, 234,
    240, 270, 330, 337, 338–39, 340, 342–
    43, 350, 352, 357–58, 360, 493. *See
    also* Debating societies: in Camden;
    names of debating societies
Debating societies: in Camden, 26. *See
    also* names of debating societies
Debt, 134; as crime, 101, 261–62, 263
Decatur Coffee Shop, 324
Delacour's: discussions at, 222, 226, 240,
    323, 345–46; visits to, 220, 222, 225,
    229, 236, 323, 333
Delaware, 67–68
Democrat: editor of, xiii, xix; writing for,
    88
Democratic Club, 78
Democratic party, 145; campaigning and,
    189, 211, 289–90, 333, 455, 456, 457,
    460, 472, 473; caucuses and, 427–28,
    432, 506; club for young men of, 78;
    conventions, national and, 427, 427
    n.15, 449–53; conventions, state and,
    426–27, 472; elections and, 38, 42, 48,
    73, 89–90, 95, 97, 109, 125, 129, 231,
    233–34, 236, 240, 289–90, 323–24,
    334, 335, 407–8, 463, 464, 490; fac-
    tions of, 162–63, 228, 233, 335 (*see
    also* "Hunkers"; Loco-focos; "Young
    Democracy"); involvement in, xvi,
    126, 127, 159, 285, 287, 289–90, 294,
    295, 324, 325, 330, 347–48, 385, 397,
    456, 457, 472, 473, 493 (*see also
    Eagle*); involvement, family in, xv
    135, 237, 427; issues and, xvi, 17, 17
    n.12, 26 n.39, 147, 211, 213, 218, 245,

440–41 (*see also* Camden County:
    creation of; Constitution, New Jersey:
    revision of; *Eagle*: positions taken by);
    Loco-focos of, 103 n.65, 218; meetings
    and, 73, 76–77, 88, 211, 323, 385, 404,
    406, 426–27, 470; Native Americans
    and, 454, 457, 460; nominations, local
    and, 127, 182, 218, 232, 331; nomina-
    tions, national and, 136–37, 179, 182,
    210, 254, 267, 324–25, 403, 403 n.104,
    420–21, 425, 430–31, 440–41, 440
    n.56, 446, 454, 454 n.96, 455; nomina-
    tions state and, 455; and patronage,
    499, 505, 506; press of, 170, 226, 228–
    29, 287, 324, 325, 329, 330, 332 (*see
    also* names of party newspapers); rad-
    ical faction of, xvi, 162, 163, 193, 199,
    228, 243, 354; supported, xv, 26, 26
    n.39, 53 n.3, 60, 76, 125, 126, 147–48,
    157, 197, 214–15, 254, 267, 433
Democratic Review. *See United States
    Magazine and Democratic Review*
Dental Care, 272, 273, 276
Depression of 1837. *See* Panic of 1837
Diary, 40, 257, 287, 297; keeping of,
    xxi, xxiv, 40, 43, 45, 51–52, 78, 111,
    117, 192, 347–48, 382, 410; uses of,
    3–4, 51–52, 88, 175, 298, 348
Discipline: in school, 22, 23
Dorr's Rebellion, 284, 284 n.55, 285,
    358, 457
Drawing: assessed, 132; examples of, 7,
    28, 93, 156, 178, 236, 262, 312, 378,
    442, 508; occupied with, 35, 44, 132,
    135
Dress. *See* Clothing; Fashion
Drinking. *See* Alcohol: use of; Drunken-
    ness
Drunkenness, 387; celebrations and, 39,
    132–33, 161, 161 n.75; decried, 27, 54,
    224. *See also* Alcohol: use of; Temper-
    ance
Duelling: advocated, 328; instances of,
    36–37, 38–40, 39 n.66; meeting on,
    35–36
Dwarf, 355, 358. *See also* Freaks

Eagle, 331, 337 n.125, 423; editor, offi-
    cial of, 418, 421, 422, 423, 425, 437,
    471, 472, 479; editor, unofficial of,
    xvi, 330, 333, 334, 336, 337, 350,
    357, 361, 382, 404; epithet, Whig for,
    439; and *Mail*, 332, 335, 336, 421,
    426, 427; positions taken by, 425–26,
    429, 427, 441, 457, 464; writer for,
    330, 335–36, 337–38, 341, 342, 349,
    352, 353, 380, 382, 383, 404

Eagle Hotel, 449, 449 n.75
Earthquake, 426
Eclipse: of moon, 120
Editor: of *Democrat*, xix; of *Eagle*, xvi, 330, 333, 334, 336, 337, 350, 357, 361, 382, 404, 418, 421, 422, 423, 425, 437, 471, 472, 479
Editors, prominent, 257, 337, 337 n.127
Egyptian Hall, 450, 450 n.81
Egyptian Saloon, 450, 450 n.81
Electioneering. *See* Campaigning
Elections, 109; in Camden, 89–90, 129, 506; in Camden County, 471, 485; in Camden Township, 234, 334, 407; congressional, 48, 48 n.2, 408; in Gloucester County, 234, 334, 408; in New Jersey, 42, 42 n.71, 89, 95–96, 335, 408; in Pennsylvania, 38, 89, 196, 234; in Philadelphia, 89, 95, 233–34, 289–90, 290 n.63, 334; presidential, 75–76, 95–96, 231. *See also* under names of political parties
Eliza and Ruth, 7
Elocution, 56, 477, 506. *See also* Rhetoric
Elysian Fields (New York), 396, 396 n.94
Empire Club, 501, 501 n.81, 505
Empire of Troy: as transportation, 465, 465 n.128, 469
Engine, steam, 44
England, 110; acts of, 37, 182, 184; United States relations with 131, 144, 222, 275
Entertainment. *See* specific forms of entertainment
Episcopal Church: attendance at, 21, 27, 181, 310
Episcopal Sewing Society, 254, 293
Evening Post, 5
Exchange Hotel, 497, 497 n.67
Excursions, boat, 186, 187, 218–19, 304, 398

Faneuil Hall, 392–93, 393 n.84
Fashion: in activities, 196; in dress, 188–89, 480–81. *See also* Clothing
Fencibles, Pennsylvania State, 322, 470; balls of, 263, 358–59, 481–82; exercises of, 322–24; funerals and, 448; on parade, 190, 190 n.121; in riots, nativist, 444, 448, 459
Ferries, 17; in Camden, 25, 26; as transportation, 32, 41, 41 n.70, 46, 264
Finances, 12, 12 n.24, 19, 19 n.16, 268
Firefighting, 25; instances of, 12, 38, 274. *See also* Fires
Firemen: and temperance, 339–340

Fires: reported, 12, 38, 256, 274, 309–10, 405; riots, nativist and, 444, 445. *See also* Firefighting
Fireworks, 199, 298, 305
First Baptist Church, 152. *See also* Baptist Church
First Congregational (Unitarian) Church, xvii
Fiscal Bank bill, 213, 214, 215, 216, 217
Fishing, 290, 291–92, 295
Floods, 112–13
Florida: Seminole War in, 37, 37 n.59, 268
Foreign influence, 480–81
Fort Mercer, 53, 59
Fort Mifflin, 53, 65, 74–75
Fourth of July, 52–54, 178–79, 192–93, 294, 295, 298, 382, 457
Fourth Street, 445
France, 110
Franklin Debating Society, 32, 35, 40
Franklin Institute, 44, 336
Franklin Park, xiv
Freaks, 221–22. *See also* Dwarf
Frenchmen, 138
Friends, Society of. *See* Quaker; Quakers
Friends Meeting-house, 3
Front Street Theatre, 450, 450 n.81, 451
Funerals, 90, 101–2, 146, 150, 203, 204, 279, 289, 424, 424 n.10. *See also* Burials
Future: of America, 119; predictions of, 382 (*see also* World, end of)

Galvanic battery, 479, 479 n.20, 480
Games, 252. *See also* names of games
Gardens, public, in Camden, 25. *See also* names of gardens
Gathering spots, male, 111, 118–19. *See also* Delacour's
German: study of, 272
Gloucester County (New Jersey): elections and, 234, 334, 408; history of, 322, 423, 426, 429, 431, 438 (*see also* *Reminiscences of Old Gloucester*)
Gloucester County Temperance Society, 415
Gray's Ferry. *See* Gray's Public Garden
Gray's Public Garden, 186–87
Greek: study of, xiv, 105
Green Tree Tavern, 471, 471 n.148
Greenwich Point, 58

Hackett's. *See* Union Hotel
Haddonfield (New Jersey), 3, 127–28, 415
Harboard's. *See* Decatur Coffee Shop

Haydn Music Club, 403 n.103. *See also* Camden Haydn Society
Hazzard's band, 283
Henry Institute: debates at, 112, 118, 139, 163, 169, 179, 181, 184, 234, 270, 328, 332, 335, 337, 338, 340, 342–43, 350, 352, 357–58, 360; founding of, 98, 100, 102, 104, 104 n.67, 263; meetings of, 104, 116–17, 160, 211, 326, 368; members of, 104, 104 n.67, 111–12, 326
Herald, 49
Heyl's Billiard Rooms, 123, 127, 247, 252, 323
Hibernia Fire Company, 284, 284 n.54
Hibernia Greens: nativist riots and, 458, 458 n.105
Hibernia Hose Company: nativist riots and, 443, 443 n.58
Hicksite Quakers, 271–72
Historians, 344, 390, 452, 492, 492 n.54
History: books on, 4, 8, 118, 370; of Camden, 24, 391, 439, 439 n.49; of Gloucester County, 322, 423, 426, 429, 431, 438; of New Jersey, 23, 164–65, 242, 245, 278, 352, 391, 411, 438, 439, 439 n.49, 440, 474, 494; references to, 29, 32, 52, 53, 59, 65, 127–28, 242, 389–90; of United States, 16, 19, 23, 391–93, 394; of Woodbury, 177–78. *See also* Research: historical; Writing: of history
Hoboken (New Jersey), 396, 397 n.95
Hoe-down, 304
Holiday observances. *See* specific holidays
Horse: as transportation, 428, 429, 460. *See also* Riding, horseback
Horse market, 21
Horse races, discussed, 11, 92, 171–72
Howard Beneficial Society, 156
Howard Hotel, 396, 396 n.93
Howard Temperance Association, 281
Hudson River, 465
"Hunkers": defined, 455 n.98, 505 n.88; patronage and, 505; references to, 455, 472, 488
Hydrophobia, 399
Hypnotism. *See* Mesmerism

Ice Cream and Refreshment House, 187, 187 n.16
Ice merchants, 262, 268
Illness: instances of, xviii, xix, 11, 34, 45, 54, 55, 60, 73, 74, 75, 76, 94, 194, 221, 241, 312, 320, 357, 361, 370, 373, 422. *See also* Dental care: received; names of ailments

Inauguration, Polk, 492, 497–502
Indian Queen (hotel), 497, 497 n.68
Indians: debates on, 114–15, 270, 340, 350, family and, 178; references to 164, 178, 401, 440, 485
International affairs, 37, 110, 131, 143–44, 144 n.53, 222, 231, 275
Ireland, 37; as ancestral home, xiii
Irish: nativist riots and, 441–45; references to, 207, 212; St. Patrick's Day and, 39, 132–33

Jefferson Debating Society: speech before, 492, 492 n.56, 495–96
Jews, 138–39
Journalists, prominent, 257, 337, 337 n.129

Kaighn's Point, 4, 9, 26
Kensington Glassworks, 225, 225 n.167
Killings, 44, 187; in nativist riots, 442, 443, 444, 446, 446 n.65, 461, 461 n.155. *See also* Duelling: instances of; Murders
Kittanniny Mountains, 204

Ladies: interaction with, 5, 7, 21, 23, 32, 38, 44, 50, 62, 67, 128, 129, 133, 172, 178, 190, 237–38, 240, 252, 254, 256, 379, 478, 494. *See also* Courting: instances of; Romances; Women
Latin: reading of, 68, 73, 105, 106, 113, 116, 118, 131, 132; study of, xiv–xv, xvi, 12, 13, 14, 17, 21, 22, 22 n.27, 23, 27, 55, 141–42; translating from the, 63, 64, 70, 102, 105, 118, 119, 132; writings on, 46. *See also* Classics
Launchings, ship, 160–61, 377, 400
Law: practice of, xix, 449, 454, 471, 473, 478, 479–80, 484–86, 497, 508; practice of, admission to, 447–49, 508; study of, xiv–xv, xvi, 126, 154, 155, 158, 159, 160, 161, 167, 169, 174, 175, 176, 188, 190, 194, 195, 197, 210, 211, 213–14, 215, 218, 220, 221, 224, 225, 227, 228, 241, 247, 248, 251, 252–53, 254, 268, 270, 281, 295, 303, 315, 316, 319, 320, 321, 323, 324, 349, 351, 358, 360, 364, 368, 369, 370, 372, 377, 383, 387, 399, 400, 402, 408, 417, 418, 422, 426, 436, 437, 438, 441, 446–47, 508; study of, complimented on, xv, 227, 228, 436, 448. *See also* Court cases: discussed; Lawyers: view of
Law Association of Philadelphia, library of, 447, 447 n.72
Lawrenceville High School, 43, 43 n.79

Lawyers, 136, 177

Laziness: discussed, 106–7, 130, 368

Lectures: delivered, 331–32, 331 n.117, 333, 429; heard, 60, 100–101, 103, 104, 105, 107, 112, 117, 119, 120, 121, 123, 131, 133, 136, 140–41, 154, 155, 156, 240, 243–44, 248, 254, 255, 257–60, 261, 263, 264, 269, 270, 271, 272, 275, 276, 286, 299, 333, 360, 369–70, 392, 392 n.81, 397, 421, 427, 479. *See also* Addresses, political; Orations; Speeches; Speeches, political

Lehigh River, 202

Liberty, 79–80

Libraries, public: in Camden, 24

Library (personal), 10; contents of, xiv, 49, 55, 85 (*see also* Books: collecting of; Books: lent; Books: purchased; Reading: titles comprising)

Little Newton Creek Meadows Company: organized, 432, 432 n.31

Loco-focos, 103 n.65, 218. *See also* Democratic party; Democratic party: radical faction of

Louisiana: elections and, 460, 463

Lyceum. *See* Youth's Lyceum

Madisonian, 383

Mail: and Catholics, 464; and *Eagle*, 332, 335, 336, 421, 426, 427; writing for, 13, 13 n.29, 35, 38, 39, 39 n.64, 40, 46, 47, 48, 49, 50, 109, 269

Malaga: campaigning in, 456, 456 n.100

Manayunk, 323, 323 n.108

"Manifest Destiny," 119

Marketing: for provisions, 132, 148, 188, 299. *See also* Second Street Market

Martial law: in Philadelphia, 445, 446

Massachusetts, 391. *See also* municipalities' names

Massasoit House, 391, 391 n.77

Matlack, Mickle v.: discussed, 3–4, 36, 180 n.103, 184, 216

Mauch Chunk, 204–7

Menagerie, 305–6, 305 n.84

Mesmerism, 269, 273

Metaphysics, 82–83, 91, 123, 264–65. *See also* Philosophy

Methodist Church, 18, 27, 241, 256, 270, 293, 299, 310, 325, 341, 342, 343, 344, 438. *See also* Methodist Episcopal Church; Methodist Protestant Church

Methodist Conference, 280, 282–83

Methodist Episcopal Church, 4–5.

Methodist Protestant Church, 335, 335 n.129.

Mexico: and Texas, 275, 275 n.35

Mickle v. *Matlack*: discussed, 3–4, 36, 180 n.103, 184, 216

Mikveh Israel, Temple, 138–39, 274

Military schools, 328, 328 n.115

Militia: exercises of, 322, 322 n.107, 323–24; on parade, 373–74; in nativist riots, 444, 445, 446, 458, 459, 460. *See also* Fencibles, Pennsylvania State

Millerism, 319. *See also* World, end of

Mississippi: launching of, 160–61; viewed, 159, 159 n.70, 265

Mitchell's. *See* Ice Cream and Refreshment House

Mobs, 63, 254. *See also* Riots

Morals, 13 n.29, 26–27, 57, 110, 268, 282–83, 391, 452, 507

Moravian Academy, 203, 203 n.136

Moravian Church, 203

Moravians, 202, 203, 204

Moravian Seminary, 203, 203 n.136

Mormonism, 170–71, 173, 176, 179, 200

Mount Holly, 307–14, 347

Mount's Boarding House, 498, 498 n.69

Moyamensing (Pennsylvania), 223

Moyamensing Prison, 223–24

Mulattos, 164

Murderers: discussed, 340, 341; met, 223–24; trial of, 362, 363, 365, 366, 369, 404. *See also* Murders

Murders: reported, 48, 146, 186 n.115, 207, 210, 355–56, 357, 369, 397, 397 n.95; references to 439, 439 n.49. *See also* Duelling; Killings; Murderers

Music, 182; arranging of, 336, 340, 343, 367; composing of, xviii, 211, 230, 241, 263, 295, 340–41, 367; heard, 121–22, 147, 182, 187, 193, 215, 430 (*see also* Concerts: attended; Singing: instances of; Songs: titles of); society for, 383 (*see also names of musical societies*); titles of, 374 (*see also* Songs: titles of). *See also* Violin: playing of; Violin: study of

Musical Fund Hall, 263 n.15; ball site, 263; concert site, 367

Musicians, professional, 186, 194, 229, 229 n.173, 252, 279, 482

"Nanny-Goat Market," 443 n.58. *See also* Market house

National Hotel, 499, 499 n.74

Nationalism, 159

National Theatre, 246, 246 n.209, 396, 396 n.91, 414

Native American, 446

Native American movement, 463; in Camden, 454; Democrats and, 454, 457, 460; meetings of, 470; members

Native American movement *(continued)*
of, 463, 493; in New York, 438, 438
n.46, 454; opposition to, 464–65, 506,
507 (*See also* Sons of Liberty); ori-
gins of, 453–54; and politics, 471, 473,
476 n.9, 405; riots of, 441–46, 447,
458–60, 479; and temperance, 469
Nativism. *See* Native American movement
Natural Bridge (Virginia), 116
Navy, 287, 288, 289
Nazareth (Pennsylvania), 203
Negroes: as criminals, 345; debate on,
114–15; encounters with, 186, 194,
195–96, 273–74; references to, 155,
194, 304, 395; and riots, 314. *See also*
Africans; Blacks
New Brunswick, 5, 6
New Haven, 388–91
New Jersey: elections and, 42, 42 n.71,
89, 95–96, 335, 408; history of, 23,
164–65, 242, 245, 278, 352, 411, 438,
439, 439 n.49, 440, 479, 494. *See also*
names of individual municipalities,
counties
New Jersey Cincinnati Society, 193
New Jersey Historical Society, 478, 478
n.16
New Year: commemoration of, 14, 106,
248; resolutions for, 251–53
New York City: nativism and, 438, 438
n.46; visited, 94–95, 338, 396, 397,
465, 469–70
Niagara (New York), 467–68
Niagara Falls (New York), 467–68
Niblo's Garden, 388, 388 n.67, 469
North Carolina: elections and, 464

Odd Fellows Hall, 450 n.81
Ohio of Wilmington, 7, 8, 9
Old Christ Church, 158–59
"Old Drury," 44, 44 n.81. *See also* Chest-
nut Street Theatre
Oliver Cox's school: assessed, 107–8; at-
tendance at, xiv, 5, 5 n.8, 7, 8, 12, 13,
16, 17, 18, 21–22, 28, 29, 30, 34, 35,
107–8; discipline at, 22, 23
Olympic Theatre, 94, 94 n.58, 370 n.39
Operas, 341, 405
Orations: delivered, 495–96; heard, 17,
19–20, 21, 191–92, 197–99, 255. *See
also* Addresses, political; Lectures;
Speeches; Speeches, political

Pacific Hotel, 388, 388 n.67
Painting(s), 135; critiqued, 370–71; 93–
94, 134–35, 135 n.43, 159, 418

Panic of 1837, 12, 12 n.24, 19, 19 n.16
Parades, 32, 153–54, 190, 229, 276–77,
317, 363
Parkinson's Confectionary, 344
Patrol, community, 372
Peale's Museum, 12, 12 n.25, 13
Pea Shore, 193, 193 n.124
Pennsylvania (state), 189; elections and,
38, 89, 96, 234; politics in, 162–63.
See also names of individual municipalities
Pennsylvania (ship), 6, 6 n.13, 7
Pennsylvania Dutch, 201
Pennsylvania State Fencibles. *See* Fenci-
bles, Pennsylvania State
Philadelphia: described, 14–15; educated
in, xiv, 126; elections and, 89, 95, 233–
34, 289–90, 290 n.63, 334; martial law
and, 445, 446; riots, black-white in,
314; riots, nativist in, 441–46, 447,
458; riots, weavers' in, 350, 350 n.4;
visited, 8, 9, 13, 14, 15–16, 17, 19, 20,
21, 29, 32, 35, 40–41, 42, 44, 45, 49,
106, 134–35, 135 n.43
Philadelphia and Camden Race Course,
11, 11 n.23, 27, 92, 171–72
Philadelphia Library, 371, 431, 438
Philadelphia Museum, 12, 12 n.25, 13
Philadelphia Navy Yard, 6, 13, 159
Philharmonic concerts, 416, 417
Photography. *See* Daguerreotype
Phrenology, 212–13, 243–44, 247, 255,
256, 266
Police. *See* Patrol, community
Politicians, prominent, 266, 285, 337,
375–77, 414, 452, 452 n.91, 466, 498,
502
Politics, xiv, 73, 93, 271; local, xvi, xix,
72, 132, 211, 218, 267–68, 270–71,
406, 438, 438 n.46, 493–94, 506; national, 12, 12 n.24, 15, 16 n.16, 17, 17
n.12, 19, 19 n.16, 26, 26 n.39, 37, 37
n.59, 37 n.60, 37 n.61, 38, 39, 48, 48
n.2, 60, 62, 74, 75, 93, 125, 126, 130,
134, 136–37, 142–46, 148, 150, 153–
54, 157–58, 166, 175–76, 179, 182,
189, 210, 213, 214, 215, 216, 218, 222,
224–25, 225–27, 245, 254, 268, 341,
342, 382, 425; opposition party in,
125; state, xvi, 35, 38, 42, 42 n.71,
162, 236–37, 285, 324. *See also* International affairs; names of political parties
Poor, the, 130, 268. *See also* Poverty
Poplar Hill, 8, 8 n.17, 383, 386, 387, 440
Pottsville (Pennsylvania), 207–8
Poverty, 424. *See also* Poor, the
Princeton University, 389

Principles of Politeness, 151

Printing, 104, 105; of notices, 98; of newspaper, 330, 341, 422, 423, 471

Prostitution, 57, 402. *See also* Brothels

Public Ledger, 382

Puseyite movement, 393, 393 n.85

Quaker: heritage, xii, xvii, 416, 424; meeting, Hicksite, 271–72; meeting-house, 3

Quakers, 385, 414, 416, 424, 491

Races: boat, 11, 70, 401 (*see also* Regatta); horse, 11, 92, 171–72

Rail Road Garden, 25

Rail-road House: fire at, 274

Railroads, 5, 25, 32, 57, 68, 206–9, 256, 331, 331 n.120, 346, 490. *See also* names of railroads

Raritan, 377

Reading (Pennsylvania), 208

Recreation, 169. *See also* specific activities

Red Bank: battle of, 164–65, 165 n.82; visited, 53, 58–60, 65, 74–75

Red Clay Creek, 68

Reform Association (formerly Constitution Club, Reform Club): meetings of, 387–88, 398, 399, 400. *See also* Constitution Club

Reform Club. *See* Reform Association

Regatta, 401. *See also* Races: boat

Regicide's Cave, 389–90

Relatives. *See* Family

Religious intolerance: attacked, 171, 176–77; witnessed, 124, 149, 152, 173

Religiousness: indications of, 4, 18, 49, 72, 153, 185–86, 221. *See also* Church services: attended

Reminiscences of Old Gloucester, xvii; publication of, 477, 497; reaction to, 435, 506–8; writing of, xvii, 423, 423 n.61, 434, 436, 437, 467, 474, 481, 483, 484, 488–89, 493, 496, 509

Research: historical, 242, 245, 256, 371, 423, 429, 431, 438, 455, 474, 488–89, 494

Resolutions: New Year's, 251–53

Rhetoric, 54. *See also* Elocution: study of

Rhode Island: Dorr's Rebellion and, 284, 284 n.55, 285

Riots: black-white, 314; nativist, 441–46, 447, 479; weavers', 350, 350 n.4

Robberies, 156, 322, 424; of graves, 345

Romances, 41, 41 n.68; characterized, xvii, 122; discussed, 133, 134, 174, 181, 253, 266, 267, 286, 315, 347; engaged in, 177, 255–56, 270, 281–82, 284, 300–301, 302–3, 304, 313–14, 315,

321, 325, 327–28, 338, 339, 340, 344, 347, 349, 369, 374–75, 382, 400, 409, 470, 494–95, 504, 509; rumored, 372–73, 489. *See also* Courting: instances of; Ladies: interaction with

Rue's Coach Manufactory, 38

Sabbath: breaking of, 86–87; ordinances regarding, 172. *See also* Blue laws

Sailing, 4, 11, 13, 36, 53, 55, 58–60, 63–64, 65, 67, 68, 69, 74, 75, 79, 82, 88, 152, 156, 180, 222, 286, 287

St. Augustine's Church, 149, 223; in nativist riot, 443, 445

St. Joseph's Church, 382, 438

St. Mary's Hall, 111, 187 n.116

Saint Patrick's Day, 39, 133, 507

Saint Paul's Episcopal Church, 149, 155, 155 n.66

St. Philip de Neri's Church, 458

St. Stephen's Church, 42

Salem, 51; Democratic party meeting in, 77; visited, 61–62, 63

Saratoga, 465–66

Schuylkill River, 186

Scotland, 37

"Scrapio": drawings, 156, 178; poem, 64, 81, 114, 117, 139, 160, 156, 178

Secession, 337

Second Street Market, 6, 6 n.12

Seminole War: in Florida, 37, 37 n.59, 268

Serenading, 260–61, 290–91, 333, 338, 339, 358, 360, 372, 374, 399

Sermons. *See* Church services: attendance at; Quaker: meeting, Hicksite

Sherron's Hotel, 61, 61 n.18

Sherron's Tavern, 61, 61 n.18

Ships: illustrations of, 262, 378, 442. *See also* Launchnigs, ship; names of ships

Singers, prominent, 283, 283 n.51, 288, 288 n.60, 405, 405 n.107

Singing, 53, 59, 117, 147, 260–61, 278, 311, 323, 374, 415, 457

Skating, ice, 28, 32, 34, 106, 112, 121

Slavery, 115, 115 n.7, 118, 328, 328 n.114, 330. *See also* Abolition

Sleighing, 30, 31, 417, 422

Smith's Hotel, 31–32

Smith's Island. *See* Windmill Island

Smith's Tavern, 489, 489 n.47

Snowden's. *See* Trenton House

Songs: titles of, 207, 415, 453, 453 n.94

Sons of Liberty, 470; formation of, 463–65; meetings of, 471

Specie payments: resumed, 112–13, 274

Speeches: delivered, 33, 99, 102, 122–23, 349, 368, 386, 398, 406; discussed, 130, 150; heard, 33, 68, 264–65, 280–81; writing of, xviii, 22, 31, 35, 78, 81, 99, 100, 122, 127, 322, 324, 326, 327. *See also* Addresses, political: made; Lectures; Orations; Speeches, political: made

Speeches, political: made, 456, 457, 472, 473. *See also* Addresses, political: made

Sports. *See* names of sports

Springfield (Massachusetts), 391

Stage coach: as transportation, 5, 20, 21, 43, 62, 63, 201, 204–6

Staten Island, 219

Steamboats: as transportation, 5, 6, 61, 95, 121, 186, 391

Steam engine, 44

Stokes, West v., 476

Stone Chapel, 392, 393 n.84

Storms, violent, 296–97, 439–40

Sub-Treasury, 77, 77 n.40, 245

Suicides, 44, 44 n.85, 194–95, 340, 340 n.130

Summit Hill Hotel, 207

Sun, 446

Sunspots, 169

Superstitions, 218, 248, 267, 364

Supreme Court: appointments to, 487–88

Susquehanna, 19, 19 n.14

Sybyl's Cave, 397, 397 n.95

Syracuse (New York), 469

Tamany Fish House, 193

Taverns, 20; in Camden, 25, visited, 43–44, 61, 201

Teaching, 155; of violin, 381

Telegraph: Democratic convention and, 452, 452 n.89

Temperance, 271, 317, 379; conventions and, 316–17, 350–51; discussed, 131–32, 313; and firemen, 339–40; involvement in, 17, 19, 25, 32, 42, 48, 68, 131, 223, 239, 255, 261, 262, 264, 266, 276–77, 305, 317–18, 322, 323, 325, 332, 339–40, 415; involvement, as delegate, convention, 350–51; involvement in, as lecturer, 330, 331–32, 331 n.117; and Native Americanism, 469; as political issue, 271, 286

Temple Mikveh Israel, visited, 138–39, 139 n.48, 275

Ten-pins, 158, 161, 163, 179, 225, 252, 384

Texas: annexation of, 437, 437 n.44, 440–41, 440 n.55, 451, 460, 484, 500;

independence and, 37, 37 n.60, 37 n.61; Mexico and, 275, 275 n.35

Theatre: attendance at, 40, 40 n.67, 43, 44, 44 n.81, 47, 50, 94, 94 n.58, 246, 246 n.209, 286, 306, 341, 370, 370 n.39, 381, 396, 396 n.91, 401, 414, 438, 438 n.45, 450, 450 n.81, 451, 470, 470 n.142; discussed, 109–10

Tontine Hotel: visited, 388, 388 n.68

Toothache, 197; instances of, 6, 196, 197, 199. *See also* Dental care

Tornado, 56

Tractarian movement. *See* Puseyite movement

Transcendentalism, 364, 381, 395. *See also* Transcendentalists

Transcendalists, 200, 271

Transportation: in city, 230; over land, 5, 20, 21, 22, 32, 43, 57, 127, 128, 201, 204–9, 256, 287, 331, 331 n.120, 389–90, 396, 406, 428, 429, 460, 466; by water, 4, 5, 6, 9, 17, 25, 26, 32, 36, 41, 41 n.70, 46, 53, 58–60, 61, 95, 121, 180, 202, 263, 264, 265, 384, 388–89, 391, 396, 425, 490

Travels. *See* Transportation; names of destinations

Trenton (New Jersey): visited, 43–44, 256

Trenton (boat), 5

Trenton House, Snowden's: dining at, 43, 43 n.79, 256

Troy (New York), 465

Two-thirds rule: Democrats and, 450, 450 n.77, 451

Union Debating Society, 26; involvement in, 8, 12, 13, 27, 29, 33; Washington's Birthday and, 33

Union Hotel, 77, 77 n.38

Union Temperance Society: lecture before, 331–32, 331 n.117; meetings of, 264, 314; parade and, 276. *See also* Camden Temperance Society

United States Hotel, 353, 353 n.7

United States Magazine and Democratic Review, 493, 493 n.58

Utica (New York), 466

Valentines, 266

Vansciver's Coach Manufactory, 256

Vauxhall Garden, 25, 221, 405

Violin, 172; playing of, 174, 175, 176, 184–85, 186, 188, 220, 228, 229, 233, 234, 235, 241, 247, 253, 270, 273, 276, 277, 280, 282, 286, 288, 290, 295, 303,

314, 319, 322, 325, 329, 331, 333, 334, 338, 367, 379, 400, 454; study of, 172, 173, 179, 182–83, 184, 188, 194, 196, 209, 210, 216–17, 220, 221, 223, 224, 225, 227, 228, 230, 242, 252, 253, 255, 274, 303, 306, 319, 320, 321, 322, 323, 324, 325, 327, 329, 369, 370, 386, 399, 477. *See also* Teaching: of violin
Violinists, prominent, 416–17, 417 n.131

Wales, 37
Walnut Grove (New Jersey), xiv, 383, 386, 464
Walnut Street Theatre, 306, 341, 438, 438 n.45. *See also* American Theatre
Ware, Bateman v., 436, 436 n.39
Washington (D.C.), 497–503
Washington and Levin Temperance Society, 276
Washington Library Company, 24; business conducted for, 32, 122, 134; lectures sponsored by, 100–101, 103, 104, 105, 107, 112, 117, 155–56, 227, 231, 232, 233, 238–39; meetings of, 44, 45, 65, 67, 78, 127, 235–36, 345, 411; officer of, 28, 85–86, 120, 236, 277
Washington Manufacturing Company, 436
Washington Monument (Baltimore), 453, 453 n.93
Washington's birthday: celebration of, 32–33, 266, 495–96
Water, mineral: drinking of, 67, 191
Weddings, 383, 385, 387, 491
Welch's National Theatre, 370 n.39
Welsh's Circus (theatre), 370
West v. *Stokes*, 476
Whig party, 145, 150; campaigning and, xv, 75–76, 75 n.36, 89, 95–96, 108, 117, 118, 126, 212, 215, 217, 438, 438 n. 47, 440, 472; convention, national and, 440; criticized 39, 75, 89; and *Eagle*, 439 (*see also Mail*: and *Eagle*); elections and, 48, 75–76, 89, 96–97, 231, 233–34, 236, 240, 334, 335, 407, 408, 460, 464, 485, 490; issues and, 245, 440, 505; meetings of, 92, 455; nativism and, 438 n.46, 506; nominations and, 137, 189, 403, 425, 440, 473; patronage and, 99, 157–58, 189, 370, 380, 489–90; press of, 383, 383

n.55, 418 n.135; split in, xv–xvi, 210, 215–16, 224–25, 225–27, 268, 275, 500
Whippings, 121
Wilkes Expedition, 294, 294 n.69
Windmill Island, 4, 4 n.5, 13 n.29; canal through, 19, 22, 22 n.22, 29, 29 n.47, 44; illustration showing, 250
Witchcraft, 267
Women: Jewish, 138–39; Pennsylvania Dutch, 201. *See also* Ladies: interaction with; Courting: instances of; Romances
Woodbury (New Jersey): history, 177–78; illustration of, 14; as settlement site, family's, 177–78; visits to, 31–32, 57
Woodbury Railroad, 22, 22n. 22
World, end of: discussed, 364; predicted, 296, 319, 339, 361, 367
Worship: styles of, commented on, 18–19, 42, 341
Writers, prominent, 257, 353, 393, 394–95
Writing, 12; of critiques, 109, 240, 261, 269; discussed, 78, 98–99, 108, 139, 174; of history, xvii, xviii, 379, 423, 426, 438, 439, 439 n.49, 440 (*see also Reminiscenses of Old Gloucester*; Research: historical); of music, xviii, 211, 230, 241, 263, 295, 340–41, 367; for newspapers, xvi, 13, 13 n.29, 35, 38, 39, 39 n.64, 40, 41, 46, 47, 48, 49, 50, 88, 108–9, 199, 226, 240, 261, 266, 267, 269, 271, 330, 335–36, 337–38, 341, 342, 349, 352, 353, 366, 380, 382, 383, 404; occupied with, 35, 40, 42, 133, 314; of poetry, xviii, xxix, 57, 64, 81–82, 114, 117; of play, xviii; political (*see Eagle*: writer for); religious, 49; skill at, xiv, xvi, 156, 269; of speeches, xviii, 22, 31, 35, 78, 81, 99, 100, 122, 127, 322, 323, 324, 326, 327

Yale University, 389, 390
"Young Democracy": alliance with, xvi; defined, 479, 487–88; and Polk administration, 488
Youth's Debating Society, 27, 50
Youth's Literary Messenger, The, 9
Youth's Lyceum, 8, 9, 13, 20

Cooper's Creek

COOPER'S FERRY ROAD

Rail — Road

Amboy

MO

SIXTH ST

FIFTH ST

ST

FOURTH

ST

ST

COOPER

MARKET

THIRD

PLUM

FEDERAL

SECOND

FRONT ST